Catechizing Culture

COLUMBIA UNIVERSITY PRESS   NEW YORK

Catechizing Culture

Missionaries, Aymara, and the "New Evangelization"

ANDREW ORTA

COLUMBIA UNIVERSITY PRESS
Publishers Since 1893
NEW YORK, CHICHESTER, WEST SUSSEX

Library of Congress Cataloging-in-Publication Data
Orta, Andrew.
 Catechizing culture : missionaries, Aymara, and the "new evangelization" / Andrew Orta.
  p. cm.
 Includes bibliographical references (p.) and index.
 ISBN 0-231-13068-6 (alk. paper)—ISBN 0-231-13069-4 (pbk. : alk. paper)
  1. Aymara Indians—Religion. 2. Aymara Indians—Missions. 3. Catholic Church—
Missions—Bolivia. 4. Catholic Church—Bolivia. I. Title.

 F2230.2.A9077 2004
 266'.089'98324—dc22

                                                    2004047844

Columbia University Press books are printed on permanent and durable acid-free paper
Printed in the United States of America

c 10 9 8 7 6 5 4 3 2 1
p 10 9 8 7 6 5 4 3 2 1

CONTENTS

In recent years Catholic missionaries serving Aymara-speaking communities of the Bolivian highlands have offered a surprising message to their flocks. After centuries of preaching that the Aymara should turn away from their traditional cultural practices to embrace Christianity more fully, they now insist the old ways were Christian all along. To become more Christian, the missionaries declare, the Aymara must become more "Indian" and return to "the ways of the ancestors"— ways that the missionaries have come to see as local cultural expressions of Christian values. Practices once denounced by priests as idolatrous or pagan—offerings made to snow-covered mountain peaks or llama sacrifices—are seen as plausibly Christian insofar as entire communities come together to make the offering and bonds of family are reinforced through ritual sacrifice. In some cases missionaries are in the awkward position of encouraging Aymara to celebrate the very ritual practices they or their predecessors effectively eradicated. And so, some five centuries after their arrival in the New World to spread the Christian message at the expense of indigenous cultures, foreign Catholic missionaries at the turn of the millennium find themselves teaching the Aymara their own culture.

Catechizing Culture: Missionaries, Aymara, and the "New Evangelization" is an ethnography of this complex situation. It is based on field research I conducted with Aymara in a number of different communities and the mainly foreign priests who attend to them. I also focus on Aymara "catechists." These are Aymara who receive regular training from the priests and serve as permanent native missionaries in their own communities: leading Sunday worship groups, preparing members of the community seeking Catholic sacraments, and, in recent years, leading the community in the performance of newly revived traditional Aymara rituals. (The introduction begins by describing just such a ritual.)

I began my research in 1989, at a time when this new missionary message—called the "theology of inculturation"—was just being introduced to Aymara. A continuous period of research from 1990–92, as well as briefer follow-up visits in 1997, 1999, and 2000 helped me learn about the story I want to tell here. In the telling I have found it helpful to place this story in historical and comparative context. Ethnography is most effective when it is properly contextualized, enabling readers to appreciate both the particularity of the situation being described as well as the lessons it may teach us about situations in other parts of the world or moments in time. To that end I devote a portion of this book, including long stretches of the introduction, to drawing out broader comparative lessons in dialogue with work in anthropology and research on the Andean region. This preface summarizes what I see as the most important of these themes. Readers less interested in these claims, or less conversant with the literatures of anthropology and related disciplines, may skim over the more detailed rendering of these arguments in the main text to focus on the particular ethnographic case at hand.

Contemporary Catholic missionary activity in Bolivia—or anywhere else in Latin America—is the latest chapter in a long story dating from the turn of the sixteenth century. Catholicism has been a part of Aymara life for centuries. (In fact, a great irony I address in this book is that when I asked Aymara about "the ancestors," they consistently reported that they admired the ancestors for being good Catholics—not in the culture-friendly way the missionaries now celebrate them, but *really* good Catholics: knowing their catechism, reciting prayers in Latin.) Similarly, the pastoral problem of how definitively to convert the Aymara to Christianity has been a preoccupation for generations of Catholic missionaries.

In places like the Andes and among people like the Aymara the image of missionaries and "natives" immediately calls to mind long-standing discussions about the degrees of merging or separation between indigenous and European cultures. By approaching both missionaries and Aymara as the "natives" of this study, and finding that in many ways they require one another, I argue that they should be viewed as inseparably "entangled" within a single cultural context.

This does not mean that there are not important differences between missionaries and Aymara, or that there are not a number of different points of view within what I clumsily label here *missionary* or *Aymara*. Over the last half of the twentieth century the missionary concern with what they saw as an unfinished evangelization was reflected in a series of missionary campaigns undertaken by the Catholic Church in Latin America. After the Second World War thousands of missionaries streamed to the region—and to other areas of the "third world"—as part of what they described as a "second evangelization." This reenergized pastoral effort gave rise to a number of innovative and interesting missionary strategies; *liberation theology,* which taught that Christians were called upon to correct the "sinful" social injustices of poverty and oppression, may be the best known of these. *Inculturation* has followed on the heels of liberation theology.

The rise of inculturation as a missionary strategy in the mid-1980s and the related decline of the theology of liberation are coordinated with similar shifts in global politics away from class-based movements and toward identity or ethnic politics. I am interested in this book in the global contexts that help shape this shifting pastoral approach within the Church as well as the regional and national ones in which missionaries spread their message. However, I am also interested in the theology of inculturation as a particular example of multiculturalism and as an instructive point of reference for discussions of the politics of cultural identity in a range of other settings in Bolivia, across Latin America, and around the world.

In a similar way, I also approach missionization as a particular example of another sort of phenomenon: globalization. The Catholic Church is certainly a global institution; it may well have been the first global institution. As an effort to convert diverse peoples of the world to what is taken to be a universal truth, and as an effort that at the same time inevitably gives rise to a range of regionally "flavored" religious identities, global Catholicism well reflects a tension often attributed to globalization. This is a tension between homogenization and the stubborn endurance of (or the creative production of new) local differences. In my view missionization provides a remarkable opportunity to examine one kind of global process ethnographically. Among the first lessons learned is that global processes take place someplace and involve real people engaged in on-the-ground activities. I develop this misleadingly self-evident point throughout the book.

One of the ways I develop this point has important implications for the ways we think about indigenous communities in places like the Andes. If there is a core argument to this book it is that local places, like the communities where I conducted my research, point beyond themselves—that "locals" make their lives fully assuming, and oftentimes requiring, "outside" influences, which include, in this case, locally resident missionaries. To people seeking evidence of unchanging indigenous society resisting the advance of outside forces, this may seem a tragic story. And the history of the Aymara certainly reflects episodes of tragedy and injustice, some of them ongoing, that should not be ignored. But the story I hope to tell here also recognizes the ceaseless human capacity to make community and to render even the most complex and challenging global contexts relatively coherent and richly meaningful from local points of view. In this hopeful way I seek to position the Aymara I know as profoundly engaged with, rather than passively victimized by, a complex and changing world.

ACKNOWLEDGMENTS

In the Andean communities I know debt is a positive social force, a promise of future sociality, a gift. In the long course of this project I have been fortunate to become indebted to so many. My greatest debt is to the surprising number of people in Bolivia who shared their lives, their meals, and their homes with a stranger. From pastoral workers who tolerated the presence and the questions of an investigator without religious affiliation to Aymara who warily let me and my wife Ingrid become routine presences and, I hope, contributing parts of their households and their communities, this project like so many ethnographic works is built on a remarkably generous reception. For reasons that have to do with the often politicized nature of Catholic pastoral work in Bolivia and the confidences to which I was privileged in an ecclesial hierarchy of catechists, priests, and their superiors, I have used pseudonyms throughout the book. Though I cannot thank them individually here, I do want to acknowledge the support of the catechists and pastoral workers of the southern altiplano pastoral zone of the Diocese of La Paz and the catechists of the pastoral zone of Carangas in the Diocese of Oruro. I am particularly indebted to catechists and pastoral workers from the parishes of Batallas and, especially, Jesús de Machaqa. A number of these hosted Ingrid and me; many more invited us. In Jesús de Machaqa I enjoyed working relations and periods of residence in a number of communities. My thanks to the cabildo and ayllu authorities who enabled our presence, particularly to the people of Qhunqhu Milluni, Qhunqhu Liqiliqi, Sullkatiti Titiri, and Kalla Arriba. As I try to convey in this book, they have taught me much about heartfelt thanks; I offer this work to them *chuymajatwa*.

In Bolivia and beyond I have benefited from a generous network of friends and colleagues with interests in and commitments to the region and to my project. My thanks to Tom Abercrombie, Xavier Albó, Rob Albro,

Ramiro Argandonio, Astvaldur Astvaldsson, Denise Arnold, Rosanna Bar-ragán, Ricardo Calla, Dolores Charaly, Franz Damen, Laura Gottkowitz, Bernardo Guhs, Kevin Healy, Tomas Huanca, Alan Kolata, Dimetrio Marca, Luis Oporto, Gilberto Pauwels, Norman Reyes, Stuart Rockefeller, Calixto Quispe, Lynn Sikkink, Juan de Dios Yapita. At the University of Chicago, where I first conceived this project, Jean Comaroff, Bill Hanks, Alan Kola-ta, Nancy Munn, and Terry Turner were exceptional mentors. At the University of Illinois at Urbana-Champaign I have enjoyed participating in an outstanding community of scholars. Nancy Abelmann, Matti Bunzl, Alma Gottlieb, Bill Kelleher, Janet Keller, Alejandro Lugo, and Norman Whitten have all commented on portions of this book. Tom Abercrombie and Joanne Rappaport carefully read an early version of the manuscript and each offered a mix of insightful criticism and encouragement that has improved the work immensely.

Demetrio Marca, Dolores Charaly, and Rene Guttierez provided invaluable assistance transcribing and translating tape recordings in Aymara. Emma Reuter and Isabel Scarborough helped as research assistants. Steve Holland prepared the maps, figures, and photographs for this book. Nelly González has maintained a matchless collection of Latin American resources at the University of Illinois Library and helped solve some of the more challenging of the reference questions in the production of this book. At Columbia University Press Suzanne Ryan's support has helped make this book a published reality. Susan Pensak's steady copyediting has helped tame my idiosyncracies and in-consistencies and made the book better in many ways.

The longest period of field research (1990–92) was funded by a Fullbright-Hays Doctoral Dissertation Abroad fellowship. Preliminary research (summer 1989) and follow-up visits (winter 1996–97, summer 1999 and 2000) were made possible through the support of the Center for Latin American Studies of the University of Chicago Earlham College, the Midwest Universities Con-sortium for International Activities, and at the University of Illinois at Urbana-Champaign, the Center for Latin American and Caribbean Studies, The Cam-pus Research Board, and the Department of Anthropology. The Campus Research Board also provided a subvention to support the publication of this book. The Museum of Ethnography and Folklore in La Paz kindly extended institutional affiliation to me for the initial period of my field research. The di-rectors and staff of the archives of the Arzobispado of La Paz, of the Cathedral of La Paz, and of the Bolivian Episcopal Conference have afforded me access to those important resources. I have benefited in recent years from collegial relations with the Universidad de la Cordillera in La Paz.

Chapter 4 is a revised version of my essay "Syncretic subjects and body politics: Doubleness, personhood, and Aymara catechists," which appeared initially in *American Ethnologist* 26(4): 864-889.

Chapter 7 is a revised version of my essay "Burying the past: Locality, lived history, and death in an Aymara ritual of remembrance," which appeared initially in *Cultural Antrhopology* 17(4): 471-511.

And then there are the friends and family who have rolled their eyes, offered support, and for stretches of time learned not to ask about "the book." They have sustained me in more ways than they know. To my mother, Phyllis Orta, and to the memory of my father, Louis Orta, to Dave Cassuto and to Anne-Mieke and Jan Karel Smeets, I am particularly indebted.

Ingrid Melief has shared in this work from the beginning, joining me for most of my research in Bolivia. She has not joined me in my sometimes obsessive focus on this book, reminding me always that we share so much more. I cannot thank her enough. Our children, Erik and Natalie, offer me more gifts than I can count. This work is for them.

Despite the help of so many, there are surely errors in this book. I am responsible for these.

Catechizing Culture

Converting Difference

Christianity provided the Indians, above all, a new vocabulary to express their traditional beliefs in Catholic terms. . . . The subjects of the Incas, overwhelmed by the fervor of the conquistadors and the Spanish preachers, accepted the religion of the invaders without resistance. They did not understand. Defeated, they retreated into a disconcerting religious muteness. In truth, no one today knows their true religious sentiments. They know with precision when and how to organize their worship and their religious fiestas; at the desired moment, they send for the priest. And if he is not initiated in their religious customs, they explain in detail what they expect from him under the given circumstances.

—Jacques Monast, O.M.I.
Los indios aimaraes: ¿evangelizados o solamente bautizados?

On an overcast December day in 1991, the Catholic feast day of Santa Barbara, I attended a ritual in one of the Aymara communities (*ayllus*) of the region of Jesús de Machaqa, Ingavi Province, Bolivia. It was an *ayuno* (fast)—a community-level event marking the completion of the year of service provided by community authorities, an honor and an obligation long taken as a foundation of indigenous community in the Andes. Through a collective fast and an intercommunity rite of "pardon" (during which ayllu members, on their knees and weeping, embraced one another expressing reciprocal forgiveness for their trespasses of the past year), the community prepared the way for the entrance of new ayllu authorities in January. The event also coincided with the early weeks of the growing season and performed an offering to earth and sky to help secure an abundant harvest.

Beginning early in the morning, ayllu members assembled at the site of the local Catholic chapel at the base of a small foothill overlooking the community. Over the course of the rite, they ascended to the top of the mountain where a *yatiri* (ritual specialist) instructed the outgoing authorities to kneel, holding aloft a flat stone with smoldering embers. He placed an offering of flowers, fronds, and incense upon the embers to burn. As the smoke drifted into the sky, the rest of the community, on their knees, circled around the authorities and yatiri, pausing to pray the Our Father and read aloud the Christian liturgy of the stations of the cross, the Via Crucis.

The ayuno is remarkable for a number of reasons that open onto the themes of this book. Perhaps the most immediately evident of these is the stark juxtaposition of apparently "indigenous" and Catholic practices. Some readers will also note the irony that this traditional Indian rite is denoted with the Spanish term *ayuno*. Even in extended commentaries on the event in Aymara, speakers used the Spanish term. In this the rite embodies a classic conundrum of Andean studies (and anthropology more generally) concerning the merging of indigenous- and European-derived cultural forms.

To some analysts the spatial arrangement of the ayuno might disclose a fragmented, syncretic history of partial assimilation, localized resistance, and clandestine survival by which a marked Andean core endures within the perimeter of imposed Christian form. As Tristan Platt has noted, "Andean studies have long emphasized a distinction between new Christian forms and an underlying concrete logic of pre-Columbian origin, suggesting that pagan mythic thought, accompanied by many practical concepts and ideas, has been able to survive unobtrusively till today, beneath the deceptive appearances of a dominantly European public aesthetic" (1987a:141).[1] The yatiri kneeling with brazier aloft is an enduring symbol of indigenous religiosity. Like the fabled idols hidden by natives behind Christian altars or Monast's image of Indians superficially baptized but not authentically evangelized, the burnt offering encircled by the Via Crucis appears as an index of a historically derived state of relations.

But a thicker description of the event cautions against mistaking this for a steady state. Also notable about this ayuno performance is that the event had been all but abandoned in recent years. In part, this was a product of sometimes violent interreligious tensions in the region during the 1960s and 1970s as a growing number of Protestant converts and an emerging movement of neo-orthodox Catholics publicly denounced what they saw as idolatrous and fraudulent traditional beliefs and practices. Intersecting with these developments has been a more general decline affecting a number of traditional practices: like the ayuno, fiesta celebrations in the region were suspended or reduced and a host of regalia marking ayllu authorities was abandoned. Indeed, the very site of the ayuno celebration bears the mark of apparent cultural decadence: stone cairns that once sequenced the space up the side of the foothill behind the chapel in accordance with the stations of the cross have been destroyed (or allowed to tumble down), a *calvario/apacheta* (a small structure at the top of the hill, a ubiquitous complement to such chapels in the Andes) is similarly in ruins. The crumbling calvario walls were the site of the yatiri's offering and the focal center of the circular Via Crucis.

The ritual I witnessed in 1991 was continuous with a period of ethnic revitalization beginning in the 1980s in which a number of practices abandoned in previous decades reappeared. Coordinate with this ethnic resurgence have been shifting pastoral postures of the Catholic Church. This book is about this complex and surprising intertwining of local practices, ethnic revitalization, and the missionary efforts of the Catholic Church.

THE "THEOLOGY OF INCULTURATION"

The ayuno I observed was a direct result of efforts by the local pastoral team to reanimate and reinforce what they understood to be traditional Aymara cultural practices. This pastoral ideology, known as the "theology of inculturation," is part of a wider effort in the Andes and in other contemporary Catholic mission fields to celebrate and incorporate cultural difference within a universal frame of Christian identity—to catechize culture.[2] In the Andean case, local practices—in some instances practices that only a decade ago were denounced as idolatrous superstitions—are being embraced as culturally specific expressions of universal Christian meanings. In this light the spatial configuration of the ayuno embodies the ideals of inculturation: a consciously reconstituted Aymaraness constructed with respect to an encompassing Christianity.

The theology of inculturation provides much of the backdrop for this study. Let me tease out three dimensions of inculturation that I believe open onto particularly fruitful ethnographic paths. The first is that as a global missionary phenomenon, inculturation bears examination across a number of levels of analysis: from the institutional, theological, and pastoral positions of the Vatican, as well as the perspectives of various religious orders and regional and national clergy, to the more situated experiences of local parish priests and pastoral teams, as well as indigenous catechists and their communities. These catechists are the local agents of missionary Catholicism. They recruit and lead community faith groups (*grupos de fe*) and serve their communities more generally as ritual specialists and brokers of contacts with priests. In the chapters that follow I take the ayuno and related events as opportunities to examine the emergent ideology of inculturation in the southern Andes and the parish-level practices by which a cohort of catechists are trained, with rites like the ayuno reinforced and reformed. I also focus on the community-level enactment of such "revalorized" Aymara practices to examine the ways formal ritual models are accountable to particular community practices and illuminate a variety of personal and intracommunity tensions and dramas that shape and are expressed through the specificities of any given ritual performance.

At this microlevel, for instance, we find two catechists involved in the delicate business of presuming to lead a ritual they had, under the frame of an earlier pastoral ideology, once sought strenuously to abolish. One undertook this from the ambiguous standing of an orphaned younger brother, alienated from his kin and marginalized (save largely for the authority he could muster as a catechist) within his community. For the other, his ambivalent stand with respect to "Aymara culture" was all the more poignant in that among the yatiris previously displaced from the ayuno, whom he now sought to enfold in his encircling embrace, was his elderly but still vigorous father. For both men—also caught up in an ongoing rivalry, each with a loyal faction within the community's faith group—their authoritative participation in the ayuno involved them in the public performance of an embattled identity: shaped by the normative expectations and sensibilities of their community, constrained by the details of their personal histories, and also reflecting sensibilities and expectations deriving from a more encompassing sociopolitical moment (see chapters 4 and 5).

At this more macrolevel inculturation reflects and participates in the ascendance of ethnicity as an increasingly salient frame of political action in Bolivia and a broader turn toward "identity politics" evident across the globe.[3] This is the second dimension of inculturation I want to underscore. In the Andes, inculturation follows hard on the heels of a set of pastoral paradigms—including the theology of liberation—implemented since the Second World War and interlinked with a global emphasis upon development and modernization. (Father Monast was among a group of Canadian Oblates sent to Bolivia in the 1950s as one of the earliest cohorts of this "new evangelization.") Indeed, my original interest in Bolivia was as a place to build upon ethnographic research I conducted in Nicaragua in 1984 focused upon the pastoral practices of liberation theology. My preliminary inquiries in the region prompted the discouraging report that liberation theology had been tried, found wanting, and all but abandoned—at least in rural indigenous areas. Sketchy reports of the ideology of inculturation piqued other ethnographic interests that have guided my research. Yet liberation theology and the series of modernist pastoral paradigms it accompanied have remained an important point of reference. For reasons I detail in chapter 3, I approach inculturation as a specific and revealing example of a broader turn from class to culture, from homogenizing rhetorics of development to particularizing invocations of locality.

Students of colonial evangelization in the Americas will object that this is mistaking the early modern for the late, a fascination with the post blinding us to the past. This is a compelling point. The theology of inculturation is arguably but one side of an antique evangelical coin and might be seen in terms of a longstanding evangelical ambivalence toward indigenous "religions." In the early colonial Andes missionaries sought in indigenous cultural practices for *semilla verbi:* "seeds of the divine word"—evidence of God's revelation, even traces of a distant evangelization by Jesus's apostles (see Albó 1966; Borges 1960; MacCormack 1991). In a similar way the cultural decline and renaissance I describe seems to echo colonial accounts, as muscular and ethnographically savvy evangelizers frequently described extirpated practices reemerging from the rubble of smashed idols and desecrated sacred sites (Gareis 1999; Mills 1997). And here is the third dimension of inculturation I want to signal: it opens onto a long and unfolding colonial and postcolonial history and calls for an analysis that is attentive to the colonial past and its legacies while situated in developments of immediate contemporary salience. Such a claim could surely be extended to other examples of missionary activity and may well be a function of all cultural practices in postcolonial settings. In the case of inculturation, however, the institutional continuity of the Catholic Church combined with a pastoral ideology that strives explicitly to missionize "against" the colonial Catholic past to the end of a new Aymara Christianity present these themes in especially condensed and evocative forms.

For these reasons the phenomena of inculturation present analytic challenges that tap into enduring themes in Latin American studies and set in relief a number of significant current developments in the region. Approached ethnographically, they call for an analysis of Andean particularities that must also grapple with questions at the heart of anthropology as a contemporary comparative discipline. Specifically, I take this modern missionary encounter as an opportunity to examine the intersection of two vital issues. The first involves the experiences and legacies of colonialism; the second concerns our understanding of locality. To a discipline born uncomfortably of processes of European expansion and perched precariously upon claims of access to local points of view, these issues compel us to consider the foundation of our endeavor and its contemporary implications.

CONVERSION AND CONJUNCTURE

A discussion of Catholicism in a setting like the Andes quickly verges upon the topic of syncretism. As a recent anthropological revisiting of this "contentious term" notes, "syncretism" is typically taken to imply the "inauthenticity" of local practices and the "'contamination' . . . of a supposedly 'pure' tradition by symbols and meanings seen as belonging to other incompatible traditions" (Shaw and Stewart 1994:1). Despite the potentially positive connotations of syncretism as a process of intercultural accommodation, as Peter van der Veer (1994:197) observes, "It is striking how pejoratively the term is often used by the defenders of 'the true faith.' It is seen as a loss of identity, an illicit contamination, a sign of religious decadence. . . . Syncretism is seen as a corruption of the Truth."

Religion has often gone hand in hand with colonization, typically through the work of missionaries. Historians and anthropologists have paid fruitful attention. Studies of religion and processes of conversion have shaped our understandings of colonial and postcolonial situations.[4] The pairing of the instrumental and rational projects of colonialism, arguably a hallmark of modernity, with religion, a symptom par excellence of modernity's alter:tradition, is an uneasy one. Studies focusing on this ambiguous alliance thus reveal fissures and tensions within what may otherwise appear as a colonial monolith (cf. Stoler 1989). Similarly the spatial scope of missionary projects, which often encompass ministries at "home" as well as in the "colonies," offers an instructive vantage point from which to survey colonial metropoles and outposts, the ideological core and the front lines of colonial engagement. And where missionaries seek to transform through conversion what are taken to be among the most intimate and fundamental components of indigenous social life, analysts have attempted to assess their successes, their failures, and the syncretic results as indexes of broader processes of colonial articulation. I aim to build upon this methodological opportunity for the examination of unfolding colonial and postcolonial situations through a study of a contemporary and long-standing missionary effort.

The discipline of anthropology has long wrestled with the implications of the past for the present; that the past is an unclosed chapter takes on particular relevance for the anthropology of postcolonial situations. This truism requires additional attention in Latin America, where the legacy of colonialism has been a vexing problem and the colonial tradition itself is markedly "other" with respect to contemporary analysts. To some degree this derives from the liminal modernity of the baroque Iberian colonial project (Maravall 1986). This ur colonial moment appears at times incommensurable with the more fully Enlightenment-driven projects of the eighteenth and nineteenth centuries. This can also be traced to the politics of the Counter-Reformation and the legacy of the Black Legend of Spanish colonial excesses in the hands of rival (and Protestant) colonial powers and WASPish academic traditions (cf. Kagan 1996). Another factor must surely be the postcolonial anomaly of Latin American nation-states, which, like their near postcolonial age mate the United States, were born of Enlightenment-inspired revolutionary ferment at the turn of the nineteenth century. Yet, for a host of reasons, this historically postcolonial region appears to remain "shackled to its past."[5]

In the ethnographic and historical academic encounters with Latin America—which intensified over the last half of the twentieth century[6]—observers aligned with the self-consciously modernizing times encountered the legacy of a colonial past that was decidedly not their own. Similarly, in the light of an emerging modernization/developmentalist perspective, the colonial legacy was radically dysfunctional. In the Andes this has been compounded by the enduring fascination with the accomplishments of pre-Hispanic societies in the region, usually seen as degraded by the impositions of Spanish colonialism. In many of these discussions, I shall argue, religion and the status of colonial conversion served metonymically to evoke the wider legacy of colonialism. In an especially strong version of the critical views of syncretism identified by Shaw and Stewart and van der Veer, the colonial legacy was seen as at once a corrupted ensemble of its source materials (Spanish and Andean) and an echo of a premodern tradition absolutely distinct from twentieth-century Western modernity.

Much of the ethnography and ethnohistory of the region has been influenced by these founding regionalist concerns. And these have also shaped a reinvigorated Catholic missionary presence in the rural parishes of the Andes, as evident in the opinions of Father Monast and his confreres, who arrived in the Andes in increasing numbers beginning in the 1940s and 1950s. By this time the colonial-Catholic past was "other" even to these descendants of the colonial evangelizers. In their efforts to complete what they saw as the unfinished evangelization of the region, missionaries came to see the enduring influence of colonial Iberian Catholicism as a stumbling block pernicious as the apparent survival of indigenous pagan customs. The chapters that follow will show that the overlapping binaries separating indigenous from European and traditional (or colonial) from modern hide a more dynamic amalgam. Yet such binaries nonetheless acquire a social force of their own, emerging as emic as well as etic ways of representing Andean reality (cf. Abercrombie 1998; Handler 1988; Herzfeld 1997). A related goal thus is to track the shifting historical and ideological situations in which such binaries are reproduced and asserted, even as I document a lived reality that is more complex. While such representations certainly have some force in constituting Andean reality, the present realities they help shape are not the enduring pasts they claim to reference.

LOCALITY

Long a basic, if often tacit, building block of ethnographic understanding, locality has become a topic of increasingly self-conscious ethnographic concern. It is, we are now cautioned, both more and less than we take it to be. More, because locality is never self-contained or self-sustaining; the local emerges in complex interrelation with other localities and overarching structures conditioning these engagements. In colonial settings and their aftermaths, locality is typically enmeshed inextricably and unequally within regional and global networks.[7] And, as other recent work has stressed, within these regional and global networks the social groups once thought to be local are better seen as translocal, comprising a range of migrants and travelers, products and ideas coming from and destined for other places.[8]

For others locality is less than we take it to be. They devalue it as a mere analytic concept, a fiction of the observer, conjured by some anthropologists in our quest for stable, bounded units of analysis. By extension it is also seen as a fiction of the observed: an invented tradition, an imagined community the double-edged blade of social theory often undercuts in jarring ways.[9] As to locality, notwithstanding the claims of locals, such approaches hold that there is no "there" there.

Anthropologists grapple with these challenges in various ways. Some turn their ethnographic gaze away from sites that smack of classic ethnographic locality, focusing on translocal phenomena of global capitalism or deterritorialized social identities such as found in diasporic populations.[10] Among regional specialists of the Andes that approach has been compounded by a subdisciplinary anxiety about a tradition of community-level studies that tend, in the view of critics, to treat local communities as bounded and enduring essences that reflect indigenous culture or a colonial trauma frozen in time.[11]

Others seek in local social life evidence of the differential reception of global phenomena, seen as a vast ecumene in which each node of the global web adds local flavor to a more dispersed monocultural order (cf. Hannerz 1992). In his introduction to a recent set of essays on the topic, for instance, Daniel Miller (1995) suggests that many of these discussions evoke a sense of locality as heroic survival, bending global forms to local wills. Miller notes as well that such discussions typically narrate the halfway point in a story expected to end in tragedy: local distinctiveness has been valiantly retained so far, but an ever more omnivorous homogenizing global juggernaut lurks just offstage.

Miller dubs this sense of local difference "a priori difference" and nicely distinguishes it from "a posteriori" forms of local diversity, by which he means "the sense of quite unprecedented diversity created by the differential consumption of what had once been thought to be global and homogenizing institutions" (3). Rather than understanding global modernity as entailing homogenization, Miller argues, "it seeks out new forms of difference, some regional, but increasingly based on social distinctions which may not be easily identified with space. It treats these, not as continuity, or even syncretism with prior traditions, but as quite novel forms, which arise through the contemporary exploration of new possibilities given by the experience of these new situations" (ibid.).

I am interested in similar questions, but my approach is different. Rather than turning away from such local settings as rural communities or households, I seek to revisit these ethnographically as the contexts for translocal entanglements. On the one hand, I take as my subject the prototypically global phenomenon of missionization. While I pay analytic attention to the translocal sweep of missionization, I also take stock of the fact that such phenomena must gain purchase at particular points of the terrain they encompass. The global phenomenon of missionization is inseparable from its concrete localized manifestation: missionaries whose personal trajectories span—say—childhoods in rural Poland, training at an urban seminary, a year of study in Chicago, three years of work with migrant laborers in North Carolina, and an ongoing pastoral stint on the Bolivian altiplano.

On the other hand, I take as my subject classical Andean locality: a set of small-scale and relatively out-of-the-way indigenous communities. Rather than approaching locality as the remote and bounded terminus of a global web, I seek to recenter locality as the situated context of social life. As such, locality is always ever emergent. The alternative analytic positions of a priori and a posteriori difference sketched by Miller share a similar conception of locality as primarily a site of consumption, receptive of global forms.[12] Implicit in this discussion, and common I think to many other discussions of locality (and, we shall see, of syncretic and popular religion as well), is a tendency to posit locality as unproblematically "already there." In the approach I take here, however, tempering this assumption of "already thereness" opens up new possibilities for thinking about locality by moving the discussion beyond binary framings of predicated locality interacting with global cultural forms and toward an ethnographic examination of the situated production of local social forms in complex situations.

Arjun Appadurai (1996) has made a similar point. Gesturing to classical discussions of ritual in ethnographic theory, he reminds us that locality, rather than a given, is in fact the ephemeral product of hard and continuous work, produced and sustained out of a variety of cultural operations. This insight cautions us away from heuristic approaches to locality as a presupposable position within an interaction. Rather than understanding locality as a prior condition to encompassing circumstances, I examine it here as an emergent product generated with respect to the circumstances of encompassment.

The Porous Production of Locality

The phenomena of contemporary Catholic missionization, and the overarching challenges of conversion and conjuncture, provide an opportunity to examine locality as porously produced. More than asserting the truism that social formations are never closed unto themselves (though this lesson still bears repeating), by "porous" I mean to evoke a condition of permeability or even saturation by external forces while simultaneously acknowledging a degree of local integrity. Porousness qualifies boundedness but does not efface it.

Qualifying boundedness suggests the sort of movement of people and culture traits familiar from classical discussions of diffusion as well as more recent literature on globalization, diasporas, and so forth. This "horizontal" movement across space—by missionaries and by Aymara, for whom, we shall see, the spatial circulation of people, objects, and other values has long been an important end of social activity—is certainly evident in the case at hand. However, correlated with this dimension of porous locality, I am interested in locality as it is porous "vertically." By this I mean the interpenetration of different conceptions and experiences of "the local," from local and translocal points of view, and their different kinds and degrees of influence. This is evident, for instance, in the spaces between the quotidian experiences of my Aymara consultants, sensibilities of social totality expressed in various household- and community-level rituals, juridical notions of community in national political organization, invocations of Aymara culture by inculturationist missionaries, or the ambiguous category of indigenous or traditional as mobilized within the contemporary politics of multiculturalism informing far-reaching constitutional reforms implemented in Bolivia since 1995. These coexisting framings of the local are structurally dissimilar, and they impact one another in ways that I explore most directly in chapters 3 and 7.

In my view the task for much contemporary anthropology (and perhaps especially for ethnography in those world areas where the discipline has traditionally erred on the side of reifying models of insular stable locality) is to account for these entanglements without losing site of the "there" there—and to account for the "there" there without falling into the trap of positing some enduring authentic locality at the capillary endpoints of global processes.

The approach I develop here builds upon a few basic axioms. The first is an understanding of culture as an ensemble of phenomena that takes place some-place, that is always enacted and emergent in a given context, that is always given situated relevance by positioned agents. A corollary of this is an under-standing of locality as never fully given but always produced by a range of coimplicated actors. A third fundamental point is that translocal and putatively foreign agents—in this case, missionaries—need to be understood as compo-nent subjects of local-level ethnography, deeply engaged in the production of locality. This last claim, complicating the units of analysis by which we discuss Andean culture, derives directly from the methodological challenges of con-ducting an ethnographic study of (mostly foreign) missionaries *and* Aymara.

A word of caution is in order here. In arguing for an empirical focus on local meaning production as a fundamental condition of culture, in stressing that missionaries be understood as component subjects of Aymara locality, and in offering this as an approach for thinking beyond binary categorizations of local and foreign, traditional and modern, pagan and Christian, I do not at all mean to minimize the force of such categorizations in shaping local experi-ences. My claim is not that these differences are absolutely erased or effaced in such complex settings; I do not take locality as a space for the cultural pro-duction of a microecumene. From different points of analytic purchase one can distill sensibilities that may accurately be cast as Aymara, Andean, West-ern, Christian, etc., and I do so, albeit self-consciously and cautiously, in the following pages. However, at the same time my analysis is based on the ethno-graphic observation that such differences are worked out and negotiated at the level of day-to-day situated practice. That is not to say there are no valences, tensions, or conflicts, but rather that this complex manifold is the presupposed frame of cultural practice, rendered coherent by situated subjects. Again, "co-herent" not in an absolute way but in the evanescent meaning-creating way inherent in most real-time, real-world cultural activity.

I am influenced in this approach by discussions in sociolinguistics as well as an overlapping literature on place and space. Both direct analytic attention to the question of context and to the social processes that produce the ground of meaningful social experience. Sociolinguists, for instance, have paid fruitful attention to the ways language users continuously generate interactional frameworks within which people are able to realize shared meanings. Through a host of resources—from gestures and facial expression to intonation and pro-nunciation—speakers routinely share and "get" the intended sense of a multi-valent word or of semantically underspecified "shifters" (indexical terms such as *that* or *her* or *now*) that are always dependent upon the context of utterance for their meaning.[13] My approach to locality is based on a comparable interest in the emergence of frames of interactional coherence encompassing an array of actors.

A related set of approaches in the literature on place and space argue that rather than inert given backdrops, these be seen as part of the culturally produced context of social life (e.g., Basso 1996; Massey 1999; Solomon 2000). Basso's examination of such place-making among the Western Apache, for instance, calls attention to the cultural processes that pick out elements of landscape as significant, imbue them with social meaning and historicity, and deploy them as points of reference for making meaningful unfolding contemporary social action. The Western Apache present an apt point of comparison for the Andean case, where other work has addressed a dense toponymic network of place deities (*wak'as*) and other potent sites as a mnemonic of history (Martinez 1983, 1989; Abercrombie 1998) and an "animated cosmos" interactive with all aspects of Andean social life (Allen 1988; Astvaldsson 1997). In the case at hand this attention to place making underscores the production of locality and calls attention both to the coimplication of multiple vantages (missionary and Aymara) for making sense of Andean places and the ways places linked largely to the actions of missionaries (churches, for instance) become integral parts of the local landscape.

Along with these useful concepts, and the metaphor of porousness, I use the term *entanglement* throughout this discussion. Why cramp a terminological field already crowded with "structures of the conjuncture," "transculturation," and "contact zones" (e.g., Sahlins 1985; Ortiz 1995 [1947]; Pratt 1985)? In part I am following other uses of the term to evoke a more nuanced understanding of colonial and postcolonial settings as they are mutually constructed (e.g., Errington and Gewertz 1995; Thomas 1991). These scholars also note that regional translocal complexity often predated colonialism—an insight that applies nicely to the Andean case. To my ear *entanglement* also conveys the unseen dangers and asymmetries of intention and power that give shape to such settings. Finally, I am borrowing from the usage of the term in quantum physics, where it seems to mark the limits of possibility for the analysis or description of discrete, individual components or particles of more complex phenomena (Zajonc 1993; Schrödinger 1956). For this is also the elusive quantum core of most social phenomena, the alchemy of culture in history: an open-ended human capacity to experience, reference, and meaningfully engage the ever changing world. While analyses that decompose colonial, postcolonial, or syncretic settings into component parts are revelatory, the fractured reality they depict does not exist. In its place I am seeking an analysis accountable at once to the asymmetries of history and the situated practices by which historical subjects realize deeply valenced settings as coherent lived worlds.

To be sure, the case I have chosen to advance these claims is privileged in at least two ways. As we shall see, the ethnographic particulars of the Andes suggest an especially porous engagement with "outside" forces and processes, a sensibility of localizing "foreign" value that has been an important factor in shaping the region's entangled history. At the same time, the phenomenon of missionization entails a sort of hyperlocalization of global processes, as missionaries typically engage in long-term residence in their mission fields. My view, however, is that, far from being atypical, missionization—arguably the mother of all global phenomena—provides a prime analytic opportunity to examine translocal processes as they are embodied and localized. Similarly, I think the Andes offer an illuminating comparative case for thinking about a range of examples of locality. That said, these, like all particularities, conceal as well as reveal. This unsettling reckoning of the forest and the trees is the constant question and the continuous contribution of anthropology.

CONUNDRUMS OF CONTINUITY AND CHANGE

I have suggested that, in the scholarly preoccupation with the Latin American colonial past, the phenomena of religious encounter have often served as the evocative part standing for the complex whole. As a number of recent treatments of the topic have noted, scholarship on missionization and conversion has tended to trade in relatively unidirectional, zero-sum models of encounter in which Christianity and "indigenous religion" are stable and mutually exclusive alternatives (see Griffiths 1999; Mills 1997; Taylor 1996). Thus Christianity either vanquished native religion or the evangelizers failed. Between these two poles lay the ground of syncretism, which, in the spirit identified above by Stewart and Shaw and van der Veer, is but a more complex form of evangelical failure or indigenous resistance.

Writing of scholarly analyses of colonial missionization in Mesoamerica, historian William Taylor (13) notes a tendency to "minimiz[e] the role of Catholic priests in local beliefs and practice (treating Catholicism as 'high religion')" and an "emphasis on the ability of native religions to add Christian traits without fundamental alterations." Taylor gestures to a closely related set of arguments stressing the orthodox "good vs. evil," "Christian vs. pagan" binaries of missionary Christianity counterposed to what is often cast as a more flexible indigenous conceptual scheme. The latter is said to enable natives to pick and choose from among usable elements of Catholicism or otherwise craft a more syncretic but fundamentally not converted cultural order. There is some truth to these characterizations. In the Andean case, we shall see, the translation of key Christian binaries (Heaven/Hell; God/Satan) foundered on an indigenous conceptual scheme keyed more on the productive mediation of contrasting categories than on their separation (see especially Dillon and Abercrombie 1988; cf. Klor de Alva 1999).

These characterizations of "how natives think" (differently from priests) also reflect analytic interests in recognizing and recovering folk or popular social and religious forms as distinguished from official or elite practices. Such has been the aim of important ethnohistorical studies of colonial situations in Latin America (e.g., Farriss 1984; Clendinnen 1987; Spalding 1984). These characterizations also participate in a related shift in analytic focus from religion as prescribed to religion as practiced and so illuminate a more creative and emergent sense of religious phenomena. For my purposes, I want to focus on and unsettle two intersecting and implicit assumptions in a good deal of this work.

The first concerns the spatial corollaries of this official/folk divide, since indigenous locality is posited as the site of popular religious practices. To return to the case of the ayuno, it is not simply the juxtaposition of a burnt offering encircled by the Via Crucis that seems to embody a syncretic history of partial assimilation and clandestine survivals. It is also the peripheralness of the ayuno event itself, performed in an outlying hamlet of a remote rural parish, that further suggests its syncretic or popular credentials (cf. Christian 1981).

Second, and alongside this sense of the popular/local as the capillary endpoint of institutional control, where formal doctrine is most subject to local alteration, adaptation, or resistance, is the assumption of the conservative, enduring nature of the popular/local. This is sometimes taken to be a locus of a sort of sui generis religiosity; this is certainly a component of the inculturationist view. Local syncretic meldings thus are sometimes taken as the continuing organic expression of pre-Christian ways.

Inga Clendinnen (1990), for instance, examines post-conquest religious experience in sixteenth-century Mexico. She approaches ritual as a swirling multisensory space of activity inducing experiences of the sacred. Taking this to be where the religious action was for the Mexicans, she argues that "for long years after the conquest" clandestine ritual acts as well as public and colonially sanctioned performances of Catholic rites served simply as variations at the level of technique expressing a more long-standing indigenous sensibility of the sacred. Other discussions similarly imply a bending of colonial form to more or less enduring local will. In his study of conversion and historical narratives in the Solomon Islands, White (1991:179) notes "Christian ideology has not been simply passively recorded on Pacific minds like a tape-recorder left running in the background of a Western conversation. It is instead actively interpreted in local contexts and put to use within culturally constituted spheres of interest and activity." Lattas (1998:xxi), in his discussion of cargo cults in Melanesia, asserts, "People gave an autochthonous form to the civilizing processes that were transforming them (cf. Elias 1939). They internalized those processes into their schemes of origin." Through these efforts to "impose new local meanings . . . these foreign processes came to be localized, internalized, and transformed" (98).

This book is in sympathy with such efforts to trace the local implications of global missionization and to rethink approaches to conversion and religious synthesis. The work I have cited by Clendinnen, Taylor, White, Lattas, like the above noted comments on syncretism by Stewart and Shaw and van der Veer participate in a turn in anthropology and other disciplines to focus on the textured nuances of broader processes of power, to render these in more fine-grained ethnographic terms. With differing degrees of success they strive to move away from all-or-nothing views of conversion and corollary claims concerning colonial and postcolonial societies. Yet, as should now be clear, I aim to do so in a way that explicitly takes locality less as a sleight of hand for cultural continuity—a preexisting end of the line for translocal processes—than as a porous product of such entanglements.

Localizing Missionaries

One of the ways I hope to build upon this body of work is through the examination of missionaries as participants in the production of Andean locality. This involves resisting the temptation to treat Catholicism as "high religion" and view missionaries as the embodiments of abstract and rigid religious ideology. The realities of most missionary experiences, which involve long-term and often intimate immersions in indigenous locality, belie this stereotype and call for a grounded ethnography that links levels of official doctrine with the messiness and negotiated nature of *doctrina* life.

An Andeanist cognizant of a violent history of extirpation and torture qualifies assertions of missionary inflexibility with some trepidation. However, it should be noted that these violent extremes typically resulted from the playing out of tensions and ambivalences implicit within the colonial evangelical project itself and in the context of unfolding local histories involving colonial administration as well as missionary-native relations (Clendinnen 1987; MacCormack 1991; Mills 1997; Taylor 1996). That is, we need to see these extreme cases not as a function of missionary single-mindedness but rather as a reflection of missionary involvement in local settings. Missionization, as a technique of colonization, entails the reciprocal transformation of missionaries, and, indeed, their routinization as component local subjects, in ways that crosscut the official/popular binary.

Big Bang Colonialism

It is increasingly common, thanks to many of the authors I have been citing, to note that colonial situations are not unidirectional processes of displacement. Anthropologists have stressed "the creative force of culture in shaping sociopolitical reality out of the dynamic interplay of indigenous and colonial elements" (White 1991:202) and approached contexts of colonial evangelization as a "long conversation" in which colonizer and colonized were locked in a "mutually constraining embrace" (Comaroff and Comaroff 1991:198).

These discussions from other world areas set in relief what I take to be a core limitation of much of the scholarship on syncretism and conversion in the Americas. This concerns a tendency to focus on formative moments of encounter, taking the dramatic and decisive decades of conquest and colonial consolidation as constitutive of a syncretic amalgam that endures to this day. In ways that accord with what I have described above as the "otherness" of Iberian colonialism from the vantage of most Western scholarship, the reciprocal process of colonial missionization is acknowledged but temporally displaced. As William Taylor (1996:53) has observed, the Americanist literature on syncretism reflects "a general view that colonial Indian communities independently achieved a more or less full and, by the mid-seventeenth century, stable synthesis, a synthesis in which Christian traits had been absorbed incrementally into native religion." Griffiths (1999:3) similarly suggests this may be linked to conventional conceptualizations of "conversion" that have "tended to encourage scholars to seek a recognizable end-point to religious interaction at which a stable synthesis is presumed to have occurred."[14]

The risk of such approaches is that they assimilate a view of colonial transformation within a new binary: in place of a presumed enduring indigenous culture locked in an all-or-nothing colonial struggle, we have an inherited amalgam generated in the earliest colonial moments set against the challenges of modernity.[15] With other research stressing conversion, religion, and identity in general as ongoing, emergent processes, I want to examine contemporary missionization within a long and unfolding history of Aymara-Christian entanglement. At the same time, these scholarly approaches to the inheritance of colonialism take on emic social force in the categories and conceptions of some contemporary missionaries and some contemporary Aymara (see chapter 4).

Translation, Metaculture, and Modernity

Recent efforts to rethink syncretism and conversion have also raised questions about issues of translatability and commensurability. Missionization typically involves communicating and finding local equivalences for Christian concepts (e.g., Keane 1996; Meyer 1994; Rafael 1988). However, local practices, like locality itself, are multivalent, subject to different readings from different vantages; translatability, in this sense, is made rather than found. Given the localizing bent of inculturation, this will be a recurring theme in the chapters to follow. A related theme concerns the translatability of religion as a metacultural concept or self-conscious experience. At issue is the familiar anthropological point that while religion appears as a more or less discrete category of phenomena in Western experience, arenas of thought and practice in other cultural settings need not bundle in immediately comparable ways.

Beyond the reflexive insights afforded by the vexed topic of religion in comparative perspective (see, for instance Asad 1993; Tambiah 1990), such discussions also caution us to be attendant to the ways that colonial and comparable encounters generate newly objectified categories of meaning and practice for all participants. Jean and John Comaroff's work, for instance, has traced the unfolding colonial missionary embrace in South Africa as generative of Tswana understandings of whites as well as of Tswana understandings of Tswana. For the present case I will advance the correlated argument that such encounters also generate shifting self-understandings among the missionaries and the missionary societies they represent.

In the Andes it is common to hear mythohistorical accounts of the origins of local culture framed as an evangelical engagement. In these cases the buffoonish, precultural ancestors of a distant age are explicitly cast as unconverted heathen; the constitutive condition of indigenous culture is the triumphant ascendance of Christianity (e.g., Dillon and Abercrombie 1988; cf. Errington and Gewertz 1994). And while contemporary "traditional" Andeans come to see their pre-Columbian ancestors as savage "gentiles," the practices and personnel of Catholicism have emerged as potent cultural symbols by which Aymara and other Andeans signal *in Andean terms* the most horrible rupture of social norms conceivable. Catholic priests are widely suspected of engaging in the theft of human body fat—poached from living Indians who typically fall sick and die or harvested from victims flayed and butchered to that end. The fat, which derives its value from an essence thought to inhere in Indians, becomes the substance of the most salient symbols of Catholicism's potent presence in the region: it is rendered into holy oil, used in the manufacture of candles and in the forging of the bells whose pealing came to sequence the rhythm of Andean life. More recently the fat has been identified as the key ingredient in medicines manufactured in Europe or the United States, thought to be used to power cars, trains, or planes, and suspected of being traded internationally to offset the national debts of Andean countries (see chapter 6).

But note that in addition to producing forms of self-consciousness and objectification anchored in a colonial encounter, processes of conversion, colonization, and missionization also involve a certain compression and interpenetration of levels of phenomena—indigenous and colonial, local and global—and correlated perspectives. Native origin myths incorporate colonial conquest as a condition of local cultural possibility. Bodily substances are taken to condense an "Indian" essence and then posited as commensurate with the symbolic repertoire of global Catholicism, the forces of industry, and the circulating value of transnational capital.

This interpenetration of levels is a direct function of such situations of encompassment and entanglement of dissimilar frames of power and practice. It is a core focus of this book, as inculturationist missionaries seek to "localize" their pastoral work through a theological alignment of Aymaraness with what they take to be universally translatable Christian meaning. However, the pan-Aymaraness that appears highly local from the global perspective of the Church and its transnational pastoral agents does not map comfortably onto the situated sensibilities of a given ayllu or parish. We shall see that the standardized "traditional" practices increasingly encouraged by the Church in fact undercut important and generative differences, tensions, and secrets across regions and pose new challenges for the local enactment of missionized religious forms. The current missionary setting thus generates conflicting reckonings of locality and reveals a number of frequently forgotten frictions and fault lines in contemporary processes of multicultural inclusion or ecumenical globalization. An analysis attendant to these coimplicated levels of analysis can better evoke the unfolding entanglements of colonial settings and their aftermaths. To build upon my initial discussion of inculturation, the analytic promise of missionization is that it cuts across levels of analysis and is integrally involved in the production and interaction of newly objectified categories.

A PREVIEW OF THE FIELD

Though I did not know it at the time, it was a beginning of different sorts for all of us. My first trip to Jesús de Machaqa in late 1990 coincided with a three-day, parishwide course for catechists conducted by the parish priest (Hernando) and a young Aymara seminarian being groomed to take over the parish.

This was the first formal presentation to the catechists of an ambitious plan to revitalize the pastoral work of the parish, seen by Hernando to have stagnated during much of the 1980s as missionaries and catechists grappled with the pastoral limitations of liberation theology and regional communities reeled from a series of disasters ranging from the local effects of neoliberal economic reforms (so-called shock therapy) to a sequence of droughts, floods, and crop-damaging frosts. Building upon lessons learned coordinating the distribution of relief aid to the region, Hernando, in concert with the Church-affiliated research and development organization CIPCA (Center for the Study and Advancement of the Aymara Peasantry), had developed a ten-year plan for the social, pastoral, and economic development of the region. His presentation to the catechists included a forceful introduction to the tenets of inculturation:

> [Here in this parish] we are beginning a ten-year plan. Ten years of agricultural work, of health education, and about women. And so, if there is not a heart, if there is no faith, there may be fights, there may be division. So, this is what we have to achieve as Christians. What does it mean for us that what God wants is that the people eat well, and what God wants is that the people be united, and God wants that the people continue progressing to have better houses, to have better water, better crops? And for this what is lacking is to have faith, to have celebrations in which the people feel united, in which the people feel they are a single community.

My wife Ingrid and I arrived at dusk with Father Hernando to find most of the catechists gathered in the dormitory of the parish center, joking and sharing a meal from the snacks of potatoes, broad beans, salted fish, and cheese carried by many Aymara when away from home for extended periods. We joined them. Afterward we helped Hernando unload supplies for the course, including a gas-powered generator and a VCR and television for evening entertainment. Hernando was looking forward to showing a comedy about a priest in a Mexican town. But the quality of the tape was poor and Hernando switched to an alternate video, *The Ten Commandments*. Unfortunately, the film was subtitled, and the small screen combined with the marginal literacy of many of the catechists made this a poor choice. After a short while we abandoned Charlton Heston and Yul Brenner to watch a documentary in Spanish about the work of the bishop of Riobamba (Ecuador), a prominent advocate of the sort of melding of social activism and ethnic revitalization being adopted by Catholic missionaries in Bolivia as the theology of inculturation. This was a big hit with the catechists—less for its doctrinal content than for its exoticism. The catechists gasped and hooted to see the strange clothes and different farming practices of the Ecuadorian highlanders depicted on the video. The next night we watched *The Misson.*

The following day the course began in earnest. I treat this in detail in chapter 3. Here I want to stress that the course involved compiling a calendar of "Aymara ritual practices": a formal register of community activities to be embraced by the catechists as local cultural expressions of Christian values. Indeed these were taken to be "the celebrations in which the people feel they are a single community", a local cultural means to realizing a universal religious end. Perhaps because the event was relatively fresh in their minds (this course took place in mid-December 1990; the ayuno is usually performed early in the month), Hernando engaged the catechists in a detailed discussion of ayunos. Catechists from communities where the rite was still celebrated were asked to narrate what activities took place. Those from communities where the rite had been abandoned were asked to recall how the event was once performed. Out of this extended collective ethnographic interview Hernando and the seminarian rendered a composite version of "the ayuno": an idealized template of the rite to be enacted by the catechists as part of the evangelical labors in their communities.

The ayuno performance described in the beginning of this introduction is one local result of this course. It is in many ways a prototype of the sorts of classical ritual to which Appadurai refers in his point about the ceaseless production of locality. The ayuno constitutes local community and, done right, ensures its material and social reproduction. However, "the ayuno" promoted by Father Hernando produces a community of a different order. It posits a standardized "Aymara community" interchangeable with any other community in the parish. Moreover, alongside this horizontal seriality, Hernando's choice of films to punctuate the course for catechists suggests a more vertical sort of replicability: aligning local Aymara experiences with those of other Andean Indians, with other contexts of Latin American Catholicism, and with founding events in the Judeo-Christian tradition. It this regard the ayuno is symptomatic of what Wilk (1995:118) has identified as the ambiguous renaissance of locality in contemporary global settings as "cultures are becoming different in uniform ways."

Toward an Ethnography of Entangled Locality

This book brings together three discussions: an ethnography of missionization, an ethnography of Andean locality, and an ethnography of embodied subjectivity and personhood. As an ethnography of missionization, the book documents a recent history (since the end of the Second World War) of Catholic pastoral practices in the region, conceived as part of a long unfolding entanglement of the Church with Andean societies. On the one hand, Catholic pastoral strategies represent a contemporary interaction of localized "traditional" cultural forms with ways of conceiving and engaging the world deeply implicated in processes of modernity and globalization. Even when posed in opposition to such processes (and we will see that inculturationist missionaries are ambivalent adepts of modernity), the modern missionary process is of a piece with projects of development, neoliberalization, and democratization. At the same time, this contemporary encounter engages a social landscape in which Christianity is already deeply implicated: a lived local world informed by a calendar of saints' days and their celebrations; a geography of chapels, shrines, and administrative towns; a folklore of foreign priests and their indigenous assistants who embody the promises and the perils of the powers condensed by Christianity. While they are certainly agents of innovation in Andean Catholicism, catechists operate within and with respect to a local tradition that itself reflects and refers to a dynamic history of cultural articulation. By the same token, however much they may hope to distance themselves from their predecessors, contemporary missionaries take part in a field heavily informed by that history.

A second discussion is an examination of postcolonial Andean locality. While the book is based on fieldwork in a number of rural parishes on the Bolivian altiplano, I conducted my most intensive research in the area of Jesús de Machaqa (Ingavi Province, Department of La Paz). I present a historical and ethnographic discussion of Jesús de Machaqa that keys on the complex condition of Aymara locality (see chapters 1, 5, and 7). Focusing particularly upon the presence of the Church in the region, and taking as a point of departure my ethnographic treatment of missionaries as component subjects of Andean locality (see chapters 2 and 3), I argue that the locality ceaselessly produced by putatively "Aymara" practices is a profoundly porous one, referencing and reproducing a translocal field in which Aymara and missionaries should be viewed as entangled communities.

The third strand of this discussion involves an ethnographic examination of personhood and embodied subjectivity. To some degree this emphasis on the body as a site of analysis and salient locus of activity is the endpoint of my broader concern with locality and correlated with my effort to rethink approaches that have tended to insulate locality. Bodily space, goes the argument, is about as local as you can get. The challenge I take up here is to link together levels of analysis spanning global processes of colonial and postcolonial missionary entanglement and their unfolding in local arenas and in the situated experiences and practices of embodied agents (see chapters 4 and 6).

This focus is also prompted by the issue of religious conversion. In ways that often intertwine with modernity, conversion involves a narrative objectification of self.[16] Van der Veer (1996:19) underscores the politics of such selfhood, noting, "The topic of conversion allows us to penetrate deeper than usual into the peculiar ambiguities of modern power. Christian conversion is a "technology of self," to use Foucault's notion, which, under modern conditions, produces a new subjecthood that is deeply enmeshed in economic globalization and the emergence of a system of nationalities." In this sense conversion to Christianity is co-implicated with incorporation into a dawning social order.[17] In a similar way, I am less interested in making propositional claims about conversion per se than I am in examining missionization as a technology of conjuncture that interpenetrates multiple units of analysis, spanning the global, the local, and the corporal.

For their part, the missionaries I came to know often expressed their evangelical concerns about an incomplete Aymara conversion in a bodily idiom: describing the Aymara as having "a foot in two worlds" or being physically "divided in two." Such comments echo classic discussions in Andean ethnography whereby local Andean spaces—rural hamlets, households, or the interior spaces of Andean bodies—remain largely insulated from external influence. Indeed, missionaries I worked with spoke explicitly of the Aymara "heart" (which they glossed with the Aymara term *chuyma*) as a site of cultural continuity apart from the veneer of Christianity adopted by contemporary Aymara. Alongside missionary invocations of their unpenetrated "heart," I consistently found Aymara consultants invoking chuyma not as an insular enclave but rather as seat of entangling engagement with the world. Keying upon these alternative sensibilities of bodily space and embodied subjectivity, I examine the ways that even the most microlevel Andean practices serve to align active subjects within and with respect to a complex translocal world. I make this case most explicitly at the center (heart?) of the book: in chapter 4. Yet the argument surfaces throughout the book, repeatedly seeking to disrupt bird's-eye approaches to syncretism and cultural conjuncture, placing us rather on the paths of the situated practices through which positioned agents realize complexly entangled settings as lived worlds.

At every criss-crossing of these themes stand the catechists. They are the primary local agents of missionary Catholicism. They are also the principal indigenous interlocutors of the missionaries, embodying the failures of colonial evangelization and the promises of newer pastoral paradigms. Indeed, drawn from communities across the altiplano, the catechists themselves constitute something of a meta-Aymara community. In interaction with this metacommunity, missionaries formalize their own visions of pan-Aymara culture. But the catechists are also complexly positioned subjects, negotiating in their own heartfelt ways their places in their families, in their faith groups, in their communities, and in the manifold world that contains them.

The following chapters are my effort to braid together these component themes. In casting this work as one of "braiding," I mean to evoke a process of separation and reunification—a simulacrum of wholeness that parallels the analytic project. Research and analysis involve separating experience into strands and attempting to weave them into a reevocation of the whole—one that is hypertextured, setting some things in instructive relief. This is a process of reentangling that only approximates and surely distorts the richness of its real-world referent. I take some comfort in the fact that I am not alone in this labor of good faith (but unavoidably distorting) approximation. I borrow the metaphor from the Aymara, spinners and weavers who refer to a range of social processes of unifying alternation as "braiding." Thus, like me (and, I dare say, you), Aymara are immersed in their own ongoing simulation of coherence, braiding meaningful order out of a complex world.

PART I

Entangled Communities

CHAPTER I

Andean Locality Revisited

In November of 1990 Ingrid and I traveled with Father Jan and Sister Marta. Snug in a late-model Toyota Landrover, we whizzed down the highway on our way to the parish of Peñas, a colonial town tucked in the foothills that rise into the Cordillera Real east of the altiplano. Behind us was the parish of Batallas, where the priest and nun resided with their respective communities. Before departing for Peñas, Jan had celebrated mass in Batallas for a small congregation composed chiefly of members of a Catholic youth group organized by a sister in Marta's charge.

Jan was relatively new to altiplano pastoral work. He had arrived in Bolivia after a year of service in his order's mission in Paraguay. He was clearly uncomfortable in his newest post. In an interview with me the day before, he expressed some frustration with the "lack of spontaneity" he found in highlanders as compared to his flock in Paraguay. He also repeated a lament I heard from many pastoral agents concerning the "excessive" value Aymara place on sacraments: fiestas, masses, etc. Blaming the work of his colonial predecessors, he complained, "The gospel message of liberation has not arrived in a profound way in the heart of the Aymara people." "We must learn the language, recuperate Aymara cultural elements," he continued, "[and] use them for a more profound evangelization."

With the assistance of Marta, Jan found the turnoff to Peñas and we left the highway for a rutted dirt road that put the Landrover to good use as we bounced and turned our way into the foothills. The mass was to commemorate two deaths in the parish. There was also a request for Jan to visit and bless a nearby site where lightning had recently struck, killing some livestock and injuring two young herders. When we arrived a large crowd was waiting in the parish office, many of them hoping to obtain certificates of baptism. Jan and Marta entered and began the laborious process of issuing the certificates. Each petition had to be confirmed against Church records: multivolume *libros sacramentales* kept under lock in the parish office. Solicitants paid 8 Bolivianos (app. $2.00) for a new certificate signed by the priest. Such certificates are necessary for Church as well as civil functions (e.g., marriage) and are often the closest thing to a birth certificate available. Many of these transactions were mediated by catechists who accompanied solicitants to the desk where Jan and Marta were working and served as translators from Aymara to Spanish.

We then entered the church, where Jan, with the assistance of local catechists, presided over a crowded mass. The mass completed, we made our way back to the Landrover to return to Batallas. (At some point Jan had decided not to visit the site of the lightning strike. It may be that the work of issuing certificates put him behind schedule, though the reasons were not clear to me.) Many in the congregation were disappointed that Jan had not repeated the names of the dead several times during the liturgy. "That's all they want to hear," observed Marta disapprovingly. Outside the church Aymara swarmed around Jan and Marta with various requests: late petitions for certificates of baptism, invitations to meetings, and requests for additional masses. A "mothers' club" (*club de madres*) was being formed in a nearby community. One of the women asked Marta to come to an upcoming organizational meeting where the women would select the group's first leader. Marta was upset by what she saw as a last-minute invitation. "If you tell me in time," she scolded, "I can come. But now it is too late: my calendar is all filled." As we climbed into the car, people continued to call out to Jan and Marta. Jan eased the car through the pressing crowd as some trotted alongside, palms pressed to the windows of the Landrover, imploring the priest and nun for attention. As we made our way back to Battallas, Jan muttered angrily, "These Aymara are like children!"

At Work in the Mission Fields

So went a formal observation of missionaries "in the field" early in my own field research. I have selected this vignette for the "everydayness" of it. There is no syncretic ritual spectacle; though I will confess to a real disappointment that Jan put off his visit to the scene of the lightning strike. There are no secret sacrifices in the shadows of the church, though such masses are but a part of set of practices, some more private, involved in remembering the dead. There is no stark confrontation between missionary and Indian. The final press of bodies is dramatic and was, perhaps, frightening to a recently arrived priest. But, for the most part, it was merely annoying: the pragmatics of Aymara politeness in such situations call for a wheedling, whining tone. They scrambled and pushed to make contact with the priest and nun or impassively watched the scene unfold and compelled it to continue by crowding in front of us or with their feet by one of the wheels of the jeep. Jan and Marta did not abuse the Aymara. There were no epithets shouted; none of the crowd were pushed or hit.

The pastoral changes at the center of this book must be understood against the routine day-to-dayness of Jan and Marta's visit to Peñas. To be sure, not everything went smoothly. Jan was clearly frustrated. I thought I detected a hint of amusement in the more seasoned Marta's observations of her recently arrived coworker. Some Aymara were visibly uneasy making requests of the priest, and there was a whiff of the "weapons of the weak" (cf. Scott 1985) in the crush of bodies that penned in the Landrover. And there were certainly elements of misunderstanding as the mass failed to fulfill local desires to have their dead remembered by having their names more frequently intoned. Still, I want to begin by situating Jan, Marta, and the Aymara they mean to serve as mutually presupposable participants in a single social situation. Their misunderstandings, fears, and irritations notwithstanding, Jan and Marta and the men and women in the church made sense to one another; their presence was assumed, their interactions required. In this chapter I present the local historical, geographical, and ethnographic context of the study with two additional and interlinked goals: 1. the presentation of missionaries as component subjects of local-level Aymara ethnography and 2. an emphasis on the ways locally constitutive practices and sensibilities generate and reference a skein of translocal entanglements.

By stressing the integrity of this sociohistorical formation and the complicated and coimplicated positions of the missionaries and Aymara within it, however, we should be careful not to mask the power relations that suffuse it. To argue that the situated production of locality references and renders coherent an entangled social order is not to claim that local actors make the world as they wish or that they (or I) approve of the world they reference and reproduce. As we glimpse in the above vignette, this routinized encounter itself references and performs bureaucratic power asymmetries evident in the documentation missionaries control—documentation that can enable or impede interactions with the Bolivian state.[1] Similarly, mothers' clubs are vital channels for assistance from the Church and other nongovernmental organizations (NGOs), which are increasingly important in Bolvia (Gill 2000); they often require indigenous communities to constitute themselves in specific ways. The imprimatur of Sister Marta is not strictly necessary for the club to form, but her requested presence suggests that Marta and the powers she represents serve as something of an implicit audience for the act of forming a mothers' club. The history I relate in this chapter is of an entangled locality produced within sharply constrained contexts under highly unfavorable and sometimes threatening conditions.

A MAP OF HISTORY

Where should "Andean culture" be found? How should we know it when we see it? Should we even presume it is there? Andeanist scholars wrestle with these and other questions as we work in an area classically defined by key historical moments and canonical disciplinary questions deriving largely from the heyday of "area studies" in the middle decades of the twentieth century.[2] Such wrestling becomes especially contentious given the critical questioning, ongoing for more than a generation in anthropology, of the presumptions of bounded and stable culture areas implicit in much of the classical ethnographic canon. The challenge for students of the Andes is to finesse the claim that a regional cultural "there" there exists without falling into the trap of positing a homogeneous or enduring Andeanism. A corollary challenge of particular urgency is to learn from intraregional comparability without becoming so mired in this discussion as to lose sight of broader and more pressing frames of comparison with other world areas and a set of global historical processes.

It is useful to begin with the observations that the Andes are not something found but rather something made. The commonalities and differences across the region—and, indeed, even the geographic self-evidence of "the Andes"—compose a map of history (cf. Gade 1999). Thus, for instance, the distribution of indigenous languages in the Andes, in which Quechua and its related dialects predominate, reflects the status of Quechua as both the language of the Inca Empire and the indigenous administrative language of the Spanish colony.[3] The endurance of the Aymara language in portions of the southern altiplano is a function both of the relatively late incorporation of Aymara-speaking groups into the Inca Empire and of the fact that a number of these groups were awarded the distinction of serving the Inca in armed combat and exempted from other sorts of acculturative practices by which other Andean populations were incorporated within the empire.[4] That said, pockets of Quechua speakers in the fertile valleys to the east of the altiplano and near the mining area of Potosí reflect the interest of the Inca and the Spanish in these regions.

One can similarly plot variations in social structure within the altiplano region of Bolivia. From northern areas around Lake Titicaca to the vicinity of Potosí in the south, there is a tremendous range of sociocultural forms, spanning small-scale social groups on the order of a community and large-scale groupings comprising thousands of people and dozens of such communities. This variation likely reflects the differential incorporation of some Aymara polities within the Inca state. It also reflects the disparate impact of agrarian capitalism in the area during the nineteenth century, when the more fertile lands around the lake were systematically converted into haciendas. A land reform implemented in the 1950s abolished the haciendas and parceled out land and local socioeconomic control, generating a landscape of apparently discrete communities in stark counterpoint to the more large-scale social structures found in the south.[5]

Finally, archeological and ethnohistorical data suggest that many highlands polities on the altiplano routinely maintained access to a wide spectrum of ecological products, often through outlier communities in ecological zones along the eastern and western slopes of the Andes.[6] This pattern was sharply but not totally constrained under Spanish colonialism and Republican governance, which tended to conceive of (and insist upon) population groups as fixed to bounded contiguous territories. However, there are areas in the region where a considerable degree of "ecological verticality" can be maintained within a contiguous territory. This is the case for some areas in Northern Potosí, Bolivia, where forms of verticality combined with extant large-scale social structures have been taken by some to offer a glimpse into pre-Columbian ways.

Ayllus and History

One key function of these interregional variables then is the scope of local Andean social structure, particularly the ayllu—long a central unit of analysis in Andean studies. The concept is remarkably elastic: in some areas, *ayllu* might be roughly translated as "close family," in others it refers to social units comparable to "communities" or larger, more dispersed groups comprising thousands of individuals.[7] Despite distinctions in scale, these extremes have much in common. They share a pattern of nested social groups: a Russian-doll-like hierarchy of ever more inclusive units. These ayllus, moreover, tend to be bisected by moiety divisions, creating complementary social groups paired as "upper" and "lower," "right" and "left," or "male" and "female." In one of the prototypical examples, the Quechua-speaking Macha of Northern Potosí, Platt (1986) borrows Evans-Pritchard's (1940) terminology for describing the segmentary structure of the Nuer political system, describing minimal, minor, major, and maximal ayllus that stretch from community-level units to complex confederations of multiple communities.[8]

In the Bolivian highlands this range of social units can be plotted along a continuum stretching between two geographical poles. In altiplano areas south and west of the Río Desaguadero—the northern reaches of the present-day

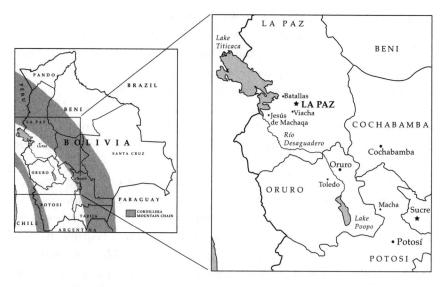

MAP I   *The Bolivian altiplano (highland plateau)*

Department of Potosí and portions of the Department of Oruro—larger levels of ayllu organization along with what have been seen as other vestiges of pre-Hispanic social organization predominate. Perhaps consequently, research in these areas has tended to key on the ongoing integrity of large, precolonial social structures and the survival of forms of ecological diversification otherwise evident only in archival data.

On the other hand, the more densely populated region bordering Lake Titicaca on the south and east was greatly impacted by the expansion of haciendas. Although located at the challenging altitude of 10–14,000 feet above sea level, the area has long been characterized by intense agricultural production as well as herding. Historian Herbert Klein describes it as "one of the richest agricultural zones in the South American empire of Spain" (1993:3). Beginning in the middle of the nineteenth century, the revival of Bolivian silver mining, the related growth of urban markets, the construction of a railway infrastructure to transport foodstuffs, and a series of market-oriented governments combined to create an economic, (il)legal, and military environment that enabled the expropriation of Indian-held lands and the emergence of large agricultural estates. Between 1846 and 1941 the number of ayllus (now defined principally as freeholding communities) in the highlands provinces of Omasuyos and Pacajes declined from 716 to 160, while the number of haciendas expanded from 500 to 3,193 (Klein 1993:119, table 5.2).

This situation was compounded in the middle of the past century, as the victory of the Nationalist Revolutionary Movement (Movimiento Nacionalista Revolucionario, MNR) in the revolution of 1952 occasioned a set of agrarian and related reforms intended to integrate and modernize Bolivian national society. The core of the reforms was the abolition of haciendas and the various forms of debt servitude that tied landless and small-holding Indians to the estates and the redistribution of much of the hacienda lands to the Indians who worked it. The reforms also reorganized and modernized the judicial character of indigenous communities, creating local community organizations—*sindicatos*—modeled after industrial labor unions and organized in a nested hierarchy linking the communities within the political structure of the MNR and a national framework of counties, provinces, and departments.[9]

So fundamental was the impact of these changes that some have characterized the MNR reforms as a second wave of assaults on indigenous communities, comparable, ironically, to the expansion of haciendas it sought to rectify and responsible for displacing and deforming traditional structures of governance (e.g., Rivera 1986, 1990). Within the rhetoric of the reforms—which has shaped political discourse in Bolivia until the present—the Indians were transformed into peasants (*campesinos*), echoing in a class-inflected idiom of modernization Bolivar's unrealized proclamation of the previous century that there were no longer any "Indians," only "citizens." Coordinated with these changes was the creation of new markets and roads in the countryside (see Preston 1978).

Logically, the lake region—most affected by hacienda expansion and closely linked with the seat of government power in La Paz—was most affected by the reforms: the impact of sindicato organization and the establishment of regional market towns and rural schools. In contrast, such reforms were slower in reaching nonhacienda areas and those more remote from La Paz.[10]

Beyond presenting some regional historical context for this book, I offer this in illustration of my suggestion that we can "read" the variations across Andean space as a map of history, reflecting not only the permutations of Andean social structure but also the differential local impact of translocal entanglements common to the region. But such a map also presents other opportunities, challenges, and temptations that bear directly on the ethnographic consideration of Andean locality and shape my own efforts to revisit it here.

Local Ethnography and the Colonial Past in the Andes

As Tom Abercrombie (1998:xvii) has observed, "much of Andeanist ethnography aims to reconcile the pre-Columbian past with the postcolonial present." From this vantage Andean locality has typically served as an anchor for a "Mendelian" view of history (cf. Harris 1995), a kernel of authenticity more or less buffered by encompassing social structures, a locus of a cultural logic detectable across the history of engagement with Spanish colonialism and fledgling nation-states (e.g., Platt 1987b). The variable scope and history of the Andean ayllu form has been significant in this regard, and a tension in Bolivianist ethnography between community-based research carried out in the lake region and work focused on larger ayllu structures to the south is instructive for considering approaches to locality in the Andes.

Community-based ethnography in the region typically addressed contemporary processes of social and cultural change involving processes of development, the impact of land reform policies, shifting ethnic identities, and/or the challenges of out migration to cities.[11] Yet, for reasons I have detailed in the introduction, such discussions often cast the contemporary challenges confronting indigenous communities as an engagement of enduring (albeit colonial corrupted) indigenous form with a late-arriving modernity. Drawing upon models of "closed corporate communities" (e.g., Wolf 1955), these studies present the community as a set of boundary maintaining processes that, at least until the present wave of changes, had enabled the reproduction of traditional culture in the face of shifting external threats.[12]

Alongside this work, research focused on large-scale ayllu structures has keyed on formal similarities between these contemporary social groups and those described in the earliest postconquest documents.[13] These scholars have usefully addressed the limitations of community-based research: contextualizing ethnographically and ethnohistorically contemporary Andean "communities" with respect to the fragmentation (in the face of Incaic, Iberian, and Republican rule) of older, more comprehensive Andean polities.[14] They have also found in large-scale ayllu structures a potent record of the moment of colonial contact and the impact of colonial institutions. In my view such research has often risked reproducing by a different route the essentialism of earlier generations of scholarship, finding in contemporary ayllu structures glimpses not of a pristine Andean culture but rather of a primordial colonial moment.[15]

Perhaps as a consequence of the sort of historical data available to them, these discussions present something of a bird's-eye view of colonial and postcolonial processes in the Andes, yielding a coarse historical periodization of epochal transformative moments, and an analytic focus on large-scale phenomena: regional systems of leadership, regional ritual practices, and long-distance networks of trade and exchange. From this vantage a dichotomy appears between a public, outward-looking interface with nonindigenous society associated with more large-scale ayllu practices and more local, private practices that appear to be relatively buffered from such changes as well as generative of an Andean cultural logic.

I draw appreciatively from much of this work throughout this book. At the same time, with other recent work on the region (e.g., Abercrombie 1998), I seek to revise "temporalized" misreadings of Andean culture as a composite of original and imposed social forms and to revisit Andean locality—as it is historically derived, to be sure, but also as it is complexly produced. Taking a situated approach to Andean locality, I shall focus on the ways the most microlevel practices presuppose and reference encompassing circumstances of entanglement and on the ways "outside" cultural agents and their influences are interwoven within the fabric of the most private experiences of Andean social life.

ANDEAN LOCALITIES AND ETHNOGRAPHIC FIELDS

My research included fieldwork with pastoral agents and catechists in settings across the Bolivian continuum of community-level and large-scale ayllu structures. Batallas, the home of the communities of Jan and Marta, is an example of a market town created in the wake of the agrarian reforms as an economic anchor for a group of communities/sindicatos in an area once dominated by haciendas (Preston 1978). It is located along a paved highway and served by frequent transportation to and from La Paz. That Batallas is now the hub of regional pastoral activity is certainly a function of this convenience as well as the fact that many Aymara from surrounding towns visit Batallas for its weekly market. In this sense the pastoral teams serving such areas are component subjects of local histories, entangled in the production of Andean locality. Prior to the arrival of the current pastoral team, the area was served by Maryknoll missionaries based in the town of Peñas. Once a significant colonial town,[16] Peñas is now off the beaten path and bypassed by recent events. The present pastoral team left the massive colonial temple of Peñas and constructed a new parish house in the young town of Batallas from which they serve four parishes: Batallas, Peñas, Aigachi, and Puerto Perez.

This group of parishes is itself part of a larger pastoral zone known as the *altiplano sur* (southern altiplano). At the time of my longest period of field research (1990–92), this was part of a group of rural pastoral zones—also including the Yungas valleys to the east and the northern altiplano on the eastern flank of the lake—under the guidance of the auxiliary bishop, Mons. Adhemar Esquivel, a charismatic indigenous bishop, who in the course of his career had served as a priest in a number of the parishes now under his care.[17] The

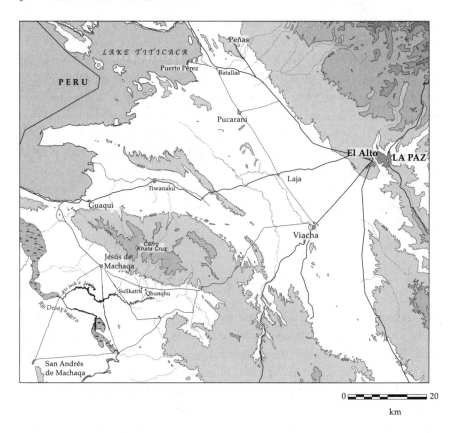

MAP 2   *The southern altiplano pastoral zone*

altiplano sur comprised some twenty-two different parishes. In the early 1990s perhaps fifteen were routinely active in interparish activities. I conducted much of my research with catechists from this "southern zone," with the bulk of my time spent in the parish of Jesús de Machaqa.

Alongside my work in the lake region, I conducted research with missionaries and catechists in the pastoral zone of Carangas, in the Department of Oruro—also the location of Jaques Monast's pastoral and ethnographic work. This arid area is among the regions where large ayllu structures remain intact, and this is reflected in the organization of the pastoral work. Some four priests, assisted by two brothers, two seminarians, and five nuns, attend to a dispersed population of highland herders (seventy-six thousand at the time of my initial field research) in an area of some thirty thousand square kilometers. Coordinated largely from the town of Toledo, which houses a training center serving the catechists from across the zone, missionaries shared responsibilities for attending to some eleven parishes spread over six different provinces.

My discussion draws upon fieldwork with missionaries and catechists in parishes across this geographic and sociocultural range, with a focus on the parishes of the altiplano sur. Regional pastoral events and especially missionary courses became important sites of my research, as these brought together catechists from many parishes. Interwoven with these discussions, however, is an ethnography of Andean locality—both in the conventional sense of an intensive and situated study of a community or region and as a site for the contextualized examination of missionaries, catechists, and their faith groups. In this regard I draw from an intensive research focus on the region of Jesús de Machaqa (Ingavi Province, Department of La Paz).

The parish of Jesús de Machaqa, along with the neighboring parish of San Andres de Machaqa, composes a single pastoral zone. One priest and a brother, assisted by a small community of nuns and a lay pastoral team, care for a pastoral zone of over 2,000 square kilometers including more than 110 communities. In the 1960s and 1970s a pastoral team residing in Tiwanaku served Jesús and San Andres de Machaqa along with four other parishes in the area—Tiwanaku, Taraco, Laja, and Tambillo—in a model of pastoral organization similar to that found in Carangas today. The current arrangement in Jesús de Machaqa reflects the impact of post-MNR reforms in the region as well as changing pastoral strategies and the particular histories of the members of the Tiwanaku pastoral team. I detail these intertwined histories in chapter 2.

The case of Jesús de Machaqa usefully complicates the tension in recent generations of scholarship between community-based studies and studies taking supracommunity ayllu structures as their unit of analysis. Jesús de Machaqa is located geographically and structurally between these two extremes. Though part of the pastoral southern zone, the region is situated on the margins of the altiplano heartland: more southwest than southeast of Lake Titicaca. While the nearby city of La Paz has had a strong impact on the region, the area never fell under the control of *hacendados* and a complex ayllu structure links its component communities. The ethnographic reputation of the area has long been one of cultural retention and resistance.[18] Yet a close look at the region's history suggests the porous and complex condition of this putatively traditional Aymara locality.

THE CASE OF JESÚS DE MACHAQA

Like many highlands regions, Jesús de Machaqa was once part of a larger social unit, comprising contemporary San Andres de Machaqa and Santiago de Machaqa on the opposite bank of the Desaguadero River. The earliest colonial accounts of the region describe a population of "Aymara" and "Uru"[19] organized in a structure of nested dual opposition: on the west side of the river, what the Spanish dubbed "Machaqa la grande" (greater Machaqa) comprised present-day San Andres and Santiago de Machaqa; on the east side, "Machaqa la chica" (lesser Machaqa), later Jesús de Machaqa, was the complementary moiety half (Choque 1991, 1993, Choque and Ticona 1996, Mercado de Peñalosa 1965).

The three Machaqas were part of the pre-Incaic polity of Pakaxe. This indigenous structure retained a good deal of its integrity as a province of Inca administration and Spanish colonial governance. *Machaqa* means "new" in Aymara, and some historians speculate that the area housed vanquished and resettled populations, placed under the rule of a powerful family of altiplano rulers, named Guarachi, who had married into the Inca line. An alternative theory holds that the Machaqas emerged out of disputes between neighboring highlands polities, prior to Incan expansion, and the Guarachis (who went on to rule the region) represent the victors.[20] Like its bipartite component, the ethnic polity of Pakaxe was itself organized into "upper" and "lower" halves. The Machaqas were part of Urqusuyu (upper, lit. "male" part) of Pakaxe.

The fifth viceroy of Peru, Francisco de Toledo (1569–1581), is credited with a massive effort to consolidate Spanish administrative control over the recently conquered and then still poorly understood Incan Empire. As part of this effort, Toledo, with protoethnographer missionaries and administrators in tow, embarked on a massive tour of inspection (*visitas*) throughout the Andes. It was in the course of such visitas that the Machaqas were given their Christianized names. Another curious thing happened in the course of Toledo's inspection: Jesús de Machaqa was designated as *hanansaya,* with San Andres and Santiago designated as *hurinsaya.* Hanan and hurin are ubiquitous Quechua designations for the ranked moiety divisions of upper and lower halves; *urqu* and *uma* or *alax* and *manqha* are corresponding terms in Aymara. Of note here is the viceroy's effort to extend to the Aymara heartland the Quechua appellation gleaned from his experiences in the Inca capital of Cuzco. This is a quibble; I have no doubt that the binaries in Quechua map fairly neatly onto the binaries in Aymara; this worked well, after all, for the Incas. Yet it reflects a moment in a longer history of the production of Machaqueño locality under often contested conditions and should draw our attention to the ways locality is conceived and engaged by a range of actors with a range of points of reference. More significant from a historicist perspective, I think, is that the valences of the binaries were reversed by Toledo. The prior local distinction between Machaqa la grande and Machaqa la chica—which corresponds to a pattern observed elsewhere along the Desaguadero water axis with superior halves to the west (see Bouysse Cassagne 1987)—was inverted as Toledo dubbed Jesús de Machaqa the superior half.

I am not aware of historical data that enable more than speculation; however, it should be noted that the half nominally valued by Toledo was arguably the choicest parcel of land: largely flat and well irrigated by rivers and streams extending from a range of foothills south of Lake Titicaca southwest to the Desaguadero River, with areas near the foothills relatively protected from destructive winds and frost. In contrast to this fairly fertile river plain, the lands of San Andres and Santiago are somewhat colder and dryer, more suitable for the sort of dispersed highlands herding that can be found there today than intense agriculture. Similarly, it seems significant that in the initial division of the spoils of conquest it was the lesser Machaqa (superior, in Toledo's eyes) that was given in *encomienda* to one Capitán Juan Remón, with the western lands of Santiago and San Andres designated for the crown. The administrative authority and responsibility of encomiendas (which included the right to receive tribute from Indians residing on the apportioned lands) were typically quite profitable for the recipients and were effectively rewards for service at arms. It is likely that the choicest swag was apportioned (or claimed) by the upwardly mobile adventurers who composed much of the conquering frontlines in the Andes, with the remainder apportioned for the distant authority of the crown. It was the crown's concern about this sort of maneuvering by the first wave of colonial neoelites that led to the appointment of the muscular administrative reformer Toledo.

And a muscular reform it was. Toledo's visitas did more than ratify and incorporate preexisting indigenous society within the colonial framework. He reconfigured the social and political landscape of the Andes, establishing model towns (*reducciones*) and frameworks of local governance (town councils [*cabildos*] operating alongside indigenous nobility) based largely on idealized Spanish views of social order and explicitly designed to maximize the efficiency and legibility of colonial tribute collection, the forced draft of indigenous laborers for the mines, and Catholic evangelization.[21] The intertwining of cabildo and related forms of local governance with the practices and places of Catholic evangelization are particularly salient to my discussion.

Precolonial Machaqa, then, appears as part of a classic highlands polity, controlling land on either side of the river and maintaining access to lands across a range of ecological zones on the western and eastern slopes of the Andes (Bouysse Cassagne 1987; Murra 1967, 1975). These regional networks were deeply linked with cultural values stressing the circulation of distantly derived products. Under the colonial state, Jesús de Machaqa appears as a discrete administrative division: constituted as an ecclesial unit and a bounded locus of indirect rule through native intermediaries (Choque 1986, 1991). From the eponymous central town of Jesús de Machaqa, priests and a host of colonial functionaries administered the various outlying communties/ayllus that composed the region.

LOCALIZING THE CHURCH: CACIQUES AND THE MEDIATION OF COLONIAL VALUE

In 1808 the bishop of La Paz undertook a review of the accounts of the parish of Jesús de Machaqa. The review came on the heels of the appointment of a new parish priest—José María García—who had arrived in Machaqa in December of 1807. For nearly twelve months prior to his arrival the parish had been administered by Diego Fernandez Guarachi, one of a line of Guarachis who had served as *caciques* of the region. Throughout their colonies the Spanish relied on the mediation of such caciques, whom they saw as an indigenous "nobility" that might command the allegiance of the native masses and lend the colonial project a measure of legitimacy deriving from the historical accomplishments of the Inca state (Spalding 1984; cf. Chamberlain 1930).

The bishop's report is mixed. On the one hand, finding the Church blessed with considerable capital, he ordered the yearly celebration of a set of parish festivals and anniversaries commemorating the deaths of notables in the Church, ranging from the popes and the Catholic kings of Spain, through bishops and priests who had served the parish, to the "founders" of the parish and the faithful who had lived there. He also ordered a number of improvements to the parish's *beaterio*—a convent for Indian girls constructed alongside the matrix church. The bishop further instructed the new priest to find an abbess for the convent and to establish a school for the *beatas* and other girls of the pueblo where they might be taught to read and write and learn Christian doctrine "with perfection." To support these works, in addition to the liquid assets on hand, the bishop ordered the church to sell a number of hacienda lands it held in other areas of the Andes, including one of three haciendas that supported the convent.

The bishop also ordered the priest to collect from those owing money to the parish. Prominent among these debtors was "Cacique, Don Diego Fernandez Guarachi." Particularly striking about Don Diego's debt was that the moneys owed (2,309 pesos and 1/2 real) were funds to which he had access while briefly serving as *mayordomo de fábricas* (treasurer) of the parish.[22] He had assumed that position in 1807, temporarily filling a void left by the death of the parish priest. Under apparent scandal Don Diego stepped down from the administration of the parish accounts. At the same time, he resigned a similar position he had held as administrator of the beaterio. The debt went unpaid until 1826, at which time it was reckoned as 2,413 pesos, 1/2 real. Some 1,726 pesos were paid in cash, with additional payments made in the form of clothing and embroidery. Curiously, Don Diego then returned to his position as administrator of the parish's accounts. Appointed by the bishop, he served the parish church from 1829 to 1840.[23]

Don Diego was the last in a powerful Guarachi line of caciques who had a tremendous influence on the articulation of the region with the Incan Empire, Spanish colonial administration, and the early decades of the modern Bolivian nation-state (from 1825). Archival documentation I have seen, along with the work of other scholars—most notably the Bolivian historian Roberto Choque Canqui—suggest the authoritative presence of the Guarachis dating from the late sixteenth century. The genealogy of Guarachi authority illuminates the porous production of the region across these shifting political contexts. It is a genealogy of decline: from heroic and powerful caciques asserting their legitimacy in Andean and Spanish terms to the likes of Don Diego, whose questionable fiscal integrity seems to have served only his own interests. It is also a genealogy of entanglement: the machinations of the "last Guarachi," Don Diego, reflect the achievements of his forefathers, whose legitimacy derived largely from the successful conversion of pre-Columbian forms of value into meaningful rights and powers within the political economy of Spanish colonialism and the harnessing of newly emergent forms of power to the production of Machaqueño locality.

The Last Guarachi and the Scandal of Postcolonial Entanglements

While colonial rule severely constrained the region's access to distant ecological zones, the Guarachis successfully converted traditional rights to distant lands into property rights within the Spanish juridical system. Perhaps the most powerful of the Guarachis were Don Joseph Fernandez Guarachi (1677–1734), who used the honorific title *maestre de campo,* and his uncle (*tío abuelo*) Gabriel Fernandez Guarachi (16??–1673) (ACLP/CC t.21, ff. 193–203v Choque 1979). The latter's testament successfully claimed as personal property—and transmitted to Joseph—a variety of lands within the region of Jesús de Machaqa, lands in the vicinity of Lake Titicaca as well as valley lands in the provinces of Larecaja and Inquisivi. The range suggests a continuity of the pre-Columbian pattern of integrating multiple ecological zones.[24]

But there is more than tenacious and wily continuity at hand here. The Guarachis' success in negotiating emerging forms of colonial power within the idiom of local structures of value made them enormously wealthy in both traditional and contemporary terms. In addition to maintaining access to the valued produce of ecologically distinct regions, the Guarachis brokered Machaqueño access to new values including cash and intercourse with colonial power. Thus what became ratified as Guarachi holdings in distant valleys were exploited not only or always for their produce but were also rented out or their produce cultivated for sale in colonial markets. Similarly, the spatial reach of the Guarachi holdings took on new meanings as points of articulation with colonial power: a house in La Paz and the means to wear the finery of indigenous nobility took on added significance with the emergence of the city as an administrative center and a nucleus of interaction between the indigenous, creole, and Iberian elite.[25]

This had two remarkable results. Thanks to their great wealth—maintained through the adept use of the Spanish legal system and enhanced through marriages with other lines of caciques—the Guarachis were able to purchase the lands of Jesús de Machaqa in a series of transactions in 1587, 1645, and 1746.[26] Documents from the late nineteenth century indicate that Machaqueños successfully (and creatively) invoked records of these transactions by the caciques to establish their rights as collective property holders in terms compelling to the liberal economic ideologies of the Melgarejo and Frías governments.[27] These were the governments that implemented the anti-ayllu reforms that led to the spread of haciendas over much of the northern Bolivian altiplano. Jesús de Machaqa's resistance to the incursions of hacendados, long held as a mark of its traditional integrity, is thus equally a function of its porous production within the shifting contexts of colonial domination.

The Guarachi family also had a remarkable relationship with the Catholic parish of Jesús de Machaqa. They were the "founders" of the parish, listed for ritual commemoration by the bishop in 1808. The matrix church in the central town—a large and impressive structure that stands to this day—was financed and overseen by the caciques. Initial arrangements for the construction of the church appear in the testament of Gabriel Fernandez Guarachi (d. 1673). After his death one of his daughters, Lucretia Fernandez Guarachi, purchased lands, the production of which went to finance the project (Choque 1979). Joseph Fernandez Guarachi oversaw the actual construction; he appears as patron of the church—along with the then parish priest Juan Antonio de Infantas y Mogrovejo—in canvasses (dated 1706) that once adorned the building depicting the "Triunfo de la Inmaculada" and the

FIGURE I.I   *The construction of the church in the central town was financed and overseen by the Guarachis*

"Triunfo de Jesús" (Gisbert 1980:93). The temple was not inaugurated until 1754, some twenty years after Joseph's death (Bonilla, Fonseca, and Bustillos 1967:37); the initial gilding of the church was completed only in 1777 (AALP JDM/lf).

Similarly, the convent that was renovated at the orders of the bishop in the nineteenth century was constructed with Guarachi support over the course of the eighteenth century. The 1734 testament of Joseph Ferndandez Guarachi includes a gift to the beaterio of two thousand head of sheep from the Guarachi-held hacienda of Qurpa, which lay within the territory of Jesús de Machaqa. Later documentation makes it clear that entire hacienda, along with two others that lay outside of the region (one near Taraco and one in Cavani) were turned over to the convent as a perpetual source of income.[28] Construction of the building for the beaterio was completed in 1778; it stood adjacent to the Church and functioned until 1841. It closed under scandal, the story of which returns us to the last of the Guarachis, the disreputable Don Diego.

During the early decades of the nineteenth century, Don Diego maneuvered with varying degrees of success to retain his position of influence in

parish affairs, including the management of the beaterio. In 1825, returning
to the position he had renounced amidst scandal in 1808, he appears again as
administrator of the convent. Perhaps taking advantage of the upheavals of
the independence struggle, Diego asserted his right to manage the beaterio as
a *cacique de sangre,* a descendent of the original "benefactors" of the parish, obligated to protect their intentions.[29] (It may be that his renewed access to the
convent's accounts enabled him, in 1826, finally to pay off his debt dating
from his stint as mayordomo de fábricas of the parish).

The story of the fall of the beaterio is murky—it is repeated by Bonilla,
Fonseca, and Bustillos (1967) and, with more caution, by Albó and equipo
CIPCA (1972). The source account appears in the work of the Bolivian folk-
lorist/lawyer M. Rigoberto Paredes (1955). As he tells it, in 1841 Guarachi
began to liquidate the capital assets of the beaterio. He sold haciendas held in
distant areas and, with the proceeds, endowed a number of scholarships in a
seminary in La Paz. He then contracted a music teacher for the beatas, a vio-
linist from La Paz named Marcelino Mariaca. Don Diego enlisted the musician in a plot to seduce one of the secluded women. Mariaca (*no mal pareci-
do,*—not bad looking—reports Paredes), was successful, and two of the beatas
were soon pregnant. Don Diego, citing the founding intentions of the benefactors that the beatas remain free from scandal, denounced this situation,
prompting the bishop to close the beaterio and return the remaining hacienda of Qurpa to the control of the Guarachi family. Significantly, the hacienda
was subsequently transferred through two generations of female descendents
of Don Diego: his daughter Isabel and her only daughter, Justa Pastora Galdo.
Paredes reports that her son, Don Diego's great-grandson, eventually sold the
hacienda to an Italian family in the 1940s. They subsequently lost it in the 1953
agrarian reform. It has since been incorporated as a component ayllu of the region. More recently, wanting to be closer to the communities they served, the
current pastoral team moved its headquarters from the shadows of the
Guarachi-funded church in the central town and constructed a new compound in the ayllu of Qurpa.

‡ ‡ ‡

In the machinations and accomplishments of the Guarachis we can see the
ways the emerging colonial context offered a new field of constraints and
possibilities for establishing the sorts of translocal mediations that were highly valued by Andeans. Access to remotely derived goods is a good thing, and
the ability to harness or incorporate distant powers is an important index of
local authority. Among the distant values harnessed to local ends by the
caciques was the Church. Over the course of the colonial period, Catholic

ritual and the sociopolitical legitimacy it conferred became integral to the production of local indigenous social orders. Priests emerged as indispensable local ritual authorities.

The construction of the church in Jesús de Machaqa pueblo was part of a wave of such church construction in free communities of the altiplano during the mid-eighteenth century (Klein 1993:120). To some extent this reflects the adaptive capacity of caciques to harness capital, engage urban markets, and compete with haciendas in the shifting colonial economy of the time.[30] To some extent this reflects the establishment of the Church as a prime value in local terms. Similarly, the machinations of the last Guarachi illuminate the entanglement of indigenous locality within broader spheres of power and politics. While the details of the closing of the convent may be apocryphal, the decades after independence were a time of considerable anticlericalism by the nascent Bolivian state. Independence also marked a watershed for the caciques, who were seen as a colonial inheritance, and gradually saw their power wane in the face of other forms of regional political administration. In this light Don Diego's efforts to take his capital and "run" suggests a savvy reading of the political signs of the times.

In underscoring the caciques' ability to control emerging forms of value during the colonial period, I do not mean to minimize the brutal impositions of colonialism. After all, the position of the colonial caciques was itself predicated on various forms of colonial extraction of tribute and labor. Nor do I mean to suggest that the caciques operated without constraint or that they represent in some transparent way the interests and will of the Indians they helped govern. The caciques, like contemporary ayllu authorities (and, for that matter, like the catechists), are conflicted ambivalent figures. In the Machaqueño oral historical tradition, the Guarachis are not always remembered fondly (e.g., Ticona and Albó 1997). They did, in essence, come to serve as the hacendados of the region. Yet their ambiguous actions are the condition of possibility for the contemporary assertion of the unambiguous traditional integrity of Jesús de Machaqa. What is more, the genealogy of the Guarachis reveals that the structures and personnel of the Church have been integral to the production of Machaqueño locality—as distant value to be harnessed to local ends and—as I shall argue in the following section—as local sites condensing such translocal connections. My aim here, then, is to frame undeniably asymmetric colonial and postcolonial historical processes as nonetheless interactive, manifold entanglements. This sort of pattern remains salient today in the ambivalent prestige attributed to similar local sites of foreign power such as rural health posts and schools. These figure prominently in a number of regional ritual performances constituting community-level sociopolitical authority with respect to such local instantiations of more distant power. It is to contempo-rary Machaqueño sociopolitical structure and the practices that produce it that I now turn.

ENTANGLED LOCALITY

Over the course of colonial history, Jesús de Machaqa emerged as a self-contained unit of indigenous social structure: a network of ayllus composed of various patrilines, anchored by a ritual and administrative center, the town of Jesús de Machaqa, a site of religious and colonial functionaries as well as an emerging population of white or mestizo residents (*vecinos*). The ayllus of the region comprise a familiar Andean moiety pattern of "complementary oppo-sition," described above, by which components of a social whole are paired as contrasting halves. This pattern replicates across Machaqueño society, from the region as a whole down to each component household. I begin by sketching this recursive dualism, taking as a starting point the community where Ingrid and I resided for much of our time in Bolivia, Qhunqhu Milluni.

When contemporary Machaqueños use the term *ayllu* it is a social unit of the scale of Qhunqhu Milluni to which they refer. In the bureaucratic language of the peasant syndicate structures that have organized rural society since 1952, Qhunqhu Milluni is a *subcentral*, composed of two *sindicatos*.[31] In the terminol-ogy of Andean moiety relations, these are figured as the upper and lower syn-dicates. A system of component "zones" (*zonas*) dovetails with the syndicate or-ganization. Milluni comprises eight zones—four to each syndicate. The eight zones reflect the fissioning in the 1970s (some informants said 1973) of a system of four zones, also called *katus*. The Aymara term *katu* suggests a "handle" as of a hoe or other tool and well evokes one function of the zones: as a way of or-ganizing communal work parties. Bonilla, Fonseca, and Bustillos (1967:60 ff.) report the establishment in the 1960s in the central town of Jesús de Machaqa of intracommunity work groups, essentially revitalizing a form of local labor or-ganization that had long existed in the region organizing the fulfillment of a range of labor obligations from road construction and maintenance to the con-struction of the church. The work groups helped muster and organize labor for the construction of a new school in the town—an outgrowth of the MNR re-forms. The reorganization of the katus in Milluni is likely linked to a school construction as well—a secondary school serving the ayllu was constructed in 1974. Schools, like churches, are metonyms of encompassing power. The emerging local social structure of zones serves in part to coordinate local labor power to the end of the entangling localization of these state institutions.

Like the syndicates they constitute, the zones are coded as upper and lower, right and left. Repeated questions about this elicited conflicting rankings. The zones are often named in a way that references the fissioning of four to eight zones: 1a, 1b, 2a, 2b, and so forth. According to some informants 1a through 2b were "upper" and the remainder "lower." This is essentially the ways the zones map onto the syndicate structure. Alternatively, some consultants suggested that 1a, 2a, 3a and 4a were "upper," with the *b*s all "lower." This arrangement of upper and lower within a syndicate was described as "intercalated" or "braided." Of course, each of these arrangements—along with other permutations—may be "correct" given that the nested oppositions yield relative positions: "upper" with respect to x (see Platt 1986; Allen 1988). One consultant suggested that the fissioned zones were initially labeled one through eight, but that the half of the first katu that was to become zone 2 insisted on being termed zone 1b. Another man—a member of zone 1a—responded to my questions by describing the zones this way: zone 1a, he said, was "completely upper," zone 1b was simply "upper," and the rest, he suggested, were "mixed." Such conflicting data reveal that the arrangement congealed administratively in the syndicates is but one understanding of a more complexly reckoned local context.

The results of my efforts to map the zones spatially were similarly mixed. While Andean dualisms can sometimes be plotted empirically—products from the highlands paired with products from the lowlands, biological men paired with biological women—the labels more often produce a difference than refer to one. Thus upper zones are not all more elevated than lower zones. Nor are the zones or the syndicates they compose contiguous. Some informants linked certain zones with particular family names—e.g., referring to the "zone of Ch'uqis"—or with specific place names, suggesting that members of a given zone are related by proximity or ritual to a significant place—a mountain or rock outcropping—in the community.[32]

Despite my determined efforts, people I spoke with insisted that names and places were not important organizing categories for the zones. In part this was a function of intra-ayllu diplomacy. I suspect that connections of certain zones to particular places or family names also reference certain hierarchies within ayllus between families of longstanding (*originarios*) and those that migrated to the region over the course of the colonial and republican period (*agregados/forasteros*).[33] When I dwelled on the theme of zones and other intra-ayllu divisions too long, Qhunqheños would invariable change the topic declaring, "We're really all just one ayllu." At the same time, their reluctance to ratify any single structural principle reveals a more dynamic tension underlying this sort of segmentary structure, which depends upon the participation of positioned actors for its reproduction through a system of rotating and alternating obligations to the community in which each household in effect comes to constitute itself as the "center" of its zone and of the ayllu.

The zones are said to be composed of ten or eleven "persons." Persons are communally recognized representatives of a given household or cluster of patrilineally linked households (*sayaña,* see chapter 5). Each zone maintains a list of its persons, used for recording attendance at zone meetings and tracking a variety of obligations from participation in community work parties to rotating positions of community service. The lists are unambiguously patrilineal. An eldest son inherits his father's position on the list, at which point the father "rests." "The son becomes a person when the father is tired," I was told. Alternatively, a group of sons may serve collectively as a single juridical person, sharing the responsibilities (and the family land) among themselves.[34] Despite the idiom of masculinity, a prime condition of such public personhood is marriage. Should a man die without sons old enough to serve, his widow continues publicly to perform his personhood (see chapter 4).

Other ayllus in the region exhibit comparable but not identical structures. While Milluni has eight zones, neighboring Sullkatiti Titiri comprises ten. Qhunqhu Liqiliqi, which borders the other side of Milluni, has four zones, and each zone is constituted as a syndicate. Kalla Arriba, which borders on the town of Jesús de Machaqa, similarly has four zones, again each constituted as a syndicate.

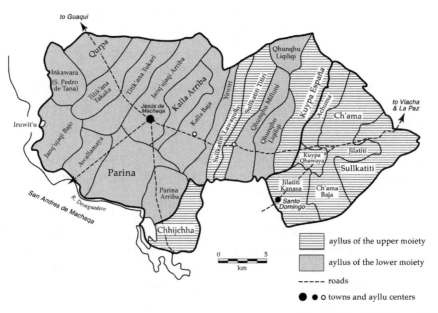

(map: after Ticona & Albó 1997 maps 1 & 3)

MAP 3   *The principal ayllus of Jesús de Machaqa*

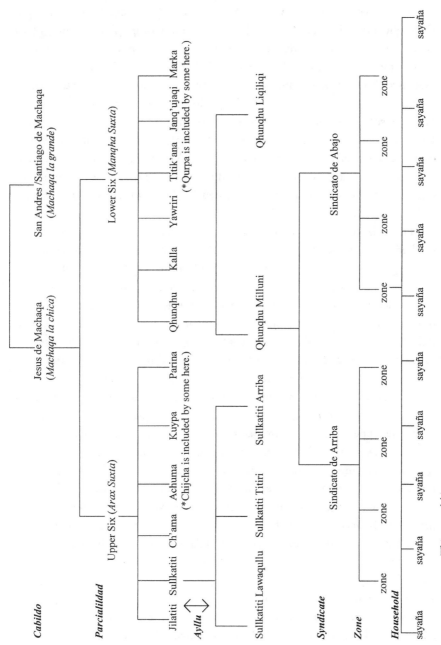

FIGURE 1.2   *This nested binary structure . . .*

As the names suggest, Qhunqhu Milluni and its neighbor to the east, Qhunqhu Liqiliqi, once composed a single ayllu. Comparable groupings (not all of them contiguous in territory) are revealed by a scan of the contemporary ayllu names: Kalla Arriba (Upper Kalla)/Kalla Baja (Lower Kalla), Yawriri San Francisco/Yawriri San Juan, etc. While there are dozens of contemporary communities "on the ground" Machaqueños tend to characterize the region as composed of twelve or sometimes twenty-four ayllus (see Albó and equipo CIPCA 1972). In colonial documents ayllus that today have split into two or more parts are referenced as a single entity—"Aillo Calla, Aillo Yahuiri, Aillo Conco."[35] Qhunqheños sometimes told me that their grandfathers were once united, and one man recalled a time when Liqiliqi held rights to a small plot of land in Milluni and vice versa.[36]

The relationship between Milluni and Sullkatiti Titiri is much more marked than that between the two Qhunqhus. There are two massive school buildings (along with barracks for teachers) built on the boundary of the two ayllus as well as a plaza (the site of a weekly market) and a health post. The ayllus celebrate a number of rituals together and also exchange visits to one another's community-level fiestas. These ritual interactions invariably end in fights between groups from each ayllu. Members of one ayllu tend to regard members of the other either as contemptible weaklings or savage murderers.

This smoldering tension makes some (regional) structural sense. The Milluni-Titiri boundary condenses a moiety organization, by which the prototypical twelve ayllus are bisected into two halves (*parcialidades*) of six ayllus each: the upper/right six (*arax suxta*) and the lower/left six (*manqha suxta*). These sets of six are internally ranked, and the resulting hierarchy indexed somatically. Together, I was told, the two parcialidades make up a human couple. Qhunqhu is considered the "head" (*p'iqi*) of the *manqha suxta;* Sullkatiti is a superior component of the *arax suxta*.[37] The Milluni-Titiri border is the principal physical boundary between the moieties of the region. It was described as such to me, and the complex relations between the ayllus further bears this out.

Braiding Locality: Ayllus in Motion

This nested binary structure (from the moieties of the region, through the relative interayllu binaries produced by the somatic hierarchy of each moiety, through the syndicates and their component zones within each ayllu, down to the "persons"/households/conjugal pairs that compose the zones) provides the framework for a set of public practices that serve to produce every level of Machaqueño society. I am referring here to the familiar fiesta-cargo or civil-religious hierarchy: a sequence of public service obligations to the ayllu through which all adults are expected to pass. Classically, these "ladders" of public service twine participation and sponsorship in Catholic saints festivals with forms of administrative service first instituted with the Toledan reforms and modeled on early modern Iberian town councils (*cabildos*). Fiesta-cargo systems thus embody the merging of colonial catechetical strategies and structures of indirect rule and their emergence as integral techniques for the production of indigenous locality.[38] The local concern to construct churches and maintain access to priests and sacraments surely reflects this.

The cabildo system and the cargo structures that fed into it served as something of a populist counterweight to the quasi-feudal authority of the caciques. The caciques' loss of power over the nineteenth century was the council's gain. Apart from a brief revival of so-called neo-caciques at the turn of the twentieth century, the local structures of rule generated by fiesta-cargo complexes have been the principal administrative interface between indigenous localities and the Bolivian state. It is telling in this regard that the last Guarachi, the calculating Don Diego, exercised his waning power by brokering access to the Church—which access was integral to the legitimacy of the fiesta-cargo system. The genealogy of the various positions in the cargo hierarchy remains murky—some positions were likely held for periods of years; participation may have been different for originario and agregado family members. The contemporary upshot, however, is a sequenced career of yearly positions, with each cargo aspirant "resting" for a period of several years between offices. In recent decades this melding of colonial practices and indigenous social structure has merged with the national hierarchy of peasant syndicate organization (Barnes Marschall 1970a, b).

In Milluni participation in the fiesta-cargo system is bound up with the status of "person" in a zone—cargo officeholders are the formal representatives of a household or cluster of patrilineally linked households within the ayllu; each turn of service publicly ratifies this position. Although the language of fiesta-cargo leadership and public personhood is starkly masculine, it bears emphasizing that such public careers—conceptualized by Machaqueños as a "path" (*thaki*)—are traversed by a couple. That said, the man is often the most public face of cargo leadership positions. The earliest rungs on a ladder of cargo service typically involve sponsorship of the annual fiesta of San Antonio in the ayllu.[39] Every year's celebration has two married couples serving as sponsors, with each representing a different half of the ayllu. The next level of service in the current cargo configuration is the position of p'iqi or head of a zone. P'iqi service cycles through the list of constituent persons; as most zones have ten or eleven persons, a household will be responsible for leading/representing the zone every ten years.[40] Until the mid-1970s p'iqis served for three consecutive years. This changed to an annual rotation at about the same time that the system of eight zones emerged.[41]

A p'iqi is responsible for mustering the members of his zone for periods of communal labor and for informing his zone of upcoming ayllu meetings. Similarly, a p'iqi is expected to maintain order among his constituents. Should someone become disruptive during a community event, people call for the corresponding p'iqi to intervene and keep the offending person in line. Finally, a p'iqi serves as a representative of his zone in delegations representing his ayllu to other communities or at intercommunity events held in Jesús de Machaqa town. Failure to perform these functions result in complaints and insults from the members of his zone and fines and other sanctions from superior ayllu authorities.

Some consultants cast p'iqi service as something of a training period, a preparation for more authoritative positions in the ayllu. P'iqis are seen as maturing men, "learning how to speak" and becoming familiar with the customs of the community. They are expected to assist ayllu authorities—*mallkus*—accompanying them in their travels or serving as a messenger in their stead. This subordinate maturing relationship was well evoked by one man who told me, "The p'iqi is the mallku's son."

The cohort of p'iqis has been adapted to the structure of the peasant syndicates introduced since 1952. Modeled after industrial labor unions, the syndicates prescribe a leader (secretary general) served by a cabinet of specialized posts: secretary of acts, secretary of justice, secretary of sports, and so forth. In Milluni the hybridity of this adaptation is much in evidence. The administrative fiction of two component syndicates (enabling the ayllu's precariously inflated claim to subcentral status) means that four of the zones compose one syndicate (upper) and four another (lower). One of the p'iqis from each set of four is dubbed secretary general, a title that rotates among the zones in each syndicate. In the communities I observed, the component syndicates are rarely autonomous political units, though they represent that potential. The remaining p'iqis all assume syndicate cabinet posts. However they serve not their respective secretaries general but the superior position of subcentral, also labeled with the Aymara terms of authority *mallku* or *jilaqata*.[42]

The mallku/jilaqata/subcentral is the maximal position of authority in the ayllu. Service as mallku completes a fiesta-cargo career. Service as p'iqi—which may or may not correspond with service as secretary general—is a precondition for mallku service. Most of the ayllus of the region have two mallkus— each one representing one half of the community. In Milluni the mallkus are drawn from those persons of each of the two syndicates who have completed their service as p'iqi. People refer to an age set (*q'uchu*, lit."cut") to describe this set of eligible couples. During certain ayllu events this pool of eligible men are formally dubbed "machaq [new] mallkus"

The two mallkus are ranked. Earlier ethnographic work in the region reports a right and left—*kupi* and *chiqa*—mallku.[43] In contemporary Milluni the ranking is marked with syndicate titles. The superior mallku takes on the office of subcentral and is formally served by a cabinet of p'iqis. The inferior mallku assumes the post of "president of the Association of Heads of Families" and is charged with mediating relations between the ayllu and the local rural school: supervising professors, enforcing attendance, managing the facilities and the institution's accounts—typically in the form of herds of sheep and cattle. These ranked positions of mallku (and note that it is the syndicate-derived gloss that serves as the diacritic) alternate between the syndicates from year to year; the subcentral is drawn from the machaq mallkus of the upper zones in one year and from those of the lower zones the next.

This pattern of alternating hierarchy is evident elsewhere as well. Recall that the schools served by the lower mallku are located directly on the border of Milluni and Titiri. There is a corresponding "school mallku" among the mallku pair from Titiri. This interayllu set of mallkus is itself internally ranked—the superior mallku overseeing all of the school's operations, the inferior mallku tasked with managing the school's herds. This relationship alternates from year to year.

Put most broadly, mallkus are responsible for community solidarity and for mediating the interactions of the ayllu with other ayllus, with the Bolivian state (police, schools, etc.), with NGOs, with the Catholic Church, and so forth. During his tenure, a mallku is expected to sponsor and host a number of feasts and ritual offerings and to settle any disputes that arise within the community. The expenses of ritual sponsorship, the continuous bounty of alcohol and coca a mallku is expected to provide, the costs of travel in service to the community, compounded by time away from herds and crops, make mallku service an especially onerous financial burden. As with all of these cargo posts, the mallku is literally a public servant—working on behalf of the community and obliged periodically to inform ayllu members of his actions. A mallku who does not perform his tasks adequately will be harshly criticized by his ayllu and, in extreme cases, may be required to serve for an additional year.

Mallkus are also responsible for the distribution of *aynoqa* land: communally controlled plots, scattered throughout the ayllu in different phases of crop rotation.[44] Most households have plots (*qallpas*) in various aynoqa tracts.[45] Though the aynoqa rotation is common knowledge for many, the mallku is responsible formally for notifying the ayllu which fields will be coming out of fallow and what will be planted in the other active aynoqa lands in the coming agricultural cycle. While many families speak of "their" plots in various ayno-qa fields, use rights to these lands are contingent upon the participation of a "person" from that family in a fiesta-cargo path. It seems fitting, then, that the rite at which a father rests and embarks his son as a newly public "person" upon a cargo path occurs during Carnival at the same time that the mallku is activating fallow aynoqa lands for the coming year.

While all the community obligations I have described involve a married couple—or at least imply a maturing household—it is in the context of mallku service that this dyad is most publicly evident. Husbands and wives serve together, with the man addressed as "tata mallku" (father mallku)—sometimes "tata subcentral"—and the woman addressed as "mallku tayka" (mother mallku) or "mama t'alla." Throughout their year of service they are, figuratively, the mother and father of the ayllu. They are distinguished throughout this year by their dress—which is to some extent an exaggerated version of traditional garb. The tata mallku wears a poncho over the jacket and dark trousers typically worn by men in the region. He also wears a *lluchu* (knitted cap with ear flaps) covered by a fedora hat. Around his neck and over his poncho he wears a cross, sometimes called a *calvario,* and a scarf. Tied to his left arm is a *ch'us-pa*—a woven purse for coca—and slung over his shoulder, its ends attached to

FIGURE 1.3   *A mallku in full regalia serves a drink to his counterpart from a neighboring ayllu*

FIGURE I.4   *A mallku tayka (or t'alla) adorned for Carnival*

form a loop, is a whip (*chiquti*) of braided strands of llama hide affixed to a
wooden handle. Some mallkus carry ornate staffs of authority (*varas*), though
this is not typical in Machaqa (cf. Rasnake 1988). Finally, a mallku wears a carrying cloth—*q'ipi*—slung across his back, containing extra coca, alcohol, and
a variety of ritual items. Among these is a cloth pouch sewn shut containing
small amounts of all the agricultural products produced in the ayllu. The mallku libates these periodically and is often held responsible for the agricultural
success of the ayllu during his tenure.

A t'alla's costume is more distinctive and more rigidly prescribed: a black
skirt and dark sweater or blouse covered by an *awayu* shawl in which the dominant color areas (*pampas*) are black. On her head, in place of the bowler hat
typically worn by Machaqueño women, she wears a *montera,* a headdress of
black cloth draped over a frame. Like her husband, she wears a q'ipi slung over
her shoulder in which she carries a variety of ritual items, including a supply
of coca and alcohol. Where men tend to use a ch'uspa purse, women store and
serve their coca in a *thari,* a small cloth woven of llama wool.

As part of their travels outside of the ayllu, mallkus go frequently to the
town of Jesús de Machaqa. Indeed, among their first acts upon entering office on New Year's Day is traveling to the town to hear mass celebrated by
the parish priest.[46] The mass is followed by the first meeting of the regional

cabildo, composed of the mallkus/subcentrals and in some cases the secretaries general of the ayllus of the region. The cabildo corresponds to the contemporary political unit of a county (*cantón*).[47] It also reflects the moiety organization of the region (i.e., the two parcialidades, upper and lower six). Each parcialidad corresponds to the syndicate structure of a "central agraria," composed of syndicates and subcentrals. The maximal position of authority in each central rotates among the component members according to the somatically indexed hierarchy of the ayllu in each moiety. Within the cabildo the moieties form an asymmetric pair. The leaders of each central are also the leaders of the cabildo, and they assume the primary and secondary posts of cantonal and subcantonal. As with the asymmetric pairings I have described at other levels of the social organization, these positions alternate across the parcialidades/centrals from year to year such that the leader of the upper moiety will be cantonal one year, while his successor in the upper moiety will serve as subcantonal the following years.

Locality and History

Beyond providing a background for coming ethnographic discussions, I have reviewed this social structural information at some length (and risked some deceptively normative claims about Machaqueño culture) in the service of three arguments. The first concerns the nested nature of Andean social structure. Social practices at the most interstitial, microlevels of Andean society are central to the production of the sort of regional, macrolevel institutions (such as fiesta-cargo systems and cabildos) that serve as the principal interface between indigenous society and colonial/foreign forms. The data from Jesús de Machaqa suggest that these nested levels of structure serve less as onionlike insulating layers than as vectors entangling the production of microlocal social forms with a set of encompassing social forces.

Seen over time, the structure of the region evokes a complex pattern of rotation and alternation at the levels of central, ayllu, syndicate, zone, with these nested levels crosscut by a set of cargo paths. The paths are directly correlated with the life cycle of households (couples typically embark on their cargo careers as relative newlyweds and complete them when their children are ready to assume their own paths) and weave that process into a field of power deeply informed by the region's colonial and contemporary history. Machaqueños themselves speak of their cargo paths as "braided," or woven together, enmeshed with other paths as with the warp and woof of other social and political processes and the unfolding histories of entanglement they condense. Though the complex contingencies of these crosscutting processes will render one man cantonal for the region and another president of the local school committee at the pinnacles of their respective cargo paths, the effect of each path is to articulate through the culturally patterned experiences of married Aymara couples the production of households, zones, ayllus/syndicates, centrals, and counties of the nation.

A second argument concerns the centrality of the Church. On the one hand, the Church is integral to these entangling social processes. Networks of ayllu, interayllu, and regional festivals compose much of the armature of the structure; Catholic sacraments and regalia are similarly crucial to the legitimacy of the public personhood and social order braided out of the paths. The ecclesial center and the annual calendar of festivals it coordinates, often involving an array of community-level chapels dedicated to specific saints, enable the integration and reproduction of the region. The paths serve to align individual and household biographies within this complexly produced social field. To be sure, elements of fiesta practice have waned in recent decades as they have waxed and waned at other times in Andean history. I track these recent shifts in detail in the following two chapters. The key point for the present discussion is the *presupposability* of the Church and its personnel: we cannot talk about the processes that generate Machaqueño locality without talking about the localized presence of the Catholic Church. By extension, we shall see, we cannot talk about changes in local Catholic practices without addressing their implications for the production of locality.

The Church itself seems to condense key aspects of regional social structure. This is most evident in the organization of mayordomos. Mayordomos—also called *alcaldes de la iglesia* (mayors of the church)—were once a post in the cargo hierarchy. Two mayordomos served annually in each ayllu: one caring for the chapel in the community, the other representing the community in service to the Church and the parish priest. This latter form of service required residence in the town for one year. Most ayllus maintained a house in the town, which was used for lodging by the mayordomo and by mallkus and others with more occasional business in the town. It is likely these same houses or others like them were used to lodge the work parties from each ayllu that constructed the church in the eighteenth century. The mayordomos' disappearance (during the 1960s) is correlated with the rise of the catechists (cf. Carter and Mamani 1982).

The mayordomo system reprised within the physical space of the church the interayllu structure of the region. The interior of the church comprises twelve named altars, including the altar table and icons located in the chancel and along the nave and side aisles of the building. Like the moieties of the region, these twelve altars are sorted into two ranked groups of six and coded "left" and "right." In similar fashion, consultants indexed the ranking with

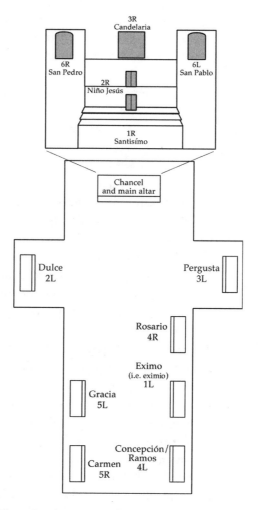

FIGURE 1.5   *The twelve altars are sorted into two ranked groups of six and coded as "left" (left) and "right" (right)*

somatic labels—*p'iqi* and *khayu* (head and foot)—and characterized the head altars of each set as *Escribano* and *Justicia*. These titles are the presyndicate-era analogues of the titles cantonal and subcantonal within the regional cabildo.

Twenty-four mayordomos served annually, one from each ayllu. In any given year twelve were active in caring for the altars. The remaining twelve were said to be "resting," although they were presumably responsible for other duties such as service in the parish house.[48] Additional responsibilities included ringing the church bell at set hours. Each of the active mayordomos was responsible for the care of one of the twelve altars. Over time, however, the correlation between ayllus and altars rotated, such that should a mayordomo from Kalla Arriba care for the altar Carmen (5R) in one year, his successor the following year would be responsible for the altar Concepción (4L). My data are sketchy, but indicate that the left and right sets of altars were intercalated to form a scale of twelve (6L, 6R, 5L, 5R, and so on) and that the mayordomos attending the altars were similarly intercalated, alternating between the two moieties according to the somatic hierarchy of the ayllus. As with analogous patterns of alternation and rotation, consultants described this as braided, *trensado*. One consultant suggested that mayordomo service was directly coordinated with the rotation of mallkus in the cabildo—that when the mallku of Yawiri San Francisco served as escribano (i.e., cantonal), the mayordomo serving that same year would care for the principal altar, Santísimo. Other informants insisted the two systems were separate, but all referred to the network of altars and mayordomos as "like a cabildo" or as a "minor cabildo" (*jisk'a kawiltu*).

I collected conflicting information as to whether the active mayordomos comprised an intercalated mix of both moieties or whether each moiety put forth an active cohort in alternate years.[49] In the case of mayordomos from both parcialidades serving together, the resting mayordomos represented ayllus that had recently served at the maximal altar Santísimo and were queued to begin the process again at the "foot" of the left altars, San Pablo. The model here is a single intercalated line cycling through the twelve altars and through a twelve-year period of rest for each ayllu. Alternate data suggest that the cohort of active mayordomos oscillated between the parcialidades—one year upper, one year lower—presumably with the ayllus from each half rotating through the hierarchy of altars. Of course this scheme, over time, preserves a braided pattern: any given altar being attended by a ranked succession of mayordomos alternating between the two parcialidads.

This latter schema takes on additional significance in the light of other comments suggesting rivalry and conflict between successive cohorts of mayordomos. Outgoing mayordomos would grease the steps of the church bell tower, making the structure hazardous to novice mayordomos. More generally, mayordomo service was considered a dangerous posting. Proximity to priests—often regarded as dangerous beings and suspected of terrible crimes including butchering Indians for their body fat—was one issue here. Former mayordomos also noted to me their fear and discomfort at having to negotiate the bell tower stairs on dark, cold altiplano mornings.

But the climate and the company were only part of the problem. The bell tower, metonymic of the entire church structure, is regarded as a potent place deity or *wak'a*.[50] Mayordomos sought to enable their proximity to such a powerful and ambivalent place through a ritual performed at the beginning of their tenure. As their wives sat in the churchyard at the base of the structure with offerings of coca and alcohol set out on cloths, the mayordomos clambered up the (greased?) stairs to the top. From there they tossed coca leaves to rain down upon their wives (cf. Platt 1986).

Here I can turn toward the third of my arguments, which concerns the complex and central position of the church—and comparable metonymns of foreign power—within Machaqueño social structure. The moiety relations of upper and lower reflect a more widespread categorical dualism often dubbed "complementary opposition" and taken as characteristic of Andean societies. The term suggests the fertile or productive merging of contrasting values, evident ecologically in the relationship between highlands and lowlands products, cosmologically in the relationship between *alaxpacha* (upper space-time) and *manqhapacha* (lower/inner space-time), and sociologically in the sorts of paired social groups I have been describing. The actions of the mayordomos and their wives at the church tower make clear these other resonances of complementary dualism: the male mayordomos ascend the tower (evocative of *alaxpacha),* their wives remain linked to the enclosed horizontal space of the church plaza; the ejaculation of coca leaves (a lowlands product indispensable to altiplano sociability) evokes the fertile circulation of upper and lower, male and female. Recall, as well, the conjugal pair serving as tata mallku and mama t'alla. *Mallku* also refer to birds (falcons) as well as to place deities associated with mountaintops. *T'alla,* which has long referred to the wives and close female relatives of caciques and other principals, also invokes feminine place deities associated with flat, or low-lying, or enclosed spaces, such as corrals.[51]

With other ethnographers of the Andes I would suggest that the end of many local social practices is the achievement of a balanced mediation of contrasting values—an evanescent state of completion, fertility, and human perfection sometimes signaled with the term *taypi* (center). Left at that, though, the story is incomplete. For this space of central completion is by no means an unalloyed indigenous site. Rather, the "centers" of the production of locality are typically marked by the presence of structures metonymic of encompassing foreign power. To illustrate this, let me return to revisit Qhunqhu Milluni, one component ayllu of the region.

Neighbors and Murderers
I was drawn to Bonifacio by his outspoken self-assurance at catechist meetings. In late January, some weeks after the catechist course described in the introduction, I took advantage of another catechist meeting in Jesús de Machaqa town to ask Bonifacio, along with a few other catechists, if I could visit them in their respective communities. Bonifacio quickly agreed, and we arranged a

visit in Qhunqhu Milluni the following week. That visit coincided with the celebration of Domingo de Tentación (Temptation Sunday, the first Sunday of Lent), the last of a weeklong series of Carnival rites. In Machaqa Carnival falls in the middle of the growing season, and much of the activities of that week turn on the celebration of the maturation and fertility of crops, animals, and human society (see also chapter 4). Ingrid and I arrived on an early-morning bus from La Paz. We stepped off the bus and right into a ritual procession.

Tentación is celebrated jointly by Milluni and Titiri. As I observed the event the following year, a group of mallku and p'iqi couples accompanied by a few friends and family marched from their houses in Milluni carrying white flags and playing flutes and drums. They converged on the large primary school that straddles the border between the ayllus (and between the parcialidades), gathering in a loose circle at the corner of the building in Milluni territory, dancing and playing music. A corresponding group from Titiri gathered in the Titiri plaza, just next to the school. After a while, the Milluni mallkus paraded onto a road connecting the Titiri plaza with the main road leading to town. On the way they merged with a procession from Titiri, and, together, the mallkus and their followers marched to the local health post also sited at the ayllus' border on the main road. (It was this part of the event that Ingrid and I stepped into the previous year.)

FIGURE 1.6   *The large primary school and the plaza at the Titiri / Milluni border (viewed from Milluni)*

FIGURE I.7   *Dancing at the school during Carnival*

After circling the health post compound, the two groups entered it, planting their white flags together in the patio. Two groups of musicians, corresponding to the two ayllus, competed musically, interrupting and trying to
play louder and longer than their rivals. The mallkus and t'allas from Milluni
greeted their counterparts, exchanging coca and alcohol. They also greeted
and served coca and alcohol to the resident health promoter and his wife and
adorned the health post with confetti and streamers.

After some time, the groups left the health post and traveled back toward
the school. They passed the primary school and continued past the secondary
school farther up the hill to enter an abandoned house patio, which served as
a corral for the herd of sheep belonging to the school. The mallkus and p'iqis
sat in an alternating fashion—p'iqis from Titiri/mallkus from Milluni/mallkus
from Titiri/p'iqis from Milluni—on a low stone bench facing the t'allas who
sat on the ground before them. Ayllu-specific music groups played in the patio
while revelers danced and pushed forward to pay their respects to the mallkus
and t'allas, who were themselves adorned with streamers and confetti. Sheep
from the corral were brought out and their ears notched in an event that parallels household-level marking rituals also celebrated during the week of Carnival. The house compound during my first visit was surrounded by onlook-

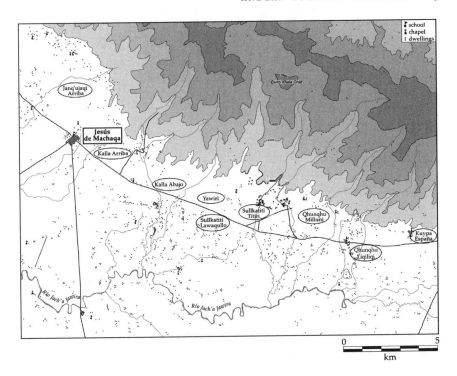

MAP 4   *Sullkatiti, Qhunqhu and neighboring ayllus*

ers, including Bonifacio, who clearly disapproved when I accepted the invitation of one of the p'iqis to join the ayllu authorities in dancing and drinking.

Later the mallkus led the celebrants in visiting the two schools that serve the ayllu. They entered the compound of the secondary school, adorning the buildings and pouring libations of alcohol. Then all returned to the larger primary school building, where the ayllus divided into separate groups dancing at their respective corners of the building. As the afternoon progressed, the authorities and accompanying dancers got very drunk indeed, some of them occasionally reeling out of the circles of dancers and stumbling or spinning until they collapsed.

The drunkenness was punctuated with violence. Some fights broke out within the cohorts from each ayllu, but the more serious battles flared up across ayllu lines. The dancing and careening veered into pushing and punching. Noses were bloodied, heads cut in hard falls to the ground, angry stumbling drunks screamed and challenged one another from across the width of the school building. In 1992, later in the evening, long after formal festivities had ceased, drunken groups loitered in the Titiri plaza looking for (and eventually finding) a fight. As I sat with Alejandro in his house in Milluni that night, his teenage son Luis came home to describe a fight between a p'iqi from

Milluni and a man from Titiri. The Titiri—his face bloodied against the door of a truck owned by a local storekeeper—had gotten the worst of it. But rumor had it that a group from Titiri was on its way into Milluni to exact revenge. Alejandro became agitated. The Titiris had "crossed the line" dividing the ayllus. This was a grave matter to be dealt with by the mallkus. His wife Rufina commented on the savagery of the Titiris, calling them "murderers" (asesinos), but Alejandro insisted that Millunis were "worse" and that one man from Milluni could fight ten from Titiri.

While this brawling and bluster seems far from the organized ritual battles—t'inkus—described in other parts of the Andes (e.g., Platt 1986), elements of these practices translate to the Machaqueño case. Platt glosses the t'inku nicely as "regenerative violence," a kind of fecund friction implicit in structures of complementary opposition. This certainly appears to be at stake in the fights between the ayllus and the sharp animosity just under the surface of most day-to-day interactions between Milluni and Titiri. Hence the enigmatic comments I collected about the events of Domingo de Tentación: consultants described it as a process of unification, effacing structural boundaries. Mayachasiñani they told me, "we will become one." On the other hand, I was told in no uncertain terms, "if blood doesn't fall, the potatoes won't grow."

From Opposition to Center

These are various voicings—one violent, the other more benign—for the merging of opposed social values. If anything becomes clear from the Andeanist literature on this topic, it is that the system of contrasting parts is not about keeping things separate but about mixing them up. To put it in highly abstract terms, we might think of this structure of valenced differences as providing a sort of symbolic potential energy, harnessed and negotiated in social practice to the ends of producing and sustaining society. The fertile promise of the opposition is realized in its mediation.

The frame of such mediation is often evoked with the term taypi (chawpi in Quechua). The term means center and stands as an implicit third term in the binaries of complementary opposition. The center is at once a component of a triadic relationship—say, the implicit border between Milluni and Titiri—and a microcosm or embodiment of a binary whole. In ecological terms taypi-rana/chawpirana refers to intermediate lands that exhibit both highlands and lowlands characteristics—e.g., where it is possible to cultivate both potatoes and maize. In cosmological terms Andean space-time is commonly conceptualized as tripartite: alaxpacha (upper space-time, merged uncomfortably with the Christian concept of heaven), manqhapacha (lower/inner space-time, merged uncomfortably with the Christian concept of hell), mediated by aka-

pacha (lit. "here/now space-time"), which is the site of human activity. This tripartite differentiation is a condition of human sociability. Research in various places of the Andes has elicited accounts of *chullpatimpu* (chullpa time), an age before the present age characterized as precultural and lacking the sorts of cosmic and social differentiation that is a precondition of human sociability. Dillon and Abercrombie (1988) describe a time of darkness; some consultants in Machaqa merged chullpatimpu with the antediluvian past of Judeo-Christian chronology and described the earth at that time as an undifferentiated flat expanse without place names. The people living at this time (*chullpas*) were without cultural knowledge; they were not baptized and had no names. Consultants described the condition of the land at this time as *puruma*—connoting uncultured fecundity. The term was also glossed as "sweet," like a "tender" young woman. In the wake of the flood the differentiated landscape of contemporary Aymara experience was formed with its complementary spatial contrasts of low-lying, flat female spaces and high, male mountains.

In the account reported by Dillon and Abercrombie the darkness of chullpatimpu is punctuated cataclysmically by the rise of the sun—likely a conflation in mythohistorical consciousness of the Inca Empire and the Iberian conquest (see also Abercrombie 1998). The result is the ordered field of akapacha (here/now) experience, poised between a dependence upon manqapacha and alaxpacha, informed by the diurnal oscillation of day and night, and—to blur their data with my own—where fully social (that is, baptized, named) actors engage in the production of society. As they point out quite compellingly, the rigid Christian contrasts of heaven and hell are here enmeshed with a cultural order requiring their constant access and mediation. "Living between the two zones of a now hierarchically ordered cosmos, today's Aymara must harness and balance through alternation, what are opposed but complementary extra-social forces, for the purposes of producing society" (Dillon and Abercrombie 1988:63).

I will return to the concept of taypi in more detail below. For the moment I want to underscore two points. The first is that taypi is at once a place and a condition. That is to say, it is never inertly there but rather is always realized or achieved through practice in the complex mediating setting of akapacha. This achievement involves engaging extralocal, extrasocial forces to local, social ends. One model for this process is domesticated growth and maturation: transforming unsocialized fertile potential (the sweet, tender, virgin chullpatimpu land) into ordered productive society. The human life cycle is a prime case of this, and the references to baptism and naming evoke some of the founding conditions of social personhood. The fiesta-cargo paths, which weave personhood through the armature of alternating contrasts, are especially crucial, and it is telling that a new thaki is opened in the setting of a rite that also served to bring fallow fields under communally ordered production.

Second, as the achievement of locality, taypi transcends itself. Taypi participates in the differentiated forces it separates; the center encompasses the margins and condenses the interpenetration of locality with extralocal forces. It is in this light that we must consider the focal presence in the Machaqueño centers of the most potent local instantiations of "foreign" power: schools, health posts, and the Catholic Church. The massive school buildings and the health posts straddling the Milluni-Titiri border are explicitly referred to as taypi. One consultant reported that the older primary school was formerly the site of a wak'a.[52] Like the church, the school is the subject of rumors identifying it as a powerful, potentially dangerous place where people are liable to fall ill. Some consultants reported that a boy and girl had been sacrificed in the construction of the building, their bodies entombed in the corners of the structure. These accounts suggest a number of lines of analysis. That the building may embody immature Aymara gender oppositions is certainly resonant with taypi. A similar link is the role of the school as a prime site of transformation and socialization of Aymara children.

But the school also evokes nonlocal power, and the accounts of sacrifice may well point to a local consciousness of extractive state practices. Similar rumors concern large buildings in La Paz, which also involve the conversion of Aymara bodily power (Aymara men perform most of the manual construction work in the city) into the brick and mortar infrastructure of dominant non-Aymara society. In addition to claims of human sacrifices entombed in foundations, the light-skinned residents and office workers in these buildings are also said to steal and sell Aymara babies. But the situation is ambiguous: human sacrifices are widely invoked by Machaqueños as characteristic of their own ancestors, and Millunis need not look as far as La Paz when evidence of antisocial savagery lurks just on the Titiri side of the local school.

A similar ambiguity concerns the very size of the building. While such large structures—like the high-rises of La Paz—seem to index modernity, they are also linked with the distant cultural past through references to archeological ruins and colonial structures such as the church in Jesús de Machaqa town. Rather than seeing in these structures evidence of the extractive and coercive power of the colonial or Incan state systems, Machaqueños typically marvel at these structures as evidence of the lost capacities of the ancestors, who are held to have been wiser, stronger, and more skilled than contemporary Aymara. In ritually adorning and celebrating these sites during Domingo de Tentación, Millunis and Titiris achieve and reference taypi: harnessing regional flows of power and potency to the end of producing locality.

As a space of translocal mediation, taypi is porously engaged with encompassing fields of power. Consider the genealogy of the Aymara concept *marka,* which today is generally used to refer to central towns such as Jesús de Machaqa or to urban spaces such as La Paz. According to historian Roberto Choque (1991), marka once connoted pre-Hispanic conceptions of sociopolitical integrity, involving the integration of ayllu structures and the coordination of a network of ecologically, politically, and ethnically different places and people. Under the Inca and Iberian states marka emerged as a unit of indirect rule— bounding and situating a subordinate population. In the wake of the Toledan reforms marka referred to a *repartimiento:* an administrative unit organizing the work of evangelization, tribute collection, and recruitment of labor for colonial mines. These relations, we have seen, were mediated by caciques.

Over time the term was further constrained to its contemporary meaning—"town"—signifying the administrative and ritual center of such a subordinated population. "With time," writes Choque, "the marka would mean the place of encounter of the ayllus to celebrate their festivals with different folkloric demonstrations and to carry out their cabildo [meetings]." Ironically, such markas are today often semi-urban towns of mestizos, sometimes contrasted with the rural Indian identity of the surrounding dispersed ayllu/communities. Choque's case is Jesús de Machaqa, and his comments call us back to the entangled colonial production of traditional Machaqueño solidarity. They also highlight the ambiguous status of the town proper as an unmarked center standing for the whole and as a component of the regional structure.

At issue is the apparent paradox of the conceptual center—taypi—not as the point of greatest local insularity but rather as a metonym of translocal engagement. To some degree the central placing of the church and the schools and health post reflect savvy colonial and postcolonial practice enabled by coercive power. But, to judge from the accomplishments of the Guarachis, local agents played important roles in locating these condensed representations and channels of foreign potency. What is more, these transcendent centers become presupposable components of local experience.

The massive church in town is explicitly held by Machaqueños to embody the spatiotemporal reach of taypi, its structure associated with the powers of the ancestors and Incas. Some consultants suggested that the bas-relief over the church's doors represented the Inca. More tellingly, Machaqueños described to me a subterranean waterway linking Jesús de Machaqa with distant churches located in Tiwanaku, Cuzco, and elsewhere.

The church not only embodies taypi space-time, it also embodies a variety of practices through which taypi is achieved—and, by extension, locality produced. I refer, on the one hand, to the discussions of the altars and the mayordomos as these condense, in the space of the church and the annual calendar and regional geography of saints' festivals, the braiding of locality out of the alternation of paths upper and lower. On the other hand, the church embodies a historical act of mediation accomplished by the Guarachis. Acknowledging this achievement may be implicit in the contemporary nostalgia for the lost powers of the ancestors. For achieving taypi—risking and overcoming the tenuous dilemma of akapacha—is the condition of possibility of localized Aymara life, a condition achieved only ephemerally.

Rosario

The Catholic festival of Rosario, undertaken in Jesús de Machaqa town, performs the integration of all of the ayllus in the region. It is an example of the sort of integrative rite, referenced by Choque, through which the marka comes to serve as "the place of encounter of the ayllus." It might further be seen as a ritual practice productive of regional Machaqueño locality. Such locality requires the incorporation of "outside" forces as component, indeed, focal elements of local. Within this entangled local setting, the production of Machaqueño locality also involves the braiding of Aymara life paths (thakis), aligning the most intimate and interstitial spaces of social life within this complexly constituted context, this local map of history. Service in Rosario (and in other, no longer extant regional fiestas) once constituted a lower rung in the cargo hierarchy.[53] Today it is expected that mallkus and p'iqis will represent their ayllus. Rosario is celebrated in October, in anticipation of the planting season and as the mallkus are on the verge of completing their yearlong tenure. The event also marks the public emergence of a set of eligible mallkus (machaq mallkus) from those who have completed service as p'iqi.

The festival as I observed it in 1991 took place over two days. P'iqis and mallkus from various ayllus streamed into town, often in trucks that plied the region's roads for the occasion. I caught a ride with a large group from Milluni. As the truck set out, the men pulled their qena qena flutes from beneath their ponchos and began to play.[54] Outside of town the driver's assistant climbed acrobatically out of the cab to tell us that passage would be free if the passengers all played loudly as we entered the plaza. The musicians obliged him as we barreled grandly into town with the truck honking its horn and circling the plaza. The plaza itself was swarming with activity—an impromptu market offered food, medicine, ceramics, bicycle parts, radios, various components of ritual offerings, regalia for mallkus, as well as livestock. The normally dust-blown and desolate town was suddenly a center (taypi) of abundance.

The truck dropped off the group from Milluni along one of the narrow streets off the plaza. We entered a house compound—called a *rancho* (ranch) or *silla*

FIGURE I.8   *The truck dropped off the group along one of the narrow streets off the plaza*

FIGURE I.9   *Ayllus dancing on the Jesús de Machaqa plaza*

FIGURE I.IO   *The kiosk*

(seat)—that was one of two such compounds in the town belonging to Milluni.
Every ayllu in the region has, or once had, ranchos in the town. In the Milluni
case, the larger of the two compounds was said to "belong" to the subcentral, the
smaller was "owned" by the president of the Association of Heads of Families. It
is within this household space, replicated in the town and enacting the ayllu as a
family, that the cohort of eligible (machaq) mallkus are publicly identified.

By mid-afternoon most of the mallkus and secretaries general had arrived,
and the cabildo gathered in the courtyard of their office off the main plaza. A
formal roll of all the ayllu authorities was called, and the assembled leaders
were reviewed to ensure that all were uniformly dressed as agreed upon at a
prior meeting. Meanwhile, in their respective ranchos, each of the ayllus was
preparing to make their formal entrance to the plaza. Many men wore puma
skin shoulder pads as well as wooden boards that hung from their necks,
adorned with green parrot feathers and pieces of colored and mirrored glass.[55]
Women put on additional skirts, giving them a heft that is greatly valued
(some of them were also wearing the parrot feather ornaments).

From their rancho each ayllu entered in a single line of flute-playing musicians and dancers. They circled the plaza just in front of the Church, dancing small loops at each of the corners and gathered at a spot near the plaza center. The plaza is divided with inlaid stones into a grid of rectangular spaces.
Each space or sayaña (the same term is used for house compounds) corresponds

to an ayllu in the region; the plaza thus embodies a microcosm of the regional interayllu structure. At the center of the plaza stands a kiosk/bandstand. The
structure was erected in the 1960s by the town's vecinos, standing as a monument to national integration inspired by the MNR revolution. It expresses the
sorts of modernizing homogeneity sought by the MNR, and, in ways comparable to the web of subterranean waterways interlinking multiple sites of
Catholic power, it established Machaqueño locality as a serial token of a modern Bolivian type.

This chapter examines the engagement of Machaqueño locality with the
Catholic Church and with other forms of exogenous and encompassing power.
To a certain extent, I have argued, the entanglement of the Church within the
region reflects the translatability of the Church into locally salient values. This
translatability is routinized in processes of regional social reproduction—particularly those involving fiesta-cargo hierarchies. In a similar vein, I have argued
that local sensibilities of engagement and mediation, reflected in historical patterns of vertical ecological integration, grounded in conceptual patterns of
complementary opposition, and evident in conceptualizations of the center as
a site of transcendent plenitude, inform Aymara experiences of the church in
their midst. These arguments blunt claims of radical separation or local Andean
insularity in the face of these tokens of foreign power. They call us to a revisiting of Andean locality in which the actions of Father Jan and Sister Marta, like
the buildings they operate in, are integral components.
      Left there, of course, this would be a deceptively benign depiction of the
local experience of often extremely unfavorable circumstances, muting both
the profound changes undergone by Machaqueño locality and the situated
sense of crisis and conflict expressed by many. It would also seem to suggest
that a certain accommodation worked out over the colonial period continues
to organize the contemporary production of locality as but a permutation of
colonial circumstances. Neither is the case. The nostalgia for the diminished
potency of the ancestors, and laments for the weakened decadent condition of
contemporary Aymara signal this. So, too, does the ambiguity and fear many
feel toward the church. The dangerous potency of the bell tower/wak'a, like
the correlated belief that the underground canals (which some mayordomos
claim to have glimpsed) are inhabited by ducks made of gold that, when
viewed, cause grave illness, suggest a localized power that contemporary Aymara nonetheless do not have fully in hand.
      The challenge, in my view, is to take stock of the porous production of
locality and yet avoid the claim that outside elements are integrated without
friction or remainder. The case of the MNR reforms is instructive here. The

impact in Jesús de Machaqa of these modernizing reforms in the 1960s and 1970s coincided with a period of heightened Protestant evangelization as well as reformed Catholic missionization. One result was the abandonment of indigenous titles and regalia for community authorities as well as the disappearance of fiesta practices. Much as with the ayuno, these recently extirpated practices revived in the late 1980s. Rumors of Andean continuities are thus greatly exaggerated. The new sindicato positions of power did not map neatly on to traditional categories or benignly fuse with them. Rather, they tangle with them, displace them, and set the terms for their constrained continuity. From the 1970s to the late 1980s the meaning of local assertions of tradition shifted profoundly.

The mapping of national fields of power upon local structures generated new regional forces and frictions in other ways. The spread of new roads, the founding of new administrative towns, and the proliferation of new market centers set in motion a variety of processes of destructuration and restructuration as locality was produced in newly entangled settings. In Jesús de Machaqa the ayllu Jilatiti (now Santo Domingo), head of the upper moiety, emerged as an important administrative and commercial center, located on an important bus and truck route. Santo Domingo in recent years has constituted itself as a new county seat, effectively hiving off much of the upper parcialidad from Jesús de Machaqa. The changes are reflected on the ground in the empty squares at each Rosario celebration and in a cabildo that is increasingly composed of mallkus from the lower moiety along with those few upper ayllus who remain tied to Jesús de Machaqa town through geographical proximity.[56]

These changes are also reflected in the efforts of the parish priest and the cohort of catechists, which focus mainly on the ayllus composing the Jesús de Machaqa cabildo. Related shifts are evident in Father Jan's residence in the newly central town of Batallas, instead of the longstanding colonially constituted marka of Peñas, as well as the move of the Jesús de Machaqa parish to Qurpa (though here the shift is in part a self-conscious move from a mestizo-identified town to an Indian ayllu.) The move to Qurpa, as we have seen, is particularly complex, as it involves a move to a community that was once a hacienda supporting the operation of the parish and later a hacienda owned by the descendents of the last Guarachi. As the cases of Qurpa and Batallas make clear, the Church is both an already integral part of entangled Andean locality—impacted along with traditional social structure by new dimensions of change—and a vector of new changes embedded within the shifting contexts for the production of Andean locality. The following two chapters take up changes in Catholic pastoral practices on the altiplano set against these shifting historical contexts and within the situated production of Andean locality.

CHAPTER 2

Missionary Modernity in the Postwar Andes

In 1955 a young priest named Jacques Monast arrived in Bolivia to begin service in the southern altiplano province of Carangas. Monast was one of a group of Canadian Oblates who arrived as part of a wave of postwar Catholic missionary activity in Latin America. This was the start of what many in the Church today refer to as the "second" or "new evangelization." In a series of published works Monast (e.g., 1972) presents both an insightful ethnographic account of Aymara society at this time and an eloquent testimony of his own transformations as a result of his pastoral experiences. Monast was clearly not your run-of-the-mill priest. Yet his reflections well condense the salient issues of the times, perhaps because he was one step ahead of them.

"If one observes a missionary recently arrived in a strange land," he wrote,

> we see that he finds himself in a state of wonder. He feels limited or disturbed by a number of things he is not used to and, in some cases, which he does not even know. He comes from the other side: he is a messenger, and carrier of a News for a people that are not even a people of God. He knows that to be understood he will need to translate his message not only into the words, but in addition and above all into the mentality of the recipients.
>
> In this way, the missionary has the impression that he must learn about life all over again, starting from zero. He knows Christian dogma or moral principles well, but he is ignorant of almost everything about the people to whom he will direct himself. Thus he attempts to be born again, if he wants the Word to be effective. (1972:253)

But the wonder of Catholic pastoral workers in Bolivia went beyond the stock missionary experience of otherness. This was not an evangelical frontier. The Aymara had been evangelized for nearly four centuries. Priests such as Monast arriving from Europe or North America found themselves confronted with neither an unconverted other nor a more familiar "Catholicism in crisis" of a sort they might have experienced in the United States, Europe, or perhaps urban areas of Latin America, where the Church found itself grappling increasingly with the challenges of modernity. The missionary rebirth in the Bolivian altiplano was through an encounter with the familiar made strange, an encounter in which the translators of the Good News found themselves already understood as old news.

This chapter is about a moment in the fashioning of an evangelical periphery, seen within the contexts of a long-standing pastoral entanglement. The shifting transcultural production of Aymara locality involved the actions and perspectives of a range of situated agents.[1] Among these agents were the freshly arrived but already familiar missionaries, operating within a renewed evangelical encounter that reflected changing global contexts.

"Baptized but Not Evangelized"

Relating his thoughts on his first night spent in the altiplano parish of Corque, as he slept on an improvised cot in the ruined presbytery and listened to the rats eat his provisions, Monast wrote:

> "The missions!" I said to myself. "How many centuries have I gone back in a single day? How far do I find myself from civilization, from that well-organized Church of our country?" The rats continued their nightly rounds. "If we had at least arrived in a new country, to a truly unharvested field. . . . But no: I am in a very Catholic country. In this presbytery in ruins!" (1972:255)

Pastoral workers arrived presupposing a recognizable Catholic identity, commensurate with their own. But Monast quickly realized that his training and his words were insufficient to bridge the gulf he was experiencing between himself and the Aymara Catholics of Corque. Such a challenge would be intelligible in an unconverted mission land, but, as he exclaimed, "I am in a very Catholic country." The Aymara professed a vibrant Catholic identity and quickly pressed the young priest into ritual service. Monast's initial bewilderment soon turned into helpless frustration as he was sought out for baptisms and fiesta masses:

> An elderly sacristan from Corque of about sixty years of age assisted with the mass, dressed in a red cassock (imported, no doubt, by the Spaniards

from the earliest times). He performed all of the ceremonies he could remember and murdered his Latin with the impertinence and disrespectful
familiarity of a choirboy. . . .

As soon as the young missionary begins to exercise his ministry in
Carangas, the poetry with which he had gilded his missionary and priestly
ideals gives way quickly to prose. The first time that my services were required for baptism, I don't know how many godparents and babies gathered respectfully around the baptismal fonts. I had spent much time preparing all of the details of the liturgy of baptism; I wanted to offer a beneficial
catechism for those in attendance. Precisely at the beginning of the ceremony, one of the little ones began to cry from hunger; it was necessary to
bring him quickly to his mother, who offered him her breast in the doorway of the Church. Another of the aspirants to baptism broke out in furi-
ous howling as soon as he saw the face of the priest; he only refrained from
his aggressions after the final "amen." Two of the godparents were drunk.
At any rate, I felt that my methods of preaching [*enganche*] were of little
use; the babies and the godparents attracted everyone's attention, such that
my words did not seem to reach anyone. My questions did not receive a
single answer. . . .

In the first months, they called me to preside over a "fiesta mass," and
I spent the week in the town in question. We can now describe in an objective way the development of a fiesta; but when a young missionary
with innocent eyes sees of this for the first time, his blood boils: the stat-
ue, the banner, the orgies, the battles. . . . When he surprises the sorcer-
er in the midst of his work; when he realizes that the animal sacrifices are
linked to the sacrifice of the mass, he says to himself: "this is the Old Testament!" and he wonders what absurd relation his ministry has with these
sacrifices. (256 ff.)

Monast found himself in a parish house in ruins. His encounter was with
what he perceived to be a degraded echo of a past evangelization. What is
more, his presence entangled him in that very degradation. In an ironic twist
on Trexler's (1984a) observation that colonial Catholic missionaries sought to
induce the natives to perform the colonial imagination, Monast, like other
missionaries of his time, found himself unwittingly performing the Aymara-
Catholic imagination. He is assisted by an aging Aymara sacristan, who,
dressed in a cassock he imagined to be of colonial origins, embodies the syncretic colonial Catholicism faced by Monast. He heard the faithful chant
prayers in barely recognizable Latin. He celebrated a mass, but found that his
actions have meanings beyond his comprehension and control. Moreover, his

efforts to engage the Aymara were fruitless: his words do not reach them; his questions go unanswered.

His experiences led Monast to posit a double decadence in Aymara religiosity—for he considered the Aymara to be profoundly "religious." On the one hand, he found that, although the Aymara declared themselves to be "very Catholic," they are "baptized but not evangelized." They participated in the external signs of a Christian identity but lacked a more profound transformation entailed in Monast's understanding of evangelization. "Christianity," Monast declared, "provided the Indians, most of all, a new vocabulary to express in Catholic terms their traditional beliefs" (18).

In other statements this contemporary missionary take on colonial syncretism is sexualized and gendered: Monast suggests that Catholicism and the "ancestral religion" have been joined together in a "concubinage":

> A religious syncretism has been in effect. In this alloying, Catholicism has the role of the concubine, and it is the ancestral religion that wears the pants. The Indians have simply conserved their spirituality, their beliefs, their myths, their taboos and—let us say it—their religion and their divinities, dressing them in the Christian style. But these "Catholic" vestments: statues, sacred clothing and objects, Christian images or words, chapels or churches, they have integrated them in their religion in such a way that it is that religion that truly lives and continues to be the religion of the people. Rather than christianize Aymara symbols and beliefs, to the end of integrating them within an authentic Indian Catholicism, the Christian signs have been "aymaracized" and integrated within the ancestral religion. (313)

This external, superficial Christianity—baptized but not evangelized; spoken but not meant—engenders relations of space and power. Christianity has proved passive and impotent: rather than actively christianize, Catholic symbols have been aymaracized. Rather than incorporating Aymara symbols and beliefs to the end of an "authentic Indian Catholicism," Christian meanings are rendered hollow, to be filled with other meaning. Rather than the Christian Word becoming Indian flesh, complained Monast, the Indian flesh has taken on the words and icons of Catholicism as an external dressing for its ancestral religion. One goal of the new evangelization is to reverse these sexualized valences, realizing an active, potent Christianity that will effectively penetrate Aymara cultural forms.[2]

Monast also suggests that while traditional Aymara belief—especially as a component of Inca state religion—approximated a true Christian revelation, contemporary Aymara beliefs have been compromised by the historical traumas of conquest and colonial evangelization. In part Monast follows a number of colonial chroniclers who found in the state religions of the New World sophisticated belief systems that offered the possibility for a profound and rapid evangelization.[3] However, from his vantage as a chronicler of the "second evangelization," Monast found that "the [colonial] dislocation of the Incaic organization brought with it a certain degradation of the natural religion" (15).

THE NEW EVANGELIZATION

The sense of the Catholic Church as embarked upon a "new evangelization" in Latin America, sometimes figured as a "second evangelization," sometimes as a "reevangelization," is a familiar one in pastoral circles, intoned in rural courses, in diocesan planning meetings, in papal statements, in the published writings of theologians, and in scholarly discussions of the Latin American Church. The terms describe what some see as a contemporary period of reanimation in the Church enabled by the "opening" of the Second Vatican Council (1962–65) and driven in large measure by the coalescence of the "Latin American Church" as evident in key meetings of the Latin American Episcopal Conference in the 1960s, 1970s, 1980s, and 1990s. This chapter and the one that follows trace this period of institutional ferment, the questions and concerns that shaped it, and the practices and experiences of foreign missionaries and Aymara catechists and deacons who have participated in this neo-Catholic missionary movement.

While I think this moment of evangelical reengagement in the decades after World War II is crucial, I want to begin by examining the limits of this periodization implicit in the term *second evangelization*. For to think of a new evangelization is to posit and bracket an initial evangelization as a flawed and incomplete foil, to imagine a reencounter with Latin America that is somehow distinct from a prior encounter. In the Andes this construction resonates with other framings of colonial contact that enable a view of Andean culture as a discrete, enduring object of ethnographic reference. While a regional intellectual history is beyond the present study, it seems likely that these views of Andean culture and history, which became canonical with the institutionalization of "area studies" after the Second World War, and the guiding assumptions of postwar Catholic evangelization are part of a larger ideological complex that might be examined alongside cold war foreign policy, development ideologies, and so forth.[4] For the moment, I want to signal two concerns. The first is the implication of a second missionary bite at an unevangelized Indian apple. The second is the implication of an empty colonial and republican middle, and a focus on a period of heroic (if ineffectual) colonial missionization, followed up only in the mid- and late twentieth century (cf. Mills 1997). Such heuristic framings do more than defy the historical record; they enable specific conceptualizations of Andean societies and the transcultural histories in which they are steeped.

As I have argued, discussions in Andean studies have too often masked our view of an open-ended process of transculturation, evoking rather a contentious dialogue between two relatively stable and intractable identities forged in a distant colonial big bang. So, too, mistaking missionary ideologies of prior evangelical failure for a historical anthropology of a complex colonial locality, it is tempting to read each wave of Catholic evangelical activity as a renewed encounter between a persistent missionary Church and a so far unyielding Andean culture. The data from Jesús de Machaqa point toward a much more complex and ongoing integration of Christianity and its representatives in local experiences.

In the wake of independence (1825), the Bolivian Church endured one of the most devastating anticlerical actions in Latin America at the hands of the republican government of Antonio José de Sucre (Barnadas 1976; Klein 1982:109 ff.; Lofstrom 1987). This chapter offers an account of the gradual recuperation of institutional power beginning late in the nineteenth century, a recuperation of power at the local and national levels that is also intertwined with the global institution of the Catholic Church and the global circumstances of twentieth-century Catholicism.

‡ ‡ ‡

With the turn of the twentieth century the Bolivian Catholic Church was on the rebound from the effects of the postindependence Sucre reforms. Spurred by Pope Leo XIII's encyclical *Rerum Novarum,* and bolstered by the return of the Jesuits in 1882 and the arrival of the Salesians in 1896, the Church undertook a reengagement with an Andean society that was slowly but decidedly emerging as a postcolonial nation.[5] These developments at the national level correlated with broader regional changes; this period also saw the first Latin America Bishops Conference (1899–1900), anticipating the later formation of the Latin American Episcopal Conference (CELAM) in 1955 (Froehle 1992:108; Bühlmann 1978:154). As the church grappled with its own colonial history, it also sought ambivalently to align itself with the slowly emerging Bolivian nation-state: constituting itself as the Bolivian Church while rejecting the premises of modern positivism underlying much of the nation-state ideology.[6]

Among the church activities was a focus on the condition of Indians within the nation. The historian Josep Barnadas (1976) has dubbed this moment the "golden age of *indigenísmo eclesiástico*" and reported the work of a variety of heroic missionaries who sought to improve the lives and prospects of the Aymara- and Quechua-speaking communities under their care. The National Pro-Indian Crusade (1926) exemplified these pastoral efforts directed toward the countryside. Essentially a rural education campaign, the clerics behind the Crusade saw themselves as addressing the Bolivian "Indian problem" by remedying indigenous "ignorance" while protecting the Indians from the dangerous anti-Catholic ideologies of positivism, liberalism, and freemasonry (Anonymous 1926; Barnadas 1976; Mamani Capchiri 1992:89). Protesting university students in La Paz denounced the campaign as reactionary. The controversy stemmed not from the basic premise of an "Indian problem" but from the Church's involvement in the solution (Klein 1969:90).

The reconsolidation of Church power in Bolivia thus emerged in tense conjunction with a broader liberal effort at modernization and national integration, and against a global backdrop of new challenges to the Church evident in revolutionary changes in Mexico and Russia. The nascent modern Andean landscape in which turn-of-the-century pastoral agents sought to reinsert themselves was marked, as we have seen, by liberal assaults on community lands, the emerging infrastructure of railways, and the reexpansion of the mining industry in coordination with the spread of haciendas and increased market penetration across the altiplano. It is within this already complexly entangled locality, steeped in projects of national building and dawning modernity, and soon to be enmeshed within a new form of global geopolitics, that the Church undertook the "second evangelization."

Battling for Postcolonial Souls: Catechists, Protestants, and the Cold War

The contemporary catechist pastoral model and related efforts to reassert a Catholic presence in rural areas of the Andes can be traced back more than four decades and reflect a reanimation of the Latin American Church that is deeply engaged with the geographical and cultural politics of the post–World War II period. The pastoral push evident in the 1950s coincides with a broader effort by the Church to reinforce its standing in the dawning postwar world order, particularly with respect to the emerging "third world" (Bühlmann 1978; McDonough 1992:218; cf. Escobar 1995). Pius XII's encyclical *Fidie Donum* (1957), calling for renewed missionary activity in postcolonial Africa, also heralded a new missionary era in Latin America (Jordá 1981:26; Bühlmann 1978).

The foreign Catholic missionaries who began arriving in the Andes were responding to a crisis of local and global, institutional and epochal dimensions. The pontiff was acutely concerned about the dangers of Protestantism and communism, which Pius XII condemned as "intrinsically evil" (Levine 1981:247). Such was the Vatican's preoccupation with the fate of Latin America that, it was said, "when the Pope thinks of Latin America in the evening, he cannot sleep that night" (Bühlmann 1978:154). Equally alarming to the Church hierarchy was the growing shortage of priests and a nagging sense of being left behind as developing nations laid their claims on an increasingly secularizing modernity. Through pastoral movements such as Catholic Action, church agents sought to consolidate and reanimate Latin American Catholic identity, creating a catechized laity organized under direct clerical control (cf. Warren 1989). This period of reanimation also saw changes in national and regional Church structures. In 1943 Pius XII elevated the bishopric of La Paz to the status of archbishopric. The Latin American Bishops Conference—CELAM—as well as its counterpart among religious clergy—the Latin American Conference of Religious (CLAR)—were formed in 1955 (Bühlmann 1978:154).

On the Bolivian altiplano, Monast and his fellow Canadian Oblates initiated pastoral work with Aymara catechists, as did Maryknoll missionaries from the United States. Arriving in the wake of the national revolution of 1952, the Oblates based their work in the central altiplano province of Carangas, in the Department of Oruro. Maryknoll's presence in the Andes was precipitated by the disruption of the Second World War, which displaced them from their traditional mission area in East Asia (Fedders 1974). What was to be a temporary relocation grew into a new mission focus. After running a minor seminary for a period of years, in the 1950s the Maryknoll priests established a center for catechist courses in Puno, in the Peruvian prelature of Juli, and soon after founded a similar center in the Bolivia altiplano parish of Peñas, where I later visited with Jan and Marta.

In addition, secular priests from a number of dioceses in the United States began arriving in Bolivia: from St. Louis (1956), Kansas City (1963), Buffalo and Rochester (1963). Religious orders with longer histories in Bolivia also experienced a wave of new priests arriving in the 1960s. Between 1956 and 1968 the number of regular and secular priests in Bolivia increased from 495 to 899. The percentage of foreign clergy—already high—increased over this time from 71 percent to 78 percent; in 1968, of 701 foreign priests, 690 came from nations outside of Latin America (Pascual and Aguilo 1968).

Liberation Theology on the Altiplano

Despite the politically and institutionally conservative bent of this evangelical effort, the pastoral experiences of these years flow directly into the emergence of the more progressive and radical pastoral ideologies of "liberation theology." A familiar narrative from Church histories of this period recounts the conversion of the missionaries, whose personal experiences of poverty, underdevelopment, and repressive governments along with news of social ferment back home in Europe or the United States proved to be a fertile growth medium for radical rethinking of their Christian identity (e.g., Cox 1984:109; Berryman 1984, 1987; Mainwaring 1989:162). Notwithstanding the influx of priests in the region, there remained a shortage of clergy. This prompted a number of pastoral innovations—including the recruitment of local native catechists and the formation of community-level faith groups. These adaptations are the precursors of evangelical experiments such as Delegates of the Word and Christian Base Communities often associated with liberation theology. The emerging regional Church hierarchy—particularly CELAM—came to play a decisive role in this process. Through its meetings in Medellín (1968) and Puebla (1979), CELAM helped shape the regional implications of the reforms instituted by the Second Vatican Council (1962–65) and highlighted many of the already unfolding premises and practices that came to be know as Latin American Liberation Theology.

As used in the Latin American context, liberation theology refers to the pastoral strategies adopted by the Latin American Catholic Church in the wake of Vatican II and the subsequent meetings of CELAM. These strategies reflect the alignment of sectors of the church with issues of social justice, human rights, and regional development (e.g., Levine 1986; Mainwaring and Wilde 1989). Liberation theology has conventionally been cast as an expression of a sui generis local popular religiosity enabled by an unprecedented opening in the Church long allied with colonial and state power (e.g., Berryman 1987). While this construction has its merits, it obscures two important points. The first concerns the more long-standing engagement of the Church with social issues in Latin America: while the political valences may be unprecedented, the engagement is not. Second, this construction of the grassroots regional authenticity of liberation theology belies the profoundly translocal contexts out of which the movement arose, as global missionary circuits contributed to the cross-fertilization of European, North American, and Latin American theological traditions as well as comparable movements from elsewhere in the developing world.[7]

Classically, liberationists have promoted a highly historicized exegetical methodology, casting Christian social action within a history of the Christian God's action in the world. Liberation theologians reject a theological division of sacred and secular histories, arguing that the work of God is ongoing and accessible within human history. The privileged site of this work is the struggles of "liberation" of "the poor" (e.g., Gutierrez 1973; Berryman 1987). Pastoral workers promote a historicized interpretation of biblical narrative deriving from various post-Enlightenment quests for the "historical Jesus."[8] This often yields a sociological and political analysis of biblical contexts as the basis for a comparative reassessment of the present local setting. Thus the contexts of Roman domination evident in the New Testament are analogized to contemporary Latin American experiences of neocolonialism.[9]

The strong emphasis placed upon historical knowing as a medium of reflection upon and witness to Christian meaning is linked to a keen interest among pastoral agents in the analytical tools of sociology and political science. Marxist analyses have figured prominently and added to the notoriety of liberation theology. In a similar vein, theologies of liberation tend to decenter the notion of sin from the individual, applying it to collective social conditions such as poverty, racism, etc. Christian identity, in this view, entails an activist commitment to denouncing and overturning such "institutional structures of sin." At stake for pastoral workers is the establishment of "partial realizations of the Kingdom of God": a calling that has produced alliances with nonviolent as well as armed movements of social change.

Consistent with other postwar pastoral efforts, liberation theologians seek to stake out a new moment—a "second evangelization"—in the religious history of Latin America, declaring themselves in opposition to the history and inheritance of a "colonializing Christianity" (Shapiro 1981; Codina 1987; Seuss 1991). In practice this has involved a condemnation of both "traditional" Catholicism and of "popular" or folk Catholicism, seen as an amalgamation of indigenous tradition and colonial Catholicism. For liberation theologians such folk practices index the failures of colonial evangelization and are dismissed as a form of "alienating piety" (Miguez Bonino 1984). They are seen as inadequate for the rational reflection upon reality "in the light of the Bible," taken by liberationists to be the liturgical formula for the realization of authentic Christian identity in the structurally sinful modern world. Inspired by liberation theology, pastoral workers have tended to minimize traditionally ritualistic styles of worship, promoting instead a rationalized, text-centered, discursive style of worship centered around small community-based worship groups (CEBs) and a transformative educational process (concientización).[10]

At the same time, and somewhat confusingly, progressive pastoral agents and theologians have characterized their work as constructing the "popular Church." This marks something of a shift from the earliest years of postwar evangelization, during which missionaries seemed bent on reconsolidating institutional orthodoxy in the region. To some extent, this turn toward lo popular was surely a function of growing pastoral experience in the field (e.g., Mainwaring 1989:162; Peña 1995:chapter 2). Yet the liberationists also employed a profoundly modern, massified sense of "popular," quite distinct from other conceptions of popular religion as a locus of traditional survival and a corruption of orthodoxy at the capillaries of institutional control.[11] In this sense the liberationist embrace of the popular Church is consistent with the modernizing aspirations of earlier cohorts of missionaries. Levine (1990:719) nicely underscores this semantic shift in Latin America pastoral work:

> Not long ago, references to *lo popular* called up images of ignorance, magic and superstition. . . . But the same reference now commonly evokes class identity (the popular as "the people"—specifically peasants, proletarians, and so forth), comes wrapped in claims to autonomy and collective self-governance by such people and is identified in ordinary discourse with values like authenticity, sharing, solidarity, and sacrifice.

This revelatory encounter with the popular has been a central legitimating claim of progressive pastoral ideologies in Latin America, which operate in the light of what they understand to be God's "preferential option for the poor." Pastoral agents report an "experience of God in the poor" (Berryman 1987:157)—a *deus ex populus* positing a potentially unmediated authenticity for liberation theology and the popular Church it champions. The popular Church represents a purified, rationalized, and condensed expression of a sui generis Christian authenticity implicit—albeit in alienated form—in popular practice.

A corollary concern of liberationist pastoral agents has involved minimizing the role of priests and nuns and empowering trained lay leaders, whose authority was based not in sacramental powers but rather in their knowledge of the Bible, their facility with resonant exegeses, and their condition as representatives of the popular. This ascendance of "evangelical discourse, with its emphasis on biblical exegesis" over "liturgical discourse" (Nelson 1986) was promoted through programs of education that have stressed literacy, and a growing pastoral emphasis on small worship and study groups.

On the Bolivian altiplano this transforming pastoral encounter was compounded by a missionary encounter with the already integral role of Christianity as a component of Andean society. While this cross-cultural dimension was certainly a factor throughout Latin America, its impact was especially acute in the Andean region, where the confrontation of Catholics from the United States, Canada, and Europe with indigenous practices gave rise to a renewed reflection on the status of indigenous Catholic identity and colonial missionary history. The issue, as Monast (1972) framed it at the time is whether the Aymara are "evangelized or only baptized." The question encodes much of the emergent pastoral ideology and its underlying presuppositions. Practically, these involved a focus on "authentic" evangelization and catechization as opposed to the celebration of sacraments. The latter were seen as superficial or external and prone to appropriation in ways that masked the endurance of traditional indigenous practices. There was an ambivalent questioning of colonial precedents in the region. On the one hand, colonial Catholicism was perceived to be the cause of corrupt contemporary Catholic practices; colonial evangelizers had been effective but misguided. At the same time, colonial missionaries were condemned as ineffective, their contemporary successors focused upon the as yet unattained "interior" penetration of a superficial Christian identity. This ambiguous sense of the corruptions of colonialism and the endurance of indigenous identity suggests a modern evangelical war waged along two fronts and smuggles into missionary experience a posited discrete enduring Andean Other accessible despite the accretions and distortions of a colonial evangelization.

"Teaching the Word in Abandoned Places"

Out of the challenges of this postwar missionary reencounter emerged the modern catechists. Today missionaries cite a range of reasons for the catechist pastoral model. The sheer number of people to reach was certainly an important factor. Catechists were seen as a way of multiplying the effect of circuit-riding priests, most of whom could visit the communities under their care only one or two times each year. A 1969 Christmas pastoral letter from an auxiliary bishop, written while traveling in the company of an Aymara catechist in an effort to recruit new catechists, celebrates the work of the future catechists who will "teach the word of God in these places that are so abandoned."[12]

In this sense the catechists represented an extension of the pastoral presence in time and space: catechists could "go to where nobody was," as one priest reminisced, and maintain a year-round presence in their communities.[13] The catechists and the weekly services they offered were to be a vehicle for establishing a routinized sense of Christian community, beyond the infrequent celebrations of calendrical and life-cycle rituals that tended to occupy much of a priest's contact with his dispersed flocks. A North American priest, active in Bolivia since the late 1960s, commented, "missioners of the '50s and '60s came to the point where they said, 'we just can't keep up these rounds of fiestas. . . . [They just] have absolutely no relationship to anything else.' So they almost said to the villages, 'we won't come anymore to do the fiestas unless you name a catechist, who becomes your delegate responsible for the continuation of the Church community here.'" The sense that periodic priestly visits merely punctuate with Catholic ritual an otherwise non-Christian Aymara life offers a temporal analogue to other notions of an incomplete evangelization. The catechists' ongoing presence, further multiplied by a community of followers in the faith group, was to serve as a permanent enactment of Christian identity in dispersed communities. The catechists were the prototypes of a newly conceived Aymara-Christian.

The selection of catechists also reflects missionary misgivings about colonial evangelization. The contemporary missionary engagement with the Aymara was equally an engagement with their colonial evangelical predecessors. Recall Monast's characterizations of Aymara culture as a degraded religiosity, debased as a function of the ineptness of colonial evangelization and the trauma of the colonial dismantling of the Incan state. But this does not imply an unambiguous embrace of "traditional Andean culture." Recall, as well, Monast's exclamations "this is the Old Testament!" "how many years have I gone back in a single day?" Like classical evolutionist anthropologists and the Enlightenment philosophes who influenced their views, Monast experienced his travel through space from Canada to Carangas as travel through time. If he disapproves of the colonial flavor of the Andean Catholicism he observes, he is no less critical of what he glimpses as autochthonous Andean culture. The result is an evolutionary conception of conversion, whereby the "Old Testament" religion of traditional Aymara culture analogically embodies the same potential and the same historical process as that condensed by the Christian tradition. Consider the following passage from a Bolivian pastoral document prepared by an auxiliary bishop for the southern altiplano pastoral zone in the early 1970s:

> We believe that the entire progression toward Christ is slow, by means of stumbles, errors, and loyalty. And thus as the Hebrew people were purifying their faith in Yahweh in contact with other beliefs, appropriating many of their values, and purifying them under the teaching of the prophets, so too the Aymara peoples, through their sacrifices—*wilanchas*—rites to the hills—*achachilas*—have gone living a deep spirituality that makes of them a contemplative people for whom everything is full of life and who for that reason respect nature as they do persons; a people, in other words, who have traveled a path toward Christ revealed in the Bible.[14]

Such comparisons are common in missionary rhetoric establishing both a necessary precondition for Christian identity and a narrative historical movement "toward Christ revealed in the bible." Nonetheless, the frequency of this characterization of the Aymara in the 1960s and 1970s also reflects the self-consciously modernizing and developmentalist tenor of the time.

Through such analogies conversion emerges as an organic and natural—rather than imposed and arbitrary—process of revelation. Missionaries further naturalize this process by harnessing it to the life cycle and dynamics of generational renewal. Colonial missionaries in the Andes and in Mesoamerica often sought explicitly to recruit native youth—and in some cases to promote the marriage of converts at young ages—in the hopes of creating quickly a converted generation that would, in time, displace their elders, who came to represent the idolatrous past (Albó 1966; Borges 1960; Orta 1993; Trexler 1987:chapter 12). Similarly, missionaries of the 1960s looked to the formation of young Aymara to displace the inheritance of colonial Christianity. This may well be a never-ending cycle in such long-term missionary settings. The youths recruited by postwar pastoral agents are now today's aging cohort of catechists; the missionaries I worked with during the 1990s saw in young Aymara a potential corrective to the mistakes they now think *their* predecessors made.

Through these evangelical constructions, the processes of social and biological maturation are linked to the work of evangelization, in the process indexing a revelation cast as the maturation of collective religious knowledge. Such constructions also create rhetorical and logical spaces to apologize for and redeem idolatrous native practice. A missionary active in the 1960s suggested to me that Aymara acts of sacrifice were acceptable from a Christian point of view as immature acts of thanksgiving in response to God's creation. They are immature in their misrecognition of the creative power as deriving from hills or stone "idols." He explained: "If the child does not yet know what is a light bulb, what is the sun, or a candle, listen, you can't demand that [understanding] of a child. Just wait until he grows. Then show him what a light bulb is, then a candle, then, ah! It was the sun all along!" As an example of this growth of faith and knowledge, he cited the child Jesus, whose life cycle indexed a theological maturation from the Mosaic Law, into which he was born, to the New Covenant, which he proclaimed as a grown man. He then went on to compare this process to the stages of a rocket, suggesting in effect that certain religious practices may be necessary for a particular portion of a peoples' historic trajectory and then can be discarded as another ideological propellant takes over. These mixed metaphors firmly bind evangelical imagery familiar from the sixteenth century with the industrialized moment of postwar evolutionary missionization.

It is little wonder that education played so large a role in this process of completing both the organic maturation of the "natural religion" and the shortcomings of a partial colonial evangelization. Courses—*cursillos*—emerged as the centerpiece of Latin American pastoral work in these years (see Berryman 1984; Cleary 1992:185; Burdick 1993:38 ff.). For Aymara catechists courses were the primary vehicles of their "formation," with profound consequences for their authoritative status.

The earliest courses for which I have seen records (1970) focused on biblical and catechetical knowledge as well as on "leadership training." These were prompted by missionary concerns that Aymara were performing Christian rituals without understanding what they really "meant." "What was happening before," explained one pastoral worker, "was ritual celebration with almost no instruction. [One goal of the catechist pastoral model was the] preparation of a nucleus of people who could teach their communities that more than just the ritual is involved in these sacramental celebrations and fiestas." This excessive focus on exterior ritual form, presumed to be without authentic content, and derisively dubbed *sacramentalismo* by pastoral works, was taken as a primary index of an incomplete evangelization.

These missionary concerns were not only about the Aymara. As pastoral agents identified and corrected the inadequacies of Aymara Catholicism, they betrayed deep disaffections with and questionings of their own faith and its place in the world. The shifting pastoral strategies over the postwar years trace a reciprocal conversion. To some degree pastoral agents responded to the superficial Christianity of the Aymara with educational efforts in keeping with those of their colonial forebears. Education was a vehicle to deepen and purify indigenous Christianity by transmitting evangelical truths to be extended through the catechists. Catechists in one parish who began their service in these early years recall the parish priest marching them around the plaza in front of the Church forcing them to memorize the Lord's Prayer, the Ten Commandments, and so forth. Catechetical songs also reflect this concern with missionary mnemonics. Missionaries published two bilingual songbooks during these years, presenting songs composed and written principally by catechists and Aymara priests. These repetitive teaching aids remain widely used today; the songs are key markers of the catechists and their followers. These sorts of mnemonics echo precisely colonial evangelical actions; it is as if the missionaries of the 1960s sought to perfect the methods of their predecessors.

At the same time, in documents and recollections of this period there is a lingering suspicion of all ritual practice that seems to transcend the historically- and culturally-specific shortcomings of Aymara Catholicism. The curricula of pastoral centers serving Aymara catechists during these years reflect sensibilities evident in Latin American Catholicism and in the Church elsewhere deemphasizing ritual and encouraging a reflection upon religious meaning to the end of principled action in the world. In the pastoral center at Laja, for instance, catechists were to undergo a program of study organized along six principal themes: Theology, Liturgy and Pastoral Practice; Evangelization and

Catechism; Family and Family Spirituality; Anthropology; and Human Promotion and Development.[15] The sequence of these themes, moving from biblical, doctrinal, and catechetical knowledge to their concrete application in contemporary life is a fine example of Latin American pastoral methodologies of that time and reflects a conversion effort aimed as much at the center of the Church as at its indigenous peripheries. As I show in the next section, a deep irony of this period of pastoral work on the altiplano is that the missionaries came to see in the catechists damning reflections of themselves.

Replicating Priestly Identity

Pastoral agents recall the earliest generation of catechists as *risiris*. The term modifies the stem of the Spanish verb "to pray" (*rezar*) with the Aymara suffix -*iri* indicating habitual action or an actor who is identified with the action as an occupation. The implication is that the catechists "merely" repeat in their communities the basic doctrinal formulae learned in courses. The term also denotes a position of religious specialist that predates the modern advent of catechists: traditional risiris—community members with a memorized knowledge of Christian prayers—were called upon by their community to pray during certain ritual occasions, especially those relating to the dead (Berg 1989:130, 1985:167). Missionaries also refer disparagingly to early catechists as *contratistas,* noting that their chief function seemed to be to contract sacraments from the priest on behalf of community members. In 1991 a priest compared these contratista catechists to "customs agents": gatekeepers who must ascertain that everyones' "papers" (in this case catechetical preparation) are in order before allowing them to go through. Similar criticisms are evident in documents from the sixties and seventies. A report prepared in the early seventies describes the first cohorts of catechists as *catequistas para,* functionaries put in place instrumentally by their communities to maintain access to the Catholic sacraments and related ritual value deriving from the Church and its representatives.[16] Recall that pastoral teams sometimes refused to attend to communities that did not name a catechist.

These criticisms reflect a range of concerns on the part of pastoral workers. Risiri suggests a homology with colonial religious practices that pastoral workers might find distressing as well as a certain superficiality implied by the idea of "repetition."[17] The notion of a contratista similarly connotes the sort of sacramental excess that was a central point of contention for the Catholic Church in Bolivia. Catequistas para, in addition to suggesting this sort of superficiality, smacks of mission and ethnographic glosses of Aymara "survival strategies": communities nominally meeting the requirements of the Church to meet their internal cultural needs while subverting the intentions of the dominant outsiders. Finally, the specter of the Bolivian customs agent conjures up not only the prospect of financial corruption (which has long been a concern of rural parishes and was a controversial issue in the development of the catechist pastoral model) but also the less than priestly image of a petty bureaucratic functionary. In its attempts to modernize, the postwar Church appears to have recreated its worst colonial nightmare.

Underlying these comments about the catechists, and at play throughout the evolution of the catechist pastoral model in the Andes, is a fundamental questioning of the identity of "priest." Here, a broader movement of experimentation and redefinition among some in the Church—worker-priest movements, priests refusing to live from the sale of sacraments, an increasing number of priests and nuns leaving behind clerical dress, an increasing number leaving the clergy for marriage—intersected on the one hand with missionaries' contemporary confrontations with their colonial antecedents and on the other hand with a pastoral effort that resurrected a colonial evangelical ideal of a native priesthood. In their invention of the catechists pastoral workers on the altiplano were struggling to reinvent themselves.

At a 1970 meeting of the Bolivian Episcopal Conference a group of priests presented the bishops with a letter reflecting on "the crisis of the priesthood."[18] The writers noted the problems of priestly poverty, which they said prevented priests from staying informed in a rapidly changing world ("a priest may not even be able to afford to subscribe to a magazine," they wrote) and forced priests to "live off the altar." A related concern was the need for priests to have a profession, to support themselves through work in the world, and so better integrate within modern society. There was a clearly expressed frustration with current pastoral work: a disappointment with their roles as "functionaries of sacraments" compounded by their confrontation with a tremendous cultural heterogeneity in Bolivia. This, they said, made it difficult to plan and coordinate pastoral work as a national Church. Priests also stated their concerns over Bolivia's "underdevelopment" and related issues of political and economic injustice. The writers noted that this situation created practical obstacles for the day-to-day labors of priests (travel difficulties, for instance). But they also cast the work of addressing these injustices as a pastoral end in itself. Finally, the priests noted their needs to better understand native languages and culture.

The letter reflects emerging points of divisions among priests: across religious orders, across pastoral context (e.g., urban/rural), across different generations, along the lines of the church hierarchy, and along the lines of national identity. There was a growing tension between national and foreign clergy throughout these years, evident in references to an *Iglesia extranjera* (e.g., Barnadas 1976; cf. Klaiber 1992:91). Broadly speaking, this tension was either between conservative national clergy who objected to the changes occasioned by the growing presence of such foreign orders as the Maryknolls or younger Bolivian priests who came to see the presence of foreign priests as another form of foreign domination. Undercutting all these discussions of the crisis of the priesthood was a profound questioning of the requirement of sacerdotal celibacy.

The issues that make up this "crisis" are contradictory. Throughout Latin America priests sought to minimize religious hierarchy and priestly authority, promoting instead democratic styles of worship with lay leadership. They downplayed priestly controlled sacramental practices as the foundation of Christian identity in favor of liturgical, text-based practices that, because they could be learned, were potentially open to all. At the same time, priests on the altiplano wrestled with a sense of powerlessness, finding themselves straitjacketed by the presuppositions of sacramentalismo.

Deacons and the National Security State

One response was to further empower Aymara Catholics. This was conceived as a continuation of the work begun with catechists. Pastoral agents sought to establish an indigenous deaconate: Aymara men empowered to celebrate certain sacraments, such as baptism and marriage, and equipped with preconsecrated wafers for the celebration of the Eucharist. From the mid-1960s there is evidence of a movement to establish an indigenous deaconate in Bolivia, which, in the words of one proponent, "is thought to be an urgent necessity for catechizing and for the administration of sacraments." In 1969 a center for the formation of Aymara deacons was established in the altiplano community of Laja under the direction of a new auxiliary bishop, Mons. Adhemar Esquivel. (Recall that Esquivel was responsible for the altiplano sur pastoral zone duing the time of my field research.) The documents proposing and defending the idea of Aymara deacons make reference to biblical sources as well as to documents from Vatican II and Medellín as they present the deacons as humble servants, invoked as at once a realization of true indigenous Christian identity and the ideal expression of humility from the Church hierarchy.

> Created by Christ and filled with his spirit, the entire Church is a priestly and prophetic people. . . . (L.G. 10). As a humble servant they announce the good news to the poor, raise up the oppressed and embrace all who are afflicted by human weakness (Lk. 4, 18). Consequently, all of the people of God, in their being and their work, are [in a condition of] service or *diaconía*.[19]

Like the catechists, deacons were to be at once true Christian everymen—prototypical converts, the end product of an authentic evangelization—and corrective alters for the Church's discontent with itself: selected, consecrated incarnations of the apostles, ambassadors of Christ, ordained by a bishop, but who nonetheless shared fully in the lives of the Aymara communities. This dual construction of these native intermediaries as prototypical converts and the embodiment of the reinvention of the priests is evident in the following comments by Mons. Esquivel in an interview with me in 1992: "We were concerned not to re-create a *sacramentalizador profesional.*" Breaking the traditional priestly mold, pastoral workers sought to constitute the deacons as servants of their communities whose centrality would simultaneously enable them to control community practice. "The married deacon," Esquivel told me, "was to be a servant of the community and the coordinator of all that was done in the community."

Underscoring these discussions are references to the deacons' facility within the Aymara culture and language: "The ordination of Aymara deacons will make it possible that the evangelization be presented in their own language and culture."[20]

For the popular masses, and above all for the people of the countryside, [who are] largely illiterate and of the Quechua or Aymara culture, there exists in addition a cultural barrier that prevents them from a true participation in the faith. Their Christian life will only be able to find its authentic existence and liturgical expression through the linguistic, musical, etc. elements of their own culture, and under the direction of members of their own society.[21]

Discussions of the time are filled with references to the defective and deformed religiosity in Bolivia, making special note of the urgent necessity of evangelization for the "popular masses of the countryside and the peri-urban areas." To speak in Bolivia of the rural and peri-urban "popular masses" is to speak of indigenous communities and communities of permanent and temporary indigenous migrants to cities such as La Paz, Oruro, and Cochabamba. Referring to the document "Pastoral Popular" from the Medellín conference of CELAM, a document of the Bolivian Episcopal Conference describes this popular/Indian religiosity as a "religion of passive resignation, of punishment, of superstition and anthropomorphisms that do not help man to seek his development."[22]

The deacons were to become an effective way to overcome cultural boundaries in the Church to the end of promoting authentic Aymara Christian communities. Missionaries selected aspirant deacons from among existing catechists with two or more years of service. In addition, candidates were to be at least thirty-five years of age, demonstrate leadership qualities, enjoy the support of their community as well as that of their local parish priest, be able to read and write [Spanish]; and, in the case of married candidates, have the express support of their wives.[23]

This last point is crucial. While it is not clear to me that marriage was a condition for becoming a deacon, discussions of the time repeatedly stressed that the deacons need not be celibate.

> The family has always been the basic nucleus of society. The reality is much stronger in the Aymara culture where only one who is married is considered a mature person. Thus the deaconate will have to be principally men with families. The deacon, by his family life, by his spirituality and union with his wife and children, by his work and prayer will give as his first benefit the example of a Christian family among the others.[24]

These themes of marriage and sexuality condense a set of important issues. This questioning of the viability and necessity of priestly celibacy resonates with the gendered and sexualized characterizations of missionization and evangelical history we have seen above. Concerns with effeminate Latin Catholicism, and the confusion over who in the missionary encounter was "wearing the pants," converged with a set of pastoral models (for instance, the family of God movement) explicitly positioning the procreative patriarchal family as a model for Catholic identity. Though it may be that pastoral agents saw the catechists and deacons as little more than culturally adept surrogates for missionaries who had failed to plant the seeds of faith, the proposals surrounding the married deaconate also evidence a growing sensitivity to cultural differences. In particular, they reflect awareness of the dissonance between Church models of priestly leadership and modes of authority in Aymara communities, where an unmarried, childless man or woman lacks legitimate public standing (e.g., Fedders 1974).

The institute at Laja preparing catechists for ordination as deacons emerged alongside the existing catechist training center run by Maryknoll at Peñas as well as dispersed parish-based courses for catechists. These local courses—offered, for instance, in parishes such as Tiwanaku, Jesús de Machaqa, Pucarani, and Viacha—were a counterpoint to the highly centralized and formalized catechist formation offered at Peñas. The local courses were more accessible to catechists and offered pastoral workers a greater degree of contact and involvement with the catechists. These parish-based courses represented an ef-

fort to go beyond what some saw as the too strictly catechetical formation offered by Maryknoll. The Laja center grew out of these parish-level courses,
prompting some concern about competition and rivalry between Laja and
Peñas. This should not be overstated—it is important to note the involvement
of some Maryknoll missionaries in the center at Laja—but does index important shifts in the pastoral ideology of the time as well as emerging tensions between groups of clergy. In general, Laja reflected the influence of Spanish and
Bolivian Jesuits and some Bolivian diocesan priests in contrast to the North
American–run center at Peñas.

The rise of the Laja center is remembered by present-day missionaries as
something of a high point in altiplano pastoral work. The center attained a
high degree of sophistication and integration: members of various religious orders, diocesan clergy, and foreign and national pastoral workers collaborated
on the courses. The Jesuit research organization CIPCA (Centro de Investigación y Promoción del Campesinado), founded in 1970, was also active in
the center. Finally, there was a high degree of coordination between Laja and
other pastoral organizations in Bolivia as well as in Peru, where similar efforts
at catechist formation were underway under the direction of Maryknoll missionary Edward Fedders, bishop in the Prelature of Puno and Juli in Peru. In
contrast with localized courses in more outlying areas, the courses at Laja provided additional amenities: blackboards; mimeographs; electric light; etc. This
reflects a considerable improvement from the picture presented a few years
earlier of priests unable to purchase magazines for their own education.

This period of ferment was short lived. The center in Laja and, ultimately, the ideal of an Aymara deaconate of married men were undone by a tangle of problems ranging from objections by more traditional and conservative
priests to the empowering of "Indians" to celebrate sacraments to the concerns
of more nativist-minded observers that investing individual deacons with such
power contradicted Aymara cultural principles that prescribe the rotation of all
community members through positions of authority. These concerns were
compounded by a set of other pressures on Andean pastoral work deriving
from reactions to liberation theology on the part of repressive military regimes
as well as the Catholic Church hierarchy. The result was the unraveling of pastoral work on the altiplano.

‡ ‡ ‡

Missionaries today widely consider the deacons to be a failed pastoral experiment. They note that despite the pastoral intentions to break the traditional priestly mold, many of the deacons ordained in the early 1970s came to

replicate negative dimensions of a priestly hierarchy. Such deacons (a few still practicing) are denounced as "minipriests," a term also used to criticize some catechists. A related point of contention concerns financial abuses by the deacons. Though they were expressly forbidden to receive payments for sacraments, and it was stressed in the planning documents that they should support their ministries from their own agricultural labors, a number of deacons charged for their sacramental services. Through this proscription missionaries clearly sought to restrict in the deacons what many came to reject in themselves: "living from the altar." But this also reflects a widely held belief among missionaries: that Indians cannot handle money, that it is a dangerous force in Aymara communities, leading to abuse and divisions.

In retrospect, it is not surprising some deacons became involved in financial abuses. Catechists saw the "promotion" to deacon as the big payoff for the considerable sacrifices of serving as catechist. (To this day a number of those who were passed over for ordination as deacons consider themselves slighted.) Ironically, these sacrifices were only intensified by their promotion. The costs of frequent travel and time away from fields and livestock put a severe financial strain on these men and their families. This pressure was compounded by a course schedule that did not take planting and harvesting seasons into account.

A related issue is the linkage in Aymara experience between formal education and wage earning. Despite the priestly ideal of deacons preparing for humble service in their communities, for many Aymara formal education is seen as properly resulting in a break with traditional, community-based life. Some catechists report being ridiculed in their communities for their longstanding attendance in courses with little change in lifestyle to show for it. Finally, an assessment of the deacons' financial practices ought to take into account a widely reported sense in the Andes that Catholic sacraments do not "work" if the beneficiary does not make some sort of offering—preferably monetary—a part of the process. Some altiplano missionaries told me that despite their refusal to charge for services parishioners often insisted on paying for masses.

Additional factors impacting altiplano pastoral work at this time were the repressive military regimes of General Hugo Banzer Suarez (1971–78) and Luis García Meza (1980–81) in Bolivia. Banzer's rule marked a reaction to a period of leftist military governments, in which climate the archbishop of La Paz had issued a number of pastoral letters calling for Christians to participate in a "permanent revolution" guided by a "new Christian ethic" that sought to walk a line between "socialism," "capitalism," and an anti-imperialist "nationalism" (Manrique 1970). Echoing the discourse of liberation theology,

Mons. Jorge Manrique Hurtado suggested a moderate overlap of Christianity and the "neosocialism" of the short-lived government of General Juan José Torres. Manrique criticized "certain individuals, unable to distinguish between unjust subversion and justified protest," who "have reacted by a stiffened anticommunism and have fomented violence." The reference is likely to Banzer, who led a coup attempt in January 1970, eighteen months before successfully seizing power in August 1971.

Banzer's coup violently contested this vision of Bolivian society. His regime and that of García Meza led systematic campaigns of state terror directed against the Church. These violent actions were part of the infamous "Banzer plan": a laundry list of dirty tricks and strategies of repression developed with the collaboration of the U.S. CIA and designed to harass, terrorize, and discredit the Church's "progressive sectors." Rural parishes were raided; clergy were arrested and expelled from the country and, in some cases tortured and murdered. Foreign priests, particularly Jesuits and Oblates—orders active in work with catechists—were especially targeted. In Bolivia, as elsewhere, indigenous leaders, including some affiliated with the Church, were targets of government violence and murder.[25]

But perhaps the most direct blow to southern Andean pastoral work during these years was a conflict with the Vatican over plans to develop, on the base of the Aymara deaconate, a married indigenous priesthood. These plans grew out of debates about the relevance of a celibate clergy coupled with the growing commitment to the catechists and deacons as the anchor of an authentic Aymara Christianity. In documents from this period priests argued that rather than a universal requirement, celibacy should be an option for priests, supported and affirmed as a "charisma" in those who choose it. They challenged the Church not to continue to oppose in theory a situation that was openly recognized as being widespread in practice. Moreover, they noted that what they saw as the relaxed sexual mores of the modern world made priestly celibacy something that diminished and inhibited their ministry. Finally, they argued that sexual continence was more difficult to maintain in rural parishes as a result of the isolation and loneliness experienced there.[26]

In 1972 Bishop Fedders proposed the creation of a married Aymara priesthood in the prelature of Juli-Puno in Peru (Jordá 1981:423). His proposal referred to advanced catechists—some with twenty years of experience—in the prelature called Catholic pastors. Fedders's report recommended, "that some of the laws that now bind as regards priesthood be relaxed—for example, concerning celibacy and the steps of preparation" (Fedders 1974:35). He stressed that the married Aymara priests so ordained would serve explicitly to celebrate the Eucharist in their local community, and so would "fulfill what is needed in the local community, namely, stability and permanence." Fedders also noted that the condition of celibacy has important repercussions in the Aymara context and cited a tradition of an indigenous priesthood, invoking Aymara ritual specialists such as the yatiri.

At about the same time, a delegation from the Bolivian Church, headed by Mons. Adhemar Esquivel, traveled to Belgium to present a report on their pastoral work (see *Pro Mundi Vita* 1974). Their travels included a visit to Rome where at least some among them raised the issue of ordaining deacons as married priests. I collected no firsthand accounts of the details of the trip, but the results apparently were a schism within the delegation (each of whom returned to Bolivia separately) and a sharply negative response from the Vatican, which resulted in a scaling back of the pastoral work with Aymara catechists and deacons and led to what many have interpreted as a period of relative silence and circumspection on the part of the Bolivian pastoral agents involved.[27]

I do not know if the Esquivel visit was coordinated with the Fedders letter. Certainly there was a great deal of interaction between the two pastoral zones. Significantly, the written response to Fedders's report made mention of the Aymara deacons in the diocese of La Paz, noting, "if married men were ordained at Juli, it would be impossible to resist the pressures for such ordinations that already exist in Bolivia, and to a certain extent in Ecuador. Already the two youngest auxiliary Bishops of La Paz are talking openly of ordaining as priests the Indians being prepared for the deaconate" (Poggi 1974).

The report, prepared by a consultor of the congregation of the clergy and conveyed by the nuncio Luigi Poggi, argued that the Aymara catechists and deacons lack the basic educational background of their European counterparts, and so would constitute a "second-class priesthood." Moreover, "the skimpy theological formation of the catechists is inadequate for exposing the follies of the superstition that is all-pervasive in the lives of the Aymaras. If the Indians had none but the married priests from among the catechists, the superstition would increase rather than decrease, inasmuch as superstition is the greatest weakness of that people." Finally, the report predicted that just as all Aymara, once contaminated by money, leave their communities for the city, so "the married Indian priests, pushed by their wives and children, would move to the cities as soon as their first enthusiasm wore off. They would thus not only abandon their communities, but would also create enormous problems for the clergy of whatever city they might go to."

The intersection of all these factors essentially undid the postwar pastoral developments that had culminated with the center at Laja, precipitating what pastoral workers today call a crisis that lasted until the early 1980s. The center at Laja was disbanded, with deacons being prepared locally in three altiplano centers for a number of years before the entire effort was abandoned.

SACRAMENTALISMO AND EXTIRPATION

A correlated "crisis" afflicting this period of pastoral work concerns pastoral agents' relationship to *sacramentalismo:* an "excessive," "superstitious," "fatalistic," "magical" focus on the Catholic sacraments. As we have seen, pastoral agents in the 1960s and 1970s found themselves confronted by what they saw as both the "Old Testament" dimensions of traditional Aymara religiosity and a defective and superficial Catholicism manifest in the Aymara focus on such Catholic rituals as baptism, marriage, fiesta masses, or masses for the dead. Missionaries on the altiplano sought to overcome, indeed to extirpate, this limited Catholicism, replacing it with a reformed Catholic practice that would both reflect a complete Christian conversion and entail a complete Christian ministry on the part of the priests. This peculiarly Andean evangelical encounter with cultural difference converged with broader trends evident in the development of Latin American progressive Catholicism in the wake of Medellín and the Second Vatican Council.

Newly arriving priests quickly found themselves overwhelmed by a schedule of fiestas and masses that left them little time for anything else. In the late 1960s and early 1970s it was not uncommon for individual priests in rural parishes to celebrate more than four hundred masses per year. Pastoral agents with their own ideals and expectations of evangelization found their time and energy completely consumed with celebrating and traveling to and from masses in rural communities. It is little wonder that, like Monast, they came to see themselves as functionaries responding to the demands of the Aymara—demands that implicated them in the very same "defective" evangelization they sought to remedy.

Beyond the frustrated ideals of novice missionaries, Catholic pastoral workers expressed other concerns over fiesta practices. Denouncing the drunkenness, dancing, or the excessive costs incurred by festival sponsors, Catholic missionaries and the catechists they trained sounded very much like their rivals in evangelical Protestant churches.[28] Writing of the northern altiplano town of Compi, Hans and Judith Maria Buechler report

In the last five years, since 1970, the Catholic Church has experienced a dramatic renewal too [i.e., in step with the growth of Protestant churches].

In the community studies [sic] the latter involved the construction of a
school and the training of one of the first Aymara deacons. These reformed
Catholics have joined the Protestants in their opposition to certain traditional practices including abusive drinking and costly sponsorship of Saints
day celebrations. As a result many traditionalists equate the "catequistas"
with the Protestants. In fact, conversions from reformed Catholicism to
Lutheranism (one of the least fundamentalist Protestant churches) seem to
be frequent. (1978:93)

The catechists served to check this sacramentalismo in a number of ways.
Through the formation of local worship groups and regular liturgical celebrations, they constituted a Christian community that was explicitly constructed as a corrective continuous evangelical background to the periodic ef-
fervescence of the fiestas. Catechists were responsible for giving classes of
formation to fiesta sponsors and godparents of baptism, and so engaged in
forms of evangelization not possible for the itinerant priests. Many catechists
required a period of participation in the faith group as a condition for receiving sacraments. It is likely that simply adding the catechists as intermediaries in the process, setting preconditions for access to sacraments, effectively
reduced the number of petitions for fiesta and other masses. Certainly the catechists helped to coordinate the number of requests: today catechists frequently organize group baptisms or weddings, arranging a date for the priest's
visit and organizing a *convivencia* bringing together catechists, faith groups, and
those seeking marriage or baptism from a number of neighboring communities. Finally, in addition to these bureaucratic obstacles to sacramentalismo
and the overwhelming obligations of fiesta masses, in many communities catechists and faith groups actively opposed fiesta practices, preaching against
them, publicly refusing to participate in them, and otherwise disrupting these
community events.

In some areas priests also reduced their complicity in sacramentalismo by
simply refusing to celebrate fiesta masses, much as some refused to attend to
communities without catechists. In Tiwanaku the pastoral team reduced the
annual number of masses from eight hundred to three hundred. In other
parishes, and especially in the northern altiplano pastoral zone of Bolivia, I was
told, pastoral teams refused to celebrate any fiesta masses. Alternatively, priests
would celebrate fiesta masses a day or two early or late, in order to be out
synch with the height of the fiesta celebrations. Some communities responded by using the local chapel space for other festival activities—in effect doing
what they could to honor the saint image without a priest. Others hired priests
from the city of La Paz to say mass.

Deeply implicated with this rejection of fiestas was a strong reaction to the worship of Catholic saints. Saints images play a central role in Andean Catholicism; as the cabildo of saints and altars in the Jesús de Machaqa Church makes clear, they are often important switch points between Catholicism and local forms of social and political legitimacy. In addition to their prominence in annual fiestas and correlated cargo activities, saints are invoked in a range of other Aymara ritual practices. They are sometimes claimed as the source of a yatiri's power, and they are often the recipients of offerings mediated by yatiris (Huanca 1989; Platt 1997). In this, like the Church tower in Jesús de Machaqa town, certain saints images appear to be analogous to more "traditional" Andean place deities—wak'as, apus, achachilas. In response to my questions about the saints, catechists typically declared: "The saints are not gods." "They are man-made." "They're only statues." "They're like photographs." This is the catechism of a modernizing "reformed Catholicism," one that remains influential among contemporary catechists. As one priest who was active in a rural Aymara parish in the late 1960s recalled, "I wanted to make new chapels without any images. I wanted to turn the altar [of the colonial Church in his parish] into a museum."

Concurrent with this rejection of aspects of traditional Catholic practice was a denunciation of apparently "traditional" Aymara practices. While the comments of Bishop Fedders invoking Aymara yatiris as models of authentic priestly ministry reflect currents of thought evident in the 1960s and 1970s and point to a longer tradition of clerical indigenismo, it is also the case that yatiris, the offerings they made, and the local place deities they engaged came under sharp attack by Catholic pastoral agents at this time. As with the fiestas, catechists and their faith groups were on the front line of this extirpation of local customs and traditions. Beyond refusing to participate in these activities, in some communities catechists and their faith groups were actively—and sometimes violently—denouncing yatiris and wak'as as "things of the devil."

One detects a strong whiff of seventeenth-century idolatry extirpation in these modern missionary practices. However, it is worth underscoring that in the postwar evangelical encounter the targets of this muscular neo-Catholicism included prototypical indigenous "idols" as well as colonial Catholicism. Can there be a clearer index of the entanglement of indigenous and Catholic forms? Yet missionary constructions of the time and subsequent pastoral ideologies continue to posit a discrete and enduring local Andean culture.

In the course of this modern-day extirpation campaign rituals such as the ayuno were disrupted and abandoned, yatiris denounced as frauds or agents of the devil, and sacred sites such as wak'as were destroyed. Similarly, catechists and priests sought to reject and control Catholic fiesta practices, removing saints' images and other ritual paraphernalia from ritual circulation. In some cases I suspect that catechists went as far as to destroy altars and saints images. Clothing and other adornments made for saints were swept off of local chapel altars. In many of the communities I visited, catechists today maintain store-rooms with abandoned (and often damaged) icons. I take these as an archive of this time. In some communities this destruction of idols coincided with the planned rebuilding or renovation of the local chapels and underscores the ethos of modernization and postcolonial development interwoven with neo-Catholic practices. In other areas, however, I collected numerous accounts of fires in the 1960s and 1970s that destroyed many—but never all—of a community's saints.

Today, many priests lament this period of secularization. Missionaries of the postwar generation who remain active today speak of these years of crisis in the 1970s as time lost. For subsequent cohorts of pastoral workers, there is a degree of resentment for what they see as the "mistakes" of their immediate predecessors. While many continue to be motivated by the social ideals of liberation theology and a number of its critical theological premises, most contemporary missionaries have come to question its application to the Andean context. By the time my field research began in the late 1980s and early 1990s, liberation theology was widely regarded as a failed pastoral experiment. The combination of national security state repression, Vatican intervention, and the cultural dissonance of the liberationist practices in rural highlands communities precipitated a sense of rupture in the early eighties as pastoral agents burned out or were reassigned (or worse), centers for catechist training closed, and a range of other evangelical initiatives ground to a halt. The emergence of the pastoral paradigm of inculturation fortified by newly arriving cohorts of missionaries, and resonant with a global rise of ethnic politics, marks a very self-conscious rupture with the modern moment of liberation theology. It is to this postliberation theology of inculturation that I turn in the following chapter.

CHAPTER 3

Local Missions, Global Alters

TWO CONVERSIONS

Father Miguel

In the beginning of [1984] I went through a very strong crisis in the sense of my work and my vocation and I came through it because of a blessing that I could transform, I could understand the . . . *my* problem. In this case it wasn't so much a problem of where I was. OK, I didn't understand where I was, I was working with complete devotion, but I brought with me in my work, in my vision, the experience I had from a different culture. And, in 1984, thanks to God I discovered that the methodology of [pastoral] work is different, that I need to be different, and that the cultural environment, the dynamic, the calendar is different from the society I come from. . . . I changed my work method, my way of seeing the Aymara themselves, and this helped me very much as I was beginning my work [in the new parish].

The speaker is Miguel, a Polish priest of the Society of the Divine Word, active since the early 1980s in missionary work among Aymara-speaking communities of the Bolivian highlands. I interviewed Miguel some six years after the personal crisis he is recounting, a moment he had come to see as something of a conversion experience. He continued:

I underwent a personal transformation, a conversion, not in the moral sense or at the level of faith. . . . I've always tried to be a believing priest [laughs] not simply an administrative cleric. . . . I believe I underwent a transformation at the personal, the human, and even the charismatic level. . . . I withdrew to the mountains for one week. I was about to leave the mission, and my continuation as a *religioso* and as a priest was in question. . . . So I withdrew with my pack and my tent to the mountain to pass a few days in the desert before making my decision, to have this contact with myself and with God. And there I discovered as a symbol of what I carried with me, of what I had been, the watch. It was like a symbol, and from that moment I left the watch behind, because my problem was the entire dimension of time, the entire industrialized society. I couldn't understand, for example, why the Aymara didn't come to mass on Sunday, why they didn't come on time. It was a complete focus of what had been my other life.

Brother Alejandro

Toward the middle of my 1990–92 stretch of field research, Alejandro borrowed my copy of Tomás Huanca's *El yatiri en la comunidad aymara* (1989). The book presents a linguistic analysis of a life-history interview with a yatiri, an Aymara ritual specialist. After some weeks Alejandro (who is marginally literate) returned the book, expressing disappointment that it was not a manual for yatiri practice. Alejandro had hoped to find condensed in the book the knowledge necessary to undertake the practices of yatiris, including the preparation of specific offerings, the divination of the causes of disease and other misfortunes, and practices of healing. I suspect that his motives were twofold.

On the one hand, he told me he had hoped to team up with a friend, himself a yatiri, and earn some cash by offering their ritual services to urban whites in La Paz. On the other, Alejandro's request reflects his own form of conversion. Before becoming a Catholic catechist, Alejandro had been an active member of a Protestant Church, which he joined in the mid-seventies. In 1985, in response to efforts by the parish priest to recruit new catechists and revitalize parish pastoral work in anticipation of a papal visit to Bolivia, he was selected by his community to serve as a catechist.

The community was eager to name a new catechist in order to counteract the power of a long-serving catechist from the community. This man, Bonifacio, had engaged in some stridently extirpative actions during the 1970s. Of course, Alejandro's Protestant affiliation involved him in a similar rejection of traditional *costumbre*. But Alejandro had a reputation as a quiet man, and he was likely viewed as relatively unthreatening by his community. On the other hand, for reasons discussed already, faith groups have been largely assimilated in Aymara communities as a variant of Protestantism, and it may have been precisely Alejandro's Protestant bona fides that made him a strong candidate for the position of catechist.

Alejandro assumed the position of (second) catechist at about the same time Miguel was undergoing his period of crisis and rethinking his Christian identity. Among the consequences of Miguel's conversion—and a set of similar missionary experiences at that time—was an intensified pastoral embrace of the theology of inculturation. One of the results of this new pastoral posture was a conversion on the part of Alejandro, as he came to see his catechist identity as a basis for acquiring and enacting prototypical ethnographic knowledge about "the Aymara." He hoped to glean this knowledge from Huanca'a book.

‡ ‡ ‡

This chapter is about Alejandro's and Miguel's respective conversions and the entangled history of Aymara and missionaries they reflect. I have three goals. The first is to continue a narrative of postwar missionary activity in the Andes, moving from the crises of the 1970s and early 1980s to a more recent renaissance of Catholic pastoral work under the rubric of the theology of inculturation. To this end I review some of the basic tenets of inculturation and present ethnographic descriptions of inculturationist pastoral courses conducted by missionaries for Aymara catechists.

At the same time, Miguel's conversion account illuminates the lived experiences of the missionaries themselves. To be sure, the drama of Miguel's narrative—as well as other accounts presented in this chapter—is intensified by the particulars of the historical moment and the sharp sense of rupture in the turn from theologies of liberation to inculturation. Nonetheless, these narratives of missionary self-transformation underscore a more fundamental dimension of missionization: the condition of missionaries as component subjects of local Aymara experience. I take Miguel's conversion as an opportunity to examine some of the strategies by which foreign missionaries constitute themselves as plausible evangelizing subjects within mission fields, the ways they imagine the Aymara as their interactants, and the means by which these identities become routinized and presupposable. This is my second goal.

In settings such as the ones where Miguel and Alejandro live, locals produce locality but they do not produce it alone. For Aymara the production of locality typically involves situating and referencing a host of translocal actors (missionaries, government officials, aid workers, etc.). In situations of long-term missionary engagement, missionaries become presupposable and necessary strangers within local frames of reference. As the cohorts of postwar pastoral workers discovered, to their frustration, this presupposability and necessity constrain missionary practices and harness them to a variety of activities integral to the production and maintenance of indigenous locality. These range from priestly participation in fiestas and intercommunity events, life crisis rites, or the investiture of local leaders to riding circuit around a pastoral zone, distributing international aid, or brokering local access to governmental resources.

This is not to suggest that missionaries merely dance to the tune of the colonial legacy. Far from inert component subjects of locality, missionaries and other strangers are directly involved in its production. Just as locality is not unproblematically already there for indigenous locals but must be sustained and generated by present- and future-oriented work, neither is it already there for the strangers who engage it. What is more, these agents tend to have their own axes to grind with regard to locality; implicitly or explicitly they assert their own vision of locality and their place within it. In this light, missionization can be seen as an intervention in the production of locality and in the production of the "subjects" whose practices ceaselessly remake locality and align it with local and translocal frames of meaning and power. To return to the case of Father Miguel, I want to examine the ways such narratives of missionary conversion describe the production of a particular kind of locality as a space for missionary practice. Miguel's conversion involves his negotiating, within the constraints of an ongoing history of missionary-Aymara interaction, a subject position enabling his participation in locality in ways that are authorized by and authorize a specific pastoral ideology: the then ascendant theology of inculturation.

Alejandro's efforts to embrace and assume the practices of a yatiri clearly reflect the exhortations of inculturationist priests. His faith in the textual condensation of Aymara tradition and his own ability to authentically embody such book-learned culture is resonant with a tendency for inculturationists to codify what they take to be local cultural tradition. The implications of this missionary standardized Aymara orthodoxy are complex. The third goal of this chapter is to examine the efforts by catechists to negotiate and control their ritual and sociopolitical authority with respect to the overlapping fields of inculturationist missionization, pastoral work in the parishes, and activities with their faith groups. This discussion serves as a bridge to part 2 of this book, "Syncretic Subjects."

In my fieldwork with Aymara and missionaries I was struck by a reciprocal self-consciousness most of them manifested, as they see themselves as they imagine others see them. This sort of intersubjective commensurability is a condition of the possibility of missionization and a telling symptom of the complexities of local spaces. Hannerz (1992) suggests it is a characteristic of the global ecumene, cast as a dense network of "takings into account" that situate locality within a skein of translocal perspectives. We have a glimpse of this in Alejandro's assumptions (likely correct) about his marketability as a yatiri in La Paz, a sense of the ways prototypical Aymara tradition is perceived and consumed by urban Hispanic society. But such intersubjectivity is also a key dimension of all social practice, including the most microlevel day-to-day interactions.[1] This chapter takes up the global ideology of inculturation and examines its manifestations in the situated practices and experiences of catechists and missionaries.

GLOBALIZATION AND THE CONVERSION OF DIFFERENCE

In recent years Catholic missionaries in the Andes have sought to codify and reinforce indigenous religiosity as part of the church's broader effort to embrace "local theologies" and "inculturate" itself within specific cultural contexts.[2] In Latin America this has followed on the heels of liberation theology, which has tended to downplay ethnic distinctions and local folk culture as corrupt and corrupting inheritances, stressing instead the homogenizing theological identity of "the poor."[3] With few exceptions mainline liberation theology, with pastoral practices characterized by CEBs and rationalized and politically radicalized discourses has failed to flourish in rural regions as it has in some urban and peri-urban areas and in proletarianized settings such as mines.

As the dominant evangelical frame for Aymara missionization today, the theology of inculturation is in part a strategic recognition of the failures of classical liberationist approaches in indigenous contexts, in part a revoicing of liberation theology in the wake of Vatican and state repression, and in part the emerging product of the "conversion" of influential missionaries affected by their experiences in the field. Simply put, inculturation strives to recuperate and revalorize indigenous culture. The ways of the ancestors, until recently denounced as idololatrous, are now embraced as profoundly Christian or at least as expressions of an indigenous religiousity that do not resist translation into a Christian frame of reference. Indeed, this revalued tradition is cast by missionaries as being "more Christian" than contemporary Aymara and Bolivian social life.

Redeeming History

First articulated in the 1970s, inculturation emerged as a response to what theologians percieve as a double tension: on the one hand, the relationship of the Church with modernity; on the other, the relations of the Church with "traditional cultures" (Suess 1991). Much like liberation theologians, inculturationists take a highly historicized view of the Bible. But where liberationists classically have sought to identify parallels between biblical history and contemporary experience, inculturationists are also concerned with the Bible as a record of a particular and particularly authentic amalgamation of Christianity with the local cultures of antiquity. As the sites of the original incarnation and the prototypical evangelization, these are benchmarks against which all forms of local conversion are to be judged.[4] By this criteria Christianity in Europe or North America—that is, the lived experiences of most of the foreign missionaries on the altiplano—reflects both a relativized particularity as well as a cultural amalgamation judged to be more genuine that that found in the Andes. Thus William, a North American priest active in Bolivia since the 1960s, contrasts North American and European Catholicism—characterized by "deep roots of faith"—with the Church in Bolivia, "where the roots of faith are not that deep. They're all superficial. They were imposed and they were not allowed to evolve and mature as happened in Europe."

In the views of inculturationist missionaries religious practice, as a consequence of shallow roots of faith, is rendered doubly opaque. "We don't know yet what people really understand by the customs that they do," noted William, adding, "*They* don't know." His concerns are echoed by other missionaries who lament a space between real meaning and superficial practical intent, such that neither (Aymara) actors nor (missionary) observers grasp the significance of local cultural practices. This is, of course, yet another voicing of the classic dilemma of syncretism; the spatial metaphor of deep roots corrects the heretofore superficial evangelization. But there is an important sleight of hand here that we should keep our eyes on. For the roots connecting deeper meanings with surface practices, serve also, within the frame of inculturation, to align a universal Christian core with a local cultural surface. These roots, in other words, are an index of a translatability (between core Christian meaning and local vernacular form) that is fundamental to inculturation.

In this way deep roots of faith are the enabling condition of a kind of socioreligious pluralism, allowing a Catholic authenticity to assimilate to a variety of cultural traditions. The possibility of multiplicity is based upon the authenticity or depth of evangelization, aligning local particularity with respect to a presupposed underlying truth. As Father William tells us, inculturationist evangelization involves making sure that "they" and "we" really understand what "they" are doing.

In the Bolivian context foreign missionaries often cast inculturation as a process of overcoming the historical creolization of the Christian faith—the long-standing link of Christian identity with a Hispanic Andean elite. *Creole* here refers to a displaced European identity: Spaniards born in the Americas, for instance, and the Christianity they practice in the New World. Father Esteban, a Spaniard with extensive rural pastoral experience, underscored these racial and ethnic implications of evangelization and conversion.

> If Christianity has presented itself up to the present as married completely with the creole religion, with the way of being creole, and the way of being creole is the way of being, let's say, important in the country, then what has resulted is that [an Aymara convert] tends to imitate the creole. . . . So the the very difficult and large and immense step that I am involving myself in in these years is really to say that Aymara ways are Christian just as creole ways. So, in this process, just as Christianity has inserted itself in creole culture, something similar has to be done. How will we insert it [Christianity] in Aymara culture. So here, in what does Christianity consist. It is a form of living Aymara culture, a different way of living the same Aymara culture

Implicit in inculturation is a process of theological deculturation: distilling and retrieving a posited pure faith message and crafting its reexpression in another cultural medium. The model for this process verges on the Christian belief in revelation and incarnation. As Father Esteban explained to me.

> What is the difference between the Christian and the non-Christian? The only difference between the Christian and the non-Christian is, for me, in the simple word "like." The entire world loves, but the Christian loves attempting to love like Jesus. The entire world works, but the Christian attempts to work like Jesus.
>
> There is a faith that tells you that the highest expression of humanity was Jesus. . . . The richness this faith has is that the reference point of my humanism is not a theory but rather a person. . . . What I attempt [in my work of evangelization] is [to announce] a Good News that has a human backing, in a person. To show that that which is Aymara—Aymara rites— can be lived as Christian . . . like Jesus. Not imitating, but retranslating, actualizing today what Jesus did in his time. What Jesus did with his Jewish culture, it is today required of me that I do that with Aymara culture or that I do that with Western culture.

At issue is nothing less than an Aymara New Testament.

The ideals of inculturation are illustrated in the following excerpt of a sermon presented by a foreign priest, Father Alonso, addressing an annual meeting of catechists and faith group members from various altiplano parishes.

Here among yourselves, you can do something that cannot be done in any other place, which is to discover and cause to grow the Good News, but from our own roots.

Sometimes they say the Good News has come directly from a distant land. It has come from Europe, from gringo-land, from other directions, perhaps from the direction of Jerusalem, from Bethlehem, from the Holy Land. [And] there are many different people, there are gringos, many, many different people come [to tell you] "what do you know. What does the word of God have to say to you?" That is how they talk. And so we think, we say "*Ay caramba,* they know [things]; we are stupid." It is not like that. That good word of God, that good resurrection of God, it is here, it is here. From long, long ago, it is here. That good word of God is here. The roots of the Good News of the Gospel is within us, since our grandparents, our ancestors, the good word of God is here. . . .

Some [go to Church] on Sunday, some on Saturday, some on Thursday. . . . There are all kinds of religions, each with its own God, and thus there is fighting. . . . But did this come from within the ayllu? No. It came from somewhere else. So perhaps this return to this unity, this oneness, this single heart can only come from us Aymara. . . .

Which was more Christian? A communal title or the way it is now, half separated with each one having his [little piece of land]. Which was more Christian? Communal or separated? Communal! And from where did this come? From our own past or from what they have brought us from outside? From what is our own! The past ways from here, were more Christian than what is coming to us now from the laws from other places. . . .

When one needs to work, but lacks something, he can ask, he says "Ah shit, I'm going to need four *yuntas,* but I only have one." What does he do? *Ayni! Ayni!* [i.e., an exchange practice common, with local variations, across many areas of the Andes]. Where did ayni come from? From Europe or was it always here? Which is more Christian? Ayni or a patron with money? He pays someone else, that way the other person turns into a peon. Which is more Christian? Ayni or that other way with a patron and peon? Ayni! This Christian thing, ayni, has been here. . . . This is much more Christian than that the rich one pays and the poor one works. The rich one with money scratching his belly, and the poor one just working. That is not so Christian.

The rhetoric of inculturation involves a metacultural focus on particular Aymara traits. Prototypical exchange practices such as ayni, highly formalized ritual actions such as the *waxt'a* (burnt offerings to place deities), the local authority of yatiris, the use of coca and alcohol, and perhaps above all the socio-ritual solidarity of the ayllu are routinely deployed by pastoral workers as metonyms for an authentic shared Aymaraness. A number of these traits are already politically charged, having been taken up in recent decades by neotraditionalist political movements and as points of conflict in community-level religious disputes arising from both Protestant and neo-Catholic evangelization.

This was evident when I observed an Aymara priest stopping to pay his regards to a group of catechists while passing through the parish where they had gathered for a pastoral course. Finding the catechists seated in the classroom passing around plastic bags of coca leaf provided by the missionaries, he exclaimed in Spanish, "Shit! This looks like a meeting of Kataristas! All you need is alcohol and some cigarettes!" The reference is to an indigenist, nationalist political movement, named after Tupaj Katari (the leader of an eighteenth-century rebellion), which has self-consciously taken up emblems of Andean culture as politicized symbols of its struggle against a state seen as complicit in the destruction, repression, and forgetting of indigenous cultures (see Albó 1987, 1994; Harris 1995; Hurtado 1986). One catechist cautiously invited the visiting priest to join them. Switching to Aymara, the priest declined, saying, "Janiwa, nayax siktawa" ("No, I am a Protestant"). The jokes dispelled the tension of an awkward moment; catechists giggled self-consciously as they chewed coca in front of a priest whose predecessors condemned the very same activity. Moreover they reference key concerns of the inculturationist wing of the contemporary Bolivian Church: to counteract the pastoral policies of the past seen as having created fragmented worship groups quite similar to Protestant congregations and, more constructively, to forge a more inclusive religiously grounded ethnic solidarity as a base for social action and change. Insofar as the revalorized practices promote communal solidarity and justice they are embraced by missionaries as local expressions of the theological and sociological values of the progressive Church.

"And I Discovered This Here"

By the lights of inculturation, missionaries witness and discover Christian truths in other cultures. Pastoral workers conceive of the Aymara as a "people of the Bible," a people enmeshed in the unfolding narrative of their own "new testament," and in so doing missionaries construct themselves as witnesses to and aspiring coparticipants in Aymara history. They posit and position themselves as subjects of revelation. "In your communal organization, you express and reveal God," declared a pastoral worker to a gathering of catechists. She continued: "You are the revealers: through your experiences you can reveal God to other peoples." In this sense inculturation is as much about the conversion of the missionaries as it is about the evangelization of Aymara.

Miguel's conversion in the mid 1980s correlates with the shift of pastoral paradigms from liberation theology to inculturation and can be read as the reorganization of the missionary self in terms of an emerging pastoral ideology. But these pastoral ideologies are never simply imposed from without. Certainly in a setting like the Andes, with a long history of missionary engagement, pastoral ideologies arise in interaction with situated practices and the local constraints and presuppositions to which missionaries are subject. There is, then, an element of truth, though a distorted one, in the missionary characterization of the experience of otherness as a motor of conversion. Yet where Miguel seems to be claiming a transparent recovery of religious meaning in his experience of the Aymara, and a corresponding rejection of European Catholicism metonymically cast off with his watch, it is clear that he is not "going native" in any simple way. Nor does inculturation effect a straightforward recognition of religious plurality. For at stake in inculturation is a discursive alignment of Aymaraness establishing not a horizontal relationship of pluralism but a hierarchical relationship of encompassment. Aymara religiosity is valorized always with respect to a posited transcendent field of Christian meaning. At issue in Miguel's conversion is not an evacuation of his Western/Christian self, not a separation from "what had been my other life," but rather a controlled and controlling alignment with otherness through a reinstrumentalized Western/Christian self. Inculturation gives force to a particular framing of this evangelical encounter and the subsequent reinstrumentalization of self.

After recounting his transformative experience in the mountains, and his pivotal rejection of his watch, Miguel continued:

And I discovered my own roots. I come from the peasantry. A peasantry that also had to struggle because it was close to and influenced by a mechanized society, an industrial society, and all these things that have to go with the watch. . . . I discovered my own deep roots in that we also, in spite of all of these things, as Polish *campesinos* and under *minifundia*—another correspondence with them—we had to defend our identity before communist power, and especially during Stalinist times . . . I discovered as well that I lived the calendar not of hours and minutes, but I also lived the calendar of seasons: seasons of harvesting, of sowing or reaping, of fallow, others that govern our lives. And I discovered this here, among the Aymara people. I threw away the watch, my life changed, my way of behaving with them, my way of working. I no longer had any problem with impatience with running around, I calmed down very much. The cultural horizon opened up much more for me. I began to understand—after I made my own calculations—how foolish I had been. The Aymara dedicate more time to God and to the Church even though they do not go to mass every Sunday like the best Polish Catholic, who, during the course of the year only dedicates one hour every Sunday for the mass. At best he is in a group [and] dedicates one more hour on Saturday. Combining all these hours, I saw that an Aymara may not go every Sunday to mass but in one season is capable [of spending] an entire week with his wife and with their children dedicated to a retreat, an encuentro, a convivencia, a prayer. And comparatively [the Aymara] has dedicated many more hours than the other [i.e. the Polish Catholic].

The irony of Miguel's calculus of Christianity—as he systematically measures time in order to justify casting off his watch—discloses precisely the sleight of hand of pluralism and universality integral to inculturationist rhetoric. Central to the processes of missionization and conversion is the production of mutual intelligibility and translatability (e.g., Keane 1996; Stewart and Shaw 1994). Such intelligibility is generated within and with respect to a range of situational constraints, constraints that take on particular force in such long-term missionary settings as those encountered in the Andes. Within these settings Miguel's conversion and comparable narratives are conditions of the possibility for establishing meaningful frameworks of missionization, aligning transcendent frames of meaning and action with the localized fields of missionary practice through the translocal biographies of missionary selves. A Christian truth, available to Miguel from his biographical past, is "discovered . . . here, among the Aymara people."

Of note in Miguel's narrative is a set of equivalences that do not involve issues of doctrinal content: in Miguel's words his conversion is "not in the moral sense, or at the level of faith." Rather, the achievement of his conversion is the calibration of the rhythm of Aymara ritual practices with his own expectations and sensibilities. His frustration about Aymara participating irregularly in Catholic ritual activities, about seasonal shifts, and so forth are soothed not by insights into the temporal sensibilities of the Aymara per se but by insights that enable a transformed understanding of himself that echoes, anticipates, and authorizes the practices he identifies among the Aymara. Miguel's nostalgic recovery of his peasant roots provides a framework for making sense of the Aymara activities that had so vexed him. The relationship of commensurability thus generated authorizes Aymara patterns of ritual activity as plausibly Catholic, but also authorizes his own localized missionary practices as continuous with an anchoring Christianity that transcends and embraces local specificity. This double process of authorization negotiates (from a missionary perspective) the positions of missionaries as component subjects of Andean locality, intelligible interactants within Aymara sociocultural fields. At the same time, and correlated with the self-conscious transformation of missionaries, such discourses convey a particular framing of Aymara locality—one that is often in tension with the practices and presuppositions of Aymara interactants.

These missionary conversions weave biography, national histories, and evangelical ideologies to constitute effective subject positions within the local Andean mission field. They enable an authoritative missionary participation in the production of locality. In place of discussions of Christian doctrine or glosses of the metaphysical content of "Andean religion," these conversion narratives are notable for a tendency to stress the day-to-day activities—riding circuit, in particular—that compose the practical marginalia of missionary life. These marginalia are not only evangelical analogues of the sorts of spatial practices that are often integral to the production of locality, they are in fact vital switch points between the production of Andean locality in indigenous and missionary terms. In this sense these missionary discourses of self-transformation focused on the situated practical routines of missionary-Aymara entanglements are analogous to what sociolinguists call "shifters." These are indexical terms such as "this," "that," "you," or "me" that are semantically underspecified and take their meaning largely from the context of their use. The referential "success" of shifters is directly linked to the generation of situationally specific frames more or less shared by interacting speakers (Silverstein 1976, 1988). In a similar way, these discourses of missionary self-discovery in the Andes are functionally oriented to the establishment of a meaning-bearing interactional context. They evidence from the vantage of missionaries the work of establishing locally plausible frames of evangelical practice.

"Living the Past Another Way"
Consider as a second case a letter also written in the mid-1980s by Father Hernando reflecting on the contrasts between his previous life as a "city person" and his present rural pastoral experience. Writing during a period of severe flooding afflicting his parish, he suggested that city life had sheltered him from the harsh realties of nature, which he was now forced to confront, and compared his missionary experiences of riding circuit to visit Aymara communities with his years in Spain, during which he enjoyed hiking and camping trips:

It is not the same to go fifteen days on a trip, sleeping every day on the ground or wherever, carrying all the essentials, and this for adventure or even with a fixed goal, as it is to go those same days to share the life of people who always sleep almost on the ground and always have only the essentials in the true sense of the word.

It is not the same to experience thirst, fatigue, hunger, tiredness, heat, cold during some "prepared" days of vacation as it is to have to pass the same [period] together with a *pueblo* that you see to be obliged to pass through all of these things "always."

From this perspective, you don't stop living the past, but you do certainly live it in another way; there are real faces whose presence transforms all of your life.

Thus, with time one goes on discovering that in the struggle for life the important things are truly "important" and the rest is secondary. And not the reverse as it usually appears to us in the other environment of the city. That is, today, when one knows that upon whether it rains or not depends whether there will be a harvest and thus whether the people will have food to eat, rain stops being only an atmospheric phenomenon and becomes a sign of life or death; it becomes something "important."

The missionary encounter provokes a revelatory reassessment of the missionary's past: things that previously appeared to "us" as "reverse[d]" are set right. This reciprocal evangelization—"the Aymara make us human," suggested one pastoral worker; "they evangelize us"—effects an alignment of the biographical past and the pastoral present: "you don't stop living the past, but you do certainly live it in another way."

These accounts also participate in a missionary construction of Andean pastoral geography, which, under the frame of inculturation, posits outlying Aymara hamlets as sites of indigenous (Christian) authenticity in contrast with central towns and cities. Missionaries are often deeply critical of Aymara migrants to these places; their periodic return to their natal rural hamlets for fiestas is seen by some as a source of cultural corruption. But this space between corruption and authenticity is also traveled by the missionaries, who tend to have comfortable parish houses in central towns and nicely appointed quarters in houses maintained by their order in the city. The transformed missionary is thus better able to transit this pastoral space and in so doing to perform the commensurability between his translocal Christian biography and the religious meaning he has encountered on the altiplano.

As with Miguel's conversion, Hernando's letter was written in the wake of a set of crises that challenged his ability to continue his pastoral work and embedded him in the production of Aymara locality in dramatic ways. Hernando directly experienced the conjuncture of Vatican and government repression against progressive clergy in the 1970s. Poor relations with the Church hierarchy forced him to keep a low profile or risk losing his parish. With the coup of 1981, initiating the brief and brutal reign of García Meza, everything came to a complete halt. Hernando was denounced by a local official and forced to flee his parish to the relative security of his religious order's house in La Paz. He returned after a few months, although his name remained on the list of those to be detained.

He cites this experience as establishing a basis of trust and solidarity in his relations with the Aymara. He noted that after his return from La Paz he was allowed to remain at a meeting of local Aymara leaders planning a blockade.[5] The shared historical event is transformative; Hernando told me he felt he was becoming no longer a stranger, he was no longer "as foreign" as he had been.

This experience was followed by another period of crisis: a severe drought that afflicted the area in 1983. The parish coordinated a range of relief efforts that built upon Hernando's base of trust and involved him in a new set of activities bringing him into contact with a wide range of Aymara. He felt that afterward he could go "to any corner of [the parish] and everyone would know me." His success in working with local community authorities made him feel that "all my years of work had served a purpose." He felt he was able to adapt external criteria of aid distribution ("aid to the neediest") to what he saw as Aymara values ("all should receive equally") and allowed a number of decisions to be made by local leaders. As a result Hernando enjoyed increased acceptance by the Aymara because he was able to demonstrate that he was there for all of them. This demonstration had a theological content for Hernando, who told me, "I think the important thing I achieved is not something of formal religion but rather that at least in a determined moment they could have experienced that God is near, that God did not fail them."

Hernando underscored his increasing proximity to the Aymara with two examples. The first evokes issues of trust and deception. He noted that although he gave local leaders a great amount of autonomy in financial dealings related to relief supplies, and despite the advice and warnings of representatives of relief agencies that the Aymara ought not be trusted in such matters, he is convinced that only a small percentage of the Aymara took advantage of him. The second example, echoing Miguel's comment that "the cultural horizon opened up much more for me," is his assertion that on the basis of this crisis-driven solidarity he was able to begin a process of learning more about Aymara culture. "If, until then," he told me, "the people had never told me what they thought but rather said, 'What is it that Padre Hernando wants to hear? That's what we'll tell him,' then from that moment on it became possible—and you have to be careful here—to be able to understand something more of them.

But without forcing it. . . . It is not a question of asking, let's say, but rather it is that, in a given situation, a theme will come up, and because [i.e., although] I am there they will not stop talking [i.e., whereas previously his presence would cause them to remain quiet]."

This growing proximity to Aymara culture is also indexed spatially in pastoral practice. Rather than visit communities for brief visits, returning to his parish house in the evening, Hernando made efforts to remain in the communities, sleeping on the floor of a local school or sometimes being hosted by a catechist.

Producing Plausibility

One corollary of the achievement of a localized subject position is a reciprocal self-consciousness. As I have noted, missionaries I spoke with tend to imagine themselves within the local field as they think the Aymara see them. Hernando's sense that the Aymara are engaged in a project of dissembling, calculating, "What is it that Padre Hernando wants to hear? That's what we'll tell him" (to which he once told me he countered by trying never to let the Aymara know what he was thinking so that they would be more likely to be sincere with him) is one expression of this. His comments reveal a sense of opacity that is potentially overcome through the subjecthoods emergent from missionary conversions. Yet, despite missionaries' concerns about Aymara opacity, many Aymara I spoke with attributed to priests an alarming capacity to monitor their activities and detect their dissembling. This sense of pastoral surveillance clearly relates an experience of priestly power, a theme to which I will return. Here I want to stress that this sort of reciprocal self-consciousness is grounded in a presupposed commensurability that is never unproblematically there but must be produced and sustained through a host of situated activities.

These discourses of conversion, like the day-to-day practices that provoke them and perform them, establish the here-and-now contexts of missionary-Aymara interaction as one suffused with evangelical potential. In this regard they function as "missionary shifters," negotiating, in the light of specific pastoral ideologies and with direct reference to the situation at hand, relative interactional coherence. The self-contextualizing character of missionary conversion involves the missionary positing and positioning himself as a plausible evangelical subject within the mission field. This plausible subjectivity turns in part on the possibility of intersubjectivity. It is this intersubjectivity, I think, that is asserted in the reciprocal self-consciousness of missionaries.

As a final example of this, let me return indirectly to the case of Miguel, through experiences recounted to me by other members of his order. In the

early 1980s they expanded their missionary activity among the Aymara, inher-
iting an altiplano parish from another pastoral team. During their first years in
the parish, the priests built a new parish house. They recounted this to me as
a significant step in their process of being "accepted" within the parish. The
construction of the house was a self-conscious performance on the part of the
missionaries of their capacity to work. For some this sense of themselves as laborers was tied to their sense of their Polish identity. They presented it as an
important dimension of identification with the Aymara. I would agree:
work—physical toil and especially house construction—is an ethnically salient
activity for Aymara. Of particular note here is the keen sense on the part of
these missionaries that they were being watched by the Aymara. They recorded the house construction with photographs and showed the photos to me as
they told me that the Aymara were greatly impressed by the sight. Their impression was confirmed independently by Aymara informants who remarked
on the industriousness of the missionaries.

‡ ‡ ‡

The achievement of such "missionary shifters" is a form of reciprocal self-
consciousness or presupposable intersubjectivity across the various identity categories coimplicated in Andean locality. This is a condition of the possibility for
missionization. It is not coincidental that these self-contextualizing accounts involve biographical memory, which, like all acts of memory, functions indexically (e.g., Halbwachs 1980). But these invocations of biography do more than
declare where the missionaries are coming from. They trade on, indeed they dis-
cursively produce, a particular alignment between the local (missionary) field
and distant missionary experiences in ways authorized by dominant pastoral ideologies. Missionary conversion accounts and correlated pastoral practices are part
of the pragmatic work of positioning missionaries as plausible subjects within a
locality and negotiating the production of that locality in terms deriving from
translocal missionary ideologies and the constraints of ongoing situations of entanglement. In the following sections I focus especially upon the particular vision and scale of locality entailed by the practices and discourses of inculturation
and examine the implications of this framing of locality for Aymara catechists.

OF MICROLOCALITY AND MACROLOCALITY

While from the perspective of the Church inculturation is certainly localizing,
in grounded practice it is deceptively homogenizing: effacing local distinctions
through metacultural reference and practice. A heuristic analytic distinction

between microlocality and macrolocality helps to bring this tension into focus. Microlocality refers roughly to the "face-to-face" community or comparably immediate units of sociocultural activity. Macrolocality, on the other hand, involves more inclusive categories of identity, such as "peasant," "Indian," or "Aymara." The localizing thrust of inculturation involves an integration at the level of the macrolocal, and this comes at a certain cost for the microlocal.

This distinction of micro and macro underscores the asymmetry of what Arjun Appadurai (1996:198) casts as the fragility of locality "when subject to the context-producing drives of more complex hierarchical organizations, especially those of the modern nation-state" or, in this case, the global Church. For, while the microlocal is figured relatively horizontally and potentially reciprocally, the macrolocal is figured vertically, producing and aligning positions of unequal order within a relationship of encompassment (for instance, the relationship of "the Aymara" to the Bolivian nation or the relationship of "the Aymara" to the Catholic Church).

At the heuristic extreme of the microlocal we have the situated contexts required and produced by all social activity, as interactants generate and draw upon mutually relevant cultural schema. At the other extreme of the macrolocal, we find a marking of difference having less to do with the relative positions of interactants and appearing more like that of ethnicity in which a marked subordinate group is encompassed by another, typically in a relationship involving ties of structured inequality (Comaroff 1987). In such relationships the dominant group acquires a certain invisibility, an absence of ethnicity, further determining the markedness of subordinate groups (e.g., Williams 1989:409 ff.; Handler 1988:chapter 7). Inculturationists' promotion of a "local theology," conceived at the macrolocal level of "the Aymara" and implemented through the microlocal practices of catechists and faith groups, ought thus to be considered against these structurally dissimilar localities. At issue for the catechists is the microlocal negotiation of macrolocalizing assertions of Aymaraness.

Missionary courses for catechists are principal sites for the enactment of pastoral visions of Aymara macrolocality. This is particularly evident in the catechist courses held at the regional centers at Laja (in the southern altiplano pastoral zone) and Toledo (in Carangas). These appear as rituals of macrolocal community, consolidating catechists drawn from across the altiplano as a coherent social body. These courses and related regional pastoral events constitute a metacultural community in which Aymara identity is asserted as a unifying feature: a salient dimension of commonality among catechists (and indigenous priests and nuns) and a unifying contextual point of reference for foreign missionaries.

Catechists from various communities within a parish are typically organized in ways analogous to syndicate organization (with a president, recording secretary, and so forth). I observed similar sociopolitical structures among catechists from different parishes who come together occasionally at the regional centers. While the authority deriving from these positions is minimal, this quoting of the syndicate model underscores a sense of the catechists as constituting a coherent and continuous (meta)community. This sense of a macrolocal community of commensurable catechists was further extended in a course I observed at Laja in 1999. Catechists from across the southern altiplano pastoral zone were gathered in preparation for an upcoming period of missionization to correlate with the end of the millennium. But, in a variation on the catechist pastoral model, teams of catechists from the southern altiplano were to travel to communities in the northern altiplano. Teams from the north would reciprocate, traveling to missionize communities in the southern pastoral zone. This interchangeability of the catechists indexes the homogenized sense of Aymaraness posited by the rhetoric of inculturation and reinforced at the level of content and practice in the mission courses.[6]

This is further reinforced by the typical course procedure, which, like styles of conferencing familiar from North American contexts, involves group lectures or demonstrations, followed by "breakout sessions" in small groups, followed by large plenary discussions. Typically, the small groups are asked to reflect on a set of questions, drawing from their own experiences in their communities. Each group prepares a report for the plenary session, delivered by a catechist serving as recording secretary. The effect is that a diversity of opinions reflecting a range of community experiences are rendered a single voice. Moreover, as each group's secretary reads their report in turn, these are noted on a blackboard by a teacher (priest or other pastoral agent), who glosses each group's comments as a normative monological statement. These synthesized perspectives are then copied down by catechists in their notebooks. Missionaries construct these verbal offerings as standing for a coherent ethnic perspective—a nascent Aymara new testament.

Latter-day Prophets

This coherent ethnic categorization is made explicit in courses through a variety of rhetorical devices by which missionaries establish the comparability between "the Aymara" and populations identified in the Bible.

In one course I observed catechists were implicitly constructed as latter-day prophets, as missionaries stressed the analogous "humble" condition of the biblical prophets who were "agriculturalists," or "herders," with little formal education. These Biblical "peasants," catechists learned, were nonetheless selected by God to "serve their communities." In some cases missionaries used maps to locate these "communities" for the catechists, implying a social, political, and cultural landscape commensurate with the catechist's own experiences.

As with the community-level specificity of the Aymara catechists, the microlocal specificity of the prophets was subsumed in courses through references to the "pueblo de Israel" and its contemporary analogue, the "pueblo Aymara." A discussion of Exodus established and underscored these parallels suggesting that each "people" is subject to foreign domination. Noting that Aymara communities are subject to national law rather than "Aymara" ideals of justice and sociability, an Aymara pastoral worker declared, "There is still no exodus [for the Aymara]."[7] As a narrative of liberation the book of Exodus has done a lot of analogical work under a variety of exegetic traditions. In the case of inculturation, emplotment within this redemptive narrative hinges upon an ethnic valence—a denotable Aymaraness.

Quintin's Parable

In November 1991 I observed a course for catechists at Laja led by Quintin, an Aymara pastoral worker of long standing who had been at the forefront of the turn to inculturation. A former catechist, who had undertaken some seminary training and who now worked for a La Paz–based ecumenical theological think tank, Quintin was widely known and admired by catechists from across the altiplano. Building upon the implicit parallel between the "people of Israel" and the "Aymara people," the course was focused on the implications of Jesus' teaching for Israel—and by analogy for the Aymara. Quintin's message condensed much of the inculturationist perspective, a perspective stressing historical ethnic continuity: Jesus' "project" is the fulfillment of the Hebrew (Aymara) cultural past, not its overturning.

Quintin condensed these points through a diagram of a tree representing "Israel marka." The roots of the tree corresponded to the "past," while the trunk was described as the "history" of the people. Together, the roots and trunk are the Old Testament. Yet, the tree is incomplete, Quintin noted. It must have beautiful branches. As a result of the carelessness of the people of Israel, weeds grew around the tree and some of the branches became twisted. Jesus' "project" detailed in the New Testament, Quintin explained, is to "complete" the tree. Jesus, he continued, did not come to toss out the ways of the past but rather to fulfill them. This fulfillment involves a twofold process of enabling the branches to grow and cutting away the deformed bad branches. "So," stressed Quintin, "Jesus' purpose is to construct this same tree, not to make another tree."

There is an implicit criticism of previous Catholic missionaries here. "For a long time," Quintin told the catechists, "they have told us, 'this [part of your culture] has to be removed, this is bad, this is not written in the Bible, the word *ayllu* is not there; it has to be removed. *pachamama* must be removed, *waxt'a* [also].' Our ancestors didn't know God, so we have to get rid of that.' And music, 'since they are not the horns of the Apocalypse, you must get rid of the *tarkas* [vertical duct flutes].'" Amid much laughter Quintin made his points, erasing branches of the tree for each word denied Aymara culture by Christian evangelization.

The tree that once represented the biblical history of Christian revelation now stands for Aymara history: the roots and trunks index an Aymara past; the severely pruned branches the engagement of Aymara culture with Christianity. Having parodied missionary priests, Quintin now assumed the voice of Jesus and, paraphrasing Matthew 5:17, told the catechists, "I did not come to cut the laws that you had since the Incas or since the Tupak Amarus or Tupak Kataris. . . . Rather I came to fulfill the laws that you had since your ancestors (achachilas). You have beautiful laws for living in community. . . . You have beautiful laws for creating solidarity." As with the Jews, noted Quintin, there are many bad customs in Aymara communities that must be removed. But he exhorted the catechists to see the Bible not as a "new project" but rather as a vehicle for fulfilling what he identified as the "historical project of the Aymara people."

Revelation through inculturation is thus cast as the end of cultural history. The Aymara are to realize their own new testament as the contemporary unfolding of Aymara history is harnessed to the narrative poetics of Christian revelation and salvation. As an Aymara priest commented, "The Holy Scripture is the fruit of a people's history. To create an Andean theology, we have to take account of our history." Yet the Aymara are also said by missionaries to "no longer know their historical memory." This rupture with the past is indexed sociologically (in the decline of community solidarity, in the westernized ways of the younger generation) as well as physically (in the declining use of traditional medicinal practices, in the increased dependence on imported foodstuffs—noodles, rice, sugar—said to be less nutritious than the native diet of potatoes and highlands grains). Inculturation and the conversion it predicates entail a recommitment to historical continuity. It organizes a range of metacultural discourses around a posited Aymaraness anchored by a newly remembered history.

‡ ‡ ‡

"You are the grandchildren of the yatiris. What are their grandchildren like?" At a course offered a few of months after his discussion of Exodus, Quintin began with this challenge to the assembled catechists. He instructed everyone to leave the classroom where we had gathered and assembled us outside around a small stone altar covered with a thari cloth and set with coca, cigarettes, and alcohol. Quintin asked one of the older catechists to prepare a ch'alla, a ritual libation of the sort performed in the context of a range of traditional ritual practices. The catechist prepared a shot glass of alcohol in which he placed three coca leaves; he aspersed the altar with the alcohol and then invited a female catechist to perform a ch'alla with the wine.[8] The older male catechist spoke to me, addressing me as "Padre." I told him he was mistaken—I was not a priest, furthermore, I informed him, I was married. This did not put an end to the matter, as he insisted that I was simply a priest who had married a nun. This became a familiar line of (teasing?) interrogation for me over the course of my research. It was performed here quite publicly before an amused audience of catechists and Quintin. When he learned that Ingrid and I did not have children—a vital public index of social adulthood—he spent some time telling me how young and immature I was and how little I knew about life. He then informed me (and his audience) that he could read coca (a capacity usually limited to yatiris) and began an impromptu coca reading workshop as a number of catechists asked his opinion about the significance of variously shaped leaves. "I can read coca better that I can read the Bible," he boasted, adding that each was the "Word of God." Quintin then led the catechists in prayer around the altar and distributed cigarettes (also important ingredients in a number of practices by yatiris), which we all smoked. We all returned to the classroom to begin the course.

These autoethnographic performances are for immediate consumption by the catechists. Quintin adeptly elicits a ch'alla from an older catechist framed by his call to the catechists to assess their relationship to their yatiris/ancestors. In addition to authorizing what for some of the catechists were scandalous practices, the ch'alla enacts a quasi-familial relationship of descent linking generations of catechists, and so reinforces both the meta-Aymara community of catechists as it underscores implicit doctrinal messages about the evangelical promise of remembered Aymara culture. Indeed, it is revealing that this catechist segued to his authoritative performance of a metonymic culture trait in the wake of making me stand for a foreign priest and publicly scorning my utter ignorance of life.

This appeal to elder catechetical authority (modeling a broader evangelical remembering of the cultural past) is risky business given the tendency for older catechists to be among those most strident in their opposition to the new postures of inculturation. In this light Quintin's orchestrated ch'alla is also an autoethnography of penance, calling catechists to align themselves anew with their own cultural past. As Quintin remarked to the catechists in the course of his discussion of Exodus and the extirpative position of many Catholic missionaries, "I remember as a young catechists telling the *awkis* [elders] to stop with their costumbres, that the culture was ruining them. I don't know who I was then."

‡ ‡ ‡

At the same time, Quintin's discussion makes clear that inculturation is an ideology of conversion. Notwithstanding the value placed on the organic unfolding of cultural traditions, when pastoral push comes to missionary shove not all the branches on the tree remain. Local cultures are to be judged in the light of "Christian values," and the resulting pastoral pruning is referred to as "purifying" cultural practices.

Human sacrifice and cannibalism were often invoked as unambiguously un-Christian practices. A missionary from Brazil confronted a group of Aymara catechists with their heritage: "It was the custom to make human sacrifices. Don't be afraid if that custom existed here. Don't be afraid that there may have been bad customs." She went on to say that the task of the missionaries was not to judge Aymara culture but rather to prepare the Aymara themselves to undertake the task of judgment. "All that which facilitates life, living in community. . . . This should be conserved and dynamized. I cannot do this [selecting] for you. The inculturation of the Gospel is for you to do. We give your the criteria."

Practices that are seen as fostering community solidarity are held to be consonant with Christian values, often contrasted with practices that cause division or "fear." Father Hernando frequently cited the Gospel of Matthew (7:16–20), "You shall know the tree by its fruits," as a reference point for catechists in assessing their culture.

> I say to you what I have always said: "When the fruit of something is fear, you ought to think, 'this must not be good.' God does not want the people to go in fear." . . .
>
> If people go to mass out of fear, because it is forced on them, although it is mass, and the mass is the greatest thing Christians have, it will not be good. If the people after a wilancha [a llama sacrifice] are afraid, then that wilancha is badly done; it is not good. You should know that anything that causes fear in people is not of God. You must go thinking what fruits these things produce. All that is good comes from God. That is the way you must analyze. It is not whether you can do or not do [a particular ritual act]. Each one of you must answer for yourself, in your heart, honestly, "I do this out of fear" or "Because I do this I am in peace, I am happy, I am

with love." There are many [Aymara rituals], so we must read them with the eyes of Jesus from the Bible.

Reading the Ayuno

Hernando's comments came as part of the parish-level course for catechists that provided my entree to Jesús de Machaqa in 1990. For Hernando this course marked an effort to revivify his work with catechists, and he described it to me as a self-conscious effort to introduce the inculturationist theme of "culture" to the catechists. This was discomforting to a number of the catechists present, some of whom directly reflected the cultural conservativism of old-line neo-Catholicism, and so found themselves encouraged to embrace practices they once had a hand in extirpating. The course was marked by nervous laughter and silence in places; the discomfort was palpable to me despite my then limited experience in the field.

The morning of the first day (after the film screening of the previous evening) began with some organizational tasks: the president of catechists took attendance and divided the catechists into working groups (for small group discussion as well as cleaning and cooking chores during the three-day course), and the secretary of the treasury collected contributions from the catechists in the form of cash and food. The catechists responsible for bringing a tank of propane for the kitchen serving the catechist training center had forgotten to do so. The task fell to Hernando and his Landrover; he drove away in a poor mood. Manuel, a young seminarian assisting Hernando, began the course.

Working at a chalkboard, Manuel drew a chart listing two categories of "ministries": those that are "ours" and those that are "foreign." He illustrated this by sketching a map showing Latin America and Europe, with arrows depicting the movement of things from Europe to Latin America. He also glossed this movement with references to "Columbus" and "conquest." "Evangelization" and "baptism" were quickly listed under the heading "foreign." The goal of these foreign ministries, Manual suggests, is "to create community." He illustrated the need for this with a pie chart representing a typical Aymara community as fraught with divisions between Catholics and Protestants, members of different political parties, and so forth. Slyly implicating the catechists in this state of affairs, he noted that baptism creates other kinds of divisions, because it excludes people who have not received the proper catechetical preparation.

As to "our" ministries, waxt'as, wilanchas, fiestas, and ayunos were listed as local practices unknown in Europe. Fiestas and ayunos, of course, are not unproblematically autochthonous; their categorization as "our" (viz. indigenous) stemmed in part from their oppositional relation with recent generations of official Catholic doctrine. We are then already on a complex composite terrain of locality, autochthony, ethnicity, and the popular, generated and referenced in contemporary interactions. From the point of view of the catechists as well, the list is a potentially scandalous one. The mention of wilancha (a blood sacrifice of a llama sometimes overseen by a yatiri) elicited a fair amount of nervous laughter that prompted Manuel to erase the term. Comparing the lists, Manuel echoed Father Alonso, asking, "Which are more comunitarian?" The answer is "our ministries." Catholic rituals such as baptism, which, despite their communal aims, sow fragmentation, were graphically depicted as standing outside the indigenous community (indexing their ongoing failure to transcend their foreign origins).

The task as Manuel posed it is a kind of a double unification. On the one hand the contemporary fragmentation of the Aymara community is to be overcome. Manuel used a variety of Aymara terms that evoke the sort of productive merging of parts characteristic of ayllu structures; mayachasiña (becoming one); sawthapiña (weaving). At the same time, this unification of the community entails the authentic placement of foreign ministries at the center (taypi) of the community. As representatives of foreign ministries, the catechists were thus challenged to position themselves at the centers of their communities. In this effort, Manuel told them, the catechists are singularly capable (and culpable). "We have been following other footsteps along another path," noted Manuel. "We have gone wrong." But, catechists know the correct path, the path of Aymara ministries "from when we were young." As if to underscore the entanglements entailed in this movement toward a more perfect Aymara-Christian future through their memory of their lived Aymara past, Manuel added, "So the Padre is going to guide us in how we will weave this together."

Hernando, who had returned during Manuel's presentation, waited at the back of the classroom as a number of catechists spoke about what they saw to be a general state of cultural decline in their communities. For the most part, their nostalgia focused on a contemporary breakdown of respect and proper sociability—as more and more young Aymara migrate to the city; as the current generation of mallkus seems less capable of leading the community than those of past decades—rather than on the decline of waxt'as and fiestas. Still, Manuel seemed to have hit his mark.

At this point Hernando intervened to sketch out his goals for this course, which were to see "how we can achieve a faith that is communitarian. These types of celebrations—ayunos or fiestas—are very communitarian. Everyone participates. In contrast, baptism, marriage, in reality this is only for me. . . . We have to do something." Hernando's efforts were linked in part with a broader project of ethnodevelopment being undertaken in the parish—a long-term plan involving initiatives in health care, agriculture and animal husbandry, education, the formation of local cooperatives to market products in the city, and the establishment of a regional radio station. The theology of inculturation dovetailed ideologically with the project, but it also presented more practical benefits as a unified community makes a better client of development.

Hernando then turned to elicit a ritual calendar—"an Aymara liturgical year"—to represent the sequence of communal (i.e., "our") rites practiced in the region. Here the course turned into an extensive ethnographic interview. Under each month of the year he listed the rituals celebrated in the home ayllus of the catechists.

As foregoing discussions of the ayllu and the regional history of Jesús de Machaqa make clear, the notion of community as a unit of analysis in the Andes is neither unproblematic nor transparent. Yet this inculturationist ethnography preselects a particular level and locus of ritual activity—the community—as a principal site of authenticity, holding foreign rites such as baptism accountable to the same sociological level. Hernando's liturgical list does not address what priests might judge to be more fragmentary Aymara practices such as the household-level rituals or indigenous analogues to baptism such as first haircuttings (ratucha). Similarly, this fabricated Aymara liturgical year codifies a set of practices as communal—i.e., making this community-constituting function the most salient dimension of the rite—when in fact such practices are differentially salient for different actors depending upon their positions in their own life cycles, in the genealogical contexts of their families, and with respect to the braided paths whose shifting configurations constitute and re-constituted Aymara locality.

More significantly, this missionary ethnography homogenized a diverse range of practices across the region, establishing a prototypical liturgical calendar as well as a prototypical community/ayllu. Hernando went on in this ethnographic encounter to focus on the ayuno, eliciting detailed descriptions of the rite from various catechists. In some cases these were narrations of extant practices. In others there was a whiff of salvage ethnography, made more troubling as the very catechists responsible for the decline of such events memorialized their passing. Hernando, who has a subtle and deep knowledge of his parish, was well aware of these variations across communities, and it is not my purpose to criticize him personally. My point is that the pastoral position shaped by inculturation trades upon a homogenized conception of Aymara locality as a serial component of an overarching (macrolocal) Aymaraness. One function of the course was to extract a generalized template of the practices being discussed; Hernando spoke explicitly of a process of cross-fertilization, suggesting that catechists may get new ideas about the ayuno after learning of the practices in other communities. This generation of a normative, prototypical version of the ritual is key, for the ayuno was being promoted as a principal ritual to be revitalized: a privileged forum for the catechists and faith group members to achieve the aims of inculturation.

"We Cannot Go with Only One": The Pragmatics of Partial Knowledge and Situated Memories

Such schematizations may be unavoidable in social practice, and the cross-fertilization or diffusion of cultural practices within a regional network is not unique. Nonetheless, the sorts of officializing, homogenizing operations evident here would be problematic in many settings. They seem to be particularly so in the Aymara context, and at times catechists explicitly rejected such efforts of pastoral agents to codify "Aymara culture." As the composite ayuno took shape, one of the catechists, Jesús, interrupted the discussion to argue against prescribing a single way of practicing the ayuno, insisting on his ignorance of the rite as practiced in other communities.

> "Very well, I too would like to speak, brothers. These examples, the way the Father has spoken to us of these things, to my way of thinking, you should not just take out one path [thaki]. Each community has its own custom [costumbre]. Pedro, in his community, in his ayllu, has just said his custom, and that must be the way it is. In Placido's community, his custom is of another kind, in my community also another kind. Now, if we take out one word, if we take out one thaki, we would have to oblige a community [to perform that custom]. No. This [tradition] should be revived. For me, this teaching is very good. With this the "recuperation of the culture" is possible, this is what we are discovering from our parents, from our grandparents. We are encountering their acts, the actions of our parents that unified. . . . Those unifications (mayacht'awinaka) have been mentioned; thus the ayuno, truly the ayuno unifies the people. . . .
>
> We cannot go with only one. On the contrary, now we are going to think. The Father is going to teach us, we will speak also, each catechist we will speak. After, thinking about this, we will reorient ourselves, align ourselves. Then each one, in each ayllu we will go to our customs, We cannot be the same. Neither in Qhunqhu, nor in Aigachi, nor in Parina can this be done. In Parina they must have a different custom, like the ayuno. Where do the people come together? Then they will be having a mink'a, a faena—I don't know."

Jesús thus accepted the premise of inculturation while rejecting its practice. The stress on a multiplicity of ayllu-level "paths" evokes local autonomy within a segmentary political structure through the same metaphor commonly used to describe braided life trajectories. This might well be read as a catechist attempting to maintain what he can of his autonomy and flexibility given his unenviable position of being exhorted to lead a ritual he once strenuously denounced. The stress on voluntary participation—that one cannot be compelled to undertake a given ritual—gestures explicitly to an interreligious détente reached in Jesús de Machaqa among traditionalists, Protestants, and neo-Catholics.

More significantly, Jesús stressed his situated perspective on this field of practice, presupposing a landscape of concealed difference. He insists upon his ignorance of the practices of other communities and his complete dependence upon the accounts provided by catechists from those areas. This is resonant with other discussions of ayllu-specific esoteric terms in Aymara ritual texts and an aesthetic of ritual potency linked to elision, secrecy, and opacity (Arnold, Jiménes, and Yapita 1992; Huanca 1989). Against this background the detailed ethnographic knowledge of other communities encouraged by missionaries is seen as rude or intrusive and potentially antisocial. Comparable concerns are evident in day-to-day complaints about gossipy neighbors, always thought to be watching one another. Intrusive knowledge carries still more ominous implications with the panoptic powers sometimes ascribed to priests and to kharisiris, who are said by some to be able to observe from afar, or otherwise undetected, the day-to-day activities of Indians. Jesús's insistence on his ignorance of the practices of neighboring communities also reflects a sensibility in which local difference and situated partial knowledge are valued over homogenization. This is one possible reading of the classic Andean theme of "complementary opposition," as contrastive relations (between genders, between ecological zones, between social groups), even when violent, are generative (e.g., Platt 1986; Allen 1988). Homogeneity, in contrast, is regarded as sterile, as an absence of potential. In this sense the prototypical community-based Aymaraness imagined by inculturationists is an unimaginable community for many catechists and other Aymara.

The Local Limits of Antinomy

The rhetoric of inculturation is also confounded by the colonial entanglement it seeks to redeem. While missionaries strive to purge Aymara practices of colonial Catholicism (characterized by rote knowledge of Church doctrine, the "superficial" performance of Catholic ritual, and the "inauthentic" syncretic juxtaposition of indigenous and Christian practices) and so recover a pristine restored Aymara tradition, in the eyes of many Aymara colonial Catholic doctrine is a vital component of ancestral tradition. When Aymara I spoke with lamented the decline of traditional culture, it was this knowledge they tended to cite. Some outdo the inculturationists and claim Christian doctrine as autochthonous: local knowledge that predates the arrival of the Spanish. More commonly, its traditional pedigree was evident in the observation that knowledge of Christian doctrine was once passed down and taught from father to son. The transmission of this knowledge was reinforced by ayllu authorities, whose obligations included Catholic prayers and mustering catechized contingents to represent the community in parish celebrations. Many cited the disappearance of these practices and the attenuation of this doctrinal knowledge as the cause of a range of contemporary afflictions, from poor crop production and unusual weather patterns to declines in Aymara sociability marked by the rudeness of the younger generations.

Catechists (even the old-school, extirpation type) are commonly embraced as contemporary revoicings of Aymara social and ritual authority. Many compare them to mayordomos, *lutriniros,* and risiris, all ritual intermediaries who harnessed and mediated Catholic power to local ends.[9] Today catechists are the principal representatives of local communities before the parish. Like mayordomos, service to the parish and maintenance of the matrix church and community-level chapels typically falls to them. They are recognized sources of doctrinal authority and ritual potency; like risiris, families wishing to commemorate the dead during All Soul's Day sometimes contract their services.

My point here is that, alongside the mission rhetoric of pan-Aymara identity and an ideology of conversion predicating a discrete Aymaraness, exist local perspectives and practices that both limit macrolocal homogenization and reveal the complex condition of Andean locality. In the following section I turn to examine the situated practices of the catechists in such complex contexts, focusing on the ways the catechists present themselves as authoritative local actors.

TRANSLOCAL FOOTINGS

Despite missionary efforts to authorize the locality of the catechists, catechists frequently negotiated their local authority in markedly translocal terms. Notwithstanding the strong inculturationist focus on the autochthonous knowledge of the ancestors, catechists often presented the knowledge circulated in faith groups as deriving from outside the community, performing their legitimacy as adepts of modernity and specialists in its esoteric knowledge.

Travel to courses and other pastoral events are crucial to the construction of catechetical capacity, which turns as much on the mediation for local use of distantly derived knowledge as on the revalorization of a local tradition embodied by the catechist. As catechists draw upon multiple footings they reference and wrestle with the entanglements of a locality that is much more complex than that imagined by the ideals of inculturation.[10]

The first example of public catechetical self-presentations is from an outdoor mass celebrated in the Machaqueño ayllu of Kalla Arriba attended by delegations from most of the ayllus in the parish. A local deacon presided over the mass alongside catechists from across the parish. The deacon, Cristobal, was among the deacons ordained during the heyday of altiplano pastoral work in the 1960s and 1970s. He is well known and widely respected in the region. The mass was part of a ritual commemorating the local martyrs of a retaliatory massacre by the Bolivian army in the wake of an indigenous uprising in Jesús de Machaqa in 1921 (see chapter 7). Among the catechists were a small group recently designated as "ministers," and empowered by the regional bishop to celebrate certain sacraments. (More precisely, there were two "grades" of ministers: "ministers of communion" authorized to distribute preconsecrated eucharist wafers, and the superior "ministers of sacraments," also authorized to perform baptisms and weddings.) This mass was among the first public performances of the ministers, in whom can be seen a reprise of pastoral interest in an indigenous deaconate. Their advent was coordinated with a more formal effort to revive altiplano pastoral work around the tenets of inculturation. Unlike catechists who go about their work in everyday clothing, the ministers were prominent in their white vestments: uniforms distributed to them at their ordination. Cristobal began the service by presenting the ministers to the assembled crowd:

OK, today we have come together once again. This is an accompaniment [retinue] of catechists, missionaries, and ministers. I believe Jesús de Machaqa is the first with ministers. That, "minister," means that the viatica are given within the communities themselves. And, in addition, deacons will soon be selected. Soon you will have deacons in the communities of Kalla Arriba, the community of . . . [he named the communities in which ministers were serving]. This is the way their [i.e., the communities'] catechists are being guided. Last year or the year before, when the pope came to the Alto La Paz, they were discussed—the ministers. From that they began. Now they are not catechists. First, they were catechists. Second, they were like missionaries. Third, they were now ministers: minister of communion, minister of baptism. Now they will go a little bit farther, and beyond that we will also prepare other communities. Jesús de Machaqa was the first with ministers, but it was said that the entire department [La Paz] should have them. They should be like the *tatakuras* [priests]. They, the tatakuras, prepared all this. Then the bishop ordained them. They are his workers, too. These uniforms were offered through his hands last year.

The statement positions the catechists along a translocal thakilike hierarchy extended to include priests, bishops, and even the pope. The authority claimed for the ministers derives quite directly from the priests (who prepared the way) and especially the bishop who ordained them and invested them with power and legitimacy. The deacon asserts a sort of collective regional pride in the ministers: Jesús de Machaqa is the first parish with ministers. Yet equally significant is the future routinization of ministers across the Department of La Paz. Here the catechists and ministers are implicated in a more ubiquitous grid of authority, positioned as representatives of a more encompassing web of power, locally instantiating an idea discussed in La Paz.

A second example stems from a fiesta mass celebrated in the Machaqueño ayllu of Ch'ama. Hernando had received a request from the community's catechist to visit for the mass and asked that a delegation of ministers and catechists from neighboring ayllus undertake the pastoral visit. Such a visit hearkened back to the original aims of the catechist pastoral model of reducing sacramental burdens on priests. It also reflected the immediate aims of inculturation (and the rationale for the pastoral experiment with indigenous ministers) to enable forms of local evangelical autonomy through which Aymara might indigenize their faith. I walked to Ch'ama with Alejandro and Marcelino, a catechist from the community of Yawriri. We took a path that hugged close to the mountains to the north. The two-hour "shortcut" took us by a number of abandoned chapels, wak'as, and evidence of chullpas—burial enclosures dating to pre-Columbian times—and provided ample time for talking.

Chullpas are a favorite topic of Andean ethnography. They seem to index, for ethnographers and natives, a pre–Columbian presence in contemporary Andean experience. In a myth encountered in various forms in the region, the age of the chullpas (chullpatimpu) was populated by a race of presocial beings, who lived in darkness. As we saw in chapter 1, the rise of the sun (conflated with the historical experiences of Incan state expansion and Iberian invasion and colonial evangelization) at once destroyed these savage ancestors and created the differentiated world of productive tensions (the diurnal oscillation of day and night, the cosmological distinction between alaxpacha and manqhapacha, the sociological landscape of families, ayllus, ethnicities) in which contemporary Aymara live.[11] As Marcelino put it during our conversation, "chullpa people didn't have individual names, they didn't even know how to pray . . . until the priests came." Alejandro opined that the chullpa people were "stupid." He then offered an interesting presentist gloss to the chullpa story, suggesting that Aymara were able to think better after the 1952 agrarian reform. Prior to that, he said, the Aymara were "without ideas . . . like chullpas."

Such chullpa talk reveals the limits of a cant of Aymara cultural continuity and highlights the entangled condition of contemporary Aymara experience. Marcelino's demonization of chullpa people is not a function of neo-Catholic orthodoxy (which would likely dismiss such "superstitious myths") but rather reflects a long-term engagement of indigenous and (colonial) Catholic sensibilities. Alejandro's comments reflect contemporary revoicing of this culturally constitutive watershed as the sociopolitical context of the post-MNR decades, including sensibilities of modernizing citizenship indexed most powerfully through a network of rural schools, become routinized components of Aymara experience—natural and presupposable, to return to the chullpa myth, as night and day. Thus even the foundational mythic genre of chullpa talk unsettles the local indigenous religiosity predicated by inculturation.

When we reached Ch'ama we joined Bonifacio (who had bicycled along the dirt road serving the region) and two other catechists. One of these was the catechist for Ch'ama, though he was inactive in parish affairs and did not lead a local faith group. The catechists conferred: dividing up tasks for the celebration, selecting songs to sing, and identifying Bible readings. They decided that of the three readings the selections from the Old Testament and from the Epistles would be read in Aymara, while the Gospel reading would be in Spanish. This was a departure from most of the rural masses and faith group celebrations I observed, which were conducted entirely in Aymara. This decision highlighted the limitations of the community in the eyes of the visiting catechists. As they reasoned, since the community did not have an active catechist, they were unaccustomed to the sorts of services catechists performed. The irony, of course, is that, in determining their need to spoon-feed the practices of inculturation to the ayllu, the catechists disclosed that the "authentic Aymaraness" inculturationists aim to recover is made rather than found.

This sense of the community as unprepared for the practices of inculturation was further underscored in Bonifacio's homily, which stressed the importance of hearing the word of God in Aymara. He praised the costumed dancers who filled the chapel, characterizing their dancing as a way of remembering Aymara culture. "With this culture, the people of God are here," declared Bonifacio. After briefly summarizing the Bible readings, he characterized the fiesta of San Roque as a day to remember San Roque as a "wise man" from the distant "days of the prophets." He linked the present fiesta directly with this past (as a tradition handed down through the generations who spoke the word of God) and he praised the community for continuing this by remembering San Roque.

Note the complex alignment he invoked between local practices, Aymara tradition, and the biblical past. In suggesting a connection of descent linking local practices with the biblical past, Bonifacio's homily exceeded the discursive alignment typically asserted by inculturationists. One result is a footing of legitimacy grounded not in (intrusive) familiarity with microlocal practices, nor in the transcultural perspective of Jesus (with its presumptions of individual moral authority), but rather in the control of esoteric knowledge of the Bible derived from beyond the community and authorized through the discursive link of locality with the biblical tradition. After praising the fiesta celebrants for maintaining this connection, Bonifacio asserted his own authoritative knowledge of the biblical past, pointing out that San Roque's real name is San Joaquin. In such moves of praising and then correcting the participants, Bonifacio asserts an authority that parallels—at the level of "the people of God"—the homogenizing ethnography of inculturation but skirts the intrusive implication of local knowledge. Bonifacio deftly performs his esoteric knowledge and asserts its local salience without compromising his ambivalent standing as a visitor to this community.

He then turned to present himself, his colleagues, and me.

I also want to say a few words about the parish. Father Hernando. He is the parish priest and he did not have time to be here today. So I have come delegated by him. I am a "minister of sacraments." [He names the local bishop], I am ordained by him. Thus I am Father Hernando's successor. So I am accompanied by you brothers ministers and together with some catechists. I am from [he proceed to identify the ministers and catechists present by community.] I am with you today. What should the people of God, the Aymara, know? To return to God, to speak the word of God. In those days, we have been seeing. [i.e., we have been seeing what the word of God says about distant days]. [Referring to me:] The brother is here. In the same way, foreign priests may come to me. In these days there are not many priests. The parishes are without priests. There are no priests. So it falls to the same catechists to lead, and today, for Machaqueños, this is a joy. In Machaqa this is called "ministers." This cargo is appearing. Perhaps now in other big towns more will be seen. Why do I say Machaqueños are happy? From Machaqa catechists appeared, those who know [yatirinaka] the word of God. First, because of this they are in all the parishes. Second from Machaqa this singing in Aymara, speaking and singing the word of God in Aymara appeared from Jesús de Machaqa, and that is two. Now from Machaqa this act of making this celebration is appearing. That is three. That is, Machaqa is more advanced than all of the parishes.

Note again the play between regional Machaqueño pride and the anchoring of minister/catechist authority in a broader pastoral domain. Machaqa is a source of leadership and innovation, which is at the same time legitimated through extension across an encompassing ecclesial structure. In both cases the speakers identify themselves and/or the accompanying ministers and catechists by ayllu, yet override this footing as visitor and outsiders by invoking their alignment with the parish. In these interactions with other Aymara outside of their own ayllus, their legitimacy stems not from their selection by their community, nor from a personal calling to serve God (although the gloss of catechists as yatiris of the word of God is interesting), but rather from their authoritative position as representatives of the parish hierarchy.

Bonifacio characterizes himself as a delegate of the priest, even claiming to be his successor. The terms suggest a subordinate position, although within a trajectory leading to the reproduction of the superior role. The catechists are compelled to replace foreign priests, who are no longer available to Aymara communities. This foreignness is ambivalent. On the one hand, Bonifacio anchors the legitimacy of catechists and ministers in their Aymaracization of Christian worship, pointing out how unique and good it is to discuss the Word of God in Aymara. This might be seen as precisely enacting the spatialized ambitions of inculturation, moving ministries from "outside" into the center of the community. On the other hand, catechists authenticate themselves in terms of regular access to outside power and thus enable the metacultural perspective otherwise precluded by their microlocal embeddedness. Bonifacio appears to derive his legitimacy largely from his routine contact with foreigners, as he notes my presence and makes me stand for a succession of priests who allegedly come to visit him. The catechists replace these outside representatives, who are increasingly unavailable to the local communities. Indeed, the presence of the ministers and catechists is justified by the absence of the priests. The necessity of these strangers for the maintenance of Aymara locality resonates with Marcelino's characterization of chullpa people, who were without the basic conditions of human sociability (most notably names) "until the priests came."

Another issue raised by Bonifacio's comments, underscored by other catechists, and condensed by Bonifacio's biography is that catechists frequently attenuate microlocal ties by describing themselves as orphaned or landless. There is clearly some correlation between such structural marginality and a tendency to serve (or to be named) as a catechist, although in a number of cases these statuses are more classificatory than real. When they do cast themselves this way, catechists typically describe their affiliation with the parish in terms of filial ties, often narrating their attraction to the Church from "when I was a young boy." Bonifacio describes himself as a "successor" to the parish priest. The expression suggests a relationship similar to that obtaining between a father and son, who will inherit his father's public personhood in the ayllu, representing his patriline through cargo service to the community. Describing himself as an "acolyte," Bonifacio once told me that he was moved to become a catechist from a very young age, when he spent much of his time with the parish priest. Catechists thus efface local patrilineal ties while transposing their connection to the Church into the idiom of kinship. Recall that the doctrinal knowledge controlled by catechists is held to be traditional Aymara knowledge, once faithfully passed from father to son but now increasingly forgotten. In a move that matches the operation of inculturation, catechists embody their translocal legitimacy as locally embedded knowledge, as the situated classificatory descendants not of the ancestors but of (traditional) Catholic priests. This is even more poignant in Bonifacio's case since his biological father is a yatiri. His alignment with the Church reflects the ambivalent conversion of the catechists: a break with local traditions but an effort to reinscribe and negotiate translocal entanglements in situated practice.

‡ ‡ ‡

Here we might return to Alejandro and his multiply ambivalent project to become a yatiri through the study of Huanca's text. Alejandro's attempted embrace of Aymara culture discloses both the objectifying operation of metacultural constructions and the ironically entangled implications of such efforts. As Charles Briggs (1996) has noted, constructivist approaches to invented tradition often have a disempowering effect on indigenous activists and scholars and have become the target of criticism by native scholars. The present case suggests that the negotiation of "discursive authority" in the assertion of indigenous identity does not only involve struggles between native scholars (and missionaries) and their deconstructivist Western colleagues. Assertions of macrolocal identities are also subject to deconstruction and transformation in microlocal practices. As catechists such as Cristobal, Alejandro, and Bonifacio struggle in microlocal settings with the macrolocalizing implications of inculturation, they negotiate and produce indigenous locality in its contentious and ongoing integration with encompassing systems of power.

Coda: Entangled Locality

The main goal of this chapter has been to trace the local implications of shift-ing pastoral ideologies and practices over recent decades and to critically ex-amine the limits in microlocal practice of the macrolocalizing vision of incul-turation. With the preceding two chapters, my aim has been a revisiting of Andean locality (and particularly the region of Jesús de Machaqa) as constitut-ed out of situations of colonial, republican, and contemporary history and as including as component subjects translocal actors such as missionaries. Of course, this complex context is not inertly inherited; it is the product of and context for an unceasing process of cultural production. This cultural process, moreover, articulates relatively immediate, microlocal, on-the-ground activi-ties as well as macrolocalizing, metacultural engagements with Andean locali-ty: assessments of the complexity of locality and the colonial and postcolonial history for which it is taken to stand. As a coda to this chapter and to part 1, I present a brief description of the fiesta of San Antonio as I observed it in Qhunqhu Milluni. Fiestas reflect the ways colonial Catholicism has become integral to practices of community reproduction; they are key techniques for producing entangled locality. As such, they are also highly sensitive to shifting local and translocal contexts (e.g., Buechler 1980). While inculturationists strive to reembrace fiestas as loci of local religiosity, a close reading of the fi-estas reveals the porous production of Andean locality.

For scholars, for missionaries, for social reformers, fiestas have long been a privileged site for assessing the legacy of colonialism and diagnosing the promis-es and limitations of Andean modernity. Fiestas have been, of course, prime tar-gets of neo-Catholic extirpation, liturgical stones in the shoes of circuit riding priests, not to mention key sites of dispute with Protestant congregations. In Jesús de Machaqa, as the numbers of neo-Catholic faith groups and Protestant churches increased over the 1960s and 1970s, this resulted in a period of up-heaval and violence, which was the painful reference for the sort of evangelical penance evident in inculturationist courses in the 1990s. People I spoke with were extremely reticent in their recollections of this difficult time. It is clear, though, that, due to a confluence of factors ranging from interreligious conflict to the impact of modernizing post-1952 reforms, the region experienced a sharp decline in fiesta celebrations and a correlated contraction of fiesta-cargo hierar-chies in many ayllus of the region during the sixties and seventies.

In Qhunqhu Milluni a complex of two ayllu-level fiestas—one devoted to the Virgin of the Snows, one to San Antonio—fell into decline during the six-ties and were completely abandoned for a period in the mid-seventies. At about the same time, titles of authority such as jilaqata were eclipsed by their syndicate analogues, and forms of dress and other practices linked with ayllu authority fell into disuse. In 1978 a man returning to Milluni after a period of work in the yungas valleys to the east proposed the institution of a soccer tournament as a public event in place of the fiesta. Around this sporting event emerged a revised version of the feast of San Antonio. This reformed fiesta was marked by a reduction in a number of extraliturgical features and the incorporation of a number of salient new dimensions. Perhaps most notable among the changes was the disappearance of a set of altars at the corners of the "plaza." These had been attended by p'iqis from each of the four zones; it is my understanding that this shift also corresponded with the change from four katus to the present system of eight zones in the ayllu. The following account is from observations of the festival in 1991.

The fiesta took place over a period of three days in mid-June. The spatial foci of the fiesta were the plaza of the community chapel and the respective households of the sponsors. It was sponsored by two pairs of *cabecillas:* young couples—one from each half of the ayllu—who prepared for the event by mustering a group of friends to honor the saint by dancing and contracting a brass band to perform. In addition, the sponsors were responsible for renting the costumes worn by the dance troupes and providing a continuous abundance of food, coca, and alcohol for the dancers and musicians throughout the

FIGURE 3.1   *The chapel, sacristuyu, and plaza in Milluni*

event. This is an onerous burden for a young couple, who typically press into service their close friends and family. Fiesta sponsorship is the first significant step on a married couple's cargo path—a precondition for service as p'iqi.

The first day of the fiesta began with a soccer tournament among teams representing different rural schools in the region. The event was hosted by the mallkus of the ayllu, who also provided the prizes: a llama for the winning team and a sheep for the second- and third-place teams. Over the course of the day the dance troupes and bands of each of the cabecillas began to congregate at their respective house compounds. Fiesta participants tend today to be young adults who have migrated to La Paz/El Alto, and sponsors usually hire a truck to transport supporters from the city. The arrivals were quite dramatic (both for the hoopla of the troupe and musicians crammed into the back of the truck and for the off-road heroics of the truck drivers who were intent upon driving across rocky and uneven terrain right up to the house patio of the sponsors). Once settled in the respective houses, the brass bands began to play. The music was audible throughout much of the community, establishing a rivalry that continued throughout the fiesta.

At dusk, with the church bells ringing, the dancers made their formal entrances, processing with musical accompaniment and led by the cabecillas from "their" house compound to the community chapel. They circled the plaza in front of the chapel (following what had been the counterclockwise sequence of the corner altars) and proceeded to the steps of the chapel. The group continued into the chapel to pay their respects to the saint. Two members of the faith group attended to the altar: Juan, a young man in his late teens whom Alejandro was grooming to be a catechist, and Oscar, a man in his seventies, who was identified by Alejandro as the mayordomo of the Church. A regular member of the faith group, Oscar was recognized as a yatiri in the ayllu. It is a telling indication of the conflicted history of the fiestas that both Alejandro and Bonifacio had left the community during the days of the festival. There was no fiesta mass celebrated. In addition to the music—an offering in its own right—the cabecillas and dancers made offerings of lit candles and flowers, which were received by Oscar and Juan and placed on the altar before the saints'images.[12] Over the course of the evening they also received offerings of coca and alcohol sent into the chapel by the mallkus and consumed "for the saint" by Oscar and Juan. Later that evening, as I sat (drinking) in the chapel with the mallkus, Oscar and Juan, the subcentral of the ayllu, compared the fiesta to a national holiday: it marked the anniversary of the community, he told me.

The dance troupe exited the Church and took their place on the right or "upper" side of the plaza. A comparable entrance was performed by the second

FIGURE 3.2   *Members of the faith group attended to the altar*

FIGURE 3.3   *The costumed dance troupes danced on their respective sides of the plaza*

FIGURE 3.4   *A group of senior men and women from Titiri visited to pay their respects*

dance troupe, which eventually took their place dancing on the left or "lower" side of the plaza. Over the next two days the dance troupes, headed by their respective cabecilla couples, danced in various configurations of male and female lines on their respective sides of the plaza. The cabecillas carried pitchers of grain alcohol cut with water, fruit juice, or sugared tea, and they served their lines of dancers and musicians many, many shots. The troupes both made two entrances the second day; each time the men donned more of the elaborate and very heavy dance costumes they were to wear. The costumes created a quadripartite color system among the men, each troupe comprising two sets of uniformed male dancers adorned with contrasting colors. The plaza emerged as a microcosm of the ayllu enacting the relationship between its upper and lower halves as well as nested relations of complimentary opposition within each component moiety and crosscutting contrasts of gender.

The female dancers wore two different kinds of costumes. Most of the women were dressed in the finery of a young cholita: an indigenous women in the city. They wore store-bought polleras, a blouse and embroidered sweater covered by a finely woven shawl, topped off by a new derby hat (cf. Gill 1994:103–109). However at the back of each troupe of dancers were two women wearing more stylized and sexualized drum majorette costumes: shiny unitards with high cut legs, high heels, colorful hats. These are the sorts of uniforms common in urban-based celebrations of Indian fiestas. Next to bikinis,

they are also a costume of choice (when any clothing is chosen) for the depictions of women used by beer companies in posters/calendars that are ubiquitous adornments to adobe walls across the altiplano. The sponsors, who
danced facing their troupes, were also adorned in urban finery: the man in a
dark suit with the Bolivian tricolor pinned to his lapel, the woman similarly
dressed in the costume of a young cholita, though with a different colored
shawl and elaborate jewelry.

There was a strong element of competition between the troupes. The brass
bands often interrupted one another and occasionally engaged in "battles"
playing different tunes simultaneously in a contest to see which band could
play loudest and longest. There was a similar element of competition among
the dancers who strutted their finery and danced energetically in an effort to
outshine their counterparts. On the morning of the third day men from each
moiety faced off in a soccer match. The upper moiety won.

During the second day a group of authorities and other senior men and
women from neighboring Sullkatiti Titiri visited to pay their respects. They
played duct flutes in contrast to the brass bands and danced in circles weaving
figure eights across the plaza. The men from Titiri dressed in stiff puma skin
shoulder pads of the sort used for ritualized dance battles at Rosario, underscoring the tense complementary relationship between the ayllus.[13] In addition
to these more formally enacted structural tensions, simmering underneath the
ritual activities is a constant threat of violence. Fiestas are notorious settings for
fights. This is why Alejandro left town.[14]

But beyond embodying the structural relations among the component
parts of the ayllu, there is a strong element of productive process in such festivals. They are, after all, sites that weave together a number of different cargo
paths in the production of locality. Fiestas are the Andean example par excellence of the sorts of formal ritual practices that get such things done.

At a number of points the fiesta of San Antonio quotes directly from key
practices of Aymara marriage: figuratively joining the upper and lower
troupes in a productive union. Fiestas are prime sites for flirting and trysts,
and many of the focal dance participants are young unmarried men and
women. On the third and final day of the festival, the rivalry between the
dance troops and brass bands picked up as they vigorously played and danced
simultaneously. Abruptly, the playing and dancing ceased and the dancers
formed two single lines and filed past each other shaking hands and embracing. This act was called sart'asi (going away). The same term denotes the visits by which the family of a bride-taking Aymara groom negotiates the marriage with the parents of the bride. These visits are initially violently rebuffed
by the bride's family, before the acceptance of an offering of coca and alco-

hol ratifies the productive merging of two patrilines in a newly emergent household. After the sart'asi the troupes returned to their houses to rest. That evening, the bands resumed playing on their respective sides of the plaza. The dancers (no longer costumed) and observers clustered informally; some couples paired off stealing into the shadows beyond the large bonfires burning in front of each band.

More broadly, the fiesta might be seen as a rite socializing nubile sexuality to the ends of ayllu reproduction. The troupes of young dancers, for instance, were metaphorically equated by some consultants with herds of llamas, which at about the time of the fiesta are returning to the lower elevations of ayllus from high herding areas where they have been kept for much of the agricultural season. These highland areas—apachetas—are considered the margins of socialized space: sites of danger and uncontrolled fertility. Accounts from other Aymara-speaking areas describe courting rites among young adults taking place in such high wild places. One Machaqueño consultant described witnessing a "troupe" of wild llamas that, during this time, had descended from the apacheta and "danced" on a fallow field. He was convinced that this imparted fertility to the plot.

The fourth and final day of the fiesta was devoted to the transfer of the festival sponsorship to the couples from each moiety who would undertake the cargo in the following year. These transfers completed, one of the troupes began climbing a large hill just beyond the chapel. They proceeded to the top, where the ruins of an old calvario (the site of the ayuno) sit before a clearing with two circles of piled stones. This place was described to me as "San Antonio's chapel." The groups sat around the circles, chewing coca and pouring libations of alcohol, while saying, "We have bought a house." In one instance I saw someone pick up a flat piece of rock and hand it to a young boy, who mimed the act of signing (as if it were title to the house?).

Suddenly a man dressed in a parody of a priest's cassock—a woman's white petticoat over his shoulders, a man's suit jacket hung inside out behind him from his forehead and secured with a scarf—appeared and stood in the ruins of the calvario, which served as a pulpit. The qhencha cura (cursed priest) was assisted by a "sacristan/catechist" who forced the assembled group to line up awaiting attention from the priest. The priest was handed a flat stone. He made the sign of the cross over this, his "Bible." Prodded by the sacristan, the line of couples and young children moved by the priest. They were seeking rites of baptism and/or marriage. The priest and his assistant engaged in a bawdy parody of the Catholic sacraments involving highly detailed marital advice and information that cast doubt on the paternity of the children being baptized. The priest aspersed the group with a sprig of a t'ola bush sprayed with alcohol.

With the bells of the chapel ringing, the group descended to the plaza, where they danced for the rest of the afternoon.

‡ ‡ ‡

The festival of San Antonio underscores (again) the integral role of Catholicism within the practices and process by which ayllu locality is produced in Jesús de Machaqa. Recall the example at the beginning of part 1: the case of Father Jan, whose angry mutterings and imperfect ritual services reveal tensions within what is nonetheless a single sociohistorical formation comprising missionaries and Aymara. The parodic mimicking of the Catholic priest (and catechist?) may well be the mocking revenge of the dissatisfied and scolded locals after the dust of the Landrover settles. Yet, notwithstanding the ambivalence of these figures within local experience, their ritual legitimacy and the sacramental techniques they control are crucial to the production of the legitimate situated subjects of Aymara locality. In this regard there is not much space between the ambivalent parody of the qhencha cura at the culmination of the festival of San Antonio and the approximations of priestly authority undertaken by Bonifacio. Both trade on the ambivalently presupposable foreignness of priestly powers even as they appropriate that potency to local ends.

And here lies the rub—at least of this present chapter, and particularly as I segue to part 2 of this book. The locality thus constituted is predicated upon webs of translocal entanglements. The fiesta of San Antonio, particularly in its reconstituted form, achieved the production of locality through practices that refer well beyond the local. The soccer tournament assimilates a key ritual of modern Bolivian identity and so reengages young Aymara men with processes of community reproduction hinging upon the social production of publicly agentive persons. These young men were increasingly opting out of community service, often as a function of migration to El Alto. Here the spatial reach of the fiesta is also significant. In addition to young Aymara living in the community, the festival also engaged a growing community of *residentes:* El Alto–based Qhunqheños who maintain ties to the ayllu. Thus a ritual that formally enacts the alignment of the households of fiesta sponsors/cargo aspirants with the chapel plaza (seen as the center of the ayllu) similarly aligns urban spaces with the socioscape of the community. Thus the heroic driving of the truck, which travels door to door from city to sayaña.

The theology of inculturation imagines practices such as fiestas as metonymic of a predicated Aymara locality that is at once self-contained and serializable across "Aymara" space. This imagining is not unique to inculturation (nor to missionary discourse) but can be situated with respect to a host of ascendant ideologies of multicultural and pluriethnic diversity. In this chapter I have examined some of the tenets and practices of inculturationist missionaries, set against a glimpse of a more complex manifold of Aymara locality. Catechists negotiate these discordant localities in the light of situated practices and sensibilities that are integral to community reproduction and the articulation of local and translocal networks of self-worth and sociopolitical authority. In the next chapters I turn more directly to sensibilities of self-worth and embodied personhood informing the experiences and practices of Aymara catechists.

PART 2

Syncretic Subjects

CHAPTER 4

Syncretic Subjects: The Politics of Personhood

Catholic missionaries on the Bolivian altiplano often describe the Aymara cate-chists with whom they work as "divided in two"—part "Christian" and part "Aymara" (e.g., Quispe et al. 1987). By extension, this "crisis of identity" and its underlying dualism are thought to afflict all Aymara. Missionaries have taken up the Aymara concept of *chuyma* (roughly, "heart") as a locus of Aymaraness and focus of evangelization, cast in opposition to a foreign and so far uninternalized Christianity seen as being only "skin deep." In this chapter I take these mission-ary characterizations of "Aymara-Christians" (Berg 1989) as a point of departure for examining additional Aymara conceptualizations of the body as these enable a rethinking of such syncretic contexts—shifting the analytic perspective away from bird's-eye approaches toward the situated embodied experiences of such complex settings. These sensibilities of embodiment cast the body as a locus of personhood and social action dynamically engaged with—rather than partially insulated from—the conjunctural world. They recast the catechist from disabled metonyms of colonial and postcolonial juxtapositions to syncretic subjects realiz-ing through positioned practice conflicted settings as coherent lived worlds.

Through such claims of doubleness missionaries reference a pastoral "prob-lem" in the Andes: an incomplete evangelization. As a somatic metaphor jus-tifying a missionary presence and commenting on a history of evangelization, the divided catechists reflect a dominant cultural construction of contempo-rary pastoral work. As I set out to examine this emerging pastoral embrace of indigenous traditions, I was struck by this dramatic image of doubleness por-traying the catechists' struggles to manage conflicting identities while simulta-neously positioning them, Janus-like, as brokers between the Church and their communities.[1]

Of course, such cultural constructions of doubleness present much more than a missionary framework of evangelization or a compassionate characteriza-tion of the dilemma of indigenous intermediaries.[2] As I have suggested, religious doubleness and comparable metaphors have been an analytic shorthand for the partial or superficial merging of cultural systems in discussions of Andean and other colonial contexts and their aftermaths. Despite the pathos of the doubled catechists' plight, in this light the missionary characterization seemed to evoke less their embodied negotiation of identity than a disembodied clash of cultural systems, with the composite catechists as the inert historical result.

What, then, can we learn from these unfortunate bisected catechists, who appear from the earliest pages of my field notes? As a rhetorical figure the doubled catechists and the oppositional religious history they embody appeared increasingly salient as an evangelical and ethnographic construct but decreasingly relevant as an analytic frame for making sense of the catechists' experiences. As I have argued in part 1, the complexity of my field sites (comprising Aymara and missionaries) pointed away from conceptualizations of catechists as brokers of discrete cultural systems, presenting instead the entanglement of Christianity and its (mostly foreign) missionary agents as component subjects of local-level Aymara ethnography. Prompted by the missionary invocation of the Aymara chuyma, I became particularly sensitive to the chuyma and related bodily bases of identity and personhood as evident in other ethnographic data. This was no great accomplishment—the people I was working with invoked their chuymas quite often. As I struggled early in my research to follow long orations in Aymara by catechists in meetings and courses, and by ayllu authorities in community meetings, I repeatedly heard the phrases *taki chuymajampi* and *chuymajatwa* ("with all my chuyma," and "from my chuyma," respectively) prefacing most comments. Why should it be that what missionaries cast as the elusive site of an insular Aymaraness appeared to me as something Aymara wear on their sleeve? I began to listen more closely and ask more systematically about the chuyma.

Just as my discussion of missionary ideology has been complicated by a certain blurring of the boundaries of data and theory (I approach the missionaries as both "natives"—component subjects of my field work—and bearers of a theoretical stance pervasive in Andean ethnography), I here present Aymara conceptions of the body as illustrative of alternative theories of embodiment in recent Western social theory. These alternative conceptions of embodiment question received binaries in a way that is not simply homologous but also fundamentally interlinked with dualizing approaches to conjunctural or syncretic settings.

Specifically, I argue for and illustrate a conceptualization of embodied identity as an open-ended process of situated and situating engagement with the world. This follows other work calling analytic attention to the situated character of social activity and the position takings by which social actors realize and reproduce culture systems as lived frameworks of meaning[3]. In this light the Aymara body is less a metonym of juxtaposed systems than a spatial anchor and instrument of meaningful social practice. Aymara personhood, I shall argue, entails the positioned realization of a complex, conjunctural setting as a lived world. The catechists are thus not brokers operating at the margins of traditions but syncretic subjects active in the making and remaking of entangled social orders.

SYNCRETISM AND EMBODIMENT

That colonial relations and their aftermaths should be cast in bodily terms is not remarkable. As Andrew Lattas (1992:35) has noted, in such settings "bodies are made to internalise and to objectify the moral economy of colonialism, the values it puts into circulation." The embodied ambitions of colonialism are intensified in contexts of Christian missionization, which, as others have noted, is closely linked with particular conceptions of selfhood.[4] Writing of the sixteenth-century missionization of the Nahuatl, Klor de Alva stresses a sort of double dualism in the Christian presentation of self: on the one hand, a radical contrast with indigenous sensibilities of selfhood, on the other, a bifurcate Christian self ceaselessly at war with its baser self. This Augustinian tension shifts the evangelical battleground from the mission field to the syncretic subject.

The subjecthood thus produced is particularly congenial to incorporation within the practices and institutions of modernity—from marketplaces to voting booths to penal systems (e.g., van der Veer 1996). I point this out, tripping too lightly between the sixteenth century and the twentieth, because this contemporary pastoral engagement stems directly from the participation of the Latin American Church in processes and projects of modernization. Thus the current missionary concern with embodied authenticity reflects the broader prominence of the body as an instrument and site of modernity—a locus of citizenship and rational subjectivity embodying ideals of indivisibility, relative transparency, and commensurability, not to mention the ceaseless self-scrutiny that seems such a part of the modern condition.[5] In this sense the self is a site of multiplex symbolic labor, spanning colonial and postcolonial processes and encoding both radical alterity and serial commensurablity. Notwithstanding its local embodied particularity, the Christian self was macrolocal from the get-go. Put differently, Christianity

was at once the problem and its solution—the source of the conflicted doubled self and the path for its amelioration.

‡ ‡ ‡

More remarkable, though not, ultimately, surprising, is that this bodily discourse should serve such a disembodied understanding of history and culture.
Christian conceptions of personhood inform and reinforce binary understandings of syncretism. The Aymara hybridity described by the missionaries is cast
less as a creative fusion than a disabling juxtaposition, wielded, as we have
seen, to evoke essentialism, insularity, and a potential authenticity to be recovered or received. I have also suggested that a comparable discourse of disjunctive syncretism has been a mainstay of Andean ethnographic and ethnohistorical work in which a highly local Andean core is typically held to have
remained unpenetrated by surrounding cultural forms. This "Mendelian discourse" of Andean cultural identity has stressed cultural continuities through
assertions of boundedness and inheritance (Harris 1995:111 ff.).

In a similar way, the composite Andean body of missionary imagination is
a metonym of colonial history, reflecting what is thought to be a partial and
inauthentic merging of cultures. The limitations of such disjunctive approaches to colonial and postcolonial contexts have been of increasing concern in
Andean studies and elsewhere. Here I want to stress that these dualizing approaches reflect a specific paradigm of personhood linked to a particular sense
of embodiment, reducing Andean bodies to indexes of historical processes. At
worst it renders Aymara inert artifacts of colonial trauma (cf. Lyon and Barbaret 1994:54). At best it limits Aymara personhood to a conservative insular
reaction: a form of boundary maintenance.

An alternative approach to embodied personhood focuses not on the body
as an inert and passive object but turns rather upon the connection of bodiliness
and subjective action (e.g., Csordas 1990, 1994; Lock 1993; Mauss 1973 [1936];
Turner 1994). This paradigm of embodiment stresses the body as the "existential ground of culture," the seat of subjectivity (Csordas 1990:5, 1994:9). At stake
is a shift from a view of the body as a product of objective contexts (e.g., in the
conception of the Aymara as double because of the trauma of conquest and an
incomplete evangelization) to an approach to embodiment as pragmatic potential (cf. Farnell 1994; Strathern 1996, especially chapters 4, 6). In this view the
body is the positioned site of social practice, a setting for the situated mediation
of complex social fields, a resource through which people realize conjunctural
contexts and their aftermaths as lived worlds. Rather than being reduced to the
"outcome of social processes," the body is seen as an "active source of social
processes and institutions" (Lyon and Barbaret 1994:49, 54).

The sensibilities of embodiment and personhood anchored in the chuyma and reflected in my field data are largely consonant with this phenomenological, interactionalist approach to the body, underscoring the status of the body as a locus of personhood and seat of identity and social agency. In dubbing these sensibilities of embodied personhood "Aymara," I do not mean to posit an enduring indigenous ideology of personhood, nor to contrast exclusively modern/global and traditional/local cultural forms of embodiment. This would merely replicate the essentialism of missionary discourse. What I identify as Aymara is itself emergent from a long history of entanglements within dominant state systems—Incan, Iberian, and modern nations—of which the missionary encounter I observed is one domain. The evangelical ideology of doubleness is itself proclaimed by many Aymara. Similarly, these alternative philosophies of embodiment belie any monolithic characterization of Western thought. Strictly speaking, we don't need "other" cultural data to problematize such dualistic approaches. If I couch this discussion as a dialogue between "Aymara" and "missionaries," it is because the missionary schema of embodiment is good to think as an ideology of Andean syncretism but less useful in understanding the positioned practices of syncretic subjects. The Aymara case illuminates additional implications of embodiment, which, counterpoised to the mission rhetoric of doubleness and turning largely on alternative readings of the chuyma, illuminate the specific negotiation of apparently radically conflicted identities by situated agents.

Just as recent discussions of embodiment take it to be a methodological opportunity to collapse long-standing dualities in social theory, including subject-object, mind-body, and language-experience (e.g., Csordas 1990, 1994; Farnell 1994; Lock 1994; Strathern 1996), the examination of embodiment here is linked to an effort to recast dualisms prevalent in discussions of colonial and postcolonial settings. This is not to deny the supra-individual and historical conditions that inform Andean life, nor the valenced structures of identities that they give force to, but to insist that such conditions are best apprehended through situated practice. It is here that such structuring forces are negotiated, their productive potential realized, their destructive implications manifest and, perhaps, overcome.

THE FEAST OF THE ETERNAL RETURN

Qurpa, it will be recalled, is the Machaqueño ayllu—once an hacienda linked to the Guarachis and to the parish—where the pastoral team serving the region now resides. On a day dampened by a cold steady drizzle, Ingrid and I arrived by bus at dusk, hoping to meet Hernando, the parish priest. We stumbled off the bus at the plaza of the community and found ourselves, unexpectedly, in the middle of a fiesta—brass bands blaring, dancers laboring under the weight of their soggy costumes, and a crowd of drunken spectators who quickly turned their attention to us. They teetered amiably as we gathered our packs from the top of the bus.

Father Hernando, alerted by an intermediary that I was interested in conducting research in his parish, had called me a few weeks earlier in La Paz to suggest that I visit to discuss my intentions. This was a fortunate opportunity and a generous invitation. Hernando was almost continuously on the move, serving the two parishes under his care and participating in a series of other meetings, workshops, and courses that took him to other parts of Bolivia and, occasionally, out of the country. In his phone call Hernando brusquely told me when he would be in Qurpa and, in a sink-or-swim style of assistance I slowly learned to appreciate, pointed me toward a section of town near the municipal cemetery of La Paz, a warren of semipaved streets and dozens of storefront bus companies running creaking buses to rural communities around the Department of La Paz. If I asked around, he told me, I could find the company running buses a few times a week to Jesús de Machaqa and some nearby roadside communities, such as Qurpa.

Declining invitations to drink and dance, Ingrid and I got directions to the parish house and set off with a dwindling escort of stumbling revelers intent on showing us the way. Hernando greeted us with a mixture of surprise and amusement and invited us to join the rest of the pastoral team in dinner. Over the course of my research I spent a number of such evenings with pastoral teams in Jesús de Machaqa and in other parishes—eating, playing cards, talking, laughing. These are typically close-knit communities of priests, nuns, lay professionals—doctors, agronomists, etc.—and other workers affiliated with the parish. They are genuinely transnational communities. International visitors—such as myself, or, say, traveling fellow Jesuits—are common.

My sense of that first dinner, reinforced by a handful of comparable experiences in other parishes, was of a pastoral community huddled inside while the tumult of the fiesta—non-stop brass band music, crowd noises and fights, the distinctive singing of drunken men and women, the occasional detonation of dynamite—roiled just outside their door. Yet this was not a matter of missionaries cut off from the people among whom they lived. The conversation around the kitchen table skipped from commentary on the fiesta sponsors, speculation as to who would inherit the sponsorship for the following year, reports of how many sheep and llamas had been slaughtered to feed the dancers, reports of which notable migrants had returned from La Paz or from the Yungas for the festival—all reflecting a degree of situated insight into the event. As pastoral team members arrived from meetings or errands, or from strolls to observe the action (or from requests to attend to the wounded), all brought updates and gossip. Hernando himself had celebrated a mass earlier that day, though he hastened to add that it was only a coincidence he was in town for the fiesta—as I took the implication, he was not a mere functionary of sacraments. The next day he celebrated Sunday Mass in the community, assisted by a recently ordained minister to whom he was trying to transfer most of the sacramental responsibility for the ayllu. The festival sponsors also attended that celebration, which culminated in a procession led by the sponsors carrying the image of the saint around the plaza.

The mix of amusement, engagement, and disapproval in these interior vigils well evokes the ambiguity of fiestas in recent Catholic pastoral thought. Huddled around their tables, pastoral agents enact less their separation or alienation from the Aymara than the complex framing of Aymaraness entailed by inculturationist discourse. Like the Aymara heart concealed by layers of impure syncretic flesh, the Aymaraness missionaries seek to reinforce is but fleetingly available to them in what they experience as a complex pastoral geography of concealment and authenticity. Priests speak of more outlying communities as the locus of a more authentic Aymara culture. In the spirit of inculturation, these are characterized as "healthier," and preferable for pastoral work, and contrasted with more central towns and those closest to roads and other arteries of modernity, seen as "folklorized" and tainted with colonial Catholicism and contact with the Bolivian nation-state.

Pastoral workers frequently expressed their distress over the cultural impact of migration to and from the city of La Paz. Fiestas are the occasion of the return of many migrants to their natal ayllus. Indeed, as in the festival of San Antonio, contemporary fiestas serve as a prime vehicle for weaving the lives of out-migrating young men and women into the practices of ayllu reproduction. Hernando referred wryly to the "fiesta of the eternal return," and, like other pastoral workers I interviewed, found in such reverse migration the source of the corruption of traditional Aymara religiosity. Such positions shift attention away from the undeniably hybrid colonial nature of fiestas to underscore a new threat from without. They thus finesse the revised moral status of fiestas under the frame of inculturation as well as a recoverable locality claimed by inculturationist thought.

One missionary, reflecting the "revalorized" understanding of Aymara ritual drinking, commented to me that he could distinguish who was from the countryside and who from the city by how they behaved when drunk: "People from La Paz will assault you immediately; those from the countryside are more amiable when they are drunk." Another contrasted the corrupt ways of urban life with the inherent religiosity of traditional rural life ways. "To be from the countryside," he told a gathering of catechists, "is to have faith." Regardless of formal religious affiliation, he went on, "if they are from the countryside, they all have faith: they raise up the name of Jesus, of pachamama, of the achachilas, of the gods of the sayañas." "In your life," catechists learned in a different course, "there is this religiosity, that permanent reverence each day."

As with the interior Aymara chuyma, this religiosity is spatialized. The center-periphery construction of pastoral geography—valorizing the margins over against the urban centers—is replicated in the communities in an opposition drawn between the local chapel and dispersed house compounds. Priests note that in many of the celebrations they preside over the act in the chapel—a marriage, for example—is only part of a more extended sequence of rites that take place unseen by them "after we drive away in our jeeps." They speak of a "world reserved for the priests" concealing a separate "world" of Aymara ritual. This sense of concealment is enhanced by their impression that this Aymara world takes place at night. The most potent locus of Aymaraness in the estimation of the missionaries I consulted is the household. Priests speak of the "closed doors" of Aymara houses, which conceal from them crucial knowledge of local life. Such local knowledge is seen as indispensable to authentic evangelization. Others recall the times they have penetrated these house spaces—for meals or lodging while riding circuit among the communities under their care—as an index of their proximity to Aymara culture.

HIDDEN HEARTS

Authentic evangelization under the rubric of inculturation is predicated upon access to the intimate, local interstices of Aymara life. The catechists, who are often the closest contact missionaries have with the Aymara, broker this pastoral access and embody these dimensions of concealment and continuity. The catechists are vehicles of missionary access to that which is concealed; when missionaries do gain access to Aymara households, these tend to be the houses of catechists. Alternatively, catechists mediate encounters between missionaries and Aymara, serving as translators or buffers against the risks of contact with priests. When priests suggest that the catechists are divided in two, they refer to the chuyma as the locus of an internal Aymaraness, relatively untouched by colonial evangelization and, like the insides of Aymara houses, unseen and unpenetrated by the missionaries. The catechists emerge as the somatic site of inculturation, a microcosm of the mission field.

Pastoral workers comment that they see only one side of the catechist: the "side" that is presented to the Church. They describe catechists as poised between their communities and the Church, managing this intermediate position through a strategy of presentation and concealment. A number of priests echoed Hernando's suggestion, summarized in chapter 3:

> For years, historically, the norm has been that when speaking to a priest, or to any outsider, before answering something, [an Aymara] would think, "How does he want me to respond?" Because this way, one is able to get by, no? So, for my part, I have wanted to create a space in which they don't know what I'm thinking. Then they don't know how to answer me.

For pastoral workers the catechists at once embody the separation between the seen and the unseen, the said and the unsaid, and negotiate the space between them. One priest suggested that it is in what the catechists do not tell him, in what they do and say while concealed in their communities, that the real work of evangelization is to be found. Evangelization is seen as mysterious and uncontrollable: realized at the margins of the missionary encounter and based on catechists' access to concealed loci of Aymara authenticity. The resolution of catechists' "crisis of identity" is linked with their efforts to more effectively penetrate the chuymas of their fellows.

Signs Over Words

During the early 1990s priests were working to modify the text-based liturgical celebrations, introduced from the 1960s, in which the catechists were infamous for speaking for hours. They compared these extended catechetical monologues to the monotonous speeches of self-important rural schoolteachers during national holidays celebrated at local schools. Missionaries exhorted the catechists to communicate in "signs" rather than words,[6] invoking as role models the yatiris, who only recently were denounced by priests and catechists. By signs priests refer to a variety of ritual objects: candles, incense, flowers, etc. These are presented as having two benefits over words. The first is familiar from other discussions of understanding and persuasion in Christian contexts: images perceived by the eye enter more directly to the heart (e.g., MacCormack 1985, 1991). The second concerns signs as vehicles for recovering meaning from the past, which can be accessed by catechists through the culturally adept use of signs. Hernando made this point for catechists using a parable: "When one is walking down a road, although he begins very clean, by the end it may be that he is full of dust and his clothing all disheveled. That is to say there are signs that—sometimes if we don't look at them a little—they may be losing their meaning. So it is important to look at them." The context was the course described in chapter 3 aimed at remembering and reviving the ritual of ayuno in Machaqueño ayllus. Although they appear idolatrous to us now, Hernando was suggesting, Aymara signs such as those used in the rites under discussion retain a reserve of (Christian) meaning through time, which can be recovered in spite of the dust of conquest and faulty missionization.

Signs are invoked as the currency of the chuyma; just as they transact meanings deriving from the (now authorizing) past, they are held to penetrate the chuyma more readily than words. The catechists embody and broker this process and the potential to resolve Aymara doubleness. Their fluency in Aymara language and culture combined with their ongoing pastoral formation in mission courses make them privileged vehicles of and to the "Aymara-Christian" chuyma.

On the one hand, catechists must reconcile their somatic duality and that of their Aymara contemporaries, aligning Aymara chuymas with external Christian identity. On the other, this conversion is informed by the pastoral geography of Aymara communities: catechists are urged to position themselves at the center (taypi) of the community, itself referred to as chuyma. Evangelization is cast as a movement of Christian identity from the syncretic periphery to the authentic center. Inculturation entails the repositioning of Christianity as local, indigenous value.

Thus far I have argued that the supposed divided self of the catechists embodies missionary perceptions of an inauthentic evangelization in the Andes. The pastoral ideology of inculturation reverses the signs of this dualism. The enduring Aymara chuyma becomes the elusive source of—rather than an obstacle to—authentic (Aymara) Christian conversion. These shifts in pastoral posture notwithstanding, the bodily idiom of this missionary characterization of the catechists reflects approaches to syncretic contexts premised upon their analytic decomposition into component parts. Indeed, these characterizations collapse two dualizing discourses—one concerned with conjunctural settings, one deriving from pervasive conceptions of the body—and so reduce the catechists to heuristic indexes of a composite world.

Much is missed by such reductions, which overlook both the active dimensions of the body as an instrument of situated practice and the grounded experience of complex contexts. An alternative paradigm of embodiment thus presents an opportunity to rethink approaches to such complex settings. In the following section I examine Aymara conceptions of the body as a source and site of identity as one such alternative paradigm. Specifically, I present a very different conceptualization of the chuyma: not as an insular, conservative site of identity but rather as an anchor for subjective practice in the world. I then turn to the catechists to argue both the obvious—they are not divided in two—and the remarkable—that, drawing on dynamic conceptions of bodiliness and identity, they realize what appears to missionaries as a situation of fragmentation and crisis as a coherent social world.

CHUYMA

Chuyma refers specifically to the lungs, although it also comprises the complex of heart, liver, and lungs. Aymara generally offered *corazon* (heart) as a Spanish gloss, although the organ "heart" is distinguished by the Aymara term *lloqo;* the liver is referred to with the term *k'iwcha.* Yet chuyma invokes more than these biological referents; together these three organs constitute a more integral cultural whole.

As commonly used, chuyma suggests an interior site of selfhood, the subjective, somatic center of social being. It is held to be the seat of the soul and the source of will (Sp. *voluntad*). The complex is said to be "for remembering" and "for thinking." Such remembering (*amt'asiña*) is a key aspect of Aymara ritual practices, which make manifest—through offerings—the sacrifier's subjective state of thinking about or remembering the intended recipient (Abercrombie 1998, 1986; Arnold 1992). While it is often associated with innate knowledge, linked to the ancestors and most powerfully manifest today in yatiris, chuyma is also the site of learned knowledge, internalized through memorization[7].

Such acts of memory are performative indexes of embodied knowledge and its transaction. Aymara seem to consider as qualitatively distinct (and highly valued) knowledge incorporated so fully that it can be recited from memory. This remembering effects a change in the relationship between knowledge and knower, a relationship often glossed with the Spanish expression *por sí.* The phrase suggests an autonomous completeness; the recitation of the knowledge removes any earlier dependence upon external sources and underscores an authentic and now self-generating performance. Men, for instance, often "tune" their notched flutes (*pinkillus*) by leaving them outside overnight in the vicinity of a wak'a or other place deity associated with musical production. After this, I was told, these flutes "play by themselves" (*por sí toca*), suggesting a sort of capacity fully incorporated from without. Alongside these telluric transactions between place deities and instruments, musicians described comparable processes of incorporation: for instance, after hearing a popular tune played endlessly over the radio, one man told me that he could suddenly played it "por sí." The rote memorization of Catholic prayer is cast as a similar process of authoritative internalization. In ways quite at odds with pastoral workers' contempt for the "mere" repetition of prayers from memory, Catholic prayer is said to be most authentic and effective when memorized and then recited "from the chuyma."

This combination of spatiotemporal indexicality, subjectivity, and historicity render the chuyma profoundly social; chuyma and social action are interdependent. While presocial beings such as infants are said to have a chuyma, it is described as incomplete, a social potential that is manifest when they begin talking and eating solid food. (cf. Gottlieb 1998) These important media of Aymara social life merge corporality and sociability. After a curing held to summon Ingrid's lost soul (to be discussed later in this chapter), she was asked how she had slept and whether she had dreamed. Dreams, like speech, are an index of the actions of the soul. She did not remember dreaming, and I ventured that she had slept "like a dead person." I was quickly corrected: she had slept "like an infant"; infants do not dream "because they cannot talk." At stake in both dreaming and speaking is a mature chuyma. Note that, far from being insular, conservative, or even body bound, this conceptualization of chuyma involves interactions across space and time and the ongoing extension of the bodily self into the social world.

As the seat of the soul, chuyma comprises a set of overlapping elements or qualities[8]. The most frequently invoked of these components are: *ajayu, animu, kuraji,* and *alwa.* While associated with the chuyma, these are embodied in additional ways, in blood, breath, and body fat. They are manifest in acts of speaking and remembering as well as other social indexes of vitality.

Ajayu and alwa (cf. Sp. *alma:* soul) are the most comprehensive of these terms; *animu* (cf. Sp. *ánimo:* spirit; soul; courage) and *kuraji* (cf. Sp. *coraje:* courage; passion) are frequently subordinated to ajayu. Together these are said to give strength (*ch'ama*) and are associated with the blood. They are also evident in body fat (*lik'i*), which can be transformed by hard work into a steam that rises in the body or more dangerously rendered "frozen" and impotent by cold or fright. That is to say, these qualities of personhood are mutable and they affect and reflect human action in the world. Another index of ajayu, also linked to kuraji, is speech and public oratory. Admired "strong" speech is said to come from the chuyma and persuasively engage the chuyma of others. As a medium of exchange aligning chuyma-centered social subjects, words interact with other media of social intercourse. Thus, if you offer coca to someone and speak sincerely, from the chuyma, your coca will taste sweet; a cigarette rightly offered will burn well.

Marcelino, who first reported this last point to me, was a man beginning his year of service as mallku of his community. His ability to put his chuyma into his work would be central to his success in the eyes of his ayllu. Marginally literate, he had already complained to me of his inability to memorize cer-

tain ritual and political formulae: oaths of office and protocols of national peasant syndicates. He insisted that it was necessary to fully memorize the text before performing it, describing the oath of office (*juramintu*) as "like a prayer."
That same year Bonifacio was serving as p'iqi. Tellingly, Marcelino sought un-
successfully to enlist Bonifacio—thought as a catechist to have superior capacities of memorization and literacy—as something of a "personal assistant.
Given these challenges, it is little wonder that Marcelino was concerned with
stressing these other extrasomatic tokens of his chuyma-based sincerity.

The ajayu, as Ingrid and I learned, is also implicated in dreaming, transcending the body-bound self by leaving the body and wandering when we
dream. Ajayus, or at least "parts" of them, may also leave the body as the result of a bad fright. They are said to "fall down," are "caught" or "trapped,"
and may remain separated from the body. Techniques of curing this soul loss
suggest that these qualities of personhood are embodied through clothing and
food consumption.

Ingrid's Lost Soul

A few months after we took up residence with Alejandro's family, Alejandro,
prodded by his wife Rufina, suggested that we needed to contract a yatiri. As
long as we were living in the ayllu and walking about its various places, he
said, we ought to make an offering to local place deities for good health and
luck with my work. In retrospect, his rationale was more complex. This was
the beginning of August (1991), a time when many Aymara households undertake such offerings to the earth or local place deities. Given his background
as a Protestant turned catechist, I do not know if Alejandro was in the habit
of routinely doing so, but with a couple of gringos under his roof and the revised good news of inculturation, it is likely that he and Rufina were interested in hedging their bets. In addition, I later learned that Bonifacio—Alejandro's rival catechist in the ayllu—was deeply offended by our decision to
live with Alejandro (a slight I regret and for which I have apologized). Bonifacio's father, it will be remembered, was himself a prominent and powerful
yatiri. Alejandro and Rufina suspected that this catechetical rivalry heightened
by my presence might have spilled over to include sorcery. The ritual we were
asked to contract would also serve to protect the entire household, all of
whom participated.

We contacted Oscar, a local yatiri, who was also, as it happened, both a
regular member of the faith group and Rufina's uncle (her father's brother).
Under his guidance Ingrid and I purchased the requisite ritual paraphernalia—
stamped sugar cakes; dried herbs, nuts, incense, desiccated llama fetuses, alcohol, wine, colored yarn—and the entire household assembled to prepare a set

of elaborate offerings (waxt'a). Before putting these together Oscar engaged in a series of divinations with coca to determine both which place deities would be most receptive to our offering and whether there were any particular afflictions in the household demanding his attention. It was in this regard that he determined that Ingrid had lost her soul.

The coca revealed that she had pain in her leg. Ingrid noted that she did have some discomfort in her knee. Further consultation of the coca revealed that this pain was linked to a bad fall on a road or a path. Indeed, Ingrid recalled that her bad knee was the result of a horseback riding accident that had occurred some fifteen years earlier in her native Holland, when her bolting horse slipped and fell on her leg while crossing an asphalt road. Oscar then determined that Ingrid's ajayu had become trapped (*katja*—literally tied?) at the site of the accident, a condition he would attempt to cure if we cared to hire him for another offering.

We did so, and a few months later Oscar returned to prepare a set of different offerings designed to call back Ingrid's soul and to convert her current misfortune into a condition of abundance and good luck. The offering, prepared on a sheet of white paper laid atop an enamel bowl, was described as a gift of "food" for the place deities. As Oscar composed the offering, he gave us certain ingredients—stamped cakes of sugar, coca leaves, etc.—instructing us to place them on the plate while naming (i.e., remembering) significant

FIGURE 4.1   *The offering was a gift of food for the place deities*

places in Holland, in the United States, as well as places Ingrid and I had traveled in Bolivia. After cleansing each of us and the rest of the family with a ritual bath—a sticky soup of herbs, sugar cakes, and water—Oscar told Ingrid and me to climb into bed, instructed Alejandro on what to do the following morning, and left to dispatch the offering and dispose of the misfortune he had cleansed from our bodies.

Ingrid's soul was to arrive at sunrise the following morning. After consulting coca leaves, Oscar reported that the soul would travel by plane and bus. Alejandro was told to burn some incense and prepare for the arrival of a "little bird," Ingrid's ajayu. Alejandro was to hit or otherwise "tie down" the bird. Ingrid had given him a change of clothes the night before, and Alejandro was to then take the clothes and quickly "enter" and have Ingrid put on the clothes. After that, she and I were immediately to eat something. I do not know whether Alejandro saw or hit a little bird that morning; he did awaken us with Ingrid's clothing and a breakfast of bread and sweetened tea.[9] Later the same morning, as we sat in the patio, Alejandro had an unexpected visitor: a man who had migrated to the yungas but had returned to Milluni in anticipation—appropriately enough—of the upcoming feast of All Souls' Day. Alejandro speculated that he had brought the ajayu on the final leg of its journey.

While the transatlantic scope of Ingrid's soul loss is unusual, the case illustrates the extrasomatic extension of chuyma-based personhood. This is evident in the extreme case of a soul trapped in a particular place as well as in the more quotidian engagement of chuymas with the spatial contexts of day-to-day life, as Ingrid and I were asked to remember places where we walked in Bolivia. The healing also involved various metaphors of incorporation. The act of calling the soul (khiwt'aña) refers both to hailing someone from a distance by waving one's arms in a circular motion and to acts of enveloping something, mixing things together, or spooling yarn, suggesting in various ways the porous entanglement of the chuyma with the lived world, its extension and retraction in social experience. Alejandro's instructions to hit or tie down Ingrid's ajayu cast this restoration as an act of hunting or domestication. His action of "entering" with (as?) the ajayu parallels common spatial metaphors describing knowledge entering the chuyma.

Additional evidence for the extrasomatic, entangled nature of personhood stem from the ways qualities of personhood are embodied and transmitted through food and clothes. Ingrid was to eat immediately after Alejandro entered with her clothing. Similarly, after my own encounter with a pack of dogs, their owner, after driving them off, placed earth on my head from the site where my frightened ajayu might have fallen. She also picked up my hat and, waving it in a circular motion, summoned my ajayu, animu, and kuraji.

When I shared this story with others, they agreed that she had done the right thing and suggested that I should also have taken some dirt from the area and mixed it with my tea to drink and restore my soul.

‡ ‡ ‡

Alwa refers to the dead. While both alwa and ajayu are said to leave the body at death, it is in the alwa that the personhood of the deceased endures. Alwas of the recently dead are a source of fertility in the form of favorable weather and abundant and healthy crops and herds (Berg 1989; Harris 1982a). They return to their communities in the years following their death to receive offerings from their families (i.e., to be remembered). The man from the Yungas, who may have helped return Ingrid's soul, was back in Milluni to remember a recently deceased relative.

Alwas are temporal extensions of personhood. They retain their social identity for a period of three years, after which most fade into a more homogeneous category of ancestors. This extended social identity remains experientially salient for Aymara in a number of ways. One is through the medium of clothing, which we have already seen to be linked with the ajayus of the living. The clothing of the dead is washed and sometimes burned soon after death. Some clothing, typically a poncho and a hat for a man and an awayu (carrying cloth; shawl) and a hat for woman, is saved and brought to commemorative masses or used as part of a household "tomb" constructed during All Souls Day.

A second medium of the enduring social identity of the dead is the house compound. Aymara households are animated, gendered structures—architectural expressions of the fertility, growth, and prosperity of their builders and occupants (see Arnold 1992). The association of house spaces with the soul of a deceased occupant is most evident in the practice of removing dirt from the floor of the house as part of the dispatch of the soul after death. Similarly, in the practices of All Souls Day the house itself—i.e., one interior gable wall— becomes the returned soul of the deceased: an inhabited altar to which offerings of food and prayer are made.

The point to stress here is that embodied personhood is far from body bound. As a physical locus of selfhood, the chuyma is both the precondition for and the principal index of an ongoing transformative engagement with the material and social world. This projection from bodiliness is a key feature of Aymara sociability; the physicality of the media of sociability—blood, breath, food, clothing—further indexes this transsomatic dimension of personhood. At stake is the mediation of interior and exterior, subjective and social, local and translocal. To illustrate this, I turn to the public organization and performance of chuyma-grounded selfhood, through formalized exchange practices and life trajectories conceptualized as "paths" (thakis).

Persons and Pathways

The temporal pattern of Aymara personhood presents a recurring condition of infantilization and social maturation. Coordinate with this process are periodic expansions of an individual's social network as an increasingly encompassing context for agentive selfhood. An often cited condition of such personhood in the Andes is the establishment of asymmetric and reciprocal relations of debt and obligation. Kin and fictive kin ties are but the most stable in a lifetime of such ties, effected through such exchange practices as ayni and mink'a. Writing of the Quechua-speaking community of Sonqo (Peru), Catherine Allen notes:

> Reciprocity is like a pump at the heart of Andean life. The constant give-and-take of *ayni* and *mink'a* maintains a flow of energy throughout the ayllu. This flow extends beyond the human community as well. The obligation extends to domesticated animals and plants, to Pacha, to the many animated places in the landscape itself, and even to the saints. . . . Labor exchanges are only one manifestation of the general human responsibility to direct the flow of energy in a positive way. This is done in many contexts—in marriage alliances, in the discharging of community *cargos,* in private and communal rituals, even in how one offers speech and how one receives the speech of others. (1988:93 ff.; cf. Bastien 1985:598 ff.)

Exchange is an idiom for the practical engagement of the chuyma with the world—an engagement at once intersubjective and translocal. Reciprocal exchange is a principal template for interactions among Aymara and between Aymara and the gods (cf. Abercrombie 1986:104, 164). As an idiom of social and ritual interaction, exchange—offering and receiving—entails the subjective positioning of the chuyma. As with words, things that are authentically (and effectively) given are given from the chuyma. We have seen that ritual offerings are cast as acts of memory. Similarly, social exchanges are often cast as transactions of sentiment: "respect" or "affection." Social seniority is characterized by a widening sphere of interactions encompassing extra-ayllu forces (the Church or national government), the dead, and the distant past. In this sense seniority is a move toward positions of both translocal mediation and located centrality.

At various points in a lifetime of social maturation, individuals are symbolically reclassified as infants (cf. Gottlieb 1998). In my observations this occurred most notably at two crucial moments: marriage and at the culmination of a couple's fiesta-cargo career, when they begin their year of service in the positions of maximal community authority (jilaqata or mallku for the man, mallku tayka or mama t'alla for the woman). The practices of these life stages, enacting concentrically widening spheres of engagement (i.e., inchoate seniority within a household joining distinct patrilines and inchoate seniority within an ayllu integrating and representing multiple patrilines), encapsulate and recapitulate the cultural construction of Aymara social selves. In each case this is a movement from muteness, dependence, and passivity to "strong" speech and effective socioritual action, a movement of actualizing the potentialities of the chuyma.[10]

The prevailing metaphor in organizing these processes is that of a path or thaki. Thaki is frequently used to describe a fiesta-cargo career (e.g., Abercrombie 1986; Albó 1991b). But, more than a communal template for life trajectories, a thaki is cast as a very individual thing. Consultants spoke of "taking out" and "carrying your own" thaki. This sense of individual possession is crucial. A thaki indexes a person's social maturation and his/her fulfillment of obligations to the ayllu and the gods.[11] With the culmination of the process, serving as mallku, a man's authority is expressed in metaphors of kinship and herding: he is *awki* (father), *jiliri* (elder brother), *awatiri* (herder), *irpjiri* (one who guides). This social potency is cosmically legitimated. A mallku invokes with pride the agricultural fertility of the community during his tenure. Conversely, when the rains are late or too heavy, if hails damage the crops or the frosts come too soon, the mallku may be held responsible. His ritual acts on behalf of the community will be scrutinized for shortcomings in technique or chuyma-grounded sincerity. Much depends upon a mallku's chuyma as he serves and embodies the community, mediating the reciprocal flow of fertile potency upon which Aymara life rests.

Blossoming P'iqis: The Day They Threw Me Out of Qhunqhu

In March of 1992, some seventeen months into my fieldwork, as I was feeling quite comfortable in my relations with a number of ayllus in Jesús de Machaqa, I was abruptly asked to leave Qhunqhu Milluni. A group of p'iqis confronted me during Carnival and told me that, as I had no official permission to reside in the community, I was obliged to leave. Now, I had negotiated my residence with the previous year's cohort of mallkus and p'iqis and had been on good terms with the current year's ayllu authorities since they had assumed office in January. Indeed, I understood myself to be an invited guest of one of the mallkus at whose house the entire ayllu was gathered in celebration of Carnival. I was, in short, pole-axed by these developments. Though he was not directly involved in the confrontation, I quickly suspected the hand of Bonifacio, who was that year serving as p'iqi. I still think this is part of the answer, though this does not fully explain the timing of my expulsion. Nor does it explain why that same week I was suddenly run out of neighboring Qhunqhu Liqiliqi, where I also had been on good terms with a range of consultants.

I had gone to Liqiliqi to observe a ritual known as *yapu laki,* the distribution of fallow aynoqa fields to be cultivated the following year, and the coordination of the cultivation of those fields currently under production. In Milluni, this takes place as part of a syndicate meeting held in the patio of one of the mallkus. At one time, I was told, the event took place in the aynoqa fields themselves, with the mallku distributing plates of food to the ayllu, as he authorized and coordinated the ayllu's agricultural labor. Consultants commented on the abundance of food, coca, and alcohol offered by the mallku and described him serving heaping plates of food to each person, saying, "This is your qallpa" (i.e., parcel of aynoqa land). I expected to observe something like this Liqiliqi. The yapu laki takes place as part of a week of activities linked to Carnival. Some brief attention to Carnival will help illuminate correlations between paths of ayllu authority, processes of agricultural production, and the very public and entangled condition of all Aymara chuymas as a function of the porous production of Aymara locality.

The yapu laki was traditionally the setting for another act called *thaki chhiphira.* The term means "opening a path" and refers to the formal presentation to the ayllu of a young man by his father, by which act the young man formally initiates his cargo path (and public personhood) and his father signals his own readiness to "rest." The act explicitly links cargo service with rights to aynoqa land. It also establishes a number of powerful metaphoric links between paths of personhood and agricultural production, as immature, budding cargo aspirants are indexically connected with soon to be cultivated fallow fields. Indeed, by some readings, "opening a path" references an agricultural act of breaking up clods of earth in anticipation of planting and evokes the newly ratified public person as a planted seed, germinating social potential.

In its southern Andean manifestation Carnival falls in the second half of the short growing season, a month or so before the earliest harvests in April. It is a "not-quite-first-fruits" ceremony: a celebration of flowers, young animals, and small potatoes (themselves described as "infants"). At stake, I think, is the celebration of fertile potential in the process of being realized, production rather than product. Carnival marks the end of the rainy season and sees the last performances of the rain-attracting pinkillu flutes.

As I observed Carnival in Milluni, Saturday was dedicated to celebrating (in) the potato fields, which were full of flowering plants with small young potatoes forming beneath the earth. I joined Saturnino and Marcela seated in the center of their aynoqa field as they made a burnt offering of *qhuwa,* an aromatic altiplano plant supplemented with incense, coca leaves, and llama fat. As they did this, they adorned a number of the flowering plants with paper streamers, an act they called "tying," as one might tie up an animal (or a soul!). After praying the Lord's Prayer and a Hail Mary, we adorned one another with confetti, and Saturnino and Marcela commenced to dig at the base of a few plants, removing small potatoes and replacing them with *lujma,* a quincelike fruit grown in the yungas. They said they hoped their potatoes would grow to the size of the fruit. Beyond this iconic significance, the lujma can be seen as imparting some of the raw fertile potency highlanders associate with the yungas. The small potatoes—babies—were carried in cloths draped over the back and "made to dance." Later that day I visited Saturnino and Marcela at home and observed streamers adorning their houses. House structures are themselves seen as animate (see chapter 5) and it would seem that houses are among the living fertile things celebrated at Carnival.

On Monday I accompanied Alejandro, Rufina, and a number of their children to one of the herding houses they maintain high in the cordillera. We were on our way to mark the sheep born in the previous year. Lighting a fire of dung in a potsherd at the center of their corral, Rufina burned a packet of qhuwa, and spread a cloth heaped with sweets and coca for the sheep in the corral to eat. The family gathered to one side before a similarly stocked cloth. Alejandro directed us to pour libations on the corners of the cloth and he aspersed the corners of the corral and the herd. The marking began with a selection of four of the most robust sheep born in the previous year. These "leaders"—two male and two female—were arranged lying on their sides upon a cloth in a configuration identical to that of a wedding between humans: the central pair were dubbed the "bride" and "groom"; they were flanked by a "godmother" and "godfather" of marriage. Alejandro notched the ears of all four according to the marks of their owners,[12] and sewed woolen tassels into their ears. These colored tassels are called "flowers" (*t'ika*). The newly marked sheep were force-fed coca and wine, adorned with streamers, and sent stumbling away by Rufina, who struck them smartly on top of their heads with pairs of lujma fruit in her hands. The remaining newborn sheep were similarly marked and adorned with tassels/flowers. (A comparable event for newborn calves took place on Wednesday of carnival week.)

Tuesday—*martes de ch'alla*—is perhaps the most significant day of Carnival; its observance extends to the city where many storeowners pour libations for prosperity and luck. In Qhunqhu it is the principal day for adorning houses (an act also known as *t'ikando* [i.e. making flower]). In a sequence of Carnival days devoted to different animals, Tuesday is the day for marking llamas. It is also the day for "marking" incoming mallkus, and this coincidence draws a number of analytic threads together.

In 1991 the main activity of the day was a visit to the households of each of the mallkus. The visits enacted the moiety organization of the ayllu—with the p'iqis and other persons from the upper zones going to visit the mallku from the lower syndicate (and vice versa) later returning to visit their own mallkus. Each mallku couple sat in their patio flanked by their advisers: older men and women who had completed their cargos. The relationship was explicitly compared to that of a godparent and was thus rather like the configuration in the marking of sheep. Visitors came to pay their respects to the mallku and mallku tayka, adorning them with streamers and confetti and with large loops of baked bread (*phillus:* crowns). There are a number of parallels with the other events of Carnival—here it is the mallkus who are flowering and, as the festival progresses, "made to dance."

Martes de ch'alla stands in revelatory contrast to a similar event—called *uywara*—carried out in January during the first weeks of the mallkus' tenure. Again each mallku couple hosts the ayllu in their house; again each couple is attended by godparent/counselors. However at the January uywara I observed the new mallkus sat silently and impassively. I was told that they were "like infants": incapable of forceful speech or action. Between the uywara and Carnival mallkus remain impotent—they are expected to be humble and mute. (No wonder I got along with them so well!) During this time a mallku should devote himself to performing libations of alcohol and consuming much of the same. The successful performance of this task is indexed by the crops. As the crops mature, so does the mallku, who blossoms with the potatoes and new herd animals. From martes de ch'alla on, the mallku is considered capable of authoritatively performing his role as herder of the ayllu. A comparable maturation is undergone by the p'iqi's, and it is in this regard that I was given the (temporary) boot by a group of p'iqis in Milluni and, a few days later, by the similarly newly activated mallkus of Liqiliqi.

Carnival week in Milluni concludes, as we have seen, with the celebration of Domingo de Tentación, when the mallkus of both ayllus are adorned in common. Domingo de Tentación also reprises the marriage and marking of the sheep, although here it is sheep from the common interayllu herd that serves as part of the capital of the school that are marked. When I observed this practice, it was also p'iqis from the two communities who brought out the sheep to be marked—like the animals they carried, these young authorities were the forceful and maturing leaders of the upcoming generation.

‡ ‡ ‡

The public performance of Aymara personhood, organized through the metaphor of a cargo path, is thus closely correlated with processes of natural fertility and agricultural production. The illustration might be extended to discuss the arc of mallku service over the course of each year: mallku couples enter like babies in January, they grow and attain a certain measure of maturity during Carnival, among their final acts is participation in the commemoration of the recently dead during All Souls Day in early November. In this last set of acts mallkus are indexically connected to the resting elders whose ranks they soon will join and, by extension, to the souls of the ancestors. The key point here is that the pathway of personhood is predicated upon the transsomatic extension of the chuyma into the social and natural world, as manifest in a set of highly public tokens of efficacious personhood. In this sense thakis may be seen as public indexes of subjective, chuyma-based processes, giving the lie to notions of insular chuymas.

A thaki is described as a movement to the center (taypi) of the community. The movement indexes the transformation from junior to senior status. Physically, a thaki entails a movement from a patrilocal house compound to the community center as well as to the parish center, where important fiestas take place and mallkus from the region meet. Alternatively, the movement to the center can be seen as constituting the mallku's household as the center of the community (it is here that the community will meet during his tenure), coordinated as it is with his transformation from subordinate son to senior father. This movement to the center is a process of embodiment: the mallku's productive physical transformation is iconic of the interlocked social and natural processes by which locality is produced and sustained; the ayllu *is* the mallku's household writ large. It is equally a process of mediation. As we saw in chapter 1, taypi is at once a microcosm of the whole and a point of encounter: between the composite moieties of an ayllu, between humans and the gods, between Aymara and the foreign powers that inform their world.

Thaki refers to additional public manifestations of embodied identity such as religious conversion. Membership in a Protestant church was described to me as a kind of thaki, while an association with what is taken to be traditional custom is frequently objectified as "the path of our ancestors" (*achachilanakasan thakipaxa*). Additionally, thaki appears as a metaphor of memory, invoked through ritual libations or ch'allas.[13] Sometimes combined into a sequence described as a "drinking path," ch'alla performances effect "pathways of memory" (e.g., Abercrombie 1986; Arnold 1992).

In these examples thaki describes the subjective positioning of Aymara actors. Whereas a fiesta-cargo career aligns individual life cycles within ongoing processes of community reproduction, the use of thaki to describe a religious identity suggests both a subjective option for an identity within a field of other possible paths and identity as not a stable thing but rather a process of experience and transformation, bound up with the public performance of personhood. The subjective anchor for such a commitment and the focus of this transformation is the chuyma. Similarly, ch'alla performances are effective inasmuch as they are authentic expressions of the state of the chuyma; they are exterior manifestations of an interior state of remembering: externalizing memory and translating it into the idiom of exchange and reciprocity. Life trajectories present a frame of engaged personhood. Like ch'allas and related offerings, they align the chuyma within a broader socioritual field. As we shall see, catechists draw explicitly on these models of personhood, bodily and social space, and subjective practice.

CATECHISTS

Thus far, I have situated missionary concerns about the doubleness of the catechists with respect to long-standing discussions of conversion and analogous conceptualizations of colonial and postcolonial settings. The supposed doubleness of the catechists parallels claims made about conjunctural contexts positing an enduring or resistant indigenous identity. Against this I have examined additional Aymara constructions of personhood. These reflect a sensibility of embodied identity that inverts missionary assumptions of an insular chuyma; here the chuyma enables a subjective engagement with a presupposed complex world. Turning now to the catechists, I start from the premise that they are not double and examine the ways these sensibilities of embodiment provide the means for them to negotiate identities—not as incomplete Christians, nor as marginal converts from Aymara tradition, but as situated actors within a manifold social world.

Subjects of Surveillance

Just as missionary constructions of catechists as double disclose a pastoral reading of conjunctural contexts, so the catechists offer a lens for examining additional perspectives on cultural articulation. Catechists are intensely aware of their intermediate position; their sense is that they are always being watched. While missionaries are preoccupied with the catechists as a locus of concealment, catechists attribute impressive perceptive powers to priests, who, although they rarely visit the community, are thought to be capable of knowing every detail of a catechist's activities. One catechist suggested that his priest has some kind of "apparatus" enabling him to view faith group meetings from afar.

Note that it is "inside" the Aymara community beyond the experience of pastoral agents—precisely where the Church feels itself to be most impotent and perceives the margins of its power to lie—where Aymara experience its most penetrative power: an omniscience that leaves every act revealed. This omniscience extends to the chuyma: as a result of the priest's surveillance, catechists claimed to feel incapable of deceiving him about their activities.[14]

This sense of being watched is not limited to relations with priests. Catechists manifest a strong self-consciousness of others' perceptions of their behavior in the community. "People are always looking at us," they told me, and some catechists routinely avoided participation in communal events, complaining about watchful eyes and gossip. Such comments reflect the pastoral vision of catechists as prototypes as well as a more widely expressed social value that a person's words should be aligned with his/her actions. This alignment of meaning and action is an index of chuyma-centered discourse, a sign of socioritual efficacy. More generally, this scrutiny may be part of the Aymara condition, living in a landscape studded with place deities and gossiping neighbors all of whom, as a condition of social existence, are embedded in relations of obligation and reciprocity. Priests and comparable outsiders are a presupposed and potent part of this lived Aymara landscape. It is within and with respect to this complex field of perspectives that catechists actualize their chuymas.

But we also find in the catechists' sense of surveillance a perspectival self-consciousness: an awareness of the ways they make sense from a range of interdependent, mutually presupposing perspectives. Such self-awareness figures in other discussions of embodiment and personhood.[15] It has also been suggested as a characteristic of globalization, (e.g., Hannerz 1992; Robbins 2001). In this sense the catechists are not dual, but complexly meaningful in a deeply valenced world. The ambivalence of the catechists is not an essential condition. Rather it is manifest in situated interactions within an entangled local setting. Much as with the case of the missionaries, who experience themselves as scrutinized by Aymara, the catechists' self-consciousness directs our attention to the ways such apparently composite, hybrid situations are realized and experienced as coherent lived social worlds.

Of Callings and Cargos: Catechists' Paths

As the concerns of the catechists reflect, a principal frame for such social worlds is the ayllu. A catechist's relations within his community are linked to the ways he became a catechist. Ideally, catechists are selected by their ayllus, but they may also be recruited by a priest or another catechist or emerge voluntarily. The distinction is significant. Those selected without community approval tend to be suspected and mistrusted by other community members. Those named by their ayllus are frequently men who have completed most of their fiesta-cargo obligations. At issue are the sorts of social and ritual legitimacy established through a cargo career.[16]

For a given individual all these modes of becoming a catechist may be "true." A faith group member recruited by his catechist or the parish priest to serve as catechist may also be confirmed in this position in a general meeting of his community. The same man may also assert that it was always his "will" to serve God and his community as a catechist. But these claims to legitimacy are invoked differentially and afford a catechist different footings in different situations (after Goffman 1981). In these shifting interactive projections of self, catechists draw upon the rhetoric of chuyma-grounded personhood and the organizing metaphor of life paths. In the previous chapter I examined some of the ways catechists anchor their legitimacy in the translocal authority of the Church, particularly in interactions taking place beyond their natal ayllus. In the contexts of their home communities, and as they negotiate their standing within the metacommunity of Aymara catechists, most catechists seek to constitute their position as a cargo—a burden imposed upon them by their communities—and describe their service as a "path" (thaki), clearly invoking the hierarchy of public offices that compose a fiesta-cargo career. A catechist's position within his community often depends upon his ability to frame his service in this way.

Tiwursio was a former Protestant pastor who left his congregation after a dispute with the members. After a period of years with no marked religious affiliation, he was invited by the catechist of the community to join the faith group. He told me he decided to join because "ever since I was young I always wanted to remember my Lord." The catechist died soon after that, and Tiwursio, who already had an extensive knowledge of the Bible from his days as pastor, began leading the faith group. This coincided with the papal visit to Bolivia in 1988, at which time a number of new catechists were recruited by the parish. A contingent of catechists and their wives, dressed as ayllu authorities, went to "receive" the pope in La Paz. There Tiwursio was given the "blessing" of the priest to serve as catechist. Coincidently, the following year Tiwursio served as mallku of his community. During his tenure the community formally named him as their catechist. In 1991 Tiwursio resigned his position as catechist, citing the expense and time commitment. His community refused his resignation, insisting that he continue his work. He took this as a vote of confidence he could not refuse.

Eusebio was a gnarled man in his sixties when I met him in 1990. Discussing his history as a catechist with me, Eusebio foreshadowed his adult service with reference to his childhood. He told me he grew up as an orphan with no relatives to teach him Christian doctrine. "Since I was a child, I searched for the Christian doctrine." In the early 1960s the parish priest began to recruit catechists. Eusebio was not the first catechist from his ayllu; that was a man called Florencio who founded the community's faith group. Eusebio told me it was Florencio who first selected him as a catechist: "Florencio brought me [to La Paz for a course]. I was an orphan." In a later interview Eusebio distanced himself from Florencio, a man who clashed severely with fellow ayllu members and ultimately turned to drinking, which, in Eusebio's recollection, led to his death. In this second, more detailed interview, Eusebio cast his emergence as a catechist as a function of his own "will" and presented the faith group as a result of his own pastoral work in the community. "The community did not name me [to serve as catechist], rather I went there myself. Myself. Myself there. With me the faith group rose up. With me we went. . . . The community did not name me. I went of my own will [voluntad]."

From the earliest years, when it appeared that everybody in the ayllu participated in the faith group, Eusebio narrated a steady decline in attendance. This is a common story. Eusebio blamed Protestants for the decline, though it is likely that his own stridently extirpative activities as well as those of his predecessor contributed to this intensifying marginalization. (Contrary to Eusebio's account, rumor has it that his predecessor and mentor was killed by the community.) The final blow to the faith group occurred in the mid-eighties when a young man from the faith group was accused of stealing a bull from another member of the ayllu. Eusebio was blamed for the youth's action—"They wanted to whip me"—and even more people left the group. Alienated from his community, and unsympathetic to the new pastoral directions of inculturation, Eusebio took some comfort from his recent ordination as a minister of communion, a validation he conceptualized along the lines of a thaki of increasing prestige and responsibility. "Now I alone am continuing from the beginning to until the end. Today not even the community wants to know [i.e., they don't participate in the faith group]. Now to have passed this service, now they [i.e., the parish] have arranged to select and they have named me as minister of communion. I only lack minister of sacraments, just this little bit is left." Eusebio died in 2000, still a minister of communion.

Alejandro, as I reported in chapter 3, had also been an active member of a Protestant congregation for some ten years when he was named by his ayllu to serve as catechist. As he told me,

> I began in 1985 to be a catechist and the community has supported me. The community has supported me, [saying] "you are going to be named as catechist, you are going to be a health promoter also." I had two cargos, now I am not the health promoter, although I continue with the courses.

"How did you begin?" I asked him. "Did you decide to be a catechist and then ask the community to select you?" He replied,

> I didn't decide. Rather, it is the community that decided. They have supported me. "He is going to be, he is going to assist us in the same work, yes, with this name he is going to help us in the community," they said to us.

"Why did they select you?"

> Because they want a humble person to be catechist. I am very humble. It depends upon the humility.

"Why do they want a humble person?"

> Because some people are bad, bad faiths, no? And they trust in that. Because it has to be a reliable person, because he has to inform them. We always have to inform the community, when there are courses, when I go to Machaqa or wherever, I always have to inform the community. I always have to advise the mallkus.

Alejandro is himself a somewhat marginal character in his ayllu. His father died when he was young, and his mother married a man from another patriline, leaving him with very weak ties to his patrikin. His elder brother also died at a young age, and Alejandro married his widow. Alejandro and Ruffina and her children (six by Alejandro, six by his brother) live in constant tension with neighboring households headed by Alejandro's FFBSs, who have pushed his family off the patrilineally controlled land, obliging them to cobble together rights to a nearby homestead.

Bonifacio must negotiate both his own contentious history within his community as well as the complexities of his relationship with his father, a powerful yatiri. In some settings, as we have seen, this involves a sleight of hand by which he appears to transfer filial ties and "successor" status to the parish priest. This is comparable to Eusebio's assertion that he was an orphan as part of his narrative describing his close relationship to the first catechist in his ayllu. In my conversation with him Bonifacio seemed to mix a number of strategies of legitimation. He first established his close link with the priest, identifying himself as an "acolyte" from the age of twelve. Significantly, before telling me about his formal decision to become a catechist, he stressed his cargo service (as p'iqi) to his community.

> I completed serving as *dirigente*. Then there was a course of catechists in Jesús de Machaqa. On my own, I was animated to go because I had heard the songs—the catechists sang beautifully. When I was young I listened to this. So, I went to Machaqa. There in Machaqa they spoke to me of the Bible, of Jesús, how he called his disciples. I listened and I informed myself, and [while praying] the Lord has called me from that moment.

Sons of a Priest

Whereas in visits to neighboring communities catechists tended to present themselves as representatives of the parish, "named" and "ordained" by the priest and

FIGURE 4.2   *A catechist and his faith group*

FIGURE 4.3   *Three catechists (in a picture they composed). The catechist in the middle was serving as mallku of his ayllu*

further empowered by their unique experiences of study and travel, within his own community a catechist is likely to emphasize the consensus underlying his authority. Alternatively, in interactions with pastoral agents or within their faith groups, many catechists tend to stress the voluntary nature of their service, often casting it as a calling from God. In faith group meetings, these sensibilities of a thaki and an individual calling converge: catechists assert an individual potency accruing from their life experience of travel and contact with Church personnel and manifest in their memorized knowledge of Catholic doctrine and familiarity with national and international current events. One catechist, exhorting his group to learn the doctrinal knowledge necessary to receive the sacrament of confirmation, aptly compared the rite to military service. As a rite of passage military service is a key index of Aymara male adulthood, and the rank hierarchy of the military is often used to explain the increasing social authority that accrues to someone over the course of a fiesta-cargo career. The comparison with military service also implies a broadening of capacities through translocal experience (recruits often serve in provinces far from home) and the locally potent knowledge this generates (cf. Huanca 1989:62 ff.).

Beyond their diplomatic value in the oppositional context of segmentary ayllu structures, these shifts across identities anchored in local communities, those anchored in translocal structures and practices, and identities deriving from more individual transactions with cosmic forces illustrate catechists' am-bivalence as it is negotiated in the terms of Aymara personhood. In stressing the voluntary nature of their service, catechists clearly evoke a chuyma-centered legitimacy; the most successful catechists are often compared to tra-ditional yatiris whose personal calling is manifest in the forms of physical char-acteristics, conditions of birth, or through such life-changing events as being struck by lightning (Huanca 1989). Although apparently in contrast with this assertion of individual capacity, being named by one's community—as people are annually appointed to positions in the civil-religious hierarchy—may also be seen, as in the cases of Tiwursio and Alejandro, as a public ratification of an interior condition consistent with the public alignment of personhood per-formed through a thaki.

When catechists I spoke with did efface local ties, they tended to do so in terms of local social structure: describing themselves as landless or orphaned. As I suggested in chapter 3, despite some correlation between structural mar-ginality and a tendency to serve (or to be named) as catechist, these statuses are more "classificatory" than "real": invoked as a way to manage translocal iden-tity. Indeed, these are the public connections of male personhood, which we have seen is inherited patrilineally. In these cases catechists often stressed their affiliation with the local parish in terms of filial ties, transposing their connec-tion to the Church into the personhood constituting idiom of kinship and de-scent. Moreover, the doctrinal knowledge controlled by catechists is held by many Aymara to be traditional Aymara knowledge, once faithfully passed from father to son but now increasingly forgotten.

The key point here is that catechists experience, negotiate, and assert their identities within the embodied idiom of Aymara personhood. In their claims of filial connections to the priests, the catechists embody Catholic doctrinal authority as locally embedded, chuyma-grounded knowledge, as the situated classificatory descendants not of the ancestors but of (traditional) Catholic priests. Alternatively, catechists may describe themselves as embarked upon a thaki: constructing their lived history of catechetical service as a process of so-cial maturation entailing embodied transformations. Newly entering catechists are referred to as "infants," junior catechists—like young men and novice mal-lkus—are said to be "silent" or "afraid" to speak. Catechists speak of slowly learning the knowledge required of them, of becoming better able to "carry" their thakis as a function of catechetical knowledge and experience entering their chuymas. One catechist, recently elevated to the position of lay minister, described his humility upon "being made to receive" the increased ritual po-tency and responsibility of his position. Rather than asserting his identity categorically as a function of his title, he sought to index his capacity in terms of his chuyma: "My chuyma now has a little learning," he said, "and my chuyma always wants to learn." He evoked this learning as an "increase" effected by "words," asking his fellow catechists, "How will these words enter (*mantitasp*) into us?" There are similar references to agricultural growth: catechists are like newly sown seeds; people are watching to see "how we will sprout" (*kunjams chillqtañani*), assessing the catechists "like a tree or a fruit, how will [we] grow?" (*kunjamats jiltapxataxa*).

As a spatial metaphor conflating conversion, descent, and seniority, thaki evokes a process leading catechists ultimately to the status of priests. Catechists see themselves positioned within a hierarchy stretching from the faith group members they supervise to the priests and bishops to whom they are accountable. The hierarchy is explicitly conceived along the lines of a fiesta-cargo career, with additional comparisons to promotions in the army and formal education[17]. Yet whereas the structural "in-betweenness" of such brokers has classically been seen as crossing a boundary that otherwise separates indigenous locality from exogenous forces and contexts, the thakis of the catechists reflect not the rupture of locality but the situated, chuyma-grounded mediation of translocal contexts.

THINKING ABOUT ALL PLACES; REMEMBERING GOD

The intercalary ambivalence of catechists is further manifest in associations with positions of Aymara social and ritual authority. I have already noted practical similarities between catechists and other intermediaries such as risiris and mayordomos. While they have their origins in missionary encounters, these positions and the Catholic doctrinal knowledge associated with them are held to be traditional, dated by some to before the Iberian invasion. In this sense catechists appear as revoicings of autochthonous cultural knowledge, the forgetting of which is lamented by contemporary Aymara.

In addition, catechists are constituted as similar to Aymara community authorities: jilaqatas or mallkus. Like mallkus, their authority is cast in metaphors of kinship and herding. Faith group members refer to themselves as "followers" (*arkirinaka*); a catechist may refer to them as his children (*wawanakajax*) or more commonly as a herd (*tama*). Among themselves, at the level of the parish, catechists enact their own relations of authority with rotating yearly posts, comparable to those of the mallkus. Similarly, catechists' declared responsibility to "think about" all the people and places under their care are resonant

with the conception of a mallku who must encompass the ayllu by constituting his chuyma as the symbolic center. One catechist, reflecting on his first
year of service at the elevated position of minister of sacraments, commented:

> Now I have understood. It is a great sadness for me, and as a [mallku] has
> sorrow, this year there has been much sorrow. How will things go for the
> people? What will be? How is a new marriage working out? There is much
> preoccupation. Do they speak, or will there be fights? What will not be
> good? What disputes will there be? It is very difficult to become like a
> good herder. One must never make any mistakes in what one does. You
> must think about everything, as I think about all places.

This sense of catechist identity as a burden—"like a great sorrow" (jach'a llak-
jamakiw)—stems from another parallel to community service: the great economic strain placed on catechists. Similarly, just as mallkus are held accountable for misfortunes occurring during their tenure or p'iqi's responsible for the
conduct of members of their zones, the experiences of Eusebio suggest that
catechists may be held responsible for the actions of their faith group members
(cf. Albó 1991a:222).

Finally, there are significant links between the identities of catechists and
yatiris. These concern the capacity to memorize and recite knowledge and
again evoke a chuyma-based view of socioritual efficacy. Indeed, the substance
of catechists' knowledge—Catholic prayers and doctrinal formulae—figures
prominently in the repertoires of yatiris and (when originating from the
chuyma) is a valued component of ritual transactions with place deities.

In the faith group meetings I attended, catechists and their followers clearly constituted their activities as chuyma-grounded transactions of knowledge
and sentiment. Not only do catechists negotiate their legitimacy in such embodied terms, but the catechizing of faith group members entails the penetration of their chuymas by doctrinal knowledge: they speak of the Word of God
"arriving" into their chuymas; of "receiving" the Word "in" their chuymas;
of "tying" the knowledge to their chuymas. These spatial relations correspond
to discussions of the chuyma from other domains of Aymara life, as does the
metaphor of tying that we have seen in the discussion of Ingrid's soul, which
here evokes the internalizing domestication or control of the knowledge. This
is not an assault on embodied insularity; the Christian doctrine does not seem
to displace other knowledge. Rather the faith group appears as a space for the
authoritative local control of the doctrine. Control is manifest through memorization: the somatic harnessing and transsomatic circulation of Christian
meaning and doctrinal formulae.

Faith group worship circulates this ritual knowledge, offering it to God. As with other chuyma-based ritual transactions, this is an exchange of memory for vitality and fertile abundance. Faith group members request health, wealth, and productive abundance of God. The potency deriving from God is typically invoked in embodied terms, often under the rubric of strength or force. Group members constantly complain of their physical debility, sometimes citing named illnesses but more generally lamenting an overwhelming weakness. This may be self-consciously asserted as a defining feature of the contemporary Aymara condition, contrasted with ancestors (whose diet and ritual capacities were a source of vitality) as well as with powerful contemporary others. Faith group participation is a channel for rectifying this condition: group members describe themselves as thin, without fat, entreating God, through the chuyma-grounded exchange of memorized doctrine, to sustain them, to complete them, to give them strength.

I detail these and other faith group practices in chapters 5 and 6. At issue for the moment is the alignment of Aymara chuymas with the word of God, an alignment mediated and embodied by the catechists. Catechists and faith group members, as a function of this mediation, engage external potency to the highly local ends of producing and sustaining Aymara bodies and communities. The catechists' intermediate positions enable them to interact with exotic but necessary forces considered threatening to other Aymara: church bell towers, paraphernalia from Catholic altars, priests themselves.[18]

Alternatively, aspects of catechists' learning are cast as the means for retrieving and systematizing ancestral knowledge. This is an ironic inversion of the theology of inculturation, for here it is rote knowledge of "colonial" doctrine rather than its rejection that constitutes catechists as instantiations of the ancestors. As a function of this nostalgia, school-based learning becomes the source of catechists' capacities to acquire the chuyma-based knowledge of yatiris. Other Aymara suggested an equivalence between catechists and yatiris turning around literacy, consonant with the observations of faith group activities presented earlier in this chapter. The difference between them was often described as merely formal: the catechist reads the Bible; the yatiri reads coca.[19]

The parallel is significant. While many catechists (who built their reputations denouncing yatiris) would reject my comparison, their denunciations reveal the fundamental identity of the contrasted pair. Thus, catechists claim, a yatiri relates to the devil as a catechist relates to God; yatiris "do not raise up the name of God"; the thaki of yatiris is "to a different side," a "separate revelation." Yet the interactions posited by this ethnotheory of doubleness are identical: acts of reciprocal exchange effected via chuyma-grounded transactions of knowledge and sentiment. Aymara burning offerings to a wak'a and those reciting prayers in the chapel each describe their acts as vehicles of re-membering. The relationship of reciprocity they entail is invoked with the same term: *katuqaña* (to receive). In this sense the thaki of religious identity indexes the interactive orientation of a chuyma, embodying a subjective perspective within a field of entangled "revelations."

The divided Aymara self of missionary discourse is thus half the story—and doubly so. On the one hand, the passive metonymic body evoking conjunctural processes is complemented by active situated selves. Such bodies are at once objects of reference and instruments of practice, artifacts of a conflicted world and socially embedded seats of subjective action through which the world is experienced and made. In this light the ambivalence of the catechists stems neither from their internal duality nor from an affliction of colonial trauma they passively bear. It derives rather from the historical interdependence and porousness of the categories of social difference they condense and mediate as well as from sensibilities of personhood that constitute identity out of a subjective history of chuyma-grounded interactions and enable the negotiation of a range of perspectives within a manifold social world. On the other hand, among these situated selves are the missionaries themselves, deeply implicated in the world they reference through Aymara bodies. At issue, then, are not structural fault lines conjoining and dividing discrete cultural systems but the complexly positioned practices out of which social worlds are constituted, apprehended, and mediated. More than reflecting history, the body is a crucial means of its making through the engagement of missionary and Aymara selves as entangled communities of practice.

That said, the categories and conflicts that missionaries map onto the catechists' bodies are certainly salient in Aymara thought and experience (cf. Gose 1994b; Sallnow 1987:15 ff.). Many Aymara articulate a highly racialized view of the world in which whites are seen as the inversion of Aymara principles of cosmic fertility and social reproduction, with priests the most long-standing local tokens of this type. In disputes with their communities the otherwise authorizing identity of catechists with priests becomes an ethnic slur: during my field stay a catechist involved in the often contentious local distribution of food aid was called a thief and accused of "stealing like a priest." More gravely, catechists are accused of being *kharikhari* (fat stealers), an accusation with deeply racial implications (see chapter 6).

Much like other brokers, the catechists are in an ambiguous, conflicted position. Their thakis trace the interactional space of such paradoxical contexts. I have argued that missionary constructions of the catechists as double reveal an evangelical perspective on conjunctural history conflating dualizing ap-

proaches to the body and a comparable tendency in the ethnographic and ethnohistorical literature on the Andes and in similar syncretic contexts. While
we need not look beyond Western data for alternative paradigms of embodiment, I have focused on the practices and experiences of the Aymara catechists
as these reflect and draw upon sensibilities of embodied identity with implications quite distinct from those supposed by missionaries. Indeed, what in the
missionary characterization appears as an inert core of Aymaraness, insulated
from the complexity of evangelization—i.e., the chuyma—appears in other
ethnographic data as a seat of translocal practice, a vehicle of positioned entanglement par excellence. Social personhood appears here as a ceaselessly unfolding process (or thaki) of situated subjective (chuyma-grounded) engagement with a complex world. Far from reifying a stable, homogeneous, or
discrete Aymara perspective within a disjunctive Aymara/Christian contrast,
my aim in this discussion has been to situate a range of missionaries and Aymara as component subjects of local Andean society. It is the situated experiences of such complex local social orders that is my concern. My claim is that
one of the ways contrasting identities are mediated and revalued is through
sensibilities of personhood keyed not on the semantic foci of oppositional
identities, but rather on the subjective negotiation of this grid of cultural difference. Chuyma-grounded trajectories of thaki serve as a counterpoint to a
dualized cultural history underscoring the translocal dimensions of apparently
local practices and organizing the situated experiences of entangling colonial
and postcolonial processes as lived worlds.

CHAPTER 5

Alejandro's House: The Porous Production of Locality

Everyone was mad at Alejandro.

His wife bitterly resented the time his duties as catechist took away from his work around the house and in the fields. And she complained often about the incidental expenses of his travels to catechist courses. The recent opening of the center for catechist training in Laja, with its frequent course offerings, only intensified this domestic friction.

Alejandro was also serving as president of his pastoral zone. There were three of these in Jesús de Machaqa: groups of ayllus organized roughly along the lines of sindicatos, with annually rotating positions of leadership. However, the other catechists in Alejandro's zone felt he was not devoting enough time to organizing events for the zone, neglecting to visit his catechist colleagues to inspire them in their labors, and so forth. When he did finally organize a zonewide meeting, it was to mark the end of his tenure, at which event, in classic Aymara style, his presidency was roundly criticized and he was reappointed to serve another year.

Alejandro was also engaged in a rivalry of varying intensity with Bonifacio, the senior catechist in the community. Bonifacio had been among the Aymara catechists aspiring to the diaconate during the first efflorescence of the catechist movement in the late 1970s. That initiative collapsed before his promotion, and he seemed to chafe at his reversion to catechist status. Bonifacio considered himself more learned and worldly than his catechist consociates. He was not pleased when a second catechist—Alejandro—was named in his community. He informed Alejandro that he would have to form his *own* faith group, and, for a period of time, there were two separate faith groups meeting in the community: followers of Bonifacio met in the community chapel, followers of Alejandro met in a small space sometimes used for meetings by the community's Mothers' Club. With Bonifacio elevated to the newly created position of minister of sacraments and frequently out of the community, the two groups met under the direction of Alejandro. Bonifacio attended meetings from time to time, often affecting the bearing of a busy supervisor-priest there to check in on his flock and check up on his subordinate. The tensions remained, and the Bonifacio faction of the faith group was often critical of Alejandro.

All of this compounded Alejandro's structurally marginal position as an orphaned younger brother. As will be recalled from the previous chapter, the deaths of his father and his elder brother along with his mother's remarriage into a different patriline left Alejandro in an intercalary position with regard to his father's family. Although Alejandro remarried his brother's widow, his family was violently evicted from the patriline's land, and Alejandro, now near fifty, lives in a state of simmering feud with his father's patrilateral parallel cousins.

And now some members of the community were going around condemning Alejandro for being stingy (mich'a). The problem was his house. Representatives of a development NGO—Plan International—had proposed two projects to the community. One involved livestock. They would introduce a larger breed of sheep to a few selected families who in exchange would build sheltered pens for the resulting hybrid herds. The second involved houses. The Plan would supply metal roofing material (calamina) to a few selected families who would construct the remainder of the house according to plans provided by the NGO. Alejandro was selected by his community to participate by building a house.

In my view this house-building project was a bad deal. Unlike typical altiplano houses—small, one-room structures opening onto an enclosed patio—the Plan house was a massive structure comprising a kitchen, a living room, and two separate bedrooms. The plans called for a cement floor, plaster-covered adobe walls, large glass windows in each room, and wooden doors between the rooms. Beyond the considerable investment of time and labor, constructing the houses according to the plan—a condition for receiving the roof—was expensive. The families involved each had to sell off some livestock to cover the costs of purchasing materials and trucking them out to the community.

When I met with the project architect to express my concerns, he told me that the houses had been planned in consultation with rural Aymara. Asked essentially to describe their dream house, they described the sorts of two- and three-story brick structures that are popular among families living in El Alto—a sprawling city of rural to urban migrants on the outskirts of La Paz. The architect had modulated this somewhat to rural altiplano reality, but retained some of the modern urban feel attractive to his Aymara consultants and the features that rendered the house ideologically appealing to the Plan. These had to do with the presumed moral and sanitary benefits of having well-lit and

FIGURE 5.1   *Alejandro's house*

ventilated rooms and distinct sleeping areas in which, it was hoped, family members could be segregated by gender or generation.

Alejandro built his house largely with the labor assistance of his family, three members of his faith group, Ingrid, and myself. He also engaged in occasional mink'a and ayni exchange relations with four other community members—including people building houses or sheep pens—though these were less frequent. The accusation of being stingy referred to Alejandro's avoidance of more widespread relations of debt. Had he invited more people to work for him, went the implicit argument, more people would have a greater claim on his labor.

I initially understood this dispute to reveal the impact of my participation in house building upon the local economy of labor prestations. I still believe this, and feel responsible in other ways for Alejandro's situation, since he was "volunteered" to benefit from a new house so he would have a proper ("urban"?) place to house the gringo who was a steady guest of his family. However, I have come to think as well that this criticism is also grounded in a more profound way in tensions inherent in the positions of the catechists within their communities.

In this chapter I focus on the apparently conflicted situation of the catechists and their faith group members, examining the ways their identity is constituted and negotiated—by them as well as by others—as meaningful and authoritative in their home community settings. Catechists and faith groups are certainly ambivalent figures in Aymara communities, publicly rejecting many traditional practices and subject to a variety of suspicions and accusations ranging from mundane claims of stinginess to more drastically antisocial acts such as stealing body fat. But this embattled identity is not a straightforward matter of tradition displaced or local integrity ruptured from without. As I have argued in the previous chapter, rather than approach the catechists as marginal converts from tradition, the task is to locate them within and with respect to the porous production of Andean locality. In this light the embattled position of the catechists stems from ambivalences and productive tensions entailed at the most microlevel, apparently traditional, settings of Aymara experience.

On the one hand, this is an elaboration of a claim I have been making about locality and the complex condition of what are taken to be the most insular sites of indigenous traditions. Alongside the foregoing discussion of sensibilities of the body as a site of entangling engagement with the world, in this chapter I examine the Aymara household. The household and its reproduction serve as a template and component of encompassing processes of community reproduction. We have seen that community authorities are figured as mother and father to the ayllu and that their service is coordinated with the cycle of household reproduction and the annual cycle of agrarian production. In comparable ways catechists draw upon templates of ayllu- and household-level authority, often casting their own ritual knowledge and potency in the idiom of local ancestral powers and positioning the faith group as a site for controlling and localizing the circulation of social value. As with any household, too much success in this is a bad thing: the charge of stinginess against Alejandro verges on a charge of incest—his faith group members are in this sense classificatory members of a single household, and so not meaningful exchange partners.

Similarly, too much success on my part in this line of analysis verges on another sort of incest: a self-perpetuating regionalist theory positing an enduring Aymara difference reproduced in challenging circumstances. This is not my aim. An important goal of this and the following chapters is to examine the shifting conditions and interpenetrations of micro- and macrolocality, as the processes that ceaselessly constitute locality and reference and reproduce the entangling contexts of its production. The locality reproduced is thus always transformed, accountable to multiple vantages and valuations of locality, from microlocal sensibilities of day-to-day sociality to metacultural assertions of Aymara identity. In this chapter I review household-level practices as a backdrop for examining catechists' relations to their faith groups and their differential participation as ritual authorities in ayllu-level events and in the worship practices of the faith groups.

HOUSES AND SAYAÑAS

Perhaps the smallest unit of social structure in Jesús de Machaqa is the *sayaña:* a plot of patrilineally held land including houses, corrals, and land used for grazing and agriculture. The term is aptly homonymous with the Aymara verb *sayaña* (to stand); a sayaña is a particular patriline's place. The quasi-private character of the sayaña is clear when the term is contrasted with the other salient category of land: *aynoqa*. Aynoqa lands are extensive tracts of grazing and agricultural land. Aynoqa production is coordinated communally through the leadership of the mallku, who determines which fallow fields will begin a cycle of annual plantings in potatoes, quinoa, broad beans, barley, etc.

Most families in Jesús de Machaqa have access to more than one sayaña. Most maintain a herding house high in the mountains: a sparse compound of corrals, a kitchen, and a few simple sleeping quarters. Some have a series of houses at different elevations and may count additional households in the community center, in Jesús de Machaqa pueblo, and in La Paz as part of their extended archipelago of sayañas.

Typically, a sayaña contains the households of a group of brothers or male paternal parallel cousins. The ideal pattern described to me was that the youngest son remain in his parents' household, while older brothers establish separate households organized around distinct patios. Two married brothers, I was told, ought not to share a house compound. The unthinkability of this has to do with the close connection between households and identity and the salience of each family of procreation as a crucial link of generational continuity; much like the chuyma discussed in chapter 4, the household is a processual locus of personhood. One upshot of this is a continuous process of fissioning within the sayaña, as it is reconfigured with each generation of new households of procreation within the patriline.[1]

A sayaña is also a named place or a set of named place deities invoked by the residing family. Typically, these include a flat place—*pampa* or *wirjin* (Sp. virgin)—coded as female, complemented by a higher place or peak—sometimes called *achachila*—coded as male. Household members claim close relations with these proximate place deities, though they may also invoke more distant place deities linked with other sayañas or with their community or region.

As with the fit between ayllu and community, sayañas do not map neatly onto the notion of household. I will be focusing here on the processes by which a single family of procreation produces a household. Borrowing from sociolinguistics, I approach the household as an emerging deictic center: an anchor point, a here-and-now center, producing, placing, and aligning household members within a sociocultural landscape. Abercrombie (1986:142) has suggested that the creation of a new household entails the creation of a new set of deities; that a new household is a new place to ch'alla to. I would add that a new household is equally a new place to ch'alla *from;* a footing for engaging the world.

Other work on Aymara households has figured them as the intersection of gendered paths of memory, termed *wila thaki* (path of blood) and *muju thaki* (path of semen) (Arnold 1992, 1997). The latter refers to patrilineal ties that root a given household to its sayaña place. The former refers to the lateral movements of women between patrilocal households. The challenge for constituting a new patrilocal household is transforming the tenuous conditions of its origins into a form of publicly ratified legitimacy. A newlywed couple must transcend their ambiguous status as not-yet-independent junior male and outsider junior female to establish a household whose authenticity rests upon compelling connections of patrilineal continuity and authorizing translocal entanglements. Specifically, the process of household production involves a coordinated process of domesticating the foreign woman (who will become the embodiment of the household center and the mother of patrilineal descendents) and engaging in the most public indexes of social legitimacy through outward-oriented paths of public service to the ayllu.

The Daily Grind

House compounds (*utanaka*) consist of multiple houses opening onto an enclosed patio. Houses are typically made of adobe and stone, with peaked roofs covered with thatched altiplano grass or with corrugated metal. The compounds include sleeping quarters, storage buildings, and a kitchen. Corrals and low adobe walls complete the enclosure. Couples often begin construction of an independent household after the births of their first children. An expanding social network of compadres and other nonkin is crucial for a functioning household.[2]

A house compound is an evolving lifelong project. It is never done. However, a young couple can be said to be minimally independent with the establishment of their kitchen and its semipublic counterpart, the *misaqala*. The kitchen is arguably the most private, intimate space in the household. Family members eat meals together squatting in its smoky warmth. Even in those households I felt on most familiar terms with, households where I was welcomed to share meals and beds, I never felt fully comfortable entering a kitchen unbidden. The misaqala is a low square table of flat stone, often set in front of a low bench (of adobe or stone) fronting one of the buildings or walls in the patio. It is a combination altar, sitting room, and food preparation center. Grains and spices are ground there with the aid of a large curved stone. It serves as a table for the final stages of butchering and the initial processes of salting and drying meat to produce *charki* (jerky). The misaqala also serves as an altar: a site of offering. Covered with a cloth, ch'allas are poured to the four corners of the stone. Other reports suggest that the misaqala is the site of buried household deities or secret bundles. Finally, the misaqala is the site for receiving guests. Visitors invited are often seated in front of the table and served from it.

This combination of practices underscore the condition of the household as a ritual site—a focus and frame of chuyma-grounded transactions of sentiment comprising interactions with place deities, formal service to the ayllu, as well as more day-to-day transactions of sociability. However, they also point us to the household as more than just a place, but as a process. The misaqala-kitchen nexus reveals the household as a site of incorporation and domestication, as reflected in the grinding down of raw materials in preparation for cooking. Among the raw, unsocialized material ground down and incorporated into the household is the young couple itself, especially the in-marrying

FIGURE 5.2   *House compounds consist of multiple structures opening on to an enclosed patio*

FIGURE 5.3 *Misaqala*

woman. Recall that the newlyweds are treated as unsocialized infants—a sort of raw potential that must, under the guidance of their in-laws and godparents, make themselves as they reproduce society. This is particularly stark in the case of the bride. In some accounts the woman is led away from her parents' house like a captured animal (Carter and Mamani 1982).[3] Related data on courtship rites report these taking place in fallow fields or highlands pastures at the limits of socialized space (Buechler and Buechler: 1971). Another important site of courtship and sexual liaisons among young Aymara is fiestas. Indeed, the fiesta enacts a marriage between the component moieties of the ayllu represented by the competing and merging troupes of dancers. Recall as well that the "troupes" of young fiesta dancers are metaphorically figured as herds of wild camelids, said to descend from the high mountains to "dance" on the flat agricultural fields and so fertilize them.

The misaqala–kitchen nexus also reveals a correlated spatial dynamic crosscutting this process and opposing the enclosed privacy of the kitchen (or of any interior house space), with the semipublic space of the patio, and the more public spaces beyond the patio walls. Other work casts the Aymara household as a concentric and gendered space: a female center encompassed by male activity (e.g., Arnold 1992; cf. Salomon 1991). And here we have the remarkable alchemy of the household as a site of domestication: the foreign woman, moving laterally along a path of blood from household to household, is transformed through the process of household reproduction into the stable center of the house. In house-building libations and other ritual references, households are referred to as "nests of gold and silver," as treasure chests and cornucopias—a sort of centralized site of wealth and fertility that is embodied by Aymara women. The Andean (male?) aesthetic preference for a woman of some girth or "substance" is well known; the look is often exaggerated through the wearing of multiple layers of clothing. The concentration of value indexed here is evident in a correlated register as women also are typically the keepers of the purse strings in their households. Among my earliest field experiences in Qhunqhu Milluni was attending a meeting of a section (zona) of the ayllu at which I observed the men vigorously debate and approve an obligatory contribution of Bs.10 (about $3) from each household to support a community project. A good number of the men then had to walk sheepishly over to their wives, who sat silently observing the action and ask them for the cash. The operative contrast here is of the woman as a fertile concentrating local center and the man as a translocal and potentially entropic, dissipating satellite. Hence the common complaints by women that men have no head at all for saving money and would waste it all away were their wives not there to hold it for them. Hence, in part, Alejandro's wife's complaint about the financial impact of his outward-oriented catechetical activities.

A house presents an enclosed gendered space that is at once a site of stored value incorporated from without to within and a source of fertile activity generated and emanating from within to without. This is the other side of the concentricity of the household: the house as a footing for outward-oriented practices. Beyond the ubiquitous public currency of sociability evident in interhousehold networks of reciprocal debt and obligation, the most prototypical of these, integrally involved in the processual production of household, is public service to the ayllu. Cargo aspirants represent their sayañas before the ayllu. The set of "persons" engaged in cargo paths corresponds roughly to the viable households in the community; cargo service, for instance, is a condition for a household's access to communal aynoqa fields. The cargo paths traversed by all legitimate social persons are thus outward paths constituting the sayaña by aligning it publicly with a "braided" network of other such paths. Far from given, households are ceaselessly produced. And these paths of personhood entangle the production of households within a complex translocal field.

Recall that a fiesta cargo path is explicitly figured as a path to the center of the ayllu. On the one hand, this involves the literal movement of people (through ritual and administrative pilgrimages) to sites of taypi: the symbolic center of the ayllu, the reduction town of Jesús de Machaqa, the city of La Paz.

On the other hand, this entails the refiguring of a given household as itself the center of the ayllu, much as the cargo couple is figured as father and mother of the ayllu. In preparation for their culminating year of cargo service, a couple often builds a new house in which all members of the community are welcomed. In cases I have observed these houses have misaqalas inside: permanent altar/tables on which coca and alcohol are continuously available. Similarly, ayllu authorities begin their terms by hosting the community in their patio, and ayllu meetings often take place at the mallku's house. Finally, note that the symbolic center of the ayllu—the location of the chapel, the site of fiestas—is itself a quasi household: the walled churchyard (sacristuyu) is marked by the presence of a public misaqala.

Shimmering Centers and the Silence of Thatch

The Aymara household well embodies the condition of taypi, a zone of completion and mediation between two complementary categories. Rather than a fixed state or position, we have seen that taypi is an evanescent achievement of social practice. And, it will be recalled, this is a good thing. For like all utopian conditions, taypi evokes both abundance and completion as well as sterile stagnation—the terrible perfection of a system based in the productive tension of contrasting values.

As taypi, the Aymara household is a space of mediation—a localized microcosm of Aymara spacetime. Physically, a house condenses and integrates a variety of ecologically distinct resources. In Jesús de Machaqa a combination of salt and aji pepper (prototypical highlands and lowlands products, respectively) are placed at the corners of the excavated site prior to setting the cornerstones or adobes. The house is also sometimes figured as stretching between the interior of the earth (manqhapacha) and the sky (glurya/alaxpacha). This mediation of earth and sky is also evident in representations of the house as an animated structure: a plant with roots underground and a flowering roof/tip stretching skyward. The grass added to the mud in the manufacture of adobes is described as "roots" (saphi), thought to grow in the house and to help it to "stand." Dung and blood are also sometimes used in the adobe mixture, the finished walls are occasionally aspersed with llama blood—all of which is held to communicate a certain vertical vitality to the structure. The roof—a thicket of grass, mud, and wind-blown and bird-scattered seed that needs little symbolic help to evoke the fertility of plant growth—is often adorned with flowerlike crosses or white flags. At least part of the attraction of metal roofing, as far as I could tell, was its reflective shimmering quality. A man who had constructed a new house as part of the same development scheme Alejandro was involved in once pointed out his house to me from a distance. The new roof gleamed. "Look how it shines," he remarked with some pride, "just like a flower."

The case at hand suggests an extension of this scope of social and spatial mediation. For the construction of Alejandro's house involved the entangling relationship of Alejandro and the community with the NGO Plan International. Beyond the transnational scope of the plan is the aesthetic of the house itself, which was designed to evoke the lifestyle of a successful urban migrant.[4] In this sense the house stands as a localized embodiment of urban values. This is not far from the aims of the development agency. (A similar case could be made about the sheep; different breeds are often reckoned in an idiom of racial and ethnic difference. Thus during fieldwork in 1999 as I was being teased by a group of ayllu authorities for traveling to Bolivia without my wife, one man suggested that they soon would be seeing a generation of taller and light-skinned children born in the area. Another chimed in that they would probably also notice a larger breed of sheep.) While I have since stayed in the house during return visits, I never stayed in the new house during my longest stretch of fieldwork, preferring to remain in a vacant smaller, warmer, and older thatched roofed structure that Ingrid and I fixed up. When the new house was completed, one of Alejandro's teenage sons moved in. Luis was a young man who spent a few months of each year in La Paz/El Alto, where some relatives helped him find work, and the remainder finishing his final years of school in Qhunqhu. After each of these periods of residence in the city, Luis chafed at the transition to life in the country. Walking around with a radio/tape player blaring (until his supply of batteries ran out), he complained to me about, among other things, thatched roofs. He preferred calamina roofs—because they were pretty and reflective and rattled noisily in the wind and rain. The noise reminded him of the city. After living there, he said, he couldn't sleep under the silence of thatch.

Time and Taypi

With the emergence of a household as a context of autonomous social life, a couple establish themselves as a productive intersection of matrilines and patrilines, a denotable point in the transactional fabric of Aymara social life, and a spatial and genealogical anchor of social identity. Households are sites of spatial and temporal mediation. Here I want to examine the household as a mnemonic of genealogical continuity, a temporal taypi bridging past and future.

Descent in the Andes is a vexed topic: the literature suggests a mix of patrilineal, cognatic and parallel descent. Most discussions agree, and my research confirms, that genealogical memory in the region is typically quite shallow: three to five generations. In a classic discussion of Aymara kinship, Hickman and Stuart describe a "*tunu:*" a three-generational exogamous unit of kinship, which they describe as a "fundamental building block" of Aymara kinship. A tunu is relationally rendered a four-generational unit as a son reckons marriageability according to his father's tunu (i.e., his father, father's father, and father's father's father).[5]

Although I did not encounter the term *tunu* in my fieldwork, this was about as far as most of the people I knew in Jesús de Machaqa could remember on their own. Yet people routinely talked about a more encompassing unit of genealogical memory spanning five generations, sometimes illustrated with the fingers on one hand (cf. Urton 1997:73 ff). They referred to this as *alchin alchipax*: the grandchild of the grandchild, which, in essence, is two tunus linked together. I want to focus on this five-generational unit of genealogical memory as it underscores the household as a site of transtemporal mediation.

For while households are always important sites of continuity in any sort of descent system, within a patrilineal, patrilocal setting, shallow genealogical memory intensifies this position of the household. Unlike larger genealogical systems with institutionalized memory of distant, focal ancestors, in a situation such as the Andes the system is more ephemeral, and the household more integral to its continuous reproduction. Indeed, the household is directly responsible for mediating the relationship between the living and the recently dead, who are the only ancestors remembered as individuals.

Now, within the frame of alchin alchipax, it is the senior members of a household—adults whose children have young children—who embody genealogical positions of taypi, who realize the greatest transtemporal mediation available to Aymara. These are men who are at once focal ancestors for an emerging tunu and the last to remember their grandparents, now ancestors long dead. The successful production of household locality entails, among other things, the achievement of this temporal continuity. What is more, given the extended sequences of cargo service, this position of genealogical taypi correlates with the sorts of spatial mediation involved in positioning the household as the center of the ayllu, a site of transpatial integration resulting from service as mallku. For the moment of greatest seniority in the cargo system—the public performance of prototypical fatherhood—often coincides with this moment of greatest household seniority indexed by the subordination of young affines who have not yet established their own independent household. To be sure, I idealize this correlation—consultants did not explicitly link them. Still, I juxtapose them to underscore the broader point about the house as itself porously produced, entangling past and present, inside and outside.

CATECHISTS AND THEIR FAITH GROUPS

Catechists' relations with faith group members are, like many other expressions of public authority, modeled on household-level relations. However, whereas the relationship of a mallku as father of the ayllu is an unambiguously positive and productive one, at the level of the faith group, as at the level of the household, this is more ambiguous. That is, a household must negotiate a fine line separating the inward-looking production of itself and the outward public service of the ayllu. To retreat from the latter is the direction of sterile and antisocial autonomy. Faith groups and their members are in an embattled and ambivalent position, but one that is translatable in terms of local notions of legitimacy and cultural production. A key dimension of this translatability concerns the harnessing of distant value for local ends.

There is a strong, quasi-familial identity between faith group members and a given catechist. In the eyes of many Aymara, catechists are metonymic of the entire religious identity: faith group members are referred to as *catequistas*. The experience of Alejandro, who upon becoming a catechist was told initially by Bonifacio that he would have to form his own faith group, further suggests the role of the catechist as a leader who must constitute his leadership by attracting a group of followers. This is often achieved through kin and fictive kin ties. Members of a catechist's family typically constitute a core group within the faith group. Through gifts of food during the shared meals that punctuate every group meeting, through labor service (i.e., preparing and serving meals at intercommunity events), through a well-placed glare silencing group members whispering during the catechist's homily, and through well-timed gossip these kin assist in the smooth running of the faith group and the establishment of the catechist's authority in the context of the group and in the wider community.

Catechists also tend to establish numerous fictive kin (*compadrazgo*) ties within their faith groups. In the Andes compadrazgo ties exceed the ritual sponsorship of Catholic-derived sacraments and include additional life-crisis rituals (such as ratucha, the first haircutting) as well as events such as school graduations and completion of military service. These ties form an important part of the wider web of relations of debt and reciprocity that characterize Aymara social maturity (see Allen 1988). In the case of intrafaith group compadrazgo ties, these are typically asymmetric, with the catechist serving as *padrino* to faith group members or their children.[6] Alternatively, when catechists are searching for godparents for one of their children, they are likely to seek out another catechist. Obviously, catechists' ritual expertise largely determines their popularity as ritual sponsors and guides as well as their own sense that only another catechist could be a fitting padrino. But two additional points can be made here. First, within this grid of debt and reciprocity catechists constitute their authority within the faith group through asymmetric group internal relations. Second, catechist operate across or negotiate multiple frames of social interaction of differing scale: one the one hand, intra-ayllu and intrafaith group connections, on the other a regional network of catechists that constitute a meta-Aymara community. While mediating such levels of social phenomena is not new (ayllu authorities accomplish this), the mission practices and catechist pastoral models pose shifting implications for moving across these levels.

The cohesiveness of the faith group as a social unit is further underscored by a tendency to exchange labor within the group. I refer here to ayni- and mink'a-type exchange relations, whereby labor is exchanged for a delayed repayment of labor in kind (ayni) or for an immediate repayment in food or goods with a delayed obligation to reciprocate the relationship by reversing its terms at a later date (mink'a). Examples that I observed include trading turns in the distribution of water for irrigation; loaning pack animals for the transportation of sand and gravel from a distant riverbed for use in house construction, or loaning labor in the construction of a house. The latter cases were termed mink'a, as the work parties were feasted and "paid" with a large cake of cheese, which was reckoned according to its exchange value in the city of La Paz: three *bolivianos*. For the most part, these are situations in which faith group members are working on behalf of the catechist and his family, as in the case of Alejandro's house.

Catechists thus appear as an interactional nexus of relationships and obligations binding faith group members to them and to one another. As with ritual kin ties, the balanced reciprocal ideal of such exchange arrangements is attenuated; I observed few direct acts of reciprocity (e.g., a catechist going to assist a faith group member in constructing a house). Rather, the labor prestations I observed tended to be reciprocated indirectly: e.g., through visits to faith group members' houses for special prayer services. In these practices catechists' ritual expertise is taken up within a network of exchange practices constituting Aymara social relations. At the same time, a catechist's asymmetric position of authority within the faith group, and the relatively endogamous nature of the exchange practices I have been outlining, indicate the apartness of the faith group as a social unit. This figurative endogamy is what left Alejandro vulnerable to the charge of being stingy.

In chapter 3 we saw some of the ways that catechists position themselves as authoritative local representatives of translocal power. At the same time, and in ways that run counter to the efforts of inculturationists to purge Andean Catholicism of its colonial trappings and embrace an indigenous religiosity, many Aymara figure colonial Catholic doctrinal knowledge as a key component of ancestral ritual tradition, a tradition on the verge of being forgotten. In positioning themselves as descendants of the priests, catechists come to embody a double mediation: localizing translocal knowledge and bridging past and present such that remotely derived ritual knowledge is authorizing as both an esoteric product and a recovered local tradition. In the next section I turn to examine this complex catechetical footing as it was evident in the performance of the ayuno mentioned in the introduction, returning at the end of this chapter to discuss the worship practices of the faith groups. This balance is comparable to that involved in the production of households; while beyond their ayllus the catechists may construct themselves as classificatory sons of the priests, within their ayllus they strive to constitute the faith group as their house.

Consider the following exchange I had with Tomás, a faith group member in his forties. In the course of a discussion about the various prayers Tomás had learned in the faith group, I asked him if the ancestors (achachilas) knew how to pray. "The achachilas must have known," he said. "No one taught me prayer. I came to this side, to the catechist path [thaki]. Since then I am learning this prayer. At first I was learning incorrectly."

Tomás's comments cast conversion to the faith group as a path (thaki) suggesting both the sense of an orientation within a multidimensional world and a process of self-transformation. I have reported similar statements by catechists conceptualizing their advancement along their thakis as a function of knowledge and experience gained through mission courses. Bracketing for the moment the issue of the faith group as a frame of self-transformation, note that Tomás suggests that his conversion to the "catechist path" reconstitutes his connection to ritual knowledge (of Catholic prayers) that ought otherwise have devolved from a more organic connection to the ancestors, but did not ("No one taught me prayer"). Indeed the point was clarified for me by two other faith group members, who heard Tomás's comments to me and interjected in Spanish:

Raul: He is like an orphan.
Mario: Some people have a father and mother . . .
AO: Yes?
Mario: These have taught their children to pray in that way, and some never [do that].

The Porous Production of Locality

The ayuno performance described in the introduction reflects the gradual assimilation by catechists of the premises of inculturation and the increasing exposure of Aymara in the region to a range of other discourses of cultural revalorization. In chapter 3 we saw the ways the ayuno was codified in pastoral courses as a generic rite replicable across a presumed homogenous Aymara space. We also saw the ways the catechists positioned themselves within this pastoral effort. Turning now to the performances and practices of the catechists in their communities, I want to consider the ayuno along two analytic dimensions: first, as a capillary performance of a newly officialized practice; second, as an example of the cultural practices by which situated agents produce locality. The catechists are implicated across both of these dimensions, at once negotiating their own complex positions and as objects of reference for others.

To review, the ayuno is an intracommunal event correlated with the beginning of the planting season and with the completion of the tenure of annually rotating community authorities. I was unable to collect much information on the performance of the ayuno in years past. It was a contentious issue; my links with catechists did not help. As I understand it, the ayuno had been practiced as an annual event directed by the yatiris of the community according to the wishes of the mallkus. The ayuno had effectively been extirpated in the mid 1970s by Bonifacio, who, significantly, was a son of one of the most powerful yatiris. It is unclear to me whether the ayuno was completely abandoned or displaced by some form of worship, hymn singing, etc., involving the faith group and catechists. I suspect the latter.

As I began my fieldwork, the region was reeling from a series of disasters ranging from the impact of neoliberal economic structural adjustments (aptly dubbed "shock therapy") to floods, droughts, and, in the 1990–91 growing season, devastating frosts. More than a few people muttered that this was a consequence of forgetting the ways of the ancestors. This fear of further punishment motivating some to revive the ayuno practice was the opposite of what missionaries intended (indeed, for some missionaries the litmus test for sui generis cultural legitimacy was that rituals be undertaken not out of fear but out of reverence, faith, and solidarity), but it clearly reinforced a discourse of "recuperating and revalorizing culture" that was seeping in from many sides. Another factor shaping the recuperation of the ayuno was that one of the mallkus serving that year was a Protestant. This is more remarkable than may be apparent. Among the duties of a mallku are regular use of alcohol and coca throughout his tenure; activities prohibited by most Protestant churches and, until recently, by catechists and faith group members. In the current case the mallku complied with his obligations to the community, explaining that for the current year he would drink and chew coca and then return to the life of temperance. His ecumenism further enabled the self-conscious performance of the ayuno.

The morning of the ayuno began with intense interactions between the mallkus and Alejandro, with whom they had arranged to celebrate the ritual. I went early with Alejandro to the chapel, where the principal community authorities, along with a handful of faith group members, were already waiting. They joined Alejandro as he opened the chapel, swept the floor, and rang the bell to call people to the church. Then began a discussion between Alejandro and the mallkus (who ascended the raised chancel). I did not hear all of this, but my impression was that the mallkus were looking to Alejandro for an explanation of the ritual, to get a sense from him about what an ayuno involved. Alejandro punctuated his characterization of the rite with "como de costumbre, como nayrax." (as [was our] custom; as before).

Other community members arrived, including a group of yatiris invited by the mallkus. The mallkus exited the chapel to the sacristuyu (an enclosed space in front of the chapel), leaving Alejandro and the faith group inside. Three spatial groupings were taking shape at this point: Alejandro and the faith group inside the chapel (like a family—or pastoral team!—huddled in their home?); a larger group including ayllu authorities and yatiris in the sacristuyu gathered around the misaqala that serves as the socioritual focal point of the enclosure; and a third group outside this space, looking in. Among these detached spectators was Bonifacio, the other catechist from the community, who had been responsible for the extirpation of the ayuno.

As the event began to cohere, the principal mallku addressed those in the sacristuyu. (Alejandro and the faith group members emerged from the chapel to watch, but remained apart). The mallku praised the community for celebrating the ayuno, stressing repeatedly that this was a "sacred" ayuno and that it be undertaken "voluntarily." There is much to examine in these assertions. Most notable is that the stress on voluntary participation reflects a sort of interreligious détente reached in the region, turning on the assertion that no one should be compelled to participate in any ritual. This reflects the refusal by Protestants and neo-Catholics to participate in some practices, and so ratifies a certain weakening of tradition. It also suggests a specific vision of personhood as the discrete rational basis for legitimate ritual participation. Finally, it indexes the contentious multifaceted social frame within which the ayuno performance and consequent production of locality is achieved.

The lead yatiri (Bonifacio's father, Cornelio) began the preparation of a complex offering composed principally of flowers and ground copal (incense).

The flowers were presented by p'iqis representing the eight zones of the community. The yatiris bundled these together. The chunks of copal were similarly offered and then ground into a fine powder by an assistant to the yatiri. This was done in a bowl resting upon the misaqala using a rock as a pestle. Cornelio then invited each member of the community to spoon the copal into a bowl. This was typically done as the community member muttered prayers for a good year to come and invoked place names of significance to his/her sayaña. The offering thus embodies a merging of the community into a single homogenous totality composed of people differentially aligned with various microlocalities (households) within the ayllu. But note that the ayllu (of interest both to the missionaries and to the various participants in the ayuno) is neither unproblematically already there nor a monolith, but produced out of and with respect to a complex, translocal social field. For instance, in preparation for this stage of spooning, Cornelio had sent an assistant into the chapel to request of the catechist some palm fronds and a bowl. He accepted the palm frond, but rejected the bowls from the chapel as "too dirty" and dispatched his assistant to his own house for a clean bowl and a "silver spoon." In this ironic inversion of the stereotypical missionary obsession with hygiene and cleanliness (and compare here too the concerns behind the spacious ventilated houses promoted by Plan International), we can see a certain contestation of ritual authority and appropriateness and a certain displacement of legitimacy from the chapel and catechist-led faith group to the dispersed households represented by the ayuno participants.

Indeed, by one reading it is precisely the interpenetration of households and ayllus that is at issue, as the ayuno produces ayllu locality from a diversity of households. Within this frame of the production of the ayllu, inculturation challenges the catechist to negotiate a new footing for themselves, transcending their positions as fathers of their household and fathers of their faith group. In the catechist course presenting the ayuno, Father Hernando exhorted the catechists to position themselves at the "center" of the ayllu; the resonance with the authority of mallkus and yatiris is not, I suspect, unintended. At the same time, the structural ambiguity of the faith group hobbles the catechists in these efforts, even as it provides a space for other agents in the community to make sense of them.

As this offering bundling the community into a single body was completed, Bonifacio (who had entered the ritual space when his turn came to spoon copal) intervened—in effect, taking control of the ritual. Using the oratorical style of a community meeting, he greeted all those present and declared his desire to speak. Noting that it was getting late, he said it was time for people to decide how they wanted to do the ayuno. Appealing especially to elders in the crowd, he offered to explain the ayuno "according to the word of God." Essentially he presented a cultural menu of three variants of the ayuno (thus softening the single prototype generated by Hernando). One began at 10 AM with the community reciting the rosary until 11 or 12. This would be followed by a Via Crucis and by a *letanía* (litany). "Then we will do. . . . [long pause] . . . then that with the flowers probably gets done," he said, alluding uncomfortably to the offering prepared by the yatiris. After that comes "the rite of pardon, and when that is finished we are going to enter here and celebrate the Mass of the ayuno. On top of that there is a [communal meal]" he concluded. The two other types are abbreviated versions of the first: one without the initial praying of the rosary, the other without the Via Crucis and the burnt offering of the yatiris.

There was a period of debate as various ayllu members voiced opinions about the ayuno and about the catechists. The matter was decided by the mallku, who effectively ceded control of the event to the catechists, stating,

> Now pasados and by the same token mother pasados, all brothers and sisters, just as in the previous community meeting, we said that today is Santa Barbara and so perhaps we could fast, the entire community in the zone. And in that all of you have come, it is truly good. We the authorities [say] to you, "Very good." . . . We know in this community that from long ago we have been Catholic in our customs. But it appears that the entire community is not of the true Catholic religion. It is not that way with each sect today. Yes it's like that these days. Yes, above all, all of this is clear, and so this morning we spoke with Alejandro, "Each year you direct the ayuno. We count on you to say a few words. You have all the right [i.e., to speak and guide the ayuno]. This must be why we set you up on this path. Because in the community [we have] a voluntary ayuno, and sacred ayuno. This is what we have remembered. Above all, you cannot tell the community beforehand how it should be. . . . We trust in you." This is how we spoke, we can clarify that. So above all, we authorities, all of the bases we can trust them, perhaps they can direct, and in that way we can complete/fulfill [i.e., the ayuno].

His speech does a number of things. First note that the mallku stressed the long-standing character of local custom as Catholic. Where missionaries see the performance of the ayuno as the re-embrace of local non-Catholic tradition, the mallku framed this popular practice as a re-embrace of Catholicism. Just as the mallku assimilates Catholicism as a presupposable local tradition, the recuperation of which is being performed in the ayuno, he also frames the catechists not as agents of foreign religious ideals but as locally delegated ritual specialists, noting that the community set them on this path as catechists. Finally, the mallku makes no distinction between Bonifacio's intervention in the event and his consultations with Alejandro earlier that morning. From his point of view they are interchangeable. From a faith group internal view, however, this is far from the case. Even as the mallku is assimilating the catechists as a component part of the local community, Bonifacio and Alejandro are performing a bitter and ongoing rivalry, with Bonifacio upstaging and humiliating Alejandro as he takes control of the ayuno.

With this, all entered the chapel under the direction of Bonifacio (to perform menu option no. 2). The offering prepared by the yatiris was set on the altar in front of a saint's image. The faith group performed a song, and Bonifacio offered some instructions for the Via Crucis. The first station was performed inside the chapel. Exiting, some people suggested that a traditional Via Crucis ought to be performed barefoot (the way the ancestors did it, they said), and so we proceeded barefoot through the remaining stations, climbing a small hill behind the chapel to a calvario at the top. The yatiri bore the flower/copal offering, and the mallkus a small cross from the chapel.

This hilltop shrine warrants further comment. Machaqueños often referred to such sites to illustrate their claims of cultural decline: the calvarios were no longer visited on fiestas (as for instance in the bawdy parody of a priest after the fiesta of San Antonio), or they were in ruin—something consistently blamed on acts of vandalism by children, who destroyed the structures and knocked down the stone cairns that often mapped Via Crucis stations up the side of the hill. (I suspect these were also targeted by catechists at some point). In this and in the enthusiasm for performing the Via Crucis barefoot, and even in the exhortation that all offerings and participation in the ayuno be "voluntary," there is a poignant self-consciousness of such cultural decline. Aymara are not as hearty as their ancestors, have not maintained local ritual sites, and cannot perform a sort of communal consensus of *voluntad* (will) believed to have once been part of the ayllu's ritual repertoire. Here the locality being produced through the ayuno is explicitly marked as a flawed, entangled, and challenged one.

The degradation of the hillside cairns turned out to be an issue. Bonifacio miscalculated, and we arrived at the calvario at station 7. To my painful dismay, the remaining stations were completed on our knees, circling the calvario three times for each station. In the meantime, the yatiris prepared a fire of dung and straw. Cornelio ostentatiously checked his wristwatch (I suspect for midday) and called the mallkus out of the procession to make the burnt offering. This was the scene I described at the outset of this book, which, as is now apparent, was an improvisation building upon multiple contingencies. It is also worth noting that Bonifacio used his improvisation of the Via Crucis portion of the ayuno to deftly braid together and acknowledge the complexity of the ayllu, inviting various authorities as well as a local Protestant pastor to perform the Bible readings at certain stations.[7] This ritual ecumenism, however, is not just the province of inculturationist-steeped catechists. The focal offering having been made by the mallkus, who held the brazier aloft under the yatiri's direction, the yatiris then called each member of the ayllu (first other authorities, then men, then women) to hold the brazier while they spooned the remainder of the copal onto the embers. The effect was for each participant to transit the apparently composite space of the calvario.

After the offering of flowers and incense, the community divided into male and female groups and engaged in an act of pardon. The pardoning completed, the faith group gathered off to one side where they sang a few hymns. Cornelio completed his sacrifice with an offering of wine arced high in the air toward the mountain peaks and sky. He later told me the offering was for the harvest and compared the wine to the offering of llama blood arced against a house wall in a wilancha sacrifice.

The group then returned to the chapel, where the catechists performed a liturgical celebration, including the distribution of preconsecrated hosts. After the service, all retired to the churchyard, where we were fed at the misaqala by the mallkus, who had brought bread and wine—a traditional obligation of authorities at such events, I was told. At this point the spatial segregation evident at other points in the ayuno was largely overcome: Bonifacio and Alejandro, along with Cornelio, sat next to the mallkus. Bonifacio took over the distribution of the bread and wine, imitating the act of communion: he dunked each piece in the wine, before handing it to the recipient intoning *Kristun aychipaw* (flesh of Christ). This was followed by a communal meal, provided by the mallkus, to which Bonifacio invited everyone, saying, "Now we have forgiven one another, we are a single family."

The event bears discussion along a number of dimensions. The ayuno links the renewal of the growing season with the rotation of cargo posts. It is effectively the last act of the current mallkus, preparing the way for the next cohort of ayllu authorities, who, for the first months of their tenure will be considered to be like newly sown and sprouting seeds. This is significant, for the next year Bonifacio was obligated to represent his zone serving as p'iqi. One informant suggested that the rite of pardon was a way for incoming ayllu authorities to prepare themselves—i.e., by feeling humility and remorse for their past conduct—for the task of service ahead. Leaving aside the focus on humility, Bonifacio's intervention may have stemmed in part from his anticipation of a more public persona in the community.

The event might also be read as reinforcing many of the values and intentions of inculturationist pastoral workers. The ayuno is patently about performing community solidarity and it is well chosen by the missionaries in this respect. The configuration on top of the hill might be read as valorizing the putative indigenous core of Andean Christianity. More significant, I believe, is the way the catechists moved from their respective peripheral positions in the event to positions of centrality. The scene of mallkus, yatiris, and catechists all serving their community is an inculturationist's fantasy, fleetingly embodied in the course of the ayuno. Bonifacio's improvised transubstantiation of the bread and wine (comparable to his father's offering on top of the hill of wine as blood) would probably make many priests uneasy, and certainly exceeds his authority, but inasmuch as it entailed an insertion of his ritual authority within the context of a communitywide and community-producing practice, it conformed completely with messages conveyed by missionaries.

But this integration was not solely the objective of—nor solely controlled by—the catechists; neither did it imply the same things for all participants. The mallkus were also involved in situating the catechists as their delegates. Similarly, the yatiris recruited the catechists and the ritual paraphernalia they control as part of their offering. Who is centering whom? Whose locality is being produced?

In any event, this integration was fleeting, and highlighting it may lead us to overlook significant fissures in the event. There was a deep dispute within the faith group. Bonifacio had publicly upstaged Alejandro. Alejandro's wife and his other followers in the faith group were left seething, and in the following weeks Alejandro repeatedly attempted to criticize Bonifacio for screwing up the spatial arrangement of the Via Crucis. (A position for which I, with my still sore knees, had much sympathy.) There also remains Bonifacio's problematic history in the community; the mallku's diplomatic, cautious, and repeated stressing of the voluntary nature of the ayuno underscored the contentious ambience of such practices, and, despite the heroic integration of the catechists, the faith group repeatedly disengaged to huddle off to the side clutching their dog-eared Bibles and songbooks. Finally, there is Bonifacio's relation to his father. This yatiri-catechist pattern is not unique.

But that this integration should be only fleetingly achieved underscores the insight that the production of locality is a constant, open-ended, and manifold concern. The point here is neither to argue for nor against an "optimistic" (inculturationist) reading of the ayuno. The intent of the missionary ayuno is premised upon a particular construction of indigenous locality as the site of an authorizing popular religiosity with specific social and political implications. However, the performance of the ayuno underscores both the complexities of this missionary construction and suggests a very different vision of locality—not as an embattled site of primordial cultural authenticity but as an evanescent project continually produced by a range of situated actors.

Though by one line of analysis the ayuno and the catechists' participation in it are continuous with sensibilities of cultural production evident in such classical loci of Aymara authenticity as the household, the locality that is produced does not transcend the shifting contexts of its production. Missionization, and the frame of inculturation in particular, is just one example of a translocal cultural feature that entails the revalorization of dimensions of inside and outside, past and present, and asserts a specific sense of locality and of the articulation of past, present, and future. While the achievements of the ayuno certainly reflect the porous resilience of Andean locality and the longstanding practices of entanglement referenced by such indigenous concepts as chuyma, thaki, taypi, and even sayaña, the ramifications of inculturation at the level of this ayuno performance involve other kinds of interpenetrations as well. To return to the heuristic distinction of microlocality and macrolocality introduced in chapter 3, at issue here is the negotiation in a microlocal context of the macrolocalizing implications of inculturation and comparably transforming alignments of Aymara locality with encompassing fields of power. Through references to cultural decline, through objectified menus of traditional cultural practice, through repeated invocations of the voluntary nature of ayuno participation, through the stubborn endurance of crosscutting identities—faith group, Protestant secta—poised uneasily between the levels of household and ayllu and resisting the homogenizing grinding of the yatiri's misaqala, the porously produced locality is not what it used it be.

‡ ‡ ‡

The mallku's insistence on voluntary participation is particularly telling. He stressed the voluntary nature of the ayuno to ease the concerns of Protestants, neo-Catholics, Mormons, and others in the ayllu who may have felt compelled to participate in the rite or who may otherwise be subject to criticism from other ayllu members for refusing to participate. On the one hand, this polite and tolerant exhortation verges on the tautological in the Andean context. As I have argued, all ritual acts, insofar as they are effective actions, are voluntary, i.e., chuyma-grounded or sincere. At the same time, the statement seems to reference a posited past in which such niceties were not necessities—a past of uniformly aligned chuymas. As data, such nostalgia sheds most of its light on the present and draws our attention to the self-conscious alignment of situated subjects engaged in the production of locality. In the next section I focus on the faith group itself as a site for the production and circulation of a particular type of Aymara selfhood: a self-consciously embattled identity authorized largely with respect to sensibilities of chuyma-grounded offerings and processual paths of identity, while at the same time enmeshed in translocal grids of power.

FAITH GROUP PRACTICE AND CONVERSION

Like the Aymara household, the faith group appears as an ambivalent site of cultural practice. Membership in the faith group is a marked identity; participation in the group signals a conversion. However, as Raul and Mario helped Tomás explain to me, conversion to the faith group is often cast in the idiom of a local sociology of cultural reproduction, and the practices of the faith group are conceptualized in terms of local forms of value. While faith group members often represent their participation in the group as a conversion to an authentic Aymaraness, this is not the pristine cultural core imagined by inculturationists but rather a sort of fluency with colonially derived doctrinal knowledge that many contemporary Aymara associate with the ancestors.

My goal in this section is to examine the sort of converted Aymara selfhood produced and asserted in the context of the faith groups—to examine the persons produced in Alejandro's house. On the one hand, notwithstanding their embattled positions within their ayllus, faith group members assert a sort of selfhood that is largely consonant with other domains of Aymara practice (e.g., the house). At the same time, the converted selfhood that is asserted in the faith group is deeply entangled with the changing contexts of its production, referencing the shifting complexities of the production of Aymara locality. Conversion typically involves a temporalized or narrativized self-consciousness, a break with a previous condition. In the case at hand, however, we have less a separation from an objectified past self than a nostalgic realignment with that self. By way of evoking this complex subjectivity enmeshed among structurally dissimilar invocations of locality, I turn here to the weekly grind of its production, presenting a composite rendering of numerous faith group meetings observed in a range of communities.

Faith Group Meetings

Weekly faith group meetings typically last from mid-morning Sunday to mid-afternoon. Meetings take place in and around the local chapel.[8] I often arrived early to find a few group members just outside of the east entranceway to the sacristuyu, enjoying the warmth of the strengthening morning sun. Others trickle in, joining them or gathering inside the walled compound. With the arrival of the catechist, some of the group help him to ready the chapel: bringing water from a nearby stream to wet the earth floor and keep down the dust as they sweep the chapel with handfuls of altiplano grass. Older group members gather near the misaqala (where the ayuno offering was prepared) to gossip and joke, while younger members hide just out of view, eavesdropping, flirting, and sharing jokes of their own. The windows of the sacristuyu wall are put to good use as they offer a clandestine view of morning activities in the community. I was consistently amazed by Aymara ability to identify by name what appeared to me as distant specks on the horizon and determine whether they were coming to church, going to a meeting of a Protestant group, off to one of their fields, or perhaps on the way to meet one of the community authorities to discuss an ongoing dispute. These observations were often the grist of animated gossip. The musicians—typically young unmarried men—tend to gather separately, tuning their instruments and practicing a few songs, while flirting shyly with young women in the group.

Once the chapel is ready and with no distant specks thought to be group members on their way to service, the faith group files into the chapel. Men sit along the west wall of the chapel ("right" looking out from the altar) on narrow lengths of wood, resting atop single bricks of adobe. Women sit along the east ("left") wall atop cloths spread over the ground. The catechist's wife generally sits closest to the altar on the left side; on the men's side the musicians gather closest to the altar. The catechist stands upon a slightly raised chancel, behind a wooden table and before the altar with its collection of saints images, mirrored woodwork, candle holders, and standards. The table is covered with cloths: a multicolored awayu, on top of which is often spread a smaller thari, the type of cloth used by women to carry coca leaves and, more generally, to store important things: ritually treated money; documents; etc. Catechists often keep important items of their practices in such a cloth: crucifixes, a Bible, water and salt, or, for those who have the authority to use holy oil and consecrated communion wafers, these Catholic ritual items. Bibles, songbooks, and other liturgical materials are placed on the table in front of the catechist. Candles and other items such as a crucifix are often brought forward from the altar and placed on the table, the candles lit.

The catechist consults a liturgical calendar to determine the readings for that day. He reads the chapter and verse citations aloud for faith group members to note down. Some produce notebooks in which they record the readings, and much time is spent verifying that the information has been transcribed correctly. Many carry Bibles and try to find each reading in their book; some pass their books to the catechist for him to mark the passage. As in the game of "telephone," this process of repeating the citations often results in interesting transpositions of chapter and verse, with the result that a significantly different set of readings may ultimately be read.

Once the readings are announced and assigned to (literate) group members, the meeting formally begins with songs selected by the catechist or by one of the musicians from two published songbooks used by the faith groups. The songs are a vital part of faith group worship, and selecting them is an important responsibility.[9] The ideal is to combine popular liturgical songs with less well known hymns, and the ability to select songs with appropriate messages, encourage participants to learn new hymns, while at the same time maintaining group enthusiasm by calling for old favorites is highly valued. Invariably three "songs for entering" are performed; the catechist may offer a brief prayer after each song, with the final prayer followed by the catechist leading the faith group in the sign of the cross.

The remainder of the celebration follows the format of a Catholic Mass. The catechist speaks the lines of the priest, and the faith group responding with "amen" or reciting prayers such as the Our Father or the Apostles' Creed. In other places catechists insert their own prayers, often combining and modifying fragments of doctrinal formulae. These are punctuated with additional songs, drawn from sections in the song books that parallel the structure of the Mass: e.g., "Songs of Forgiveness"; "Songs of Glory." This is followed by the Bible readings, each followed by a song of response. For the reading of the Gospel, all stand. After the final song the catechist begins his homily, usually commenting on each of the readings in turn. On a few occasions I have seen catechists engage in Socratic dialogues with their groups, but extended sermon is the dominant style. If other catechists are present, they will offer additional interpretations of the readings. Extended participation from group members, beyond answering questions posed by a catechist, is uncommon. The exception tends to be younger members of the faith group who have been socialized into such practices within a parish youth group. For the rest, much of the authority of the catechist is enacted in the asymmetry of his capable speech.

Upon the completion of the homily, the catechist leads the group in the recitation of the Apostles' Creed. This is followed by the *Oración de los Fieles* (Prayer of the Faithful): a series of petitions voiced to God. After a number of standard petitions (for the welfare of the Church, of the Pope, of the president of Bolivia), all those present are invited to voice their petitions. This is by far the most interactive part of the celebration, and almost everyone speaks at least once. After each petition the entire group intones, *mayipxsmaw tiyus apusay* [We ask you God our Lord]. A song or two follow, sometimes separated by an additional prayer by the catechist. The catechist then leads the group in praying the Our Father, after which all greet one another with an Embrace of

Peace. When a minister of communion is presiding, he performs a modified liturgy of the Eucharist. Faith group members line up to receive communion wafers consecrated by the parish priest. Yet another song is followed by a final invocation by the catechist, who sometimes blesses the faith group members—making the sign of the cross over them or occasionally aspersing them with water[10]—as they kneel before him. The liturgical celebration is brought to an end by three final songs.

The faith group files out of the chapel and gathers around the misaqala in the sacristuyu. The men tend to sit upon the benches that line the wall, the women upon the ground. The catechist sits in the middle of the line of men, directly in front of the table, as the group shares a midday meal of a type common to many Aymara social gathering. Each person has brought some form of prepared food—broad beans, fresh potatoes, *ch'uñu* (freeze-dried potatoes), *qispiña* (small cakes made of cooked quinoa), boiled maize kernels—that is laid out on top of the misaqala in its own carrying cloth. More select food items—dried fish, dried meat, cheese, a fried egg—are distributed directly by the donor, who is likely to keep the food concealed in a carrying cloth or skirt, producing only the morsel offered to each person. Drinks are rarely served, the exceptions being when visitors to the group take it upon themselves to feast the faith group.[11] Alcoholic drinks, coca, and cigarettes were never consumed

FIGURE 5.4   *Gathered around the misaqala in the churchyard, the faith group shares a meal*

during meetings I observed. The meal is a time of socializing and gossip, often dominated by the catechist, who may hold forth describing his recent travels or performing his insider knowledge of upcoming events in the parish. The meal is capped by a concurrent expression of thanks, as each person thanks every other person. A brief break allows people to steal away to pee, warm up in the sun, or kick a soccer ball around.

After the meal, the group returns to the chapel. The afternoon session begins with three songs, often picked by the catechist as new songs to be learned by the group. The catechist leads members in the sign of the cross and offers a prayer, after which attendance is taken, recorded in a book maintained by the catechist. The structure of this portion of the meeting often parallels the syndicate protocol of a community meeting. Catechists sometimes announce a formal agenda. The review of the attendance list heightens the similarity, and faith group member who will miss a meeting, or who have to leave early, may check with the catechist beforehand to obtain permission for their absence. Indeed, the faith group itself is organized along syndicate lines, with a rotating hierarchy of offices changing annually. In addition to learning new songs, the afternoon session is usually devoted to reviewing or teaching catechetical knowledge, which is accomplished through rote learning: repetition of prayers or lists of commandments. This is often in preparation for sacraments, although the learning of new songs sometimes takes on the flavor of a rehearsal, as when the groups are preparing for periodic convivencias: parishwide, faith group gatherings at which each group performs songs for the others in attendance. A catechist may also use this time to review for the group the contents of a recent course he has attended or to plan for an upcoming event or project in the community, pastoral zone, or parish. The final act of the faith group meeting is the catechist leading the group in the sign of the cross and a series of songs, after which all file out and go on their way.

In the meetings I observed, attendance ranged from fewer than half a dozen to twenty-five people, with even larger groups attending during All Souls Day or when the sacraments of baptism or marriage were being celebrated. An attendance list for one of the faith groups from 1988 indicates the regular participation of some two dozen members. This appears to be the low ebb of a movement that initially involved a much larger number of people. Like Eusebio, a number of catechists narrated to me the decline of their faith group from a successful beginning, in which some groups claimed more than one hundred members, to the present, in which some catechists meet only occasionally, with their families and a few followers. Members of one faith group told me that they once boasted a large band of musicians as well as a soccer team (the Sacred Heart of Mary), and I gather there were sports competitions among the groups in the parish.

Catechetical Authority

A catechist's position of leadership within the faith group hinges on a range of markers of social and ritual efficacy. These turn around his knowledge of Christian doctrine, which in turn reflects both a catechist's capacity to memorize and enact knowledge as well as the life experiences of travel (i.e., to courses) that generate and transact that knowledge. As the case of Alejandro (previously a member of a Protestant church) demonstrates, this potency need not be derived strictly from the Catholic tradition; indeed, among the most striking things about the phenomenon of the catechists is the translatability of potency and legitimacy *across* what are often characterized as discrete systems.

In faith group members' comments on catechists, oratory emerges as an index of authority and a source of respect. Sylverio, a man in his mid-twenties, and a member of Bonifacio's faction of the faith group, contrasts the celebrations conducted by Alejandro and Bonifacio. With Bonifacio, he said, "there was more respect." He praised his ability to run faith group meetings efficiently and linked this discipline with his capacity to teach. "We learned everything: prayers, songs, Bible." Unlike the brief ramblings of Alejandro, "the explanations [homilies] of Bonifacio were not for a short while. [His comments on] two verses [lasted] for the entire day. We could not respond. But we were well taught, strictly well." "With him," he added, "we conduct ourselves well, we understand, we listen well. Now the idea enters into our heads." Much of the authority of the catechist is thus embodied in the asymmetry of his capable speech: clarifying and illuminating meanings to the group members who sit passively and "do not respond." In contrast, Sylverio described Alejandro's oratory as "incomplete" and suggested that under his direction there was confusion in the faith group. He told me that people did not want to sing: an indication of sadness. In contrast, "when Bonifacio is there, I enjoy it more."

Pleasurable Offerings

When faith group members described their activities in the group to me, liturgical songs were usually the first thing mentioned. They also cited songs as examples in response to my question "what do you learn in the faith group?" Songs do form a large part of every faith group meeting. While these are certainly catechetical texts, consciously deployed by missionaries as mnemonics for Christian doctrine, the musical medium conveys its own messages as well. Faith group members describe the songs as a source of happiness. Indeed, songs can be seen to index and make manifest happiness, as in Sylverio's comments that, under the direction of a less competent catechist group members did not want to sing. Songs are also described as directed to God. They are a pleasurable offering.

In general, Aymara musical practices are gendered and restricted. Men play musical instruments, and these performances are usually limited to certain kinds of occasions, such as fiestas or other community-level or intercommunity events. The performances I witnessed in Jesús de Machaqa were often performances of ayllu-level solidarity.[12] For instance, musical groups tend to serve as interayllu delegations, as a group of musicians from one ayllu will pay (play?) respect to a neighboring community's saint during a fiesta celebration. Music also is a medium of rivalry and competition at intercommunity events, where musical groups from each community engage in battles, attempting to play better and longer than their neighbors.

In faith group meetings the instrumental accompaniment to the singing is fairly sparse: only two or three musicians on markedly nontraditional instruments: e.g., a drum, mandolins, a guitar, or an organ, as opposed to the seasonally varying repertoire of Andean wind instruments. However, in public performances, and especially during visits to other faith groups or as part of parishwide events, the mandolins are complemented or replaced by seasonal flutes as all of the men in the faith group become musicians, often donning color coordinated ponchos for their musical performance.

Less gendered, but perhaps more restricted, is vocal performance, which is relatively uncommon among Aymara speakers (Turino 1993:49,52; Buechler 1980:97). While men certainly sing, the activity seems to be skewed a bit toward women, who are often described as taking the initiative in singing and said to know the songs better than male participants (Buechler 1980; Abercrombie 1986:137 n.20).[13]

Singing is more commonly associated with the activities of adolescents and with the practices of courtship and fertility (e.g., Beuchler 1980:97; Berg 1989:62 ff.; Abercrombie 1986:137). This linkage with courtship and adolescence suggests that singing is an activity even more restricted for adult men and women. (The only occasions in which I have seen older women or men singing have been ritual celebrations when they were very, very drunk.) Here the faith group offers older women and men a space in which to sing and perform musically, and much of their stated enthusiasm for the liturgical songs may stem from this highly pleasurable and significant activity otherwise unavailable to them. Indeed, beyond these meetings, musical performance is even more restricted for faith group members as a result of their (typical) renunciation of fiesta practices.[14]

Similarly, like fiestas and other rites that serve as settings for musical per-formance—and that are the principal occasions for flirting and trysts—faith group meetings are a place for a considerable amount of flirtation and courtship. Adolescent group members, who are otherwise almost always silent, spend much of the meetings making eyes at one another and preening and perform-ing for each other during the songs. Young men tend to be the musicians play-ing during weekly services. There may also be a more long-standing link be-tween Church practices, catechism, and courtship. Older informants recalling lutriniro-led catechisms during Holy Week reported boys and girls covertly flirting and tossing stones at one another behind the back of the lutriniro.

In this sense faith group membership is an almost indulgent activity. As neo-Catholicism prohibited the excesses of fiestas and other rites practiced a few time a year, it created a weekly ritual space for highly pleasurable practices and quasi-familial intimacy. This indulgent nostalgic mood seems particularly apt for the intimate sleight of hand at the core of faith group participation: the circulation of ritual knowledge held once to have traveled most authentically along the paths of semen and blood that constitute and reproduce Aymara households. Yet this nostalgia and the transformative alignment with the past it generates are double edged. For this alignment is a source of authentic self-hood that patently references its own eclipse. At the same time, this nostalgia generates a connection with the past conceived as the ground for an enabled subjectivity within the entangled present.

Keeping the Word of God

Faith group members stress their participation in the group as a means of ac-cess to specialized ritual knowledge and a special relationship with God. Tomás suggested that the group performed a sort of custodial function: "What do you do in a faith group meeting?" I asked. "We take care of [waqaychapx-txa] the word of God." Like Sylverio, most members I interviewed said that prior to their participation in the group they were unable to understand "the words of God." "We didn't understand that," said Filomena, a woman in her sixties or seventies.

> Because of that [listening to the word of God in faith group meetings], we now understand well. The word of God was good. Before we were not able to go to the side of God. We went about a little like fools. And now it is very good to be in this side, to believe in God was very good. From this we have been very happy. Sometime [when we are] sad we are unable [i.e., to act in the world], we are in a great sadness. . . . Then we listen very well to the words of God. We worship God very well. We sing. Like

that—we sing. For us our hearts [*chuymanakajax*] are left clear/uncovered. God [is?] in us. We sing to God. That makes our hearts very happy.

This internal transformation is key. Faith group members describe a movement from a situation of sadness, of incomplete knowledge, leaving them debilitated, paralyzed, and unable to go about (*sarnaqaña*) like "normal" people, to a situation of happiness and understanding manifest both through their passive penetration by the effective words of the catechist and their active interchange with God through song.

The shift is often indexed through spatial metaphors: references to the "side" (*tuki*) or the "path" (*thaki*) of God or of the catechists; related directional suffixes (e.g., *-sa* [side], *-ru* [toward]), and the use of the verb *saraña* ("to go"). Frequently combined with the crucial concept of a "path," the sense of agentive locomotion expressed by saraña is a vital metaphor for Aymara life experience, comprising motion, habit, behavior, custom, or state of being. We have seen such references above, as when Eusebio opined that a catechist should "walk straight" or when he criticized one of his predecessors for being a man of "two paths." Similarly, a spatialized vision of religious affiliation is evident in discussions of Protestant "sects," which cause Aymara to "look to the other side." It is within this spatialized relational field that we must view group members' characterizations of themselves as "going to the Lord."

CONVERSION AND INDULGENCE

The act of "going to church" thus invokes more than traveling between house and chapel. On the one hand, I am suggesting that the faith group represents a household of another order. On the other, the path to (and of) the faith group is a transformative one: a conversion. In part, this conversion makes manifest a complex nostalgia similar to what Battaglia (1995) has characterized as a "practical nostalgia"; a "nostalgia for a sense of future." Beyond pining for an objectified absent past, practical nostalgia involves "transformative action with a connective purpose," an alignment with the past that carries with it context generating consequences for the present and the emergent future. Battaglia is concerned with the reenactments of gardening practices and ritual displays of yams undertaken by Trobriand Islanders residing in Port Moresby, Papua New Guinea. Such acts do more than connect migrants with their remembered home, they problematize their contemporary senses of self in ways that intersect with experiences of national belonging and related "postcolonial rhetorics of identity" defining subnational cultural groups.

As an Aymara household of another order, as a site for the realization of colonially derived doctrine and practices, as expressions of indigenous tradition ramifying to the most intimate contexts of Aymara life, and as a space for the circulation of the macrolocalizing discourses of inculturation, the faith group sets in relief a comparable Andean interplay of practical nostalgia and a set of rhetorics of postcolonial identity. For many members faith group participation effects a satisfying link with a perceived past otherwise lamented as lost. Weaving together their subjective desires—desires shaped by the conflictual legacy of previous pastoral ideologies—with the objectifying rhetoric of inculturation, group members hearken to a moment of cultural integrity and continuity productive of model Aymara selves. From some vantages this looking to the past might be seen either as a renouncing of the present in favor of a naive traditionalism or as a savvy strategy of spin control fabricating a traditionalist high ground to shore up an embattled separatist identity. While each of these claims bears some weight, I want to argue that something else is going on as well. For, in their nostalgia, group members reference without fully rejecting their deeply compromised present. Far from restoring the past, this recuperated selfhood is imagined as the basis for a productive transformative engagement: an ancestrally aligned thaki along which to undertake the situated production of the future.

Patient Chuymas

None of this mitigates the embattled nature of faith group identity. This is evident in group meetings, where members complain about abusive treatment by others in the community. In one meeting, in the course of the petitions, Lucia, a widow in her late forties, complained about a dispute she was involved in with one of the authorities of the community. She extended her complaint to report, "This week we were insulted by people; we encountered drunken and foul-mouthed people." Lucia used an exclusive first-person plural (*nanaka*) set in opposition to unmarked "people" (*jaqi[naka]*). She went on to request (for this declaration was couched as a petition to God) that God grant faith group members a "patient *chuyma*." This is linked to the patient suffering of Jesus, but is also resonant with ideals of Aymara sociability that value the transparency of a *chuyma* unencumbered with resentment over against the opacity of a covered *chuyma* entangled in disputes. The patient chuyma she seeks is more than a suffering one; it is a resourceful one.

The faith group meetings involve the formation and circulation of complexly converted selves. Group members position their struggle not as a break from Aymara community but as a struggle to reattain it. At the same time, the transspatial reach of the patient/unencumbered chuyma for which Lucia strives exceeds the field in which positioned Aymara selves typically circulate. Here the self-consciousness entailed by conversion to the faith group must be seen as a consciousness explicitly situated with respect to a wider entangled context.

The Classes of Christians

The relative separation of the faith group from the wider community is also marked through a set of distinctions made by faith group members about types of Christians. These assertions serve the ambiguous ends of anchoring Christian identity within the wider community and declaring the faith group to be the (translocal) fulfillment of that (local) Christian identity. The following case is taken from an extended commentary offered by a faith group member seen as being on the verge of catechist status as the result of his extensive experience with a parish youth group. Nestor's case is interesting both for the content of what he has to say and the nuances of his efforts to adopt the footing of a catechist in his relation to the group. As we shall see, he was not entirely successful. Nonetheless, his efforts reveal the complex tensions of a faith group thaki, which transcends and transforms the microlocal setting of its production.

Nestor had returned to his community from the yungas, where he spent most of the year, to help his mother with the harvest. He was warmly welcomed back to the faith group. During his second meeting with them, he was invited to say a few words to the group. This turned into an impromptu course on the classes of Christians.

First, he defined "Christian" most basically as someone who follows Jesus Christ, who wants to fulfill His words. A second type of Christian is baptized: "from there we begin to be Christians, from when we are little, we begin." Yet, he noted, these Christians may not come to Church every Sunday; they do not know their priest, their bishop, their deacon, or their catechist. They come only for baptisms, or when there is a mass, or for masses for the dead. However, when they come, Nestor complained, "they cannot make the sign of the cross, they cannot pray the Apostles' Creed, they have forgotten, they know only half." Nestor called these Christians, "false Christians" (k'ari kristiyanunaka) contrasted with "us," who "are true Christians" (chiqa kristiyanutanwa). A third type of Christian is indexed by knowledge of the "signs of Christianity." These include the physical gestures of crossing oneself. Nestor noted that in the faith group people routinely perform some of these, but not all of them. In contrast, he claimed that these practices were well known by the ancestors: "The ancestors knew well how to do this; up to this day they have always taught their children and grandchildren." The fourth level of Christian identity described by Nestor involves a range of knowledge and experience grouped by him into four criteria: 1. knowing the Apostles' Creed, 2. complying with the commandments of God; 3. receiving the "third sacrament" (i.e., confirmation [see below]), and 4. knowing seven prayers. Here Nestor listed the Lord's Prayer; the Apostles' Creed; Hail Mary and Yo Pecador as prayers the faith group knows, naming others—Señor Santo, Le beso Maria, Bendito—as the prayers they still "lack."[15]

Nestor's sorting of Christian practices established a hierarchy of Christian identities corresponding to knowledge of and experience with Christianity. The knowledge is anchored in the cultural past as something that is properly genealogically transmitted, but more often forgotten. Nestor twined this sense of cultural forgetting with a Christian view of human degradation from a state of infantile purity when he suggested that "false Christians," who predicate their Christianity on their experience of being baptized as children, have "forgotten" the knowledge they once knew or should have been taught by their parents, grandparents, and godparents. The comments suggest a rupture in Aymara sociability that ought otherwise serve to transmit Christian knowledge. Yet it also posits the lived past of faith group members—their own childhood—as a locus of authenticity, forgotten by others but preserved in the faith group. In these characterizations the faith group emerges as a privileged space for reconnecting to this authenticating past.

Yet even this valued knowledge of the ancestors falls short of the more complete Christian knowledge and identity described by Nestor; they seem to place roughly at the level of the third type of Christian in his schemata. Indeed, although they are grounded in the past, Nestor, in ways comparable to other catechists, is sketching out future-oriented paths of identity—"the paths of the Doctrine" (*doctrinan sarawinakapa*). Here the faith group offers an unprecedented opportunity for fulfilling Christian knowledge, largely through the position of the catechist as a local adept of ritual knowledge at once indigenous and exotic. We can now place the faith group within the vision of the catechists' authority as constructed along the dimensions of a thaki. Faith group members, by this reckoning, appear more complete than the "false Christians" in the community, perhaps as complete as the ancestors,[16] but nonetheless incomplete with respect to the knowledge professed by the catechists. Similarly, those who have been with the faith group longer are classed as more advanced along their thakis than those who have recently joined. These latter are said to be "afraid." When faith group members ascend to the chancel in the presence of the "false Christians" from the community, their situation is not only embattled but, in certain contexts, privileged and superior.

The faith group is a venue for the transfer of that knowledge, for the completion of Christian identity. It is marked by the teachings of the catechists, by regular experiences of faith group meetings and by access to sacraments. A further look at the case of Nestor brings a set of relevant issues to the fore.

In the course of his presentation to the faith group, Nestor stressed the importance of the sacrament of confirmation as the condition of the completion of Christian identity. The sacrament is not often celebrated in Jesús de Machaqa. This is in part because visits by a bishop are few and far between, but also because the use of oil in confirmation, more so than its use in baptism, is a source of great fear and concern: some link it with rumors of kharikhari fat extraction. Nestor described confirmation as a means of receiving knowledge from God; he paired it with baptism as a second bestowal of the power of the Holy Spirit upon Christians. Though many find it difficult to learn all of the knowledge required for Christian identity, confirmation, he suggested, makes such learning easy and renders one an adept in the faith group.

> Then, each one of us, we will have strength (*ch'amaniñani*), we will have ideas (*amuyuniñani*). You will feel the song here [pointing to his chest]. "Let's sing a song, brother, we will sing this song, brother," but he will feel what the song is for the entrance, for the *gloria,* for the response, meditation, and communion, Yes, that is already there. He will have it in his chuyma.

Although one may not be able to read and write, after receiving confirmation, Nestor promised, one will know "all the words completely." "One who receives confirmation . . . he will speak these words with ease, very easily, as if they were a familiar story, that is how they speak." Note again the restoration of knowledge—otherwise accessible only through laborious processes of reading—as innate or chuyma grounded; there is no better metonym of such ancestral knowledge than "a familiar story."

Nestor was presenting himself as a potent authority, and his comments were peppered with asides about how unprepared and incomplete the faith group was. These verged on attacks on the catechist, who was accused of not teaching enough. Nestor tempered these brash assertions by occasionally casting himself as a younger man, subordinate (at least in other frames of reference) to older men in the faith group. He referred to them as "uncle" and cited their accomplishments in completing their cargo service to the community. For his part, the catechist—Manuel—joined with Nestor, chastising the faith group for not listening to his teachings. Manuel distinguished himself from the group by addressing them in the second-person plural (*jumanaka*).

Yet Nestor did not fare so well with other group members when he asked for their reaction to his course. A number of people criticized him for his spotty attendance with the group and pushed him to make a commitment they knew he could not make to visit and teach them more often. Juana, a middle-aged woman from the group, was particularly critical. She was offended by his claim that Christians without confirmation and those who do not come regularly to faith group meetings are, as she paraphrased him, "making fun of God." She argued that she was not confirmed, and sometimes missed meetings, yet was not making fun of God. Rather, she ran down a list of obligations that interfered with her weekly attendance and said that she could think of the word of God while tending her sheep. Moreover, although she is not confirmed, she noted that she heard the bishop speak during the ordination of the ministers. "I tied those words in my chuyma."

In addition to illustrating the faith group as a venue for the transmission of Christian knowledge, Nestor's encounter with the group presents a glimpse of the internal dynamics of the faith group. Nestor reveals the limits of catechists' authority, as he attempts to stake out a catechistlike position in the group and, despite the apparent acquiescence of the catechist, does not quite pull it off. His performance of subordination to senior men in the group points up the ways in which other constructions of authority crosscut intrafaith group interactions. Similarly, in presenting themselves as pastors, elder brothers, or fathers, or as mallkus overseeing a hierarchy of rotating positions in which group members serve, catechists reinforce the distinction of their primary sphere of legitimacy, even as they insist on the translatability of that legitimacy across a range of frames of Aymara social life. To assert their status as father, the catechists must constitute the faith group as their house and family. As with the characterization of the group as a herd, this is often achieved with a semantic sleight of hand: the faith group is invoked as God's children who must live together as in a single house, like a family.

Translocal Nostalgia

"The phenomena of conversion," writes Freccero (1986), "can be adequately represented as definitive only by extending what may be simply a moment of self-consciousness into a temporal sequence, which is to say, into narrative form, in which the observing self is separated from the observed." As a space of conversion, the faith group is a space of self-conscious reflection; the objectifying space opened up is informed by the complex interplay of inside and outside, tenuous links of past and present, and shifting and structurally dissimilar invocations of locality. In ways similar to the conversions recounted by foreign missionaries, faith group practices unfold at the confluence of nostalgia and entanglement generating a self-conscious production of Aymara selves in complex contexts. The selfhood produced is at once authorized through an alignment with a perceived past and plausible with respect to translocal settings that increasingly constrain or compel particular imaginings of locality and the past that anchors it.

The faith group is cast as the site of the circulation of (doctrinal) knowledge. The consequences of this are nothing less than the "completion" (*phuqhawa*) of Aymara personhood. In contrast, a catechist warned his faith group, "If you don't know the Doctrine, all else is in vain. I say this for you. I am not speaking for myself. I know. I am guarding this for myself, but I don't want to keep it for myself, thus I speak for your benefit." In circulating their knowledge, catechists' enact basic tenets of Aymara sociability, that is, as a shared offering freely given within an economy of reciprocity and complementary values out of which "completion" is achieved. Thus, when faith group members criticized his sporadic attendance and demanded that he offer them more regular courses, Nestor countered by suggesting that authentic teaching is not compelled but voluntarily given from the chuyma of the teacher. The alternative he compared to giving bread to a crying baby; the imagery nicely evokes the sense of teaching as most authentically a form of intercourse among fully social (i.e. chuyma-grounded) subjects.

A key dimension of faith group participation, then, concerns the local harnessing and circulation of the knowledge and experience of catechists. Relative knowledge is ranked along a thakilike hierarchy and is expected to reflect length of time with the group and regularity of attendance. In addition to catechists' concern with the progress of their group, faith group members actively track their learning. Songbooks and Bibles index their completion, as underlined Bible passages accumulate each Sunday and group members check off the catechetical songs they have learned by heart.

Indeed, the goal here seems to be internalized, chuyma-anchored knowledge, as evident in Nestor's comments that confirmation will enable the faithful to remember liturgical formulae and hymns from their chuymas just like a familiar story. This is also evident in Juana's rebuke of Nestor, as she authorizes her own Christianity, despite not being formally confirmed, with the assertion that she heard the bishop speak and "tied his words to my chuyma." When catechists' exhort their groups to "learn," they frequently invoke the chuyma as a somatic site of knowledge. This entails the subjective positioning of group members, who are told, as the "children of God," to prepare themselves to listen and learn with all the will of their chuymas. The challenges of internalizing such information are considerable, and the chuyma as a locus of authentic learning works in conjunction with other technologies. At times, as in the claims made by Nestor, the chuyma serves in lieu of literacy or related capacities. Elsewhere, Nestor says:

> Some, going with faith, receive chuyma (*chuym katuqapxixa*). If they don't know how to speak, they simply speak. One is very well in his chuyma. He receives. Nor does he know how to read. In his chuyma he listens. Now in his chuyma it is tied (*chuymaparuxa chint'awaykatayn*) as if it were written down.[17]

In a different faith group meeting another catechist comments:

> Although I don't think very well, the idea/understanding comes to me. . . . Although others may not have thought, they now see in their chuymas, they tie it well (*jupanaka . . . chuymanakapan chint'xapxiw suma*). He who does not know how to read, he with his head and with his chuyma he receives (*chuymamp katuqix*) that well. . . . That arrives to my chuyma.

Similarly, during the petitions a faith group member implores, "Enlighten us Father, these your words, write them in our chuymas."

I also collected many references to the chuyma functioning as a tape recorder. Bonifacio cited a course he had recently attended to stress to his group not to forget the traditions of the ancestors:

> It falls to us. We will record (*grabarakiñani*) that in our chuymas for another time. We will receive it, let's say. Just like the brother there [pointing to me] is recording, yes like that it ought to be received in our chuymas. Some don't know how to read; they receive it in their chuymas.

Similarly, a faith group member complained that the catechist ought to obtain a blackboard for writing down information. This, she said, would make it easier to "record" the information in her chuyma. Writing in notebooks was also encouraged, although few faith group members took notes beyond the chapter and verse citations. Toward the end of his class for the group, Nestor asked them what they had learned. A young man read from his notebook, "There are ten commandments; the sacraments of the Church are seven." Nestor praised him, exclaiming, "God has helped you. You have a fertile/nimble [*ch'ikhi*] chuyma."

Nimble Chuymas

The selfhood asserted in the context of the faith group is valued both for its local legitimacy within a rhetoric of chuyma-grounded and thaki-indexed authority and for its translocal translatability as a footing for plausible extensions of self across a presupposed complex world. Notwithstanding strong associations with the ancestors, the knowledge transacted in faith groups is constituted largely as coming from outside the community, deriving, for instance, from distant missionary courses. In their interactions with faith group members, catechists' present their experiences of travel beyond the confines of their community as constitutive of their authority. Indeed, the more complete Christian identity embodied by catechists and promised to their faith groups is cast as a function of this translocal experience.

At the same time, the agile translocal extension of self evident in the spatial practices of the catechists is offered as the consequence of the complete Christian identity that is the object of faith group nostalgia. One result of the transfer of knowledge from catechist to faith group is an extension of the faith group frame of reference. Notwithstanding the pastoral ethic of localizing worship, I heard catechists exhort their faith groups to learn the doctrine in Spanish and in Aymara. In meetings I attended catechists often employed both languages and filled their homilies with Spanish words, offered as highly technical, theological terminologies. This was partly for my benefit and partly to perform the catechists' status as adepts of esoteric foreign knowledge. But there was also the frequent sense that bilingual doctrinal knowledge was good for the faith group. The ancestors were said to have learned prayers in both languages. Nestor, for instance, after detailing the various prayers constituting a full knowledge of the doctrine, lamented the absence of a blackboard with which, he said, he could teach the prayers in both Spanish and Aymara:

> I could teach you in Spanish and Aymara from a blackboard. We should know the prayers that way. Here we know only Aymara; we lack Spanish. Yet when one goes to another place to make a celebration—[for instance] to a Franciscan chapel—if we go there we cannot speak Aymara: Spanish, pure Spanish. Then it is necessary to know the liturgy in Spanish.

Such linguistic capacities promise to enhance the spatial extension of faith group practices, as they reflect the spatial reach of catechists.

Faith group participation obviously does expand people's horizons. Although they travel less frequently than catechists, faith group membership does provide opportunities for travel: to neighboring ayllus for group baptisms, to the parish center for Holy Week celebrations, or to more distant parishes for regionwide pastoral events. Recall again Juana's reply to Nestor. She invoked her own travels within the frame of faith group participation, which put her in direct contact with knowledge being circulated by the bishop and so authorized her own assertion of Christian identity. Similarly, in a gathering of catechists, Alejandro commented on the strong impression made on his faith group members by a visit to an interparochial meeting of faith groups (a convivencia).

> And with respect to the convivencia, the faith group has thought a lot about this, how here in Machaqa they carried out a big convivencia. The new brothers who came were amazed [musparapxanxa]. "We are not used to seeing this. You really know how to do things well," they said. "Now I have seen this," they said. There is one older brother, Felix, no? He was really very amazed. "I had never been over to see those parts" [he said].

Another dimension of travel concerns less the movement of the catechist or faith group members than the movement through space and time of the biblical knowledge they seek to transact and localize. I have already discussed the highly spatialized imagery of words arriving to a person's chuyma. The composition of the Bible, particularly the epistles, reinforced these transspatial dimensions. Alejandro was especially fond of invoking my presence to illustrate the epistles as transspatial verbal transactions, comparing my traveling to Machaqa to the letters, which bring words to them across a great distance. In this sense the Bible contains words directed to the faith group. The public reading of the Bible puts these words into circulation and was an important part of the faith group service. The homily of the catechist was often framed as a process of making the group remember the words they had just heard. This, of course, completes the circulation, indexing the chuyma-based receipt of the words through their remembering. The Bible was also compared to the documents produced by a syndicate recording secretary. Similarly, people in the Bible, especially prophets and apostles, were often described as catechists. In constituting biblical knowledge as something to be received, such comparisons constitute it as something produced within an intelligible social context. This exegesis is resonant with missionary teaching, but also reflects approaches to the Bible as transacted knowledge, localized in faith group interactions.

The catechists thus effect a sort of vertical ideological integration, localizing exogenous forms of knowledge (cf. Murra 1972). At stake is the establishment of a positioned taypi integrating or harnessing to local ends ritual potency seen as spatially or temporally distant to the here-and-now present of situated practice. Consider again the taypi-resonant trope of domestication and incorporation evident in the figure of "tying" the words of the bishop, of the Bible, or of the catechist to one's chuyma. The possibility of completion linked to a future-oriented thaki of growing pastoral experience points toward yet another sense of taypi, the centralized seniority of a *pasante* who has successfully secured for his community the necessary extralocal values for local re-production. The completion effected through knowledge of the doctrine sug-gests the complementarity of distantly derived values: a center where all that is needed is present.

Remembering God: An Offering of Tears

In this light, faith group meetings appear as offerings, acts of chuyma-grounded sacrifice. At the most mundane level we have seen that members stress the connection between faith group practices and the perpetuation of basic Aymara sociability. Just as exchange relations among Aymara serve as a template for relations between Aymara and the gods, so the engagement of faith group members with the Christian god—performed every Sunday—is seen as integrally implicated in day-to-day Aymara social life. Without baptism as a sign that we are "children of Christ," declared a catechist to his group, "perhaps we would live like animals." He uses part of his address to the group to exhort them to live according to the words of God throughout the week. He takes as an example the issue of greeting. Greeting, and especially the lack of proper respect shown by younger generations for their elders, is an often-cited index of cultural decline; it was a favorite example among catechists, al-though by no means limited to them. To drive home his point about living according to God's words, the catechists suggested that not to greet others is the same as neglecting to greet God.

The activities of the faith group are cast explicitly as offerings: future-oriented reciprocal transactions. The vocabulary is identical. Faith group mem-bers describe themselves as standing in a relationship of *katoq* with God. The term is from the verb *katoqaña,* which means to receive or to be handed (some-thing). Alejandro, once described various religious affiliations—some people, he suggested, worshipped the devil; some made offerings to apus and wak'as; others worshipped God—as so many different expressions of katoq. I take him to mean so many different orientations of essentially the same kind of chuyma-grounded mediation.

Faith group participants implore God to give things to them and speak of what they receive from God. They may refer to receiving the word of God (*Diosan arup katuqapxañani*) or they may refer to receiving the blessing or the power of God (*tatitun ch'amap katuqañataki*). Conversely, faith group members speak of being received by God. The entire meeting may be framed as an of-fering that is "extended" to God. The term *luqtaña* (reach, or extend) is often used with respect to other forms of offering. I recorded a number of cases of the term being used in connection with faith group practices, as in the follow-ing statement by a catechist, introducing the final song ending the morning service: "OK, in order to offer/reach/extend [*luqtañataki*] this, we will sing a song" (cf. Gose 1994a:211 ff., 293, n.35). Finally, like all forms of Aymara offering, faith group meetings are cast as acts of memory. Members contrast themselves with others in the community who do not remember God: "We always remember; some do not remember but others, we, remember. He listens, and what we ask he gives that also."

After the songs the petitions or the Prayer of the Faithful are the most participatory practice in the faith group meeting. The texts of these clearly reflect the extent to which faith group practices are experienced as activities of offering, receiving, in the context of reciprocal relations with God.

1. To you, Father, these children [of yours], we give to you Holy Father God, good Father. You alone give me a well-understanding chuyma, Holy Father, God, good Father. Many families are going to all different parts. Unlike these children, I remember you, Holy Father. I give over to you; I extend [*luqtansma*] an offering to you, Holy Father. And many times I remember, Holy Father, while I inform you, Holy Father, you watch over these children for me, you are a pastor to them at all times of day and night, our Holy Father.

2. Now I truly ask you, Holy Father, since God, good Father, life in these parts here is not good, Holy Father . . . there is nothing to prepare [a reference to agricultural hardships]. But, God, good Father, you receive/accept us [*nanakar katuqist*] Holy Father, besides I always give thanks to you, Holy Father, God good Father, but now, Holy Father, show us well your hand, in that way we ask you good Father, fill/complete us Holy Father, God, good Father.

3. Father, good father, truly remember [*amtisiritaw*] the poor, the orphans, the orphaned children, the orphaned women, Holy Father. Truly in the world there are all kinds of poor. Truly, remember them, Holy Father, remember the orphaned children, Holy Father, also the poor, the sick. I remember you, Holy Father, you, Father, I ask you, Father. Truly remember us, each one of your children, Holy Father; this is what we ask.

Such communicative acts constitute the faith group practice as a positioned relationship with God. In 1, a catechist speaks to God on behalf of his faith group, underscoring a reciprocal relationship with God. He appeals to God's debt to the faith group, stressing that while many others no longer remember God, here, in the faith group, "unlike these children, I remember you." There is some slippage here between the first-person plural of the group and the agentive mediation of the catechist, whose actions of remembering and offering come from the group. This is especially evident at the end of his petition, where he invokes the return from his ritual efforts of remembering to redound upon the group, as God is asked to "watch over these children for me." Here the ritual authority of a catechist approaches those of mallkus and yatiris as his acts represent the group in reciprocal if asymmetric engagements with distant powers.

Examples 2 and 3 are petitions by faith group members. The concern with poverty, scarcity, and illness is ubiquitous in such petitions. In 2 the shortages confronting the Aymara are contrasted with the promise of a reciprocal relationship with God, who is implored to yield abundance and completion to his children by extending to them his generous hand. Example 3 illustrates an interactive sleight of hand in the economy of remembering. God is implored to remember the poor, the orphans, and the sick. This request is authorized with the assertion, "I remember you." The petition concludes with the rememberer appealing to God to remember her in turn. This is similar to the mediation effected by the catechists.

The centrality of memory, and this rhetoric of sacrifice, returns us to the issue of the chuyma, which remains the legitimating anchor for all faith group practices. Just as the chuyma is the receptive locus of a reciprocal engagement with God—faith group members receive the word of God in their chuymas or God gives them "a well understanding chuyma"—so the chuyma serves as a basis of extension, as an offering to God. "I give my chuyma to Jesus," declares a catechist to his faith group, "and Jesus helps me." Faith group worship is sometimes glossed as "inclining/submitting [alt'aña] our chuymas [to God]." The expression underscores not only the subjective chuyma-grounded orientation of such belief but also the spatial valences of subordination resonant across other fields of Aymara experience.

These two dimensions of the chuyma—a site of positioned offering and positioned reception—are evident in the following example from a catechist's homily, stressing, again, the need to live well with the entire community:

As if we were to speak of the entire community, that is what it means. So we will think/study well. We cannot unite ourselves. We are looking to different sides. We are scrutinizing others. In our chuymas, we do not pay attention. It must be like that. So the words of God do not arrive to our chuymas.

The speaker expresses an ideal of community solidarity, to be sure, but also at stake is an ideal of a chuyma unentangled in disputes with others. At issue is a value of transparency, of sincerity, of full chuyma-grounded engagement. This taypilike state of authentic positioned mediation is a precondition of authentic faith group worship. One who does not have faith is said to have a closed or "covered over" chuyma. In contrast, faith group members strive to "open our chuymas" to God. Faith group members repeatedly stress their status as subject to the omniscient scrutiny of God, who "knows everything about us," who "knows our chuymas." "God knows each one of us. God knows how I live in my house." A complaint about how some people live badly, mistreating their children and their animals, is followed by the assertion, "you see us all, Holy Father."

On the one hand, such claims assert for God a sort of omniscience comparable to that ascribed to wak'as (or the parish priest). This vigilance is a check on faith group sincerity, illuminating the interstices of participants' lives. It is also a resource, harnessed to members' needs. In one case, recorded during petitions, a man told a story of becoming "lost" for two days—apparently an illness or at least a period of time for which he had no memories. He suspected that someone had done this to him and appealed to God to reveal to him "who carried this out." The appeal is similar to requests to wak'as through coca to help find lost objects or identify thieves. The position of catechists as intermediaries also recalls these sorts of oracles. In his homily on the thakilike gifts of vocations specific to each of us, Bonifacio repeatedly stressed his personal ignorance of each person's true gift, while at the same time underscoring the knowledge circulated in the faith group and the division of tasks that he oversees as the setting for realizing and enacting each person's gifts.

On the other hand, in asserting total subjection to God, faith group members claim an authentic alignment of chuyma within the act. The efficacy of the their ritual practice depends upon this. This alignment is performatively displayed in faith group meetings. Happiness is one index of sincerity, as catechists exhort participants to sing with joyous chuymas. The confession and silent prayer of the Catholic mass are significant here as well; the act of "remembering our sins to God" is said to have a "calming" effect, perhaps related to the sort of chuyma-centered clarity so crucial to faith group activity. But the most salient index of sincerity in faith group practices stems from weeping and related displays of emotion. I observed weeping in the faith group most often in the context of petitions and most often on the part of women, but not exclusively in either case. To cite one exception: during a faith group meeting in which (for my benefit, prompted by their catechist) a number of members offered testimony of their involvement in the group, a man began weeping as he related the beneficial effects of faith group participation in healing him of health problems stemming from a bus accident he was involved in a number of years ago.

More commonly, however, weeping occurs during petitions in the course of laments over the difficulty of life. Returning to the cases above, it will be noted that the petitions reflect a fairly regular parallel structure of lines punctuated by the names "Holy Father, God, good Father." These discourse forms, especially when performed by women, often manifest a clear pattern of microtonal rising: each phrase stated at a slightly higher and breathier pitch, followed by an intake of breath. In other studies of discourse, such microtonal rising has been cited as a pragmatic cue for manifest emotionality. In the present case it should be noted that the climax of such microtonal rising, which is by no means always achieved, is weeping (see Urban 1991).

Weeping is a public index of sincerity. When people cry, suggested one catechist, it shows that they really feel something in their chuyma. He glossed crying, often referred to with the verb *jachaña*, with the term *chuymat ch'alljti*, which parses roughly as "a ch'alla from the chuyma." Recall as well the comments of the woman who took Nestor to task, invoking her own experiences of the bishop's words, which she tied to her heart. Underscoring the profundity of this internalization, she finished her recollection of the bishop's words by saying, "I remember those words well. I could cry." Weeping carries other connotations. The earliest rains, falling around the time of All Souls' Day, are said to be the tears of the dead. It is a common joke throughout the rainy season to tease people when it is raining: "Why the hell are you crying so much?!" Such comments point up the fertile potency of tears, as of all bodily fluids, implicated within a hydraulic economy connecting living and dead bodies with atmospheric and agricultural processes (Gose 1994a; Arnold 1992). It is within these frames—as indexes of chuyma-grounded sincerity and tokens of fertile potency—that the tears and near tears of faith group members can be seen as offerings. "Whoever prays crying to God," declared a catechist to his faith group, "will be received by him."

‡ ‡ ‡

The embattled identity of the faith group is neither a simple rejection of Aymara tradition or identity nor a romantic separatist return to indigenous roots. While faith group membership certainly signals a break of some sort, and entails a rejection of elements of Aymara practice, the faith groups also reflect the ongoing continuation of a number of sensibilities—of identity, of practice—that can accurately be cast as "Aymara." Like an Aymara household, the faith group stands as a site of microlocal cultural production that is also the anchor for paths of practice interweaving local and translocal phenomena. As a site of conversion and the explicit self-reflection this involves, the faith group is a space of translation, negotiating the commensurability of local sensibilities of personhood, integrity, and value in contexts that portend and compel shifting valuations of locality. The chapters in part 3, "Dismembering and Remembering Locality," look in detail at the tensions generated by such dissimilar conceptions and implications of locality. In the following chapter, for instance, I examine my view of the catechists as adepts of the negotiation of local and translocal forms of socioritual values against the susceptibility of the catechists to charges of fat stealing, conventionally seen as revealing the evisceration of locality by external forces.

PART 3

Locality Dismembered and Remembered

CHAPTER 6

Seductive Strangers and Saturated Symbols

When Roberto's wife died suddenly, her family accused him of killing her. Specifically they accused him of being a *kharisiri*. Kharisiris or *kharikharis* are dangerous beings who extract the fat from unsuspecting Indians. Their victims fall ill, weaken, and, according to most reports, die. Roberto was distraught as he reported his situation at a meeting of his fellow catechists. He wept as he told them of his wife's two-week illness and run-ins with his in-laws in the wake of her death. The catechists listened uncomfortably and decided that a delegation of them would travel to Roberto's community the next day to offer him their prayers, support, and company.

Roberto's wife was from a different ayllu in a neighboring province. These structural fault lines often make for contentious affinal connections and surely shed some light on this accusation of fat stealing. But unlike witchcraft accusations in other places, which seem to be routine components of sociostructural tensions, claims of fat theft are exceptional.[1] As Roberto's colleagues knew too well, catechists were often the subjects of kharikhari suspicion, sometimes to their own mortal peril. With his in-laws at some distance, and his relationship with his own ayllu relatively stable, Roberto was in little danger. But catechists elsewhere on the altiplano had been beaten, imprisoned, and lynched as a result of kharikhari accusations.[2]

Evidence of fat stealers (also known as *pishtaku, ñaqaq, likichiri*) is available across the Andes in a rich set of rumors, folktales, and news reports. One prototype of the fat stealer seems to be a Spanish friar, operating in some cases with the grisly assistance of his sacristan. The extracted fat is thought to be used to make communion wafers, candles, and especially holy oil. The extension of the suspicion to the catechists makes sense here. Indeed, by a remarkable coincidence, among the topics discussed at the catechist meeting in the moments before Roberto's emotional address to the catechists was an upcoming visit to the parish by the bishop, who would be performing the rite of confirmation.

(This was the visit for which Nestor sought to prepare his faith group.) While a number of priests I met told me they sometimes forego the use of holy oil when conducting baptism (to avoid the anxiety about the sources of the "grease"), it was understood as indispensable for the sacrament of confirmation. The impending visit of the bishop thus placed the catechists in the uncomfortable position of having to broker to their faith groups and their communities the circulation of this troubling and mysterious fat.

Some efforts to ascertain the origins of kharikhari beliefs point to the early modern Spanish battlefield practice of dressing wounds with fat (taken from the bodies of enemy soldiers?) and the earliest hospitals run by Catholic monks. From this vantage, kharikhari folklore marks the indigenous perspective of horror at these primal scenes of conquest. Today most accounts extend the suspicion to other whites and foreigners—mining engineers, commercial vendors, rural school teachers, and health promoters—with the fat now used in medicines, in fine soaps, or applied to machinery as a lubricant or fuel. According to rumors prevalent in Peru and Bolivia in the 1980s, the extraction was the work of government agents, with the fat used to pay down the national debts. Playing powerfully on the resonance of fat stealing to gloss other kinds of extractive and violent political and economic relations, many analysts suggest that the kharisiri embodies an autochthonous Andean commentary on a radically alien Western social order.[3]

These are evocative and insightful readings, resonant with colonial and contemporary ethnic polarities in the Andes. But such polarities, as emic theories about the social world (whether they be the perspectives of missionaries, of native Andeans, or of ethnographers), are imperfect representations of a messier, porous, entangled reality, and the situated practices and experiences through which it is apprehended, referenced, produced, and transformed. This chapter addresses the widespread suspicion that catechists steal the body fat of their neighbors against the backdrop of my own suspicion of analytical approaches to Andean locality steeped in polarizing models of postcolonial society.

But before dissecting the slippery subject of fat stealing, I want to juxtapose against the concern that the catechists are kharisiris a second set of rumors involving wak'as. Counterpoised with the catechists, who invite suspicion as local agents of what is historically an invading foreign religious tradition, these place deities are prototypical emblems of traditional Aymara identity and symbols par excellence of local sociopolitical integrity. What interests me here is that in a variety of rumors and suspicions about them, wak'as tend to manifest their power in the guise of unmistakably foreign people and places.

Wak'as are typically named places with which people enter into more or less balanced exchange relations, making a variety of offerings and receiving in return crop and animal fertility, luck, or simply avoiding misfortune. A close examination of such places would have to grapple with a fine mesh of categories and terms, from sayañas and flat fields, to rock outcroppings and local peaks, to water sources and the glacier-covered peaks that loom large in the views and thoughts of altiplano dwellers. While some consultants used the term *wak'a* (sometimes *wak'a achachila*) to pick out a particular class of place deities, others used the term to reference a general condition of potency and reciprocity inhering in certain places in the landscape. I am using the term in this less fine-grained sense, although I will focus on a particular class of wak'as— *sirinas*—below. As Ingrid and I learned when we were prompted as part of her curing to invoke local place deities from our experiences in the U.S. and Holland, such ongoing relations with potent places are considered basic components of human social experience.

What is more, despite their link with benevolent fertile potency, wak'as are also understood to be potentially dangerous and vengeful. I was warned not to touch certain wak'as, some consultants avoided watering their animals near places considered to be wak'a. In one case a bull that got loose and destroyed one family's barley field was said to have been possessed by a wak'a. I was told a story about a zealous convert to Protestantism who took a pickaxe to a wak'a on his sayaña. He was soon driven mad by the wak'a, which appeared to him in his house and pursued him into the foothills. A number of consultants described wak'as as *saxrani*. The term can be glossed as "evil" and surely conveys the categories of colonial evangelization as well as more contemporary ideologies from Protestant and neo-Catholic missionization. But the label also references the ambivalence of local place deities.

Wak'as appear to manifest their greatest powers at night. Offerings—*waxt'as*—are typically composed and burned after dark (a custom of clandestine secrecy that likely derives from early colonial extirpation campaigns [cf. Abercrombie 1998], but may also have to do with the fact that such offerings can sometimes be a part of sorcery directed against others). It was at night that the bull destroyed the barley field, at night that the unfortunate Protestant was visited in his house. I collected a number of stories about one class of wak'as known as sirina. These are typically associated with a water source. Late at night, I was told, a person passing by a sirina was likely to encounter a simulacra of a store or an inn, often staffed by an attractive young woman. Some consultants described the woman as a "señorita"—the term suggests a nonlocal ethnic distinction. The protagonist of choice in these cautionary tales was a drunken man—returning from a fiesta or staggering home after carousing with friends in the plaza.[4] Drunks seem to be especially susceptible to the temptation of entering the store or going into the inn. They fall asleep. Upon awakening, the unsuspecting victim continues home, gradually falling ill over the next few days.

A variant of this story involved wak'as—in this case a set of unusual rock formations near a path—from which light-skinned foreigners were known to emerge. "They look just like you," I was told. People encountering them were badly frightened and often fell ill. This capacity of fair skin, unfamiliar clothing, or ethnically marked accessories to frighten—and so, endanger health—was reinforced for me in other contexts. My eyeglasses were said to make children cry. Similarly, as I showed photographs of my children to people during a research trip in 2000, one woman, commenting on my son's blue eyes and fair skin, said how sorry she was that they didn't come with me. Then she suggested it was just as well, as his appearance would probably shock other children and make them cry.

A final set of rumors involves holes in the ground (animal burrows?) high in the cordillera. These holes are said to emit light. One consultant said they contain simulacra of cities, which become visible to passers-by on certain nights. People glimpsing these places are tempted to enter the hole as they view impressive skyscrapers and cars and even recognize friends and family who live in the city. Those who enter the hole fall ill. They are transformed; "They no longer walk the same," I was told. In some cases they do not return. My informant told me a story about a group of traveling musicians who were seduced by such a site when they heard a beautiful *huayño* being played. (The huayño is an urbanized, "mestizo" musical genre). All of them entered the earth except one musician who was not present. When he discovered what had happened, he went for help, which arrived in the form of a team of "investigators" from the United States. The team excavated the site, locating some of the missing musicians, who were then taken abroad for further study. In other cases, I was told that drunken men walking at night would sometimes see glimpses of a lover entering these holes. They follow, entering the earth, and awaken in the morning lying with their head and shoulders in the hole and their arms around a rock. Later they fall ill.

‡ ‡ ‡

Set in counterpoint, these two sets of rumors caution us away from facile constructions of local insularity and alterity in the Andes. Sites of indigenous authenticity (wak'as) manifest their highly local power in markedly exotic form. Similarly, I will argue, the radical otherness of the kharisiri relies on sensibilities of value and its circulation that, rather than suggest the rupture of local modes of sociability, might be seen as insisting in the strongest possible terms on their translocal translatability. In light of and in line with the analysis presented in previous chapters, I aim here to take the kharisiri rumors about the catechists less as a symptom of their exceptional in-between condition than as an opportunity to examine the porous production of Andean locality out of complex postcolonial conditions.

This involves reading against the grain of much of the existing scholarship on fat stealers in the Andes, which, in the final analysis, has taken the kharisiri to be an unambivalently negative being, the alien antithesis of productive human social relations in the Andes. Typically, fat stealers have appeared in folkloric collections of stories or in more anecdotal references that play poetically on the imagery of vampirism to comment upon colonial or post-colonial conditions (e.g., Taussig 1987; Weismantel 2001). More substantial discussions have detailed variations in kharisiri practices across shifting sociohistorical contexts (e.g., Crandon-Malamud 1986; Molinié Fioravante 1991; Salazar-Soler 1991; Rivière 1991; Wachtel 1994). Thus, while the colonial fat extractor was a robed monk, contemporary kharisiris appear as development workers and engineers, schoolteachers and politicians, working the will of such distant powers as the World Bank. In the mines kharisiris operate out of laboratories and concentration plants and may use pumps and picks to extract their victims' fat (Salazar-Soler 1991). The modern-day kharisiri has traded in his black mule for a red Toyota Landrover. There is a deep irony here, as scholarship tracing the subtle interweaving of culture and history nonetheless cleaves tightly to a presumed enduring indigenous perspective. In the case of the modern Andean fat stealer, it would seem the devil is decidedly not in the details but rather in a perduring structure of opposition between Andeans and their various Others. The kharikhari, we have been repeatedly told, stands for the fragmentation, the separation, and the opposition of two worlds.

In his 1994 book, *Gods and Vampires,* Nathan Wachtel examines a rash of kharikhari rumors in Bolivia in which a number of people—including catechists—were accused of being fat stealers and, in some cases, murdered by their communities. For Wachtel the accusations of fat stealing directed against other Indians is evidence of a radical rupture of Andean locality. He sees in these locally directed suspicions an unprecedented "extension of the outside world inside the village . . . an interiorization of otherness." "This is certainly a symptom of a profound crisis," concludes Wachtel, "the intrusion of modernity into the heart of Andean communities threatens the very roots of their identities" (1994:88).

Wachtel's comments appear as part of an insightful and reflective discussion of his return visit to Chipaya, some sixteen years after his first research in the area. His lament trades on a vision of local integrity lost, a boundedness undone by a relentless, translocal modernity. To a certain degree, this sense of traditional locality appears to be reinforced by the data I have presented from Machaqa: on the one hand, as vectors of external power, the catechists localize the alien dangers embodied by kharisiris, on the other, the alienation of local power and integrity could hardly be represented more starkly than in the specter of wak'as as site of gringo commercial power. Yet while these beliefs certainly reference changing sociohistorical circumstances and reflect a local consciousness of foreign power within a world valenced and contested along dimensions of race, ethnicity, and class, they do not signal the dissolution of local integrity. Rather, I have been arguing, it is precisely out of such complex, entangled, and contested spaces that people struggle to form coherent local orders of space and time. The challenge in the Andes—and in comparable contexts—is to examine such entangled social fields ethnographically without flattening or fracturing them.

‡ ‡ ‡

As I have suggested, the case of the Andes is particularly instructive for efforts to rethink polarizing imaginings of locality. Andean locality has long been produced out of translocal entanglements such as the various strategies of vertical ecological integration. It is likely that regional exchange networks of outliers and archipelagos fostered and routinized experiences of ethnic difference and twined these with highly translocal sensibilities of community and identity.

A related line of argument suggests that entangled difference is an ambivalent precondition of social life. To a certain degree this claim overlaps with familiar discussions of "complementary opposition" in the Andes: that is, the valenced distinction of "upper" and "lower" moieties, highlands and lowlands, "male" and "female" social positions that requires their entanglement as complementary values. Andean locality is produced through the mediation of this culturally marked field of difference. Yet, even as distant or contrasting values (including neighboring communities) are seen as at once dangerous and indispensable, unsocialized fertility to be harnessed to local ends, the acts of mediation that sustain locality are themselves ambivalent—threatening the undoing of the system. I suspect that this is in part what distressed the catechists when faced with Hernando's homogenized liturgical calendar for the ayllus of Jesús de Machaqa. Inasmuch as the contrast is where the productive action is, the mediated whole is less than the entangled sum of the parts—too much of a good thing.

This double-edged sense of mediation finds its most focused expression in the Andean concept of center or taypi: a mediating third term that encompasses and transcends the whole. The Jesús de Machaqa plaza is a graphic index of this: both a microcosm of the regional system and a hub in a network of dangerous subterranean canals, which are thought to link the local Church with a set of other temples across the Andes. In this sense taypi is the paradoxical and perilous anchor of Andean locality: at once a locally situated center and a metonym of a more encompassing integration.

Moreover, as an ambivalent frame of translocal mediation, taypi is not fixed but is rather fleetingly achieved in situated practice. This is a particular Andean instantiation of a broader claim about culture at the core of this book. The achievements of situated practice, referencing and rendering complex yet coherent worlds of meaning, stem from formal rituals as well as more quotidian actions and experiences, from the collective macrolevel as well as the body-bound microlevel. Kharisiri rumors reference the contentious relations of collective identities as well as the situated experiences of individuals within this complex field. Much of their force comes from the ways they bridge symbolic grammars evident in formalized activities of ritual and exchange with the bodily experiences of everyday practice. What is more, these rumors and accusations operate both at the level of text and at the level of telling: referencing complexities and challenges of immediate salience against the backdrop of a conflictive history generating contrasting categories of identity. My aim is not to deny this ongoing history or the damage it has done but rather to deny it the absolute capacity to render local cultural activity little more than hopelessly insular posturing of reaction and resistance. Such an approach masks in its own way the complexities of the situations it hopes to understand and the challenges and achievements of day-to-day practice in places such as Jesús de Machaqa.

Rather than taking kharisiris as a boundary-asserting ideology of self/other contrasts, I want to argue that such beliefs reveal this entangled ontology of Andean locality, which might be glossed as the ephemeral achievement of social practices aimed at the integration of ambivalent (dangerous but necessary) foreign value. The embodiment of that value is fat, a saturated symbol deeply involved in the translocal production of locality. It is to this bodily substance that I now turn.

SATURATED SYMBOLS

Fat is an index of well-being. It is said to be a source of strength—ch'ama—that enables people to "go about." While ch'ama is embodied in other ways—as blood or breath—body fat seems to be its clearest somatic index. In this sense, fat is the principal form of social potential, the energy source for the extension of self into the social and material world.

The principal symptom of fat-related illness is fatigue. Aymara who complain of fatigue often describe a pain or discomfort in their lower back. Indeed, the most potent fat in human beings is said to be located on the kidneys (*maymuru*). It is precisely this fat that is the main target of kharisiri extraction (Abercrombie 1986:176, Crandon-Malamud 1991).

Fat is also directly associated with fertility; it is a prototypically generative substance. Animal fat (llama or sheep) figures prominently in a set of offerings aimed at generative potency, in which fat and other ritual ingredients are transformed through exchange with place deities into animal fertility, cash, luck, strength, and so forth. The connection is also more literal; in some areas fat is considered to be condensed semen (Abercrombie 1986). In other accounts the fat stealer is said to have a preference for the testicles of his victims (Salazar-Soler 1991:10). Others report a belief that the castrator of animals should always be very fat himself, since he will lose some of his own fat in compensation to the animals he castrates (Kapsoli 1991).

In addition to kharisiri attack, other things can affect fat. To travel at night, for instance, is to put your fat at risk. Altiplano nights are typically very cold; a number of maladies are described as a condition of "frozen" fat. Fright is also said to affect human fat: a condition similarly described as causing the fat "to freeze." Conversely, physical labor is thought to vaporize fat, filling the body with steam or smoke.

The cover of night also aids secrecy and facilitates such antisocial behavior as fat extraction. Secrecy inverts ideals of transparent sociability, evident, for instance, in the notion that effective social and ritual action involves externalizing an interior state: showing others (people or places) that your chuyma is in the right place. In day-to-day sociability a similar sort of transparency is an ideal. Exchange practices, for instance, enact in bodily terms and in intersubjective interactional contexts forms of translocal circulation that are homologous with the more macrolevel flows of value sketched above. In this sense the body is the most localized ground for the achievement of taypi.

Fat, then, is a vital medium of circulation and transaction with both somatic and transsomatic, local and translocal implications. The circulation of fat within the body is a condition of effective productive and reproductive social action in the world, action that extends beyond the body-bound subject and entails engagements with other persons and places. As a component of ritual offerings, fat circulates with even greater reach and can be located within an economy of value deriving from a more encompassing ecological and political landscape. The correspondence between the smoke of a burnt offering and the smoke that rises in the body as a result of the exertion of physical labor highlights this connection.[5]

Notwithstanding the dangers it conceals, nighttime is a transformative and by no means unambiguously negative time. The transformative potential of freezing altiplano nights (as a productive counterpoint to the intense sun of daytime in the highlands) is harnessed to social ends in the process of making chuñu: a form of freeze-dried potatoes produced by leaving potatoes to freeze overnight and then wringing the moisture our of them and allowing them to dry in the harsh Andean sun. The resulting desiccated potatoes can be stored for years without sprouting or decaying. As suspended organic potential, chuñu is comparable to frozen fat, which is also rendered unproductive and removed from circulation.

While freeze-drying potatoes effectively suspends their generative powers, once soaked in water and cooked, chuñu is held to be an essential source of vitality. The fertile potency of reconstituted chuñu is evident in the belief that chuñu is the ideal food for pregnant women. "It has everything," I was told. Many Aymara I spoke with attributed their physical strength to their consumption of chuñu. For them the displacement of chuñu by rice and noodles in the contemporary Aymara diet is a cause of the degeneration of contemporary Aymara as compared to the ancestors, who are held to have been stronger, more knowledgeable, and more productive. The implications of this range from physical labor (the ancestors are thought to have been capable of remarkable physical feats—cultivating extensive fields and manipulating large rocks as evident in monoliths and other pre-Colombian stonework as well as the church in Jesús de Machaqa), to longevity and endurance (I was told that the ancestors could dance all night, withstand intense cold, and routinely lived to be well over one hundred years of age), to mental acuity (kids today, I was lectured, don't learn as much or as quickly as their parents and grandparents, largely because they eat a diet that is too "liquid" and full of processed foods). As an ethnic marker the ingestion of chuñu makes Indian fat qualitatively different from the fat of white people. It makes Indian fat more desired by kharisiris (e.g., Salazar-Soler 1991:10).

Nighttime is also the most propitious time for offerings to wak'as. As an analogue of human fat, animal fat is transacted in a range of offerings.[6] The transaction of this generative substance is intended to yield a return in kind: animal fertility, good health, luck, wealth, etc. Llama fat is a staple ritual component, often combined with another key ingredient: a dried llama fetus (qharwa sullu). In the offerings I have observed, the llama fetus was draped with fat and wrapped with wool. Consultants describing such offerings often referred to "giving a llama," leading me to think that they were referring to the sacrifice of a live llama. In fact, they were referring to this "reconstituted" fetus. There are important similarities between llama fetuses and chuñu: each is suspended

FIGURE 6.1   *Giving a llama. The fetus was smeared with fat and covered with wool*

in its natural processes of transformation through a process of human intervention and desiccation. Similarly, both are returned to approximations of their
natural state and so made into especially condensed symbols of these processes.
Fat is centrally implicated in these processes of transformation and exchange.

To these and other ends, Aymara, like the kharikhari they fear, are constantly
gathering and transacting fat as part of their ceaseless production of locality. Fat
can be bought at local markets. It is available along with other ritual ingredients
in large "witchcraft" markets in the cities of La Paz and El Alto. But the most
direct way to accumulate fat is to harvest it from slaughtered animals.

When a sheep is slaughtered, fat is collected and set aside. Generally, this
is gathered from around the intestines and especially from the *llika:* a membrane of fat surrounding the animal's stomach. Butchering is usually performed
by a man. While some women did participate in butchering, more typically,
they remained to the side, often in the cooking area, while the butchering
took place in the patio of the house compound.

This harvesting of fat involves yet another form of circulation, here within the sphere of the household. Once gathered, the fat from the animal is sent
to the woman in the cooking area, followed a short time later by the internal
organs and intestines as well as the blood drained from the carcass. Some of
the fat is dried and stored for future ritual use. Some is used in cooking.
Butchering usually promises a meal of *chicharron:* tasty morsels of intestine and
internal organs fried in fat. Like all things fried in fat, chicharron is a prestige,
luxury dish, linked with the city, where restaurants serve heaping plates of
chicharron made from chicken or pork. My hosts insisted that chicharron was
especially good when accompanied by chuñu.

SEDUCTIVE STRANGERS

Let me turn here to the second set of rumors: the appearance of wak'as as
powerful white outsiders, as alien sites of commerce, as cities, etc. The suspicions present prototypically local places as venues of foreign power. There are
two points at issue here. Peter Gose (1994) has linked contemporary mountain deities to precolonial ancestor cults focused on mummified bodies stored
in mountain caves and widely eradicated in colonial extirpation campaigns.
In Jesús de Machaqa such place deities are referred to as achachila (grandfather): a term that clearly conveys ancestral links. They are also referred to as
apus (lords), with connotations of political power. We might imagine that
during the colonial period, as the Andean landscape was contested and re-
fashioned to include a symbolic geography of parishes and chapels, each with

their own state-enforced graveyards, acts of burial and genealogical remembering became political (perhaps forms of practical nostalgia) in new ways (see Allen 1982:183 ff., MacCormack 1991:424–33, Salomon 1987).

This link with the dead is significant. Like the wak'as, the dead are a key source of fertile potency, associated with crop production and the arrival of the rains. By some accounts the fertile waters of highlands agriculture flow from the desiccating bodies of the dead, who yield their fatty moisture to the land where they lay as part of a hydraulic economy of circulating fertile wetness (Gose 1994a; Allen 1982).

In his introduction to the Huarochiri manuscript, a document written at the turn of the seventeenth century, likely by Andeans in interaction with Catholic missionaries, and widely taken as offering a glimpse of precolonial Andean categories of thought, Salomon (1991:16) eloquently describes this cosmological economy of moisture:

> In gross terms, then, the Huarochiri world opposes the qualities of still centricity—depth, solidity, dryness, stability, potential fecundity, womanliness—to those of a restlessly moving outer orbit—height, fluidity, wetness, movement, potential for insemination, virility. . . . Born fat, wet, and juicy, all beings eventually—in the space of dry season or a long life—separate out again into their original substances (Allen 1982). Humans like all others emerge fat and wet, but at the end of life their dried husk containing the potential for future life goes as a mummified ancestor (*mallqui*) back to earth. The function of ritual and sacrifice is to ensure a steady circulation of biological energy . . . [through] social exchange.

In the case of rains, mountains play mediating positions, circulating potency from below to above. In Jesús de Machaqa rain, hail, and frosts are said to come from specific peaks. Different mountains are responsible for different meteorological events in different years according to a rotative system known as *marani* (annuals). This rotation evokes local political offices, and, indeed, the marani are spoken of as constituting a cabildo. The analogy between mountains and (human) mallkus works both ways. Like the mountain peaks, ayllu authorities mediate the flow of fertile value. They are held accountable for the rains and crop production during their tenure and serve as the principal mediating representatives of locality with the state (and other extralocal forces). Authorities, we have seen, undertake this mediation from a position of taypi: their thakis effect a lifelong movement to the center of the ayllu, culminating in service as mallku. Mature couples are then said to "rest," assuming positions of identification with the dead ancestors, whose ranks they gradually join. The mountain lords (apus, achachilas) take on the ambivalence of these mediating elders.

Just as the applications of the fatty wetness extracted by kharisiris reflects changing historical circumstances—used to forge bells, made into holy oil, made into medicine, powering the space shuttle—the fluid values mediated by the mountains also present something of an archive of local entanglements. Alongside the accounts of cities and mountains said to contain churches of gold, I have heard stories of trains that appear in the mountains, and in May of 2000 I was told of a community in the vicinity of Peñas where the locals had found a hole in the side of the mountain from which they could extract (as from a well) a limitless supply of gasoline. This last rumor emerged at a time of considerable debate and distress in Bolivia concerning the privatization of water services. In April of 2000 hikes in rates for water service in the region of Cochabamba and the specter of charging rural peasants in the region for the water flowing through the irrigation channels they constructed prompted a series of demonstrations causing the government and the newly privatized water company to rethink their plans for the area. In the opinions of many I spoke with the following month, it was only a matter of time before a similar attempt to charge peasants for water was made in altiplano communities. For some, recent development projects modernizing the collection and distribution of water through the use of cement tanks on hilltops and plastic tubing running down the hillsides to spigots near each family's sayaña were simply the first step in an effort to alienate this resource from the control of the ayllus. It is telling that at this moment I heard rumors equating the fluid benevolence of the mountains with the liquid commodity par excellence in campesino experience.

This is one frame for considering the appearance of the wak'as as representatives of foreign power, for it is precisely the achievement of translocal mediation that renders mediators ambiguous and dangerous. In this sense wak'as may be at once ancestral ayllu authorities (the culmination of local potency) and foreigners.

This raises a second point. Not only does Aymara social and ritual practice turn on harnessing extralocal value—goods from distant ecozones; the less concrete forms of fertile potency traded in by wak'as—to local ends, but the ethnically differentiated world of white/modern power appears as a component of this more encompassing category of "outside" potency crucial to local social reproduction and the social reproduction of locality. By this light the appearance of wak'as as cities, as churches of gold, or as sociological metonyms of encompassing power—e.g., doctors, conquistadors, landowners, whites—evokes not only the ambiguity of wak'as—who are benevolent as well as destructive—but the ambiguity of the extralocal power, which is dangerous but necessary, other yet integral, distant yet central to local practices.

While I have been stressing integration and mediation over insularity and opposition, this emphasis on mediation runs the risk of masking undeniable power inequalities in what is certainly an ethnically and class-valenced social world. It is not my intention to deny these, nor to obscure the growing constraints and the profoundly unfavorable extractive relations in which Andeans find themselves compelled to participate. But, rather than asserting a radical otherness, they disclose the porous entanglement of locality within a translocal system characterized by potentially violent, extractive, and unequal relations.

This asymmetry is evident for instance in the various sorts of nostalgic statements we have seen about cultural and material decline, ranging from laments over the depletion of land and herds, to regret for the forgetting of customs and the decline of civil society, to the plight of contemporary Aymara who are frailer and less capable than their ancestors. In declaring themselves to be sick and exhausted, Aymara sense that they have little fat left to give. This asymmetry is also indexed by unequal access to the potency mediated by the wak'as, particularly in the case of churches or schools that have been classed as wak'as. To take the example of churches, in Jesús de Machaqa the matrix church is a wak'a, where Machaqueños make offerings in anticipation of fertile crops, an increase in their herds, good health, or financial gain. I was told that many "doctors" and "lawyers" from La Paz came to perform similar offerings at the church. In part this reflected the power of the local wak'a as a site of renown in the region. But the return received by the "doctors" exceeds the gain secured by local Aymara; these urban adepts receive houses and cars. There is an almost "cargo cult"-ish sense here that I shall return to below—as if urban "doctors" had found the secret to the very same system Andeans continually struggle with.

The sirina suspicions link these discussions of circulating fertility and the ethnically and class-valenced landscape of Aymara practice in revealing ways. On the one hand, the stories involve the circulation of fat and comparable value. The men who fall prey to sirinas find themselves rendered chuñu, afflicted with frozen, denatured fat. Moreover, sirinas are typically water sources to which these men are forced to yield their own fatty moisture. Similarly, this nocturnal engagement of men with the young señoritas has sexual overtones suggesting the transmission of fat in the form of semen. Finally, note that the sirina manifests itself not only as nubile femininity but also as a frame of commercial relations—stores and inns—in which basic tokens of Aymara sociability—hospitality; the gifting of food—are bound up with the circulation of cash.

At the same time, the sirina rumors are deeply implicated in acts of translocal mediation. The victims of sirinas are invariably men in the process of returning to their homes. This returns us to the gendered distinction suggested by Salomon between female stability and male motion. A similar contrast is evident in the ideology of contemporary gender relations. As I discussed in chapter 5, the Aymara household appears as a positioned site of female stability, a storehouse of value supplied by the mediating actions of masculine vitality (see also Arnold 1992). Through translocal practice men localize distant value to be controlled by women. Indeed, the woman herself is one such domesticated value, and that she should emerge as the paradigmatic center is entirely consistent with the sense of porously produced locality I am highlighting here. In marriage practices this localization is expressed in the pouring of antique coins from the hands of the groom to those of the bride. On a more day-to-day level, Aymara women typically control the family's cash and frequently complain that men have no head for money and that, without their centering guidance for accumulating and channeling wealth wisely, an Aymara man would just squander it without reflection. This is, we can now see, a multileveled concern. Money is equated with semen (and fat) as indexes of fertile vitality that are most properly channeled into the generation of Aymara households. Correlated with this is the liminal risk of mediation across space—the necessary but dangerous condition of the possibility of the production of Aymara locality. In the idealized scheme sketched by Salomon, such mediation is the work of men, who, in the absence of their domesticating women, verge always on the asocial misdirection of their resources.

The sirinas thus disrupt the right flow of vitality, semen, and cash from men to women. Their victims, as men are wont to do without the guidance and support of their wives, literally waste away. This is an exaggerated expression of a continual condition of the production of locality, referencing its complex and changing circumstances. As a metaphor of this disruption, the commercial venues of sirinas condense both the extractive inequality of the cash economy, with the encompassing spatial reach of market entanglements. The first sirina I learned about was located along a footpath to a large regional market in the town of Jiwakuta.

Fat-Draped Women and Flayed Men

There are a number of links, then, between sirinas and kharisiris. Both affect the fat of their victims. Both tend to attack victims who are drunk and traveling alone and at night. Both tend to stand for a rupture of right relations of sociability, embodying a disruption of normal social intercourse. While I did not hear the term *sirina* invoked as an epithet or accusation against specific people, two incidents from my research suggest the extension of the term in rumor and humor to characterize women who have migrated to La Paz or El Alto. In one case, as I sat talking with a group of men in the sacristuyu near the chapel in Qhunqhu, a young woman wearing pants walked through the plaza where we sat. She was, I believe a *residente:* a migrant to La Paz who had returned to the community in anticipation of the celebration of All Soul's Day, which was a few days away. Her dress, however, was extremely anomalous—even for a visiting residente—and her sudden appearance, walking alone crossing the plaza, was quite jarring. As it happens, the path exiting the east side of the chapel forks, climbing north, into the hills behind the chapel, or continuing east, crossing a small stream near a large boulder said to be a wak'a sirina. We fell silent as she passed, walking by without greeting any of the elder men (a breech of politeness) and continuing toward the stream. The men immediately began joking that she was a sirina. Although they did not seem to associate any danger with her appearance, her dress marked her as ethnically other. (Perhaps she was one of those people, seduced by the city, who return transformed.) By distinguishing her with the label *sirina,* they also refused to locate her within the grid of day-to-day sociability while still recognizing her within a more encompassing and no less locally salient landscape of power and identity.

FIGURES 6.2, 6.3   *The llika, he said, looked like the embroidered shawls worn by cholas in La Paz*

The second incident concerns a comment made by Alejandro one day as he was butchering a sheep. I often took such butchering as an opportunity to ask informants about chuyma, fat, and other bodily substances. As I was asking these interminable questions of Alejandro, he held up the llika. He commented on the patterns evident in the membrane, where thicker patches of fat formed shapes that stood out against the thinner, translucent background. The llika, he said, looked precisely like the expensive embroidered shawls worn by "señoritas" in La Paz. He referred, I think, not to white upper-class Bolivians (who are more likely to adopt their fashion from Miami than to wear Hispanic shawls [c.f. Gill 1994]) but rather to cholas: a class of successful and powerful Aymara women residing in La Paz. Among the more striking aspects of the chola Paceña is her clothing. These women wear a very expensive elaboration upon rural female dress comprising skirts, embroidered blouses, sweaters and shawls complemented by fine derby hats, jewel-encrusted earrings, and shoes. The style is replicated less splendidly by "chola wannabes": young Aymara women working as domestic servants in the city and rural women—especially young unmarried girls—for whom these clothes constitute a "Sunday best" worn for fiestas, photographs, and trips to the city. From the points of view of rural men, whose migrant experiences in La Paz may involve working for cholas as porters, bargaining with them as cash-short customers, or looking in wonder at the outsides of the houses and high-rise buildings in which domestic servants work, these women are powerful indeed. They are also highly sexualized, especially unmarried women who live far from the vigilance of their rural families (e.g., Gill 1993). These various potencies are embodied in their dress, and it is little wonder Aymara men see them as draped with fat.

This convergence of cholas and sirinas implicates migration with other forms of transpatial mediation—such as trade and offerings—and locates a range of forms of economic success and status differentiation with respect to what is locally taken as a more encompassing and apparently universally translatable idiom of increase rendered in the saturated symbol of fat. In stressing this translatability, my aim is not to smooth out or to deny the conflictive social realities of ethnic and racial difference but rather to insist that they are not radically alien to situated Aymara sociability. My contention is that it is precisely through such translocal entanglements that historical inequalities and relations of power operate. Like the sirinas, like the catechists accused of kharisiri, migrants are at once of and other to their community. Long an ambivalent component of local production, contemporary migration seems to expose Aymara to especially stark identity shifts and contradiction, even as it renders rural communities especially dependent upon translocal social networks for their on going reproduction. In the following section, I turn briefly to one example of the negotiated ambivalence of migrating others, complementing the discussion of chola-sirenas with its converse: the case of the gringo-mallku.

The Case of the Gringo-Mallku

In 1991 a man named Hugo was named to serve as one of the mallkus of his ayllu for the following year. Hugo, a man in his sixties, had recently returned to his natal ayllu after a long career in La Paz. He had served as a policeman—an upwardly mobile path toward petty bureaucratic power, corruption, and ties to political parties. Hugo told me he had also served for many years in the army, recounting his experiences of training and marksmanship competitions at U.S. bases in Panama and Fort Benning, Georgia.

Although his primary residence for many years had been La Paz, Hugo had maintained a sayaña in the community and had some family ties there. To judge from gossip, despite his physical distance, he had remained occasionally embroiled in issues of local debate, embracing some unpopular positions over the years and angering many people. He was involved, for instance, in a number of land disputes, and it appears that his access to official records in La Paz and his facility with the ways of official bureaucracy and bureaucratic corruption had given him the upper hand. Hugo was neither well liked nor widely trusted, and he was not the ayllu's first choice for mallku. However, he was technically eligible to serve, and, late in the year, as the community found that the other prospects either had compelling excuses to put off their service or found themselves conveniently far from the ayllu (working in the yungas) and unable to accept the cargo, Hugo, through a combination of obligation and ambition, emerged as one of the designated mallkus.

While, from some points of view, obliging this recently returned migrant to jump through the hoops of community service was a delicious form of revenge, a number of people in the community seemed concerned about the prospect of Hugo as a mallku. His estrangement from the community, they felt, had gone too far. "He is not from here," they said. "He doesn't know our customs." Someone suggested that he was more like the president, aligned with a political party, than a mallku serving the community. If these comments suggest a sort of total transformation of kind, that Hugo (like people who entered the holes on the mountainsides) had become something else, other criticisms reflect a sense of stunted growth. One man described Hugo as "green" or "immature." "He doesn't have experience" people complained, and so is "like a wawa (baby)." More than most mallkus, people remarked, Hugo would have to rely on his elder councilors throughout his tenure.

Other comments were more pointed. Some denounced Hugo as a "traitor." I heard one woman suggest that he would "sell the community." These sorts of comments reference Hugo's role in previous land disputes in the community. It bears noting that, for contemporary Machaqueños (and for reasons that may have as much to do with the MNR land reforms as with indigenous territoriality), the commercial sale of land is seen as a rupture of local integrity comparable to the somatic disruption caused by sirinas and kharisiris. Indeed, white visitors in the countryside are often suspected of looking to buy up land . . . or worse; I was occasionally (playfully?) teased that my briefcase or backpack were so heavy because I had filled them with earth, gold, or babies. A man who shared Hugo's patronym, and who was then involved in a dispute with him over rights to sayaña lands, called him *wiraqucha*—a mild ethnic slur typically referencing whites but apparently extendable (much like the specter of the sirina) to upwardly mobile Aymara.[7] More strongly, he described Hugo as *q'arasiri,* observing, "some campesinos who go to the city behave that way." *Q'ara* is perhaps the strongest racialized epithet in Aymara. The term often refers to whites, but more precisely denotes outsiders without social ties. The term means "peeled" connoting not only physical difference but also differences in costume.[8] The term also suggests barrenness, as in an empty, uncultivated field. Although I have encountered no other examples, the construction q'arasiri might be glossed as "one who peels (or makes barren)." It also seems to play on kharisiri, though, along with the association of q'aras with kharisiris, we should note this twist: the condition of the alien, dangerous q'ara is not unlike that of the *victim* of the kharisiri, who is said in some cases to be flayed.

From the moment his name emerged as an incoming mallku, Hugo endured continual criticism. The statements I have just reported were recorded out of his presence, but I was told of a community meeting at which he was so abused by a group of women from the ayllu that he stormed out of the meeting, leaving some with doubts as to whether he would in fact accept the cargo. His lot was no easier once he was installed in the post. He was regularly teased for adopting the traditional regalia of a mallku (poncho, coca purse, etc.), which contrasted with his former urban attire and drew attention to (and prompted addition teasing over) a large pair of aviator style eyeglasses he wore. A few months into his tenure he stopped wearing his eyeglasses at public events. Hugo upset a number of members of the ayllu by failing to observe the period of silence or humble talk expected of mallkus. In a community meeting I attended he was rudely interrupted and chastised by a woman for speaking in Spanish rather than Aymara.

Yet, as difficult as things were for Hugo, they were perhaps more difficult for his wife, Filomena. She was from another region of the altiplano—a liability under the best of circumstances. While living in La Paz—or so the rumor went—she had gone about *de vestida:* in "white clothes" (see Nash 1979; Gill 1994). As with Hugo, this heightened the ridicule to which she was exposed when she gamely donned the black skirt, shawl, and headdress distinctive of mallku taykas in Jesús de Machaqa. During and after fiestas women commented critically on what they saw as her awkward dancing and inept behavior. Some women in the community insisted on referring to her as "señora."

CATECHISTS AND KHARISIRIS

Rather than a grid of radically contrasted racial, class, or ethnic identities, rather than a bounded notion of insular locality impacted by but at some level bracketed from an encompassing national or global order, these examples suggest a continuum of presupposed, mutually intelligible identity positions engaged and referenced in situated contexts of practice. To be sure, not all positions are equally available to all actors. Moreover, these racialized identity categories have considerable force, reflecting a long history of power relations that constrain and distort social practice. They reflect ethnotheories of society, commentaries on a complex social situation. Yet while these ethnotheories posit a fractured world in which they map a space of embattled local authenticity, the differences they generate and reference are less boundaries than resources vital to apparently local practices—practices that both produce locality and reference its porous entanglement with encompassing otherness.

The parallels between the cases of Hugo and Roberto are revealing in this regard. In each case tensions of entangling otherness that are integral to the reproduction of patrilocal households (i.e., in-marrying women) are intensified by more sharply drawn structural fault lines (women from other provinces), that, while conflictive, are undeniably "internal" to Aymara society in the way that commentators such as Wachtel approach it. For a variety of reasons particular to each case—Hugo's time as a government functionary, Roberto's service as catechist—this productive tension, with a potential for conflict, is interwoven with a more absolute language of ethnic, racial, and class distinction: Roberto is accused by his wife's family of being a fat stealer; Hugo's wife is derisively labeled by his community as an inauthentic Machaqueña, a (quasi-white) "señora." Hugo is himself a near kharisiri, though the striking thing about his case is the possibility of relatively reindigenizing himself through his service as mallku.

My point is not to equate these various relations of difference as simply large-scale extensions of a single cultural logic. I have already argued that ethnic categories entail a specific grammar of difference that is not reducible to, and may often do violence to, local sensibilities of distinction. The translatability or commensurability between these frames of difference is achieved rather than found, negotiated and asserted rather than accepted. The ethnographic task is to examine this achievement in specific contextual practices. These are the practices that generate porous locality through acts of reference that presuppose its entangled condition. This returns us, at last, to the catechists, the kharisiris, and issues of spatial mediation.

Three Victims

Kharisiri suspicions are patently about transactions across space and across sociohistorically produced boundaries, be they the boundaries of the body, the boundaries of the community, or the boundaries of the nation. In some versions of the kharisiri stories, the fat extracted is transported beyond local and even national boundaries, only to be returned to the body in the form of medicine or holy oil. Note also the dislocated character of the kharisiri, who classically appears as a stranger, or as a person with few social connections. Consider as well the liminal site of most kharikhari attacks. While some kharisiris are reported to enter houses while people are asleep, or more ominously to remove fat across long distances with the benefits of new technologies, most accounts indicate a tendency of kharisiris to waylay their victims along paths or roadways, near rural schools or churches. Sometimes fat stealers enchant their victims and remove them to mountain caves where they butcher them. These are all sites of spatial mediation—settings for the practices of the production of locality. More significantly, it is not only the kharisiris who are engaged in action across bounded space. Like the men who fall prey to sirinas, the *victims* of kharikhari are frequently involved in their own transpatial practices.

Let me sketch three cases of kharikhari suspicion. The first involves the daughter of Marcela, a member of a catechist-led faith group. I interviewed Marcela to elicit details of her personal history as a faith group member. She had been a member of the faith for about ten years, though she remarked that obligations to care for her animals and fields meant she didn't always attend and thus was a bit "behind." I asked what prompted her to begin attending meetings. "I was sick," she told me, "I still am, to this day." I waited for her to continue, and she suddenly began to tell me of her daughter who fell victim to a kharisiri. "No I wasn't sick," she went on. "I had a child first. I'm going to tell you this well. My daughter Alicia worked over there [in Jesús de Machaqa town] with Father Hernando. So she was in the town. She walked in the town. Walking in the town she learned how to knit well; [she learned] all aspects of knitting. She was very accomplished in her work. And thus she died. Kharikhari butchered her. I tried in vain to cure her with medicine. It did not do anything. She simply died."

A second case stems from the regional fiesta of Rosario, discussed in chapter 1. Recall that in Rosario all the ayllus of Jesús de Machaqa dance in the plaza of the central town. The plaza is thus rendered taypi: a microcosm of the region. There is an oscillation in the rite between this encompassing unification and the violent distinctions between ayllus, with fights being very common and thought to be integral to the ritual's success. On the final night of the fiesta each ayllu retired to the houses they maintain in the town, along the streets leading away from the town plaza. I accompanied the delegation from Milluni. As the last of the drinking and dancing in the Milluni house patio subsided, we bedded down to sleep. Soon someone became aware of a stranger in the room. I had seen this man earlier, and someone identified him as being from a neighboring ayllu. Although he had been hanging around, drinking and dancing with us for much of the night, he was now aggressively confronted. One man demanded his identity card.[9] The stranger was viciously insulted and accused of having designs to "steal women." Someone yelled out that he was a kharisiri. The man himself was quite drunk and said little to defend or explain himself. At one point he simply pleaded, pathetically, "If I go outside, they'll assault me." The confrontation stopped short of physical violence. After a while the man quietly got up and left.

A third example returns us to the case of Roberto and the accusation by his wife's family that he killed her by stealing her fat. Roberto was a catechist of ambiguous standing in his community. His father was a member of a Protestant Church, and as a boy Roberto was sent out of his ayllu to study at schools run by the Church in other parts of the altiplano. He also worked for a period of time as a schoolteacher, again in other communities. Like many catechists, Roberto has a conflicted history with his own community, related no doubt to the extirpative role played by catechists in previous decades. At one point, he one told me, a yatiri accused him through coca divination of being responsible for a theft in the community. At the time of my field research Roberto seemed to be on good terms with most members of his community; to my knowledge there were no similar accusations of kharikhari made from within his ayllu.

The cases of Roberto and the stranger of Rosario point up the flexible and negotiated nature of the boundaries that are asserted through kharikhari suspicions. As I have suggested in Roberto's case, the tensions inherent across patrilines joined in marriage, heightened when spouses are from different ayllus, reemerge upon his wife's death in combination with Roberto's ambivalent history of travel, Protestantism, and service as a catechist as the basis of kharisiri accusation. In the case from Rosario, the tense interayllu solidarity performed in the Jesús de Machaqa plaza is muted within the domestic frame of the ayllu-level household; a fellow-Machaqueño, whose presence was necessary on the plaza, and tolerated in the patio, becomes in the more intimate context of the community-members' sleeping quarters a potential kharisiri. It seems likely that such accusations are always negotiated with respect to these contingently salient fault lines—as frames of local inclusion are produced and asserted situationally. We might say that the accusation was an exercise in the production of locality, especially given that Rosario ratifies the coming year's ayllu authorities and that these men were especially vocal in confronting the stranger.

A related issue concerns the ambivalence of taypi. While the suddenness of the kharikhari attack in Marcela's account of her daughter's death—"She was very accomplished in her work. And thus she died. Kharikhari butchered her"—is jarring, this narrative "jump cut" is foreshadowed by her extended presence in the town. Both Alicia's death and the scene from Rosario occur in the town: a site condensing extralocal space, and, in the case of Rosario, explicitly effacing temporarily a grid of local social difference. Whereas routine sociability entails mediation across boundaries through a range of transactions, taypi risks the dissolution of boundaries. In this sense the kharisiri embodies the terrible perfection of taypi: with no boundaries to be negotiated, there is no transaction and therefore no sociability. There is simply theft—of women, of fat.

An additional cue in Marcela's narrative is the reference to the technical skills her daughter was learning there—likely through courses offered by the Catholic parish. The salience of the parish is patent. Also relevant is the prominence of rural schools as sites of kharikhari suspicion, with particular schools earning regional reputations as dens of kharikhari, and rural teachers (who are typically Aymara from other parts of the altiplano) almost universally suspect. Schools such as Warisata, with a strong indigenist pedigree, were also cited (by Machaqueños) as places rife with kharikhari activity.[10] School buildings are themselves frequently cast as wak'a and taypi, and their function in situating distant power and value in the local landscape is key. The current climate of educational reform and political restructurings aimed at empowering local municipalities intensifies this in new ways. In 1999, attending annual festivities to celebrate the anniversary of the school in Sulkatiti-Qhunqhu, I observed a representative from the MNR donating a truckload of bags of cement for the construction of a new theater proposed by the school teachers. This was done in coordination with a speech on behalf of his party's candidate for mayor in the upcoming elections. In 2000 the mayor (from the rival MIR party) traveled from his office in the city of Viacha to participate in the same anniversary festivities. In this and other regards, schools and the practices that involve them are potent sites collapsing a range of spatialized distinctions within highly local frames of reference. National politicking and the ambivalent status of school-teachers aside, it is also worth noting that rural schools blur more local social distinctions. They often serve children from a range of communities, some-times (as in the case of the schools serving Qhunqhu, Sullkatiti and neighbor-ing ayllus) creating class cohorts that cut across supracommunity social struc-tures. The educational initiatives of the parish—including the cohort of catechists—would be additional examples of this. In this sense, too, such schools are, for better and for worse, taypi.

There is another blurring of distinction at stake in each of these discussions of kharikhari. Aymara appear as both victims of kharisiris and as the agents of fat extraction. Similarly, travel appears to render Aymara at once suspected of and subjected to kharikhari attack. Just as the classic kharikhari is a stranger without social ties, so the typical victim may appear as a solitary traveler away from home. This convergence of kharisiris and their victims is most clearly condensed by the stranger at Rosario. Even as he is accused of being a kharisiri, he expresses is own fear of being cast outside, a helpless traveler in the (dan-gerous) pueblo.

High Plains Drifters

In December of 1990, quite early in my fieldwork, Ingrid and I traveled with a catechist, Modesto, from a community in the vicinity of Batallas to attend a *centro de bautismos* in a neighboring community, called Khanapata. It was a mass baptism, conducted by a local deacon, for children from a number of com-munities in the area. I counted about a dozen children with parents and god-parents who were baptized that day. We arrived to find a number of catechists, along with some local secretaries general, parents, godparents, and children to be baptized assembled by the chapel, awaiting the arrival of the deacon, Paolo. A number of the men quickly surrounded us and began a series of questions of a sort that became very familiar and not a little annoying over the course of my field research. Along with the standard "where are you from?"-type ques-tions, I was continuously asked about the details of my travel ("Did you go in a plane?" "How much does in cost?" "How long did it take you to get here?" "How many stops does the plane make?" "Where do you get your food when you travel?") as well as details of the U.S. or Holland ("What crops do you grow there?" "What kinds of animals do you have?"). Such inquiries might be analyzed in a number of ways; they seem to betray a desire to "visit" (mi-grate to) the United States. And one common line of follow-up questions in this regard is about what sorts of jobs can be found there. The discussion of airfares was always uncomfortable; accounts of the relatively vast sums I was able to muster to visit Bolivia quickly put me in my place as I was seeking to build rapport with rural peasants. The questions about the sorts of crops we grow in the U.S. and whether we have llamas and cows are quaint but reveal efforts to assimilate—or at least locate—distant phenomena in local terms. These are useful ways of understanding my interrogation. They point, more-over, to an overarching theme of travel and mediating distance. Such discus-sions helped account for my presence and the sorts of spatial practices that brought me to the chapel in Khanapata.

But these questions were not only about me. They were also about the sorts of experiences, the itineraries, and the memories these men would have *were they* to undertake travel to the United States. In this regard these ques-tions and my answers amounted to a form of virtual travel circulating distant-ly derived experiences and knowledge. It seems fitting, then, that this early ex-perience of travel questions in Khanapata quickly veered to the topics of national and world news. We discussed the U.S. "war on drugs" and the par-ticipation of agents of the United States Drug Enforcement in the eradication of coca fields in Bolivia.[11] We also discussed the impending first gulf war and other political developments. I learned from them that Margaret Thatcher had recently stepped down, though I supplied the fact that she had been the British prime minister, not the "Queen of England." A certain fluency in this sort of information about distant events is highly valued.

It was toward the tail end of this conversation that Paolo, the awaited dea-con, made his entrance. He arrived on foot, with a beaten-up leather satchel containing his ritual paraphernalia (his stole and vest, a tin of preconsecrated Eucharist wafers, a vial of holy oil, etc.) slung over his shoulder. On a string around his neck, hanging in front of him, was a radio, tuned to the Church-run Aymara language radio station, Radio San Gabriel. The station broadcasts messages, local, national and world news, music, as well as cultural program-ming (short plays and interviews designed to promote Aymara culture). From our spot inside the walled space in front of the chapel, we heard Paolo before we saw him. Or better, we heard his radio blaring the mix of news reports over a background of music that San Gabriel broadcasts. He arrived, then, fair-ly embodying a combination of travel experience (an itinerant deacon) and the circulation of knowledge of the (distant) world.

Bonifacio's Thesis

Travel is a key dimension of the links drawn between catechists and kharisiris. Beyond their approximation of priests, catechists are first and foremost travel-ers—moving between places. Travel is a principal marker of catechists' identities. A range of informants cited it to me when I sought to elicit their impressions of "what catechists do." In their travels to distant places (mainly for church-sponsored courses), catechists accrue various sorts of social prestige. On the one hand is an experience of travel as a mode of social knowledge and a template for local legitimacy consonant with other sorts of translocal practices. Conversely, the prestige generated by catechists' travels also reflects a negative valuing of local experience with respect to the wider world of modernity. Catechists, we have seen, operate at the confluence of these contradictory ideologies, performing translocal knowledge to ambivalent ends.

I once sat with Bonifacio as he bragged to his faith group about his many travels around the country. (In addition to travels in connection with his service as catechist, military service and temporary labor migration are the main opportunities for a man to expand his travel horizon). "Where is there a place I don't know?" he boasted, claiming to have been in every department of Bolivia. He added that he kept a book in which he recorded the names of all the communities he had visited. This list of place names evokes the sorts of ritual texts anthropologists such as Tom Abercrombie and Denise Arnold have written about, in which long sequences of wak'as and other named places are invoked as part of ch'alla offerings. It also suggests the sorts of rote memorization exercises assigned to Aymara school children in their study of national geography. Mindful of my presence, Bonifacio described the book as his "thesis." More telling than Bonifacio's boasting was the reaction of his faith group, which immediately expressed concern for him. "Aren't you afraid to travel so much?" they asked him. "Don't you worry about kharisiris?" "I'd be afraid to sleep in those schools like you do." "They say the teachers in that community are all kharikhari."

As a function of their travels, as well as a function of their proximity to priests, catechists are at great risk of kharikhari attack. When priests visiting Aymara communities need to stay the night, responsibility for hosting them (and the consequent risk of kharisiri attack) is typically relegated to the catechists. At the same time, these are precisely the loci of practice that sustain accusations against the catechists. The association with priests needs no further comment. But consider the suspicion I have heard that the catechists learn the extractive techniques of kharikhari "in all those courses they go to."

Clarifying Fat

When Paolo, a member of the early cohort of deacons named in the 1970s, conducted the baptisms in Khanapata, he used a variety of the "signs" often used in the sacrament, including holy oil. I noted no discomfort or conflict during my observations of the baptisms themselves. However, additional data show that catechists anticipate such concerns and attempt, through the very same courses that supposedly teach them the nefarious techniques of fat extraction, to elicit from missionaries the "truth" about holy oil—a truth to salve their own concerns and a token of strategic esoteric knowledge for their relations with their communities. In March of 1991 I attended a course for catechists at the center for catechist training in Toledo in the Department of Oruro. The center serves catechists from a variety of provinces, including the area of Carangas where Wachtel worked, and the community of Orinoco, where a catechist suspected of kharisiri had been killed a few years earlier. At the time of the course another catechist was involved in similar accusations from his community. The course was in preparation for a period of "mission" to coincide with the quincentennial. This was a diocesewide effort, and a visiting team was giving courses to pastoral agents in a range of parishes. The team I observed, a foreign priest named Adan, who had previously served in a parish in the city of Tarija, accompanied by an urban-born seminarian, were ill-prepared for pastoral work with Aymara, seeming both ignorant of rural highlands life as well as out of touch with the pastoral posture of inculturation.

The theme of the course was "sacraments." After discussions of baptism and the Eucharist, the course turned to the theme of confirmation. The missionaries offered a discussion of the work of the Holy Spirit through history as evident in the Bible and focused on the sacrament of confirmation as a reaffirmation of the work of the Holy Spirit within the body of the Christian. This was presented as a healing presence, an important symbol of which was the anointing of the confirmant with holy oil.

The seminarian, Edgar, spoke quickly and in Spanish, only rarely pausing for translation to Aymara. (An Aymara woman, Petronila, who worked closely with the nuns who ran the center, was providing translation.) I suspect that few of the catechists followed the presentation with detailed comprehension. They did, however, seize on the mention of holy oil, and its connection with illness and curing, eventually interrupting the presentation to request a more detailed translation in Aymara.

A flurry of follow-up questions focused on the nature of the holy oil. One of the nuns intervened to inform Edgar of the prevalent concerns about kharisiris in the region and the related concerns about the safety of catechists and other pastoral agents. She noted that the priest responsible for the zone no longer used holy oil when conducting baptisms. Edgar tried to reassure the catechists, telling them that holy oil is simply olive oil to which a bit of perfume is added. The holy oil is consecrated annually during Holy Week, commemorating the treatment of Jesus' corpse with oil.

FIGURE 6.4   *Catechists attending a course (in Laja)*

The link with Jesus' death was not comforting, and the catechists continued to press for more details. The level of misunderstanding became evident
when an exasperated catechist finally asked

> [Tell us] a little more about the olive oil. Some of us Aymara still do not
> understand what an "olive" is. Is it a tree? Is it a plant? So that you might
> be more clear, so we can put this [knowledge] in our communities. And
> we will explain it, no? And there won't lack others who will ask us, "This
> olive, what is it?

A number of other catechists chimed in with related questions.
    "What does it come from, where does it come from?"
    "Where is it from? What is it?"
    "What is its origin?"
    "What do you call 'olive'? Right now, I'm in the dark, no? Because I'm
always seeing olive oil, and always perfume in this. What type of perfume? We
also need to know and explore this to explain to our communities"
    "What is olive oil? We don't know what an olive is. Is it a plant? Is it an an-
imal? We don't know. To be clear and explain it clearly, it is necessary to know."
    It is clear that the catechists were looking for information about the oil both
for their own peace of mind and for information they could strategically share

with their communities (and their potential accusers). Edgar ineptly tried to provide some more information, declaring that olive oil comes from a plant, alluding vaguely (perhaps ominously, for the catechists) to a "process of refinement" by which the oil is extracted. He reported that last year the diocese used an "expensive perfume from Paris" to make holy oil and went on to say that any type of perfume such as those for sale in a pharmacy (a site of considerable notoriety!) could be used. At this point one of the nuns who run the center cut him off. Citing her childhood experiences in Spain, she offered the catechists detailed descriptions of olive trees, the ripening olives, and the process of pressing olives. (This discussion helped clear up an ambiguity in Spanish, where "olive" [*aceituna*] is lexically distinct from "olive oil" [*aceite de olivo*]). The nun gave them, in other words, a virtual travel experience of olive plants.

In negotiating this slippery stream of information, the catechists were struggling to make sense of more than just the facts of olive oil cum holy oil. They were also struggling to place their own concerns and those of their communities (these latter coming to be framed increasingly as a mistaken form of belief) within a larger flow of knowledge and power. In comments of the translator, as well as those of other participants in the course, catechists framed their own meta-ethnotheory of kharisiri suspicion. After relating Edgar's discourse on the Holy Spirit and the role of holy oil and the laying on of hands as a sign of the communication and presence of the Holy Spirit, Petronila went on to review various kharisiri beliefs and accusations, e.g., gringos and priests butchering people who fall asleep after fiestas, reporting that her father and uncle have seen this.

A catechist interrupted this expanded translation of Edgar's explanation to say:

> Here, I can say this, look: I am a kharisiri. That's what they say in my community: "Here's the kharisiri. Perhaps these priests have been walking around, [he's?] been in the priests' house, and after that, he's had it [i.e., he's become a kharisiri]." Now how did this word [this way of thinking] appear? Perhaps now we can lose it [i.e., get rid of it]. There were not priests among the Aymara before, the Aymara didn't know [of] that holy olive in ancient times. So the Aymara invented this. Truly, they said, "where did they bring this fat to smear on people? They must have taken it from people themselves." From this it has gone, without changing. "They use human fat" they say, "we are people, therefore they use human fat." The priests restrain [*jark'asirakinwa*—also suggests "detain" or "limit"] them. The Aymara didn't see the Bible; they didn't even explain the sacraments to us. So, in their own way the Aymara invented this. Now

they say, "in the month of August, you must be careful, the priests go out to the mountain peaks and cut the people and take out that olive—yes, that olive. And with that they smear us."

He goes on to note other suspicions, for instance that ground human bone is used in making Eucharist wafers, concluding:

So they didn't explain those sacraments, you see. So in their own way the Aymara invented [their own explanations]. This is lost, each one of us thus has learned from our fathers, from our mothers; we've listened to them talk, and they continue speaking. Today, they [the missionaries conducting this course] are revealing [the truth about] the sacraments to us. They are teaching us "this is the way it was," they are saying, "now you see." Perhaps the kharisiri had always been some other thief."

Petronila, picks up this theme, adding, "Perhaps, perhaps when the conquest came a person was cut and we didn't know. Afterwards, perhaps, they said, these q'aras, they cut people, they cut people." Another catechist jumps in. "Yes, this is the way it appeared. Where did this fat come from? They didn't explain. They wielded it secretly. This [belief] grew."

This folk analysis of kharisiri beliefs parallels at the metalevel a structure of unequal relations often referenced by kharikhari accusations. Just as kharisiris embody opacity, lack of reciprocity, and unequal asocial relations, the catechists suggest that the whole problem of kharikhari is a legitimate misunderstanding on the part of Aymara stemming from the opacity of doctrinal knowledge wielded by missionaries, who controlled unequally and restrained the circulation of important ritual information. Due to their intense contact with priests, catechists are potential kharisiris, suspected of learning the techniques of butchery in pastoral courses. The catechists might agree; they embrace those same courses as sites for unlocking the secrets of kharisiris, now cast as esoteric knowledge potentially to be circulated to local ends.

The ambivalence of the catechists is grounded not in essentialized identity oppositions but in the precarious risks of constituting locality out of translocal relations. In this regard the catechist appears as a "long-distance specialist" whose travels transact esoteric knowledge from distant places otherwise beyond the control of the local community (cf. Helms 1988). As we have seen, the catechists often constitute their own authority (and are so constructed by other community members) along long-standing templates of translocal mediation: risiris, mayordomos, doctrineros. Similarly, the various parallels discussed in chapter 4 between the construction of catechetical authority and the legitimacy of ayllu authorities underscore a template of Aymara authority that is at once beyond the boundaries of locality and constitutive of its center.

This ambivalence of the catechists is matched by the ambivalence of the distantly derived knowledge they transact. Just as the wak'as appear both as dangerous foreigners and as embodiments of the ancestors, the catechists are both kharisiri Others and adepts of Catholic ritual expertise understood as vital to the production of locality and seen by many as a component of the basic cultural knowledge of the ancestors. On the one hand, the knowledge accessed by the catechists is potentially radically antisocial and destructive. On the other, within the same idiom of fat circulation and bodily integrity, their translocal experiences are often realized as locally beneficial. As we saw in chapter 5, faith group worship is typically cast as an offering to God in which catechists play a doubly mediating role: standing as authoritative intermediaries between their followers (and, in the case of some communitywide rites, such as the ayuno, their ayllu) and God, while at the same time they broker the local use of distantly derived ritual expertise. Much of the weekly faith group meeting involves catechists teaching what they have learned to their faith group. The faith group offerings of song and prayer are indexes of the distant knowledge they have internalized, resulting in new capacities to engage God. And, as we have seen, group members describe these activities with the same vocabulary used for offerings to wak'as: as acts of memory and as *katoq* (from the verb meaning to receive something).

Moreover, at stake in these transactions with God is much the same stuff at issue in offerings to wak'as: fertile potency, fatty moisture, distant value, and its more recent embodiments or tokens. "God, father," began a petition by a faith group member, "Bless us. Give us increase with your blessing. The frost and hail have wiped us out this year, God, good father. Bless us, your orphaned children, God, good father in heaven. And so now from your sweat, make a rainfall from heaven appear." Faith group members tend to cast the benefit they hope to receive from God in the form of bodily fluids: God's tears, God's sweat, God's breath are often invoked to embody the rainfall or good fortune or the strength for which people yearn. Faith group members pray in order to receive power and strength from God, attributes embodied through breath. "We speak with the breath of God," one catechist told me. "He blew this invisible breath to us. So with this we speak, with this we walk. If he had not blown on us, we would not be able to walk; we would not be able to talk. Perhaps we would be mute, without words."

Indeed, group members invariably describe themselves as scrawny, weak, and debilitated—in short, as suffering from a shortage of fat. In this world, teaches a catechist, "we are either weak and without force, or we are God's kind [of people]." "We are so tired," laments a petitioner. "Blow on this world with your breath." This debilitated state is to be corrected through the knowledge controlled and circulated within the faith group. "Good father," begins a catechist during a petition, "this morning we ask of you, we being thin/exhausted for not understanding [you]. Today, you are in our midst. Because of this, give us a good thought/understanding."

Recall that catechists themselves frequently enjoy reputations as healers, incorporating a range of curative and diagnostic strategies, turning on their communication with God. To return to the case of Roberto, he too professed an ability to heal. When I asked him about kharisiris, he affirmed that they did exist. He said that he had seen a local health promoter engaged in fat extraction. He went so far as to detail a list of symptoms manifested by victims of kharisiris, including high fever and blood in the urine. As for the accusations made against him, he denied them, insisting rather that his healing powers were especially effective in cases of kharikhari attack. He told me he had saved a number of lives in this way and had once resuscitated a four-year-old girl who had died. He recounted being called by her family and finding her body cold and without a heartbeat. Since she was unbaptized, he baptized her and prayed over her body for three hours, after which, she revived. (I learned in the summer of 2000 that Roberto had left his work as catechist and was now serving his community as the local health promoter.) Similarly, like Marcéla, most of the other faith group members I interviewed cited reasons of health (either their own or that of a family member) as a principal reason for joining the group or for their continuing faith group attendance.

Kharisiris and Cultural Emulation

Far from presenting an intrusion of modernity threatening the integrity of the community, the catechist-kharisiri reflects the ambivalent and contentious entanglement of locality within more encompassing systems of power. At stake is not the threatened preservation of indigenous locality but its complex reproduction within and with respect to a skein of networks of power, violence, and value. As translocal mediators, the catechists embody precisely the ambivalence of the porous production of locality as well as key features of its postcolonial implications. For the value they mediate is at once integral to the material reproduction of locality and threatening to it. At the same time, that such practices might provide the catechists a footing for legitimate local authority—as healers embodying ancestral control of Christian doctrine, as translocal messengers to whom the frightening mystery of the sacraments has been revealed—underscores both the deep interpenetration of indigenous and Catholic forms and an ambiguous assertion of indigenous self-worth familiar from other colonial and postcolonial contexts. That indigenous place deities take the forms of urban spaces, churches of gold, schools, or stores suggests an experience of these markers of nonindigenous power as continuous with—indeed as highly potent expressions of—local cultural values, ascribing to whites a power that verges on the radically other, by verging on the terrible perfection of the indigenous system.[12]

Considered in this light, Andean laments about cultural decline and the curious situation of the catechists, who, in learning from foreign missionaries, uncover esoteric but locally crucial knowledge and approximate the ritual knowledge and capacities of the ancestors, suggest a sort of cultural emulation reminiscent of cargo cults—with the added twist that what Aymara must emulate from whites is in large measure considered to be a reapproximation of lost ancestral capacity.[13] The comments from the course in Toledo accusing priests of keeping important information a secret from Aymara resonate more immediately with cargo beliefs. However, even here, the force of the speaker's claim stems not from a radically new or other socioritual potency but rather from the long-standing entanglement of Catholicism and the Aymara, whose ancestors, operating without crucial knowledge, understood things as best they could. In such lights we might see kharikhari rumors as less about the rupture or inversion of locality than as an assertion of commensurability across shifting situations of entanglement.

FAT THROUGH THICK AND THIN

The Andean fat stealers can be set uncomfortably within a more comparative set of discussions about vampirism, organ theft, and related visceral renderings of local perspectives on complex and conflicted sociohistorical settings. I say "uncomfortably" because in this rich confluence of bodily metaphors, existential anxieties, and colonial and postcolonial experiences the productive tension between global comparability and local particularity, between macro- and microlevels of analysis is often sacrificed for the seductive sense that these local concerns speak for themselves in a language that takes its translatability and force from the potent global experiences of colonialism, capitalism, and racism. To cite one recent effort, Mary Weismantel (2001) has sought to situate Andean fat stealers as tokens of a universal type of "racial bogeys" made commensurable with rumored organ stealers, vampires, and dangerous white strangers the world over as reflections of partial, imperfect perspectives on the global economy. Such broad and generalizeable global processes are certainly crucial referents of kharisiri and comparable beliefs. Yet my own view is that such limited readings, though evocative and instructive, come at a high and hidden cost—the cost of locality.[14] Well-meaning analytic efforts to reference global structures of pressing and legitimate concern may serve to eviscerate and flatten the local concerns they presume to champion, yielding a thin description of processes that warrant a more robust documentation and understanding.

From Evocation to Ethnography: The Local Vitality of "Things That Never Happened"

Stressing the authenticity of "colonial vampires" and related "things that never happened," Louise White (1997) insists that such discussions call us to an examination of colonial/postcolonial settings in the terms and experiences of the subjects themselves. Rather than taking these images as "generalized metaphors of extraction and oppression," the task for making sense of such beliefs entails examining them in their situated thickness and in the scalar thickness of their situations—unpacking these vital, visceral symbols on the ground. Working in this vein, anthropologists have approached such evocative embodied phenomena as they conjoin local and global orders of meaning and experience, economics and physiology, and illuminate, in local form, local experiences of entanglement with translocal forces and processes.[15]

Discussing reports of greedy people who steal and sell other people's blood, Weiss (1996:204) notes that such rumors "seem to speak to the uneasy tensions that local cultural orders experience in the face of global political economic processes." Yet these "iconic forms of evil" are only partly commensurable with similar phenomena elsewhere. Fat stealers, electric vampires, and zombies may well reference a shared global system, but they do so in the contexts of the production of particularly entangled localities. In my view the task of anthropology, building upon the unique insights afforded by ethnography, is to remain accountable to these multiple levels of phenomena through an analysis focused on situated local frames of action and experience.

This is not to propose a return to insular constructions of locality but rather to insist that locality be approached as a porous space of entanglement. The Haya forms of consciousness Weiss examines are not discrete from global processes but integrally enmeshed with them. Nor am I suggesting a retreat from comparative ethnography or from a political engagement with big-picture issues of globalization. But anthropological comparison is best built upon case studies, each anchored in the contextualized specificity of ethnographic research. Rumors about organ theft are a powerful analytic metaphor for reflections on global capitalism and its articulation with biomedicine. And some such rumors may well reference national and transnational trafficking in illicitly "harvested" organs. Such activities, as well as biomedical discourses and other practices concerning organ donations, are vital areas of study. But such an analysis does not replace the need for studies examining local understanding of the body and body parts in peri-urban Brazil, or rural Guatemala—indeed, such an analysis ultimately is not about such local forms of consciousness.[16] On the other hand, an examination of local forms of consciousness is most certainly to be partly about global processes.

It is worth underscoring that in the comments I have recorded no one dismisses the kharisiri as a fiction. Gabriela cites her father and uncle as witness to a kharisiri's victims. The catechist in the Toledo course, explaining the misinterpretations of his ancestors, does not doubt that people are "cut" He questions the attribution of responsibility, alluding to the possibility of other "thieves." Roberto claims to have witnessed a health promoter engaged in kharikhari; many others with years of experience traveling at night or in out-of-the-way places accumulate stories of "close calls." That fat might be transacted in dastardly ways is a self-evident reality. The challenge for Aymara as for other analysts is to understand what such conceivable acts might mean about themselves and the world they live in.

‡ ‡ ‡

To argue against a priori understandings of indigenous locality as enclosing coherent and enduring ethnic perspectives on the world, to insist that these spaces and vantage points are neither fixed, as timeless autochthonous locales, nor imposed subordinate positions, to focus on locality as an evanescent, always emerging cultural process is not to deny the structuring weight of the past, not to ignore the unequal force of different imagining of locality (such as those, say, from the vantages of the nation-state or the Catholic Church), not to belittle the potency of categories of class, race, ethnicity, or gender to shape local lives and senses of worth, not to imagine naively that local Aymara (or anyone else, for that matter) produce the world as they would like. It *is*, rather, to say that all these factors operate ultimately in and through situated social experiences and in and through complex and complexly lived social spaces.

The following chapter turns from the contentious politics of dismembered bodies to the political complexities of remembered bodies.

CHAPTER 7

Burying the Past

On March 12, 1921, Aymara from the ayllus surrounding the town of Jesús de Machaqa attacked the town's residents and government officials. The attacking Indians burned and looted houses and killed some sixteen vecinos.[1] A number of the victims were burned to death, "roasted" alive in their blazing houses. In urban circles the event was imagined as a cannibal feast; remembrances recorded from indigenous Machaqueños in the 1990s depict the uprising in similar ways.[2]

The Aymara were responding to increasing pressures on their lands as a result of the expansion of haciendas throughout the region during the late nineteenth and early twentieth centuries. A related factor was a series of abuses committed by the corregidor of the region, Lucio Estrada—the focal victim of the attack in Machaqueño oral histories. Estrada had a reputation for corruption and mistreatment of Indians. The news of his appointment as corregidor, in 1919, prompted a letter of protest from Machaqueño leaders to the prefect of the Department of La Paz.[3] The proximate cause of the attack was likely the death of a local Aymara man in a jail cell in Jesús de Machaqa.

Prominent among the rebels were a father and son: Faustino and Marcelino Llanqui. They were part of a broader movement of Quechua and Aymara leaders from across the altiplano who had taken on the title of cacique, once used to refer to the local indigenous nobility (such as the Guarachis) who played a prominent role under the Spanish colonial system of indirect rule. Neo-caciques like the Llanquis constituted a multifaceted effort to defend the interests of rural indigenous communities in the shifting contexts of the Bolivian nation-state (see Soria 1992; Condori and Ticona 1992).

When survivors of the attack brought news of the uprising to the city of La Paz, President Bautista Saavedra ordered a reprisal raid. Twelve hundred Bolivian army troops garrisoned in the nearby town of Guaqui sacked the communities around Jesús de Machaqa, killing some fifty Aymara, burning houses, and looting herds and fields. Leaders of the rebellion, including the Llanquis, were captured and imprisoned.[4] The army set up a temporary garrison in the community of Qhunqhu Liqiliqi. Soldiers remained camped in the region for one month.

On March 12, 1991, I observed the second annual performance of a ritual in Jesús de Machaqa commemorating the "massacre of Machaqa."[5] Though the phrase appears in official documents from the 1920s referring to the attacks by Indians against the vecinos, today the phrase recalls the army's reprisal against indigenous Machaqueños. In a series of events including a vigil on the eve of the anniversary, a Catholic mass, a march to the town of Jesús de Machaqa, and a demonstration in the town plaza, indigenous Machaqueños sought to remember the uprising and the violent response from the state. The Llanquis were commemorated as heroes and martyrs; the assault on the vecinos of the town was cast as a reminder of the cruel and unjust treatment of Aymara by Bolivian national society that provoked it.

This commemorative ritual emerged primarily with the support of the local Catholic parish and Church-affiliated regional development organizations, such as CIPCA. The event is continuous with inculturationist aims to galvanize regional and Aymara-wide ethnic solidarity. The emergence of the commemoration coincided with a multiyear initiative coordinating the work of CIPCA and the pastoral innovations I have been describing to the correlated ends of ethnic consciousness, evangelical renewal, and regional socioeconomic development (Ticona and Albó 1996). As I noted in chapter 3, Hernando's efforts to recuperate the ritual practices of ayunos in the region (and the serial communal solidarity such "Aymara" practices were thought to generate) were another part of this initiative.

In Bolivia the practices of the church converge with a growing movement of pan-Aymara ethnic identity. Within this context "the massacre of Machaqa"—along with comparable events elsewhere in Bolivia—has been taken up within an emerging indigenist historiography as a canonical event of Aymara resistance to the injustices of the Bolivian nation-state. The uprising and retaliatory massacre has been the subject of a published history by an Aymara historian from a neighboring province as well as the topic of oral historical research by an Aymara sociologist.[6] The events have also been presented in a more popular format through a variety of Aymara language radio programs broadcast by the Church-run Radio San Gabriel in La Paz[7]. In these treatments indigenous Machaqueños are invoked as martyred tokens of a heroic Aymara type, commemorated as part of a political sensibility stressing the recuperation and revalorization of a past that is thought to unify all Aymara.

Yet my observations of the commemorative events challenge this assumption of a seamless link between a recuperated past and ethnic solidarity. For while on the surface these events had all the hallmarks of a rally of politicized pan-Aymara solidarity, with the massacre condensing a history of conflictive relation between the Bolivian nation-state and the Aymara, the event culminated not with an assertion of the ethnic distinction promoted by the organizers but rather in an improvised performance of Bolivian citizenship. Similarly, despite the involvement of various indigenist organizations in the event, less scripted aspects of the commemoration appeared to contest precisely the sorts of mass mediated versions of the uprising authored and produced by these collaborators. These counterspaces of ethnic identity and historical memory seemed to have run afoul of the local actors whose perspectives and sentiments they hoped to channel.

My interest here is not merely in the fact that the oppositional implications of ethnic solidarity vis-à-vis the nation-state anticipated by the organizers did not come to pass. That ethnic solidarity need not be antithetical to national belonging is unremarkable—particularly against the backdrop of Bolivia, which is increasingly conceptualizing itself as a "pluri-ethnic" nation-state. Rather, I want to focus on the assumptions that take Machaqa as a local token of a presupposed serial ethnic type and examine the ways the commemorative ritual calls us to a new understanding of locality.

Constructivism, Primordialism, and the Iconicity of the Local

This chapter is about the complex and contentious condition of locality with respect to ethnic and national frames of inclusion. Specifically, I take these events as an opportunity to examine the relationship between memory and history and to explore some of the ways contemporary Machaqueños assert meaningful connections between the past and present and so imagine and enact locally compelling forms of ethnic and national belonging. To these ends I pursue two intersecting lines of analysis.

The first has to do with the relationship between official history underlying the scripted framework of the event and other memory forms. By "official history" I am referring to the revisionist retelling of the massacre by indigenist scholars and activists through the genres of academic history and the media of books, pamphlets, and radio broadcasts. As a topic of activist scholarship, the massacre bridges the work of secular cultural movements and inculturationists, each engaged in the production and assertion of (macrolocal) "Aymara culture" within national and transnational arenas.[8] The alternative memory forms of interest to me here involve a range of practices linked to the burial and commemoration of the dead in Aymara communities. These were especially salient in the vigil preceding the march and rally and impacted the experiences and reactions of many of the participants in ways unanticipated by the organizers of the commemoration.

The second line of analysis concerns the locality that is produced and asserted through the various acts of memory in the commemorative ritual. Building upon discussions of Andean locality in previous chapters, I am interested here in the ways local social groups produce and align themselves within and with respect to more encompassing identities.

Social science has long taught that public rites have remarkable force in constituting popular sentiment, often examined at the level of the nation-state. Following Durkheim, social scientists have been attuned to the ways such rites produce a homogenizing collectivity—insiders united by attributes that extend across space and time. Radio and print media and officializing discursive arenas—such as public education—are similarly taken to be integral to the building of nation-states by forging and correlating collective sentiments (e.g., Anderson 1983; Luykx 1999; cf. Harris 1995). The past is a key resource mobilized and officialized in such processes (e.g., Hobsbawm and Ranger 1983; Errington and Gewertz 1994; Connerton 1989; Handler 1988; White 1991).

Locality is another critical resource in such collectivizing projects, sometimes cast as a site of primordial identity, available as a basic building block of group sentiment. In this sense the solidarity to be forged in such rites is thought to be "already there"—a resource to be mobilized in ways that often extend beyond the local. Influential work on nationalism has underscored this paradoxical interdependence of supralocal identity and local distinctiveness (see Anderson 1983; Chatterjee 1993; Garcia Canclini 1995; Handler 1988).[9] In ways that parallel the situation I have described as the macrolocalizing implication of inculturationist discourse among the Aymara, this interdependence typically involves generalizing cultural distinctiveness across an (invariably more complex) national space.

Writing in a related vein, Herzfeld (1997:29) points out that "nationalism shifts emphasis from indexicality to iconicity," from a stress on the contextual specificity of place and interpersonal relations to a situation in which the importance of these particularities is effectively muted by overriding assertions of sameness. That is, nationalism is predicated upon relations of similarity taken as the basis of serial belonging that transcends face-to-face contexts of sociality and unites spatially and temporally distinct contexts as commensurable tokens of a national type. National political campaigns often rely on such claims. U.S. presidential candidates, for instance, have tended to lard their speeches with anecdotes of the experiences and concerns of peoples they "meet" in the course of their campaign. The effect is an assertion about the very nature of "the people," as a single mother in the state of Washington, a retired couple in Minnesota, or a high school student in Baltimore come to represent (iconically) a crosscutting contemporary Americanness. Other examples have been starkly evident in the wake of the September 11, 2001 attacks on the World Trade Center and the Pentagon. A memorial service held on the University of Illinois campus the weekend after the attacks, for instance, featured local firefighters in firefighting gear. This was an early reproduction of a now familiar icon, metonymic of the tragedy, and asserting similarities across a vast national community by replicating an identity that has come to embody the best qualities of a presupposed national character.

Of course, as the above examples make clear, iconicity does not exist independently of other modes of signification (cf. Peirce 1955). Candidates seek to index their closeness to "real" Americans; the everyday heroism of local firefighters merges the iconic reproduction of images from the scenes of destruction on the East Coast with the more situated interpersonal experiences of midwestern community life. Herzfeld's focus on iconicity serves to draw productive attention to the ways apparently self-evident (iconic) relations of similarity are culturally and historically produced. I find his phrasing also instructive for the present consideration of the tensions of singularity and similarity entailed in the posited building block primordiality of locality with respect to translocal frames of inclusion.

In parallel fashion, discussions of globalization have examined the ways "cultures" are organized as iconic of one another: "different in uniform ways," as Richard Wilk (1995) has put it. A different assertion of iconicity stems from discourses of ethnic identity, as these leverage local distinctiveness to the end of wider solidarities (e.g., Appadurai 1996:chapter 7). In such situations analysts stress the role of indigenous media and scholarship as crucial arenas of political contest, reinforcing ethnic solidarity and providing important channels for mobilization around mass mediated (iconic) representations of local distinction (e.g., Aguilar 1992; Albó, Greaves, and Sandoval 1983; Rappaport 1994; Briggs 1996; Harris 1995; Warren 1998).

As we have seen, the pastoral strategies of inculturation condense such developments in revelatory ways. Missionaries seize upon what they take to be representative Aymara practices or concepts and embrace them as metonyms of a pan-Aymara culture. In the case at hand, the local sociality and solidarity thought to be reinforced by the recuperation of such activities as the ayuno and by the efforts of catechists to position their work at the taypi of their ayllus is, in the context of the commemoration of the massacre, intended to be extended as a frame of region- and nationwide Aymara ethnic solidarity.

In preceding chapters I have explored some of the limits of this pastoral strategy, focusing on indigenous catechists and their rejections of the pan-Aymara replicability posited by inculturation. The present case further illuminates the limits of ideologies of ethnic inclusion, as the homogenizing standardized memory of historical events as foci of ethnic sentiment are contested by other memory forms. However, this contest does not mean the failure of large-scale solidarity. My argument throughout this book has been that local and supralocal solidarities are made rather than found. My aim here is to examine the ways the alternative assertions of locality, though offered in rejection of homogenizing models of ethnic solidarity, ultimately generate through a different ritual route imagined Aymara and Bolivian communities; communities that look like, but are produced in ways quite different from, the "imagined communities" of the literatures on nationalism and ethnicity. Though they contest iconic constructions of supralocal inclusion, assertions of local indexicality serve as pragmatic and persuasive resources for imagining and enacting ethnic and national belonging.

REMEMBERING LOCALITY

In this commemoration of "Aymara" resistance to state violence, local actors consistently rejected any straightforward homogenizing recollection of the uprising, instead asserting as valid forms of memory available only to a select, highly localized group. For the Machaqueño participants the achievement of local and supralocal solidarities involved negotiating the complicated entailments of who remembers the past and how they remember it (cf. Harris 1995).

But to insist on local, indexical distinction is not to posit a resistant or insular locality. As I have been arguing, locality is established out of often unequal relations with translocal formations: colonial and postcolonial states, transnational religions, and the economic and intellectual currents that "underwrite" the documentation or broadcast of "indigenous history." The Andean case serves well in this regard. Machaqueño space is shot through with sites and representatives of extralocal forces—as the uprising and its aftermath make clear. Rather than an insular space under siege, I am approaching locality as a positioned perspective within a wider social field presupposing translocal entanglements. Among these entanglements in the present case are relations of pan-Aymara ethnic identity and Bolivian citizenship.

This approach to locality dovetails in fertile ways with classic and recent discussions of memory. Following other work illuminating the indexical or self-contextualizing character of memory as symbolic practice (Halbwachs 1980; see also Wachtel 1986; Davis and Starn 1989), I want to examine the ways in which locality is produced and asserted through acts of memory in the contexts of commemorative ritual. Anderson's (1983) study of nationalism turns largely on the ways a primal solidarity he ascribes to the face-to-face community is extended to create a translocal "comradeship" that seems inevitably to transcend and efface the protonational (or protoethnic) community. Yet, whatever the persuasive force of the nation, community or comparable contexts of face-to-face immediacy do not go away. My concern here is with the ongoing entailments of such "face-to-faceness" for specific forms of historical memory and the local and supralocal solidarities they help generate and express.

Through situated memory forms social groups produce and align themselves within and with respect to more encompassing identities. At stake in such alignments is more than a shift in segmentary scale familiar from discussions of Andean social structure and regional pilgrimage sites (such that certain shrines stand as organizing foci for more encompassing social groups)—though these are certainly factors (e.g., Platt 1986, Sallnow 1987). The commemorative events at hand draw our attention to issues of authority, through the officializing genres and media of historical discourse as well as efforts to assert the legitimacy of alternative local rememberings, and to the different engagements with the past that are achieved and asserted through different memory forms.

Lived and Learned History

In the Machaqueño case this situation is complicated by a crisis of memory. Like their neighbors who participate in the faith groups, many other Machaqueños consider themselves to be estranged from their past. In this light, local memory forms are incomplete. Machaqueño participants in the commemorative rite sought to braid together local and nonlocal discourses as part of their public performance of locality. The resulting matrix of memory was mobilized by participants in the commemoration of the massacre to produce a qualitatively unique engagement with the historical events and actors of the uprising, an indexical connection that was in their opinion not available for iconic (pan-Aymara) generalization to other Aymara or to the indigenous and nonindigenous historians who consider themselves their allies.[10] This contrary remembering of local specificity became the paradoxical basis for an alignment of locality with more encompassing frames of ethnic and national inclusion. At stake is the interaction of multiple discourses about the past in constituting and referencing ethnic groups and their relations within postcolonial nations, specifically the engagement of local and mass-mediated memory forms: "lived history" and "learned history."

In his seminal work on social memory, Maurice Halbwachs distinguished "lived history" from what he variously called "national," "written," or "learned history." Influenced by Durkheimian sociology, Halbwachs approached memory as a social fact. For Halbwachs memory is a subjective act that effects and reflects the alignment of an individual consciousness within a wider social field comprising a range of social groups. "A person remembers," he wrote, "only by situating himself within the viewpoints of one or several groups and one or several currents of collective thought" (1980:33). His notion of "social group" remains vague, but a key point is that the subjective act of memory is a function of the objective position and perspective of the individual within a complex social milieu. Memory thus appears as an exercise of identity: a positioning of a remembering subject within and with respect to social groups through a socially constituted relationship to the past.

"Lived history" for Halbwachs is a connection to the past that participates in this intersubjective, social field–constituting quality. In contrast, "learned history" (sometimes "historical memory") is the transmission of the past without such qualitative engagement. Halbwachs situated learned history at the sociological horizon of his theory, the vanishing point of the affective community of the Durkheimian social group—the nation. Lived history is the qualitative precondition for the authentic, meaningful transaction of pasts beyond individual experiences. In particular, Halbwachs invoked the family as an example of a social group that constitutes a "living and natural framework" (1980:69), bringing into the experiences of younger generations ancestral events and past epochs that exceed their individual experiences (cf. Munn 1990). As he had it, learned history involves representations of the past that are in no way anchored in the life of the group. In Sapirian terms (Sapir 1924), lived history is genuine, official or learned history spurious. This distinction is useful for making sense of the commemorative event, with localized and localizing mortuary practices providing key frames for asserting what Halbwachs might embrace as lived history. But where Halbwachs appeared to insist on the affective authenticity of lived history over learned, I borrow these terms to mark heuristically what I am examining as interacting and interpenetrating genres of cultural practice.

The Porous Past

In chapter 1 I examined Machaqueño entanglements across colonial Hispanic and postcolonial Bolivian history. I return to a portion of this history here to underscore the (already) complex engagement of Machaqueño locality with the Bolivian nation-state as evident in the 1921 uprising and the neocaciques who led it.

As we have seen, multiple generations of the caciques Guarachi had a tremendous influence on the articulation of Jesús de Machaqa with the colonial and Republican states. The Guarachis successfully converted traditional rights to lands in distant ecological zones into property rights within the Spanish legal system. Their success in negotiating emerging forms of colonial power within the idiom of local structures of value made them enormously wealthy in both traditional and new terms. In this light I have argued that the emerging colonial context offered a new field of constraints and possibilities for establishing the sorts of translocal mediations that were highly valued by Andeans.

Over the last decades of colonialism and the first decades of independence (from 1825) the position of cacique was phased out. In Jesús de Machaqa Guarachis such as the conniving Don Diego remained powerful but were increasingly displaced by a system of annually rotating ayllu-level authorities conjoining the communities of the region under the mediating leadership of a regional council (cabildo). During the late nineteenth century the Bolivian government embarked upon a period of infrastructure improvements—constructing railways, for instance—and an assault on the colonially established land rights of Indian communities to the benefit of an emerging class of hacienda owners (Klein 1993, Rivera 1986). Coordinate with this, the city of La Paz expanded as the financial center of the country and the nearby agriculturally productive lands south and east of Lake Titicaca emerged as a prime target for exploitation by hacendados. This increased pressure on ayllu lands sparked a number of uprisings across the altiplano, including the 1921 action in Jesús de Machaqa.

These developments had three implications for Jesús de Machaqa. First, the interayllu council successfully fought "legal" incursions on the lands, invoking the transactions of the Guarachis to establish their title to their lands. This fortified the interayllu solidarity of the region and laid the basis for a contemporary Machaqueño reputation as a bastion of tradition resisting colonial and postcolonial encroachment. Second, while close to La Paz and the lake, the region is largely isolated from them by a network of mountains and foothills. The area was bypassed by the main rail lines and commercial routes and, by the early twentieth century, many of the non-native town residents had moved out—an exodus hastened by the uprising of 1921.

Third, the period saw the emergence of neocaciques such as Faustino and Marcelino Llanqui. Neocaciques self-consciously invoked their colonial predecessors and may be seen as engaged in similarly ambiguous work: defending encroachment upon community lands and protecting local interests while simultaneously facilitating local entanglements with foreign resources (see Soria 1992; Condori and Ticona 1992). These resources included forms of cultural capital deriving from education and literacy.

Marcelino Llanqui took on the title *profesor ambulante* (itinerant teacher). Rural educational networks had been in place since 1905, reflecting both a national concern with the "Indian problem" keyed on civilizing and integrating Indians within the nation state as well as the political mobilization of indigenous leaders such as the neocaciques who linked the struggle for land rights and social justice to a struggle for indigenous access to education and, especially, literacy (Luykx 1999; Choque et al. 1992). From the points of view of rural vecinos and government functionaries, such educational activities were threatening. The work of neocaciques and rural educators prompted sanctions and violent repression. Invoking a curious allegiance to Aymara "tradition," the ill-fated corregidor Estrada accused Marcelino of being an inauthentic Indian, a "hybrid cacique" who dressed in an urban style. He speculated that Marcelino had spent too much time in the city of La Paz and there fell under the sway of Protestant pastors. He also noted with alarm that Marcelino had learned and was now teaching the local Indians how to fire revolvers and Winchester rifles to the end of exterminating the white race (Choque 1986).

The schools of the neocaciques did serve as a meeting ground for planning the uprising, although this took forms the corregidor could not have imagined. Prior to their assault on the town, the Llanquis created a hierarchy of Indian authorities paralleling positions held by mestizos—e.g., corregidor, judges—even appointing a local yatiri to serve as "Catholic priest" (Choque 1986). The rebels thus sought to overthrow their oppressors even as they legitimated and reproduced the very channels of their subordinate connection with the state. This is a classic issue in the Andes: producing and asserting locality by reproducing encompassing hierarchies. In many ways, I think, their descendants did the same thing in 1991.

As a final point underscoring the entanglement of the 1921 rebels with the Bolivian state, note that on the morning of March 12, the rebels entered the town shouting slogans of the Republican Party (Albó and Barnadas 1990:160). The cry "Viva Republicanos" may have served as a password enabling some residents to escape unharmed (Perez 1962:74). The cry recognized the government of Bautista Saavedra, who had come to power through a coup in 1920 and a national convention in January 1921. As a young lawyer he had famously defended a group of Indians who massacred soldiers during Bolivia's Federalist Revolt some twenty years earlier. Seen as an ally of the burgeoning indigenous cause in Bolivia, Saavedra received (but did not acknowledge) the allegiance of the Llanquis shortly after his 1920 coup. He would eventually send the army on its reprisal raid.

The Social Structure of Memory

Returning now to the commemorative events themselves, I want first to review their spatial structure as I observed it in 1991 and 1992. The sequence of events in the rite moved across increasingly public spaces, establishing a pragmatic framework of memory forms situating the participants and the past they sought to transact within ever more encompassing social groups, ranging from family and community structures to the Bolivian nation. This is reminiscent of discussions of other translocal spatial practices (e.g., pilgrimages) and segmentary social structures in which the situational salience of locality diminishes with respect to ever increasing frames of inclusion: thus the shift from the indexicality of the local to the homogenizing iconicity of the nation. Yet within this familiar performance of scalar belonging, I turn in the following sections to examine the ways certain participants in the commemoration rejected the dissolution of local specificity apparently entailed by such processes, asserting instead highly localized forms of memory and mobilizing these as the authorizing anchor for the entire translocal framework of memory produced by the commemorative events.

The initial event—the vigil—occurred not in the town of Jesús de Machaqa but in one of its component communities, Kalla Arriba: birthplace of the caciques and the site of Faustino Llanqui's grave. The vigil took place in the community chapel and was structured along the lines of both a community meeting and household practices concerning the commemoration of the dead. I return to these mortuary practices in more detail below. These initial activities were focused not on a regional Machaqueño identity (i.e., the idealized twelve communities) but rather at the level of a single ayllu, an identity, as we have seen, that is often figured rhetorically as a single household or family. Community authorities presided over the event in coordination with descendants of the caciques. Vigil participants discussed preparations for the following morning, when Kalla Arriba was to host delegations from all the communities in the region. The mallkus of Kalla Arriba engaged in the sorts of exhortations used in other contexts to unite the community for communal work projects. Community leaders encouraged everyone to share in the hard work of hosting and preparing meals for the visitors and cautioned Kalleños to be alert for potential conflicts stemming from visitors from communities with a reputation for stealing herd animals or, in one case, a man from another ayllu said to be courting a woman from Kalla.[11] Such comments signaled this community-level footing, even as they underscored a concern to mute structural fault lines between communities to the end of a regional interayllu solidarity in the next phase of the ritual. This solidarity—the self-conscious "function" of the ritual for the participants—was clearly not a given, but approached as a task requiring considerable effort.

The events of the following morning did enact a solidarity of a more encompassing order. The action moved from the interior, houselike space of the chapel to the more public arena of the community plaza, where the entire regional council eventually came together. They did so progressively, arriving as delegations from neighboring communities, and gradually constituting themselves as two groups, corresponding to the intercommunity moiety structure. The two groups, on different sides of the plaza, established the space as a microcosm of the region as a whole. Later they joined together as a single body, as an attendance list of council authorities was formally read aloud.

Local catechists and a deacon from the region then presided over a Catholic mass commemorating the dead from the massacre. The mass, held outdoors in the plaza, further established these sorts of encompassing regional frameworks as, for the first time, the names of additional "heroes and martyrs" of the uprising and massacre from other communities were called out. Afterward the host community of Kalla Arriba ceremoniously fed their visitors. The group divided into two large circles—one of men and one of women. As assistants to the Kalleño ayllu authorities distributed food and drink, distinctions of patriline, community, and moiety were effaced by the crosscutting oppositional relations of gender and the comunitas of comensality.

I want to be careful not to suggest that some enduring Andean principle of social structure—i.e., nested dualism—is driving this event. As I have stressed, Machaqueño solidarity is neither a given—it requires explicit effort—nor is it an enduring constant—the meaning of Machaqa varies in shifting historical conditions. The idealized structure of Machaqueño interayllu relations is itself an objectified cultural trait, invoked as part of efforts to mobilize regional and Aymara-wide ethnic solidarity.[12] To some the uprising appears as the embodiment of an empowering unity sorely lacking today; the commemorative rite might be seen as a nostalgic enactment of a sort of robust regional coordination infrequently attained.

It is notable, then, that these levels of structural inclusion were explicitly marked in the course of the commemorative rite—people commented on them, noting the solidarity of an ayllu or the joining together of different communities. Inviting the participants to share in the meal after the mass, the mallku from Kalla Arriba addressed the *cantonal,* head of the regional council, stressing the goal of interayllu unity: "Brother cantonal, I ask you, we will not distinguish each type here, rather we have come together from different places, from all parts." I mean to argue that this metatext helped organize the sequence of events, effectively constituting ever more inclusive frameworks of interaction for the participants. These frameworks radiated out from Kalla Arriba, fixing and declaring local identity across a range of contexts.

After the meal the participants marched to the town of Jesús de Machaqa, some thirty minutes away. Their arrival heralded by charges of dynamite and the ringing of the church bells, the Indians entered the town and circled the principal plaza. The march clearly recapitulated aspects of the uprising; the reinvasion of the town was underscored by the circling of the plaza. This literal encompassment—reminiscent of the entrance of the truck carrying revelers into the town for the feast of Rosario—is part of the spatial vocabulary of regional ritual practice. When ayllus dance on the plaza at the culmination of Rosario, moiety divisions between neighboring communities—Milluni and Liqi Liqi, for instance—are often subsumed as the "upper" half encircles their inferior counterpart, creating ultimately a single body of dancers.

The town is a prime site of regional solidarity: it is here that the council normally meets. The plaza has also been a venue for a variety of intercommunity rituals. Of these the October feast of Rosario is the only one still extant. In this light the very structural scope of the performance might be taken as an index of a generic ritual form quoting and objectifying traditions associated with the ancestors and increasingly seen as forgotten in the contemporary Aymara world. By the same token, inasmuch as the events celebrated the leadership of the neocaciques, who were recalled as great men who successfully united the ayllus of Jesús de Machaqa, the event replicated this achievement over the course of the ritual. There may also have been an element of ethnic contest in this quoting of nearly abandoned practices. A number of Machaqueños I spoke with were of the opinion that such regional festivals in the central town, with their drinking and brawling and their ceaselessly playing brass bands, offended and angered the remaining vecinos in the town. Their objections are widely cited as a reason for the reduction of such fiestas from three to one.

Implicit in such ethnic valences is the place of the town plaza as a frame for an articulation of a more encompassing order: not a microcosm of regional locality but a metonym of translocal engagement. As I have suggested, this

FIGURE 7.1 *Jesús de Machaqa viewed from Kalla Arriba*

FIGURE 7.2   *They gathered at the kiosk*

is a key dimension of Aymara social practice: the construction of the center not as the point of greatest local insularity but rather as a site of remarkable spatiotemporal reach, condensing the entanglement of locality with extralocal forces and processes.

Rather than on the community-specific sites around the plaza, the marchers gathered around a kiosk in the center of the plaza (though the delegations from some communities would lunch on their particular spots at the conclusion of the commemorative rite). The kiosk was erected in the 1960s by the remaining vecinos in the town and may be seen as a monument to national integration, inspired by the political reforms implemented in the wake of the 1952 MNR revolution. The kiosk expresses in spatial terms the sorts of modernizing homogeneity sought by the MNR. Although built by vecinos to the end of aligning the rural town (iconically) within a revitalized landscape of national inclusion (i.e., a landscape dotted with historical markers, market towns, new town and the local peasant syndicates that have structured post 1953 political participation), the kiosk resonates deeply with the sensibilities I have sketched out around the Aymara concept of taypi: a condensed center of translocal entanglement. The kiosk was adorned with a Bolivian flag and with a number of *wiphalas:* symbols of pan-Aymara ethnic identity. It served as a stage for speakers and dignitaries, including indigenous authorities, the local police commander, schoolteachers, representatives of NGOs, and the Aymara author of a history of the uprising.

While much of the ritual traded on a discourse of lived history, asserting a highly local identity over against other nonlocal histories of the uprising (I will return to this observation in a moment), the events culminated around the kiosk in a set of practices reinscribing localized history within the expressive genres of official history and national identity. These took the forms of rituals of citizenship enacted during national holidays and typically performed in connection with local rural schools. A schoolteacher was invited to lead the crowd at the commemoration of the massacre in a performance of the Bolivian national anthem, while a descendant of the Llanquis raised the Bolivian tricolor on a vecino-erected flagpole over the town plaza. Similarly, patriotic slogans, often shouted with the names of Bolivar or Santa Cruz, now rang out as "Long live Marcelino Llanqui" or "Glory to the martyrs of the massacre of Machaqa". As a final act improvised at the end of the demonstration, a man called for a "patriotic parade," arguing, "If we do this for other national heroes, we should do it for our heroes." In response, while the dignitaries remained on the kiosk, the male participants lined up to march once more around the plaza, passing by the kiosk—now a reviewing stand—in goose-stepping military fashion. The only other instance of these practices I witnessed were at rural school festivals that culminated in a similar parade of children (and adults) past the *altar patriotica*: a stage adorned with a tricolor and portraits of Bolivar and Santa Cruz from which school teachers and the authorities of the community reviewed the procession. Such performances of national identity insert the dead caciques within the pantheon of Bolivian national heroes and assert the newly remembered local history as a footing for mediating translocal identities.

DRINKING TO REMEMBER: MEMORY AND SPATIAL MEDIATION

These telescoping spatial frames of the commemorative ritual are familiar from discussion of other Aymara memory forms, focusing on so-called drinking paths effected through ch'allas (e.g., Abercrombie 1986, 1998; Arnold 1992). These, it will be remembered, are offerings of alcohol—partially or entirely consumed by the sacrifier—invoking, or remembering, places, persons, and sources of fertility in a sequence of increasing spatiotemporal reach. In the case of house-building rituals discussed by Arnold, ch'allas effect the remembering of the sources of origin of the various components of the house structure—

from the local sites of mud and stone, to the more distant sources of grass for making adobes and thatched roofs, to the low-lying valleys yielding wood for the roof beam, to the Japanese factory where the corrugated metal roofing used in some houses is manufactured. These and other recollections are mediated by alcohol. As Abercrombie (1986) puts it, Aymara drink to remember.

More generally, we have seen that memory is a principal medium of Aymara ritual practices; consultants referred to offerings ranging from prayers to llama sacrifices as acts of "remembering." For the purposes of the present discussion, I want to underscore three points.

First, memory is a productive act establishing beneficial transactions with other people, places, and powers. Memory effects in the register of sacrifice the sorts of productive integration of difference evident in patterns of ecological verticality as well as in the Guarachis' actions as colonial brokers in Jesús de Machaqa. At stake, in other words, is the transaction of distant resources, the mediation across space of values crucial to a situated locality.

My second point elaborates upon this localizing function of memory. Memory serves as an index of sincerity, anchored in the chuyma, as the somatic seat of personhood and will. Remembering might be glossed as "thinking about" or "bringing to mind/heart." As an act of memory, a successful offering externalizes and circulates this interior condition, creating a sort of transparency that is a highly valued quality of Aymara sociability. In contrast, dissemblance or secrecy, like refusal to participate in networks of reciprocity, result in social sanctions ranging from accusations of stinginess to accusations of kharisiri. In ritual practice, they may result in disaster rather than the desired fertile abundance. In one case I observed, immediately after receiving the obligation to sponsor a saint's fiesta for the following year—if done right, this may result in increased herds and financial rewards—the house of the new sponsor caught fire. Speculating upon the cause of the fire, a relative of the sponsor suggested to me that her family had received the obligation reluctantly (i.e., their hearts were not in it) and so invited the punishment of the saint.

As ritual practice, then, memory engenders an authentic subjective alignment within the act. This is my third point. Beyond any referential representation of the past, memory in these Aymara practices first and foremost legitimates action in the present through the alignment of remembering agents within a social context. The translocal force of these acts is thus based upon the highly localizing implications of memory.

In a similar way, I am arguing, the increasingly inclusive frameworks of memory generated by the commemorative ritual did not subsume local structure within more encompassing units nor subordinate local history with respect to national history. Rather, the spatial practices of the ritual anchored the alignment of historical memory across social structures with respect to a newly localized center authorized by these sensibilities of memory. Through the events of the commemorative ritual, Machaqueños ultimately contested the authority of official history and appropriated it as a performance of national inclusion anchored in local forms of remembrance. At issue is the realignment of frameworks of memory. As we shall see, Machaqueños were less concerned about *what* was being remembered than *who* was doing the remembering, less about where the historical events of the uprising and massacre unfolded than how and where their *recollection* was taking place. In rejecting nonlocal accounts of the uprising, Machaqueños were debating not the details of history but the deictics of historical remembering.

BURYING THE PAST: LIVED HISTORY AND THE TECHNIQUES OF MEMORY

It is to this underlying anchor of localized, lived history that I now turn, focusing on the presence in these commemorative events of mortuary practices and related beliefs about the dead. The dead remain present and accessible in Machaqueño experience for a period of years after death. They are regarded as an ongoing source of agricultural, animal, and human fertile potency and are remembered through periodic offerings of food, coca, alcohol, and prayers. Aymara remember their dead primarily at All Souls' Day (November 1) in a set of acts that stress the locality of the souls, which are said to return to their community with the arrival of the spring rains. The souls are embodied in elaborate altars constructed along the gable walls of their former houses as well as at their gravesides.[13]

On All Souls' Day a family commemorating a recent death constructs an altar in the deceased's house. They wait in vigil into the next day, as others in the community come to visit and offer prayers to the deceased, referred to as a "soul" (alwa). In return the visitors receive food, coca, and alcohol, which they consume on behalf of the soul. A senior descendant of the soul, or an attendant working for him or her, acknowledges the prayers, distributes food, and may demand additional prayers remembering more distant ancestors. The senior mallku is expected to visit all of the households remembering a soul. He is joined by an entourage of p'iqis, young children, and a group of elder men who have fulfilled their service obligations to the community into whose ranks he will formally pass upon completing his own year of maximal community service. The remembering of the dead is typically repeated for three years, after which the soul fades into a more homogenous category of *laqa achachilas* (dust ancestors), to be remembered by name only when appended to rites focused on more recent dead.

The vigil of the commemorative rite correlated with these practices in a number of ways. The events I witnessed were the second and third annual performances of the ritual hosted by Kalla Arriba. Upon the completion of Kalla's ritual service, the vigil was to be hosted for the following three years by another ayllu, commemorating their own martyrs of the massacre; the expectation at the time was that the commemorative rite would rotate through all of the ayllus of the region.[14]

To one side of the community chapel, a table much like the altar erected during All Souls' Day was set up: adorned with cloth, flowers, food, and alcohol as well as a plaque with the names of the caciques. People entering the chapel first went up to the table to pray for the caciques, turning next to their descendants to request that they receive the prayers on behalf of the souls. The practice continued the following morning as visiting delegations arrived and silently proceeded to the chapel to pray to the souls before emerging to greet their hosts. This also followed the format of All Souls' Day vigils, when visitors are expected to enter the house uninvited and ignore their corporeal hosts as they present their verbal offering to the soul, said to be the "owner of the house." During All Souls' Day the heaping plates of food and other items given to those who come to pray are couched as a payment for the verbal offering. However, in a sleight of hand familiar from other Aymara ritual contexts, the "payment" is at once reciprocation for the prayers and an additional offering made to the soul, by its descendants, and mediated by the visitor, who, from the moment of her or his arrival is addressed as "soul." I was scolded during All Souls' Day for saying thank you upon receiving such a plate of food. "What are you saying 'thank you' for?" growled my host. "It's not for you!"

The commemorative vigil was also marked by exchanges of food and related symbolic media. Throughout the night ayllu authorities and descendants of the caciques distributed heaps of potatoes and broad beans, bowls of soup, bags of coca, bottles of alcohol, and cartons of cigarettes to those who had come to remember the Llanquis. The double nature of such offerings was clearly evident in this feasting. One mallku expressed his regret that I had only been served three bowls of soup—it should have been four, he said: two for Marcelino and two for Faustino. I could only groan my reassurances of the abundance of the offering. Similarly, as a relative of the caciques distributed cigarettes to those present in the church, Ingrid declined, saying she did not smoke. "That doesn't matter," he said, handing her a cigarette and moving on.

Two of the descendants of the caciques were especially prominent: a grandson of each man, the eldest now a very senior man himself. Both these men wept during the vigil. They formally received the prayers offered to the souls, sometimes addressing those gathered in the chapel as their "accompaniment"—a term also used to refer to friends who join a family throughout their All Souls' vigil.

Their genealogical position is significant. Recall that the three generational relationship between grandchildren and grandparents (tunu) is marked in a variety of ways among Aymara, whose genealogical memory is typically quite shallow. A number of consultants reported learning much of their own knowledge of what today is objectified as "tradition" either directly from or passively through witnessing their grandparents. As I noted in chapter 5, this relationship is replicated in a more encompassing folk model of genealogical connection invoked with the term *alchin alchipax,* the grandchild of the grandchild. In ways quite resonant with the Halbwachsian notion of lived history, the term doubles the parameters of lived genealogical experience.[15] Specifically, the concept constitutes senior men—who are at once grandfathers (focal ancestors for an emerging tunu) and grandchildren (situated with respect to their grandparents, now ancestors long dead)—as the key mediators between the living and the dead, the present and the past.[16] This position of seniority emerges as a temporal analogue of *taypi,* a central mediating position akin to the synthetic encompassing reach of the central plaza of the town. Recall here the visit of the mallku accompanied by children and elders on All Souls' Day. On the cusp of senior status, he leads a delegation spanning three generations in the commemoration of the dead. The presence of children in rites associated with the dead is common in ethnographic descriptions of the Aymara; in some accounts they dress as old people, sometimes donning the clothing of the dead (e.g., Buechler and Buechler 1971).

This genealogical connection to the caciques, mediated by their grandchildren, was repeatedly invoked and systematically extended to all of the participants in the commemorative event. All but the most senior men and women present were identified by others and referred to themselves as children or infants (wawas) or, in some cases, as alchin alchipax. In the mass the relationship was harnessed to the paternal image of the Christian God, as an Aymara deacon reading the names of various martyrs of the uprising said (i.e., to God), "They are your children. We, the grandchildren of their grandchildren [alchin alchipax] are remembering them today."

Additional similarities with All Souls' Day were evident in participants' concern to secure the benevolent attention of the souls of the caciques. They were entreated to "guide the community" and to "clothe us with your blessings." A number of speakers asserted that the caciques were in fact not dead but just resting or sleeping. One of the grandchildren reported that he was praying every night for the souls, asserting, "because of this they will be reviving from the dead." Such assertions reconfigure the caciques from historical persons long dead to souls active and potent in the Aymara experiential world. These acts of remembering establish a local framework of copresence with the ancestors, a footing for lived history, a legitimating memory center with respect to which the telescoping pragmatic reach of the ritual is aligned.

During the course of the vigil, a number of male participants rose to make speeches. The following portion of one of the speeches condenses a number of salient issues in the event:

[After greeting the participants and the descendants of the caciques,] I want to say a few words right now on this our day, elders of the community. . . . Last year in this same community there was a small act of remembering. This seventieth [anniversary of] the carrying out of the uprising and later the massacre of Jesús de Machaqa, brothers. In these days we have spread this history about, so that sometimes, when I arrive at my house, three or four times I hear [it] on the radio. This history has been completed and made very big, brothers. I want to say [this] as one of the community. And we are one community. We are really of one community. Here we are really an ayllu. This is our grandfather. Last year is not far away [from us]. How did we remember? From what places did we remember? Where did we speak? Which of the community's leaders spoke? I say a history should be written. Nonetheless it is others who write our history. This is not good. We know how to read and write. I say it is proper that we ourselves should write. . . . How is it going to be this evening? Compared to last year there are more of us. Next year perhaps we will be even larger. The soul truly is living. His body must be lying in its grave.

The speaker establishes relations of social inclusion around an authorizing relationship to an ancestor. Note the progressive construction from "I speak as a member of the community" and "we are all one community," through the more ethnically marked term *ayllu,* to the claim made pointing to altar table: "This is our grandfather." I want to focus on two related issues. The first concerns the speaker's final point about the body "lying in its grave." I suggested at the outset a broader Machaqueño concern over their attenuated relationship to their past, manifest here as an ignorance of the history of the uprising. In the terms of Aymara ritual such forgetting is also a disengagement from the ties of intersubjective copresence and reciprocity established through offerings effected in acts of memory. Machaqueños lament the fact that while others discuss the historical events associated with the dead caciques, "we their children

FIGURE 7.3   *Faustino Llanqui's grave*

don't know what happened." During the vigil, a number of participants spoke of the history as being hidden or covered over. One man, echoing the suggestions quoted above said, "We ourselves ought to take out with our own words what happened, where it happened. . . . Of course, unfortunately in years past this must have been kept covered." The term he used—*imataña*—refers to something kept or concealed like a secret. The sense of interiority and hiddenness or opacity inverts the sort of transparency achieved through acts of memory and suggests both a rupture of obligatory and beneficial connections with the past and a breakdown of the preconditions of productive sociability in the present. But the term also means "buried" like a body, and so suggests not only a loss or concealment but also a latent possibility. I take this as an apt gloss for the commemorative ritual as a whole. While Machaqueños lament their forgetting of the buried past, it is by remembering their buried ancestors that they regain that past, replacing historical events with the bodies of genealogically locatable historical agents.

The second issue concerns the speaker's rejection of mass-mediated accounts of the uprising (books, radio, and press were mentioned at various times), coupled with his proposal that Kalla produce its own study. In part the concern was the inauthenticity of others' accounts of their past. The book by a non-Machaqueño Aymara historian was good, I was told, but incomplete; another booklet about the uprising was denounced as "false." In contrast, Machaqueños, and especially those from Kalla, were thought to have privileged access to the facts of the past. This was asserted in two ways, each of which might have been taken directly from Halbwachs. The first was their genealogical connection to the caciques. The second was their topographical link to the history, as speakers invoked the places where the Llanquis walked. Toponymns figure prominently in accounts I have collected remembering the retaliatory massacre and may be taken as key mnemonics of lived history (Martínez 1983; cf. Basso 1988).

Others stressed the inappropriateness of outsiders presuming to talk about things so intimately Machaqueño. One speaker proposed the creation of a document for posterity, noting, "It is also not good that those who are not from here [not from our marka], that they say what has been happening, how we eat. . . . They are saying we have caused everything to be lost [i.e., forgotten]." Here history is akin to gossip, with additional resonances of disempowerment: "You are incapable of remembering your past—or even preserving your customs—so we will remember for you" (cf. Harris 1995).

A number of participants called for the production of such a study, described by some as a "letter." It was expected that the document would embody the pragmatic extension of the rite: going "out of the community" to impact La Paz and other parts of Latin America as well as influencing future generations. At least one participant framed the writing as a medium of violent encounter with outsiders: "Yes, brothers, we should work. We will select a few words. Then we will write. Only we will write good or bad. And we will bring all the remembrances together to confront those wiraquchas with their writings."

HISTORICIZING MEMORY AND MEMORIZING HISTORY

The events in the Jesús de Machaqa plaza included performances of rites of citizenship linked to rural schools: the national anthem, the raising of the flag, the patriotic parade. The borrowing of these ritual forms from rural education is understandable: schools are prime sites for the engagement of national and local practices and identities. They are also the principal site for the circulation of learned history and its technologies: Spanish, literacy, and forms of memorization involved in rote learning. These practices were invoked in the vigil as well, and it seems significant that for the occasion the chapel was filled with desks and benches borrowed from the local school. For, while the participants were concerned with remembering their history, the process was deeply linked with efforts to historicize their memories.

Examples range from exhortations by ayllu authorities that Kalleños memorize the dates of birth and death of each cacique, tokens of official history—lest they be caught unable to answer questions posed by visitors from other regions—to a broader concern to entextualize the remembrances transacted by the rite. And there were other efforts to situate the uprising within the frames of official history. "The history of Jesús de Machaqa is big," declared a later speaker, who described the uprising as "the first Bolivian revolution"—anticipating the 1952 MNR revolution—with implications for all of South America. The toponymic resonances of lived history were also officialized. One participant at the vigil proposed building a "monument" for Faustino Llanqui in the Jesús de Machaqa plaza. During the demonstration in the town, speakers repeatedly characterized the plaza as the "plaza histórica de Jesús de Machaqa." In addition to echoing other inclusions of the caciques within the pantheon of national heroes, this merging of history and landscape in monuments and tourist attractions (Jesús de Machaqa is out of the way but occasionally visited by tourists interested in colonial churches) is a potent form of learned history and central to projects of national identity formation.

During the vigil the participants nominated a young man as a scribe to begin preparing a local history of the uprising. There was an explicit concern to find a young man for the task: young people are more likely to be literate, but the recording was also cast explicitly as a cross-generational transaction between "children" and grandparents. Speaking to the elder of the two grandchildren of the caciques, he assured him, "I will only write what you tell me." There were other references to the old guiding the young and "filling them up" with their knowledge.

Yet, a formal narration of the events of the uprising never occurred. One effort to have Faustino's grandson begin to tell the history was interrupted when someone went off to find a notebook and a pen. To the best of my knowledge, no written local version of the rebellion was generated. Rather, the scribe proceeded to entextualize the commemorative ritual itself: recording the events of last year's rite and the planned program for the current year's remembrance. (Recall here the aforementioned speaker's interest in details of the previous year's event: where did we remember? who spoke? etc.). This is in part a reflex of similar scribal functions in peasant union political structures in Bolivia in which a recording secretary maintains a written record of community meetings following a highly formalized agenda. The resulting record books are part of the regalia of local leadership, transferred to each cohort of annual ayllu authorities. But the textual focus on the commemorative events also suggests that the *act* of memory is as crucial as its *contents,* that the framework of memory achieved and asserted by the ritual is as notable as the temporally distant events it references.

CONCLUSIONS AND CODAS: LOCALITY, MEMORY, AND THE CASE OF THE ANDES

The commemorative ritual presents an opportunity to examine at once the interplay of memory and history in Machaqueño practices and the situated engagement of local identities with respect to ethnic and national identities. This is a fruitful analytic intersection both because of the ambivalent condition of locality with respect to imagined identities of broader inclusive scope and because of the similarly ambivalent status of historical memory. On the one hand, historical memory is a highly self-contextualizing act of presencing the past. On the other, the invocation of the past may serve as a focal point for a more inclusive assertion of national or ethnic solidarity (cf. Gillis 1994). In each case the tension is between affiliations generated primarily indexically and those emerging principally through iconic replication as a relatively homogenizing proliferation of tokens of an authorized type. The invocation of locality to ethnic or national ends objectifies distinctive local qualities as a template or yardstick of what is taken or willed to be a more widespread condition (cf. Handler 1988; Herzfeld 1997). Assertions of a national or ethnic past similarly trade on a standardized remembering. To be sure, the indexicality of acts of historical memory (as of all social acts) remains. However, at issue here is the iconic standardization and large-scale extension of the experience. As Gillis (1994:7, 9) has put it: "National memory is shared by people who have never seen or heard of one another, yet who regard themselves as sharing a common history. . . . The past offer[s] a screen on which desires for unity and continuity, that is, identity, [can] be projected."

My effort has been to look at the ways various memory practices are aligned to assert identity in the present through a relationship to the past. I have focused especially on the spatial pragmatics of the rite, on the techniques of memory evident in a range of Aymara offerings, and on commemorative practices associated with the dead to argue that these dimensions of the ritual serve to anchor local remembrances within the sorts of situated frames Halbwachs might refer to as lived history and to extend the interactive frame of remembrance to engage pan-Aymara ethnic and Bolivian national identities. Much of the literature on memory and history, on local community and nation, and on the scalar ambiguities of ethnicity in a moment of macroethnic politics suggests a qualitative change of state entailed by such an extension: the displacement of lived history by learned history, the effacement of the local community by larger frames of inclusion. It is telling that efforts to think beyond the iconic uniformity of European-derived nationalism have placed great stress upon "community" as a space of alternatively conceived solidarity. Following Chatterjee's (1993) criticism of "Eurocentric" notions of civil society (in which "there is not space or allowance for 'community'"), LiPuma (1995:48 ff.) examines recent nation-states in Oceania, where

> the narrative of community and local culture remains decisive; it stands in opposition to both the centralized state and the formation of civil society. . . . The dynamic of community is subversive because it is the counterweight to the naturalization of the concepts of nationhood and national identity. The existence of a local culture, founded on its own concepts and conventions, provides a reminder that the nation-state is arbitrary.

Assertions of "community" as subversive of a logic of nationalism tending toward a civil society of iconic individuals are fraught with risks; such arguments surely romanticize and reify "community" in ways continuous with nationalist projects. Yet they provoke fruitful rethinkings of nationalism, and it is tempting to add the Andes to the counterexamples listed by Chatterjee,

LiPuma, and others. But the binary of counterexamples reinforces a claim that there is somewhere a total nationalism, a pure civil society, and seems to pose the complexity and imaginative possibility of "community" as a condition of non-Western postcolonial distinction. In my view the value of such counterexamples stems less from juxtaposition with a (straw man) pure nationalism, than from the ways these various voicings of community, variously entangled in national projects, shift our perspective to one in which nationalism is seen as always engaging multiple modes of identity across various scales of social phenomena. A similar case can be made for discussions of ethnicity, harnessed in comparable ways to an imagined primordial community and asserted in contest to nationalist claims. Taking stock ethnographically of positioned locality as a scalar phenomenon engaged in mutually constitutive ways with more encompassing identities, and of the sometimes competing and contradictory dispositions toward nationness (or ethnicity) found at each level (see LiPuma 1995:49), requires an approach to such conflicting dispositions not as the failure or the limits of nationalism (or ethnicity) but as an indication of the perspectivally negotiated and situationally achieved nature of even the most presupposable identities. This is not to deny the compulsive force of certain identity categories but to stress that their meaning, their salience, and their interaction with other categories is a shifting product of situated social practice.

Whipping the President and Writing History: Two More Rememberings of the Massacre

Although I have not attended a commemoration of the massacre of Machaqa since 1992, a recent publication (Ticona and Albó 1997) including accounts of the commemorative rite in 1994 and 1996 as well as interviews I have conducted in 1999 and 2000 offer a glimpse of the ritual in subsequent years. The original plan to have the vigil hosted by other ayllus for periods of three years went unrealized. Instead, the vigil has remained at Kalla Arriba, the site of Faustino Llanqui's grave. This has been a source of mild friction and turf battles between Kalleños and Machaqueños from other communities with their own martyrs to be remembered. One consultant spoke of a vigil held at the rural school on the border of the communities of Sullkatiti Titiri and Qhunqhu Milluni, near the site of the Bolivian army's temporary garrison in the region in 1921. He reported that people from other ayllus did not want to attend.

In 1994 the regional council, in coordination with the parish and the development organization CIPCA, invited the Bolivian vice president, Victor Hugo Cardenas, to attend the commemoration. Cardenas, an Aymara with longstanding ties to pan-Aymara political activism, who once worked in the region for CIPCA, accepted the invitation. The government soon announced that the president, Gonzalo Sanchez de Lozada, would be attending as well. The Sanchez de Lozada government was on the verge of implementing sweeping political reforms—the Law of Popular Participation (LPP)—aimed at a mixture of neoliberal political and economic decentralization and multi-ethnic national inclusion.[17] The LPP is a vehicle for codifying the relationship between Bolivian civil society—viewed as a multiethnic assemblage of local-level social groups—and the national government. In the terms of the present discussion, the LPP constituted an iconic relationship between diverse localities, standardizing their position within a structure of decentralized governance. Thus rural ayllus such as Kalla Arriba as well as urban neighborhood groups in La Paz or El Alto were rendered structurally equivalent as territorial base organizations; they were to be articulated with the nation-state through a network of "municipalities."

Sanchez de Lozada sent a key component of these reforms to Congress in February 1994. In March he and Cardenas were embarked on a massive publicity drive, visiting localities across the country to promote their proposed law. They saw the commemorative event as a forum to do just that. The president was under the impression that there would be twenty thousand Aymara in attendance; local leaders did not correct the misunderstanding. The turnout to the event was sizable, but the two thousand Aymara in attendance (nearly double the crowds I estimated at the events of 1991 and 1992) surely disappointed the president. He must have felt even more hoodwinked when the mallku at the head of the regional council launched into a speech that the president perceived as both insulting and threatening. The mallku, a man named Saturnino Tóla who had worked closely with CIPCA for a number of years, eloquently voiced the panindigenous politics of the commemoration, linking the history of Jesús de Machaqa with the "originary nations of Bolivia, the Aymara, Guarani, Moseteño, Quechua, and Uru peoples." From this footing he criticized the Bolivian government for corruption, misuse of resources, and mistreatment of the indigenous populations. He segued into a discussion of the problems confronting Jesús de Machaqa and listed local development initiatives underway in Machaqa. He concluded by observing, "Mr. President, you carry in your hands the staff (*bastón*) of leadership of the country; in contrast, we wield the *chicote* (whip) to guarantee what has been promised to us. The vice president knows that in our culture it has always been this way" (Ticona and Albó 1997:368 ff.).

The president took offense. He denounced what he saw as a narrow list of demands that avoided the larger structural issues addressed by the law he had come to promote; his anger was intensified by what he perceived as the low turnout.[18] It is telling that the government's enthusiasm for participating in this prototypically Indian event turned on their imagining the event as a vehicle of access to an indigenous mass of twenty thousand and remarkable that their efforts to "pitch" a set of reforms premised on the structurally homogenizing embrace of difference were so quickly tripped up by Machaqueño specificity. Similarly, Mallku Tóla's speech was remarkable not only for his deft weaving together of pan-Indian rhetoric and the local concerns of Machaqueños but also for its masking of the multiple frictions and positions out of which Machaqueñoness is ceaselessly remade. Indeed, this may have been necessary in order for him to invoke regional "Aymara" culture in the course of his speech. Tóla's speech recounted the recent history of ethnic revitalization in Jesús de Machaqa, casting this as a collective process of maturation and response to a set of challenges to the region: a devastating drought in the mid-eighties, difficult access to credit for local development initiatives. The effect was both to present Machaqa as a unitary subject and to stress the indexical particularity of Machaqa's relationship to the state based in a regional history. In a similar vein, the reference to potentially punishing the president with whips, understood by Sanchez de Lozada as an insulting threat, might be read more constructively as an effort to invoke at the level of relations between the local region and the state the sort of face-to-face accountability that informs the exercise of legitimate local political authority. As manifest through cargo careers, for instance, political authority is typically cast in the form of service to others. The chicote whip, as we have seen, is an instrument of discipline wielded at times by ayllu members to enforce their expectations of a mallku and to punish his transgressions. Though these comments by Tóla capped a speech that began by recounting the uprising against regional vecinos, the prospect of whipping the president was not a gesture of defiance or rejection of the nation-state. It was a contentious affirmation of a different kind of relationship between locality and the state.[19]

If the commemoration of 1994 underscored the contentious relationship between the iconic extension of locality in the imaginings of the nation-state (or panethnic politics) and the situated particularities of local concerns, the commemoration of 1996 returns us to the shifting, contingent, and ephemeral nature of locality itself. In commemorating the seventy-fifth anniversary of the uprising, rather than march to the town of Jesús de Machaqa the participants marched from Kalla to Sullkatiti-Qhunqhu, where they gathered at the site of the large primary school that straddles the border between the ayllus. In the course of the rally CIPCA made a formal presentation to the council leaders of an ethnohistorical study of the uprising by two Aymara scholars (Choque and Ticona 1996). Where some Machaqueños in 1991 had been critical of Choque's previously published work on the massacre (Choque 1986),

the current volume included a revised version of Choque's material complemented by extensive oral historical interviews with Machaqueños. Nearly one
half of the volume's 350 pages comprise primary data: reproductions of news-
paper accounts, transcriptions of archival documents, and transcriptions of interviews conducted with members of the ayllu Qhunqhu Liqiliqi. In his introduction to the appendix containing this transcription, Ticona notes that the
"the community itself was concerned to 'write its own history,' and decided
to do this in the month of September of 1990, bringing together those who
could best remember the event."

But, as we learned from the events in Kalla in March of 1991 (the second
commemoration of the massacre), such rememberings often call into question
the unitary Machaqueño frame they are taken to invoke. The Qhunqheño
urge to remember suggests an intraregional counterpoint to the Kalla-focused
events of the previous March (i.e., the first commemoration of the massacre).
And the commemoration of the seventy-fifth anniversary of the massacre in
1996 embodies, in its march from Kalla to Qhunqhu, the turf battle between
multiple sites and centers of memory and highlights the plural compound condition of Machaqaness. It is fitting, then, that the events in 1996 were attended only by delegations from communities of the "lower" Machaqueño moiety. A process of political fragmentation within Machaqa had been underway
for some time, with portions of the region hiving off and constituting themselves as separate administrative entities. Preexisting moiety divisions have
been one fault line for this process. This appears to have been intensified by
the reforms of the LPP and reflected in the relative indifference of the ayllus

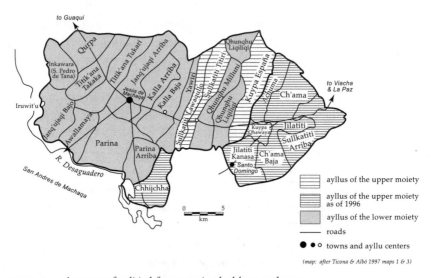

(map: after Ticona & Albó 1997 maps 1 & 3)

MAP 5   *A process of political fragmentation had been underway*

of the "upper" moiety to this commemorative ritual of putatative Machaqa-wide solidarity.

In addition to these local political machinations, unleashed by processes of political decentralization, frictions remain evident even among the ayllus constituting the lower moiety. In the years since 1992, the vigil has become separated from the more public commemorative rites enacted on March 12. Kalleños and other Machaqueños now cast it as something particular to Kalla. The remaining ayllus come together only for the rally in the town. In 2000 the anniversary of the uprising fell on the concluding day of Carnival week (*Domingo de Tentación*). In many Machaqueño ayllus Domingo de Tentación is a day of ayllu-level festivities, celebrating the production of new crops, the birth of new animals, and the reproduction of the community itself. Yet, far from inward-looking community celebrations, we have seen that such festivities often take place precisely at local sites of translocal entanglement: rural schools and health posts. Nor is it simply coincidence that Domingo de Tentación, or the days leading up to it, are typically the moments when families ritually mark the return of their young men from obligatory military service. Though the people of Qhunqhu and Sullkatiti refer to their joint celebration of Domingo de Tentación as an act of unity (*mayachasiña*: "to become one"), the tense and ephemeral nature of such interayllu solidarity is evident in the fact that fighting between celebrants from the two communities is a frequent and even expected element of each year's festivities. Organizers of the commemorative rite wisely suspended the 2000 celebration, advising each community to schedule a moment of silence in the course of their own local-level ritual.

Remembered Locality and Its Entangled Futures

The contentious position of locality in the face of supralocal projects such as nationalism or processes of globalization has received considerable comment and compelled a fruitful refocusing upon the once-taken-for-granted space of anthropological inquiry (e.g., Appadurai 1996; Gupta and Ferguson 1997; Kearney 1995; Miller 1995). Recent political developments, such as the LPP in Bolivia, and the correlated rise of ethnic politics set this rethinking of the local, its pasts, and its futures in new relief. This chapter stems from an observation of the apparent limits of constructivist efforts to appropriate Machaqueño locality as a primordial basis for pan-Aymara ethnic solidarity. This is neither to discourage nor to dismiss the possibilities of such collective mobilization nor the participation of Aymara as such within a national political forum increasingly conceptualized as multicultural, but rather to draw attention to the ways such alignments are negotiated and impinge at the most microlocal levels of experience and practice.[20] This discussion has underscored other observations that the social frameworks of ethnic identity are not given in the world but produced historically and achieved and asserted in positioned practice. At the same time, I have shown that the achievement of collective or translocal frames of identity is not necessarily at the expense of locality but may rather be with respect to locality.

The articulation of local and regional identities or local and national identities—for instance, through spatial practices such as pilgrimage (e.g., Sallnow 1987) or the politico-economic ritual of tribute/tax collection (e.g., Platt 1982)—is a theme of long standing in the Andes. From a comparative perspective the Andean case is particularly instructive because Andean locality has traditionally been predicated upon translocal entanglement. I have attempted to situate this sort of translocal engagement with respect to long-standing Andean sensibilities concerning the mediation of distant values, and with respect to colonial and postcolonial historical processes wherein the nature of this translocal mediation and the values at stake have shifted.

This chapter presents an approach to Andean locality as a porous frame of positioned practice presupposing and effecting translocal entanglements. Alongside this approach, efforts by the contemporary Catholic Church to forge pan-Aymara ethnic identity represent different (and perhaps unprecedented) translocal aspirations. Yet the entanglements of Aymara locality do not stack up neatly within the frame of ethnic affiliation. On the one hand, the marked indexicality of the former contests the homogenizing iconicity of macroethnic solidarity. On the other hand, the indexically generated entanglements of Aymara locality enable assertions of national inclusion that cut across the typically oppositional footings of ethnic solidarity. In ways ironically like the uprising it recalls, the commemorative ritual defies simple categorization as an act of resistance or ethnic inclusion. In referencing the past, this commemorative ritual does something in the present: constituting locality and its engagement within a wider field of social action or, better, constituting locality *as* an engagement within a wider field of social action.

Locating the Future

During my most recent trips to the altiplano (in 1999 and 2000), pastoral agents remarked ruefully to me that rural Aymara communities are becoming "communities of the elderly." They referred to intensifying out migration and reported their impression that young Aymara are increasingly electing to make their lives in urban areas such as El Alto—the sprawling city perched on the edge of the high plain above La Paz—or perhaps to seek their fortunes in lower lying valleys to the east, long a focus of national development schemes encouraging settler agriculture and, in recent decades, a land of additional opportunities due to the boom in the production of coca. My own impressions confirm this as well. Many in my networks of research contacts have become urban based; I am, at least, as likely to encounter them in La Paz, El Alto, or the city of Viacha as I am in their rural ayllus. The day-to-day chores of rural agrarian life increasingly fall almost exclusively to older and sometimes elderly Aymara, at considerable physical and emotional cost.

These observations might well frame a classic ethnographic departure story. In this formulaic concluding device, the ethnography presents a glimpse of the translocal forces that threaten to eclipse the local world just evoked. In the Bolivian case these pressures are considerable. Alongside the perennial challenges of dividing and subdividing lands with each successive generation, and the compounding of these challenges to agricultural subsistence by rains too scarce or too abundant or by damaging frosts and hails, the reorganization of the nation-state under the decentralizing neoliberal reforms of the Law of Popular Participation has created, fairly rapidly, new pressures and the appearance of new opportunities for many in Bolivia, with real consequences for the texture of local life in places like Qhunqhu. Increases in the frequency of transportation between Machaqa and urban areas as more buses and vans risk the rutted roads, the intensifying growth of the city of El Alto where so many dream of having a wage-paying job and living in a two-story home (a rude imitation of which Alejandro was compelled to build for his visiting gringo), an explosion of NGOs offering services that might help people realize such neoliberal dreams—all orient the thakis of many Machaqueños in new ways. There is merit to these worries.

But an ethnography of rural locality need not be rendered nostalgic by its conclusion. The aim of the foregoing chapters has been a revisiting of Andean locality to different ends. Taking my cue from other insights into the human capacity of culture, I have sought to frame an approach to locality seen as an evanescent and porous production in the process of which locals wrestle with and refer to a skein of translocal entanglements. This productive process, I have argued, involves a range of situated agents: local Aymara as classically defined as well as locatable foreigners such as missionaries. All of these are component subjects of Andean locality, presupposable and necessary to one another and engaged in the production of an already complex space comprising sites such as churches or schools that condense the porous condition of locality. And, we have seen in settings like the one at hand, the production of locality involves the interpenetration and negotiation of structurally dissimilar and unequally compelling imaginings of the local.

The challenge for a work like this, it seems to me, is to honor the unfolding achievements of cultural practice without lapsing into a pollyannaish sense of meaning making as a panacea for historical traumas and challenges. My aim has been to attend ethnographically to myriad ways people realize complex sociohistorical conditions as the contexts for coherent lived worlds without loosing sight of the facts that such complexities are often tragically unfavorable for some and that coherence is not a source of contentment, let alone justice. A converse set of challenges stems from an analytic interest in a set of translocal forces –embodied here in the global Church—and the temptation to allow an analytic set on the sweeping scale of such phenomena mask the particularities of their placement or render such sites merely inert terminals of transcendent processes. I have strived to braid together three modes of analysis, all ethnographic, and brought together with just these balancings in mind: an ethnography of missionization, and particularly the postwar pastoral ideologies and practices culminating in the theology of inculturation, an ethnography of Andean locality, cast as a revisiting of a once classical research site to contemporary analytic ends, and an ethnography of bodily practices and positioned subjectivities, serving here as an anchor for my examination of locality as an entangled product of ceaseless cultural processes. The three sections of the book coordinate and shape these strands of analysis. In part 1, "Entangled Communities," I presented, historically and ethnographically, the contextual complexity of Andean locality comprising missionaries and other Machaque-ños as well as manifold imaginings of the local. In part 2, "Syncretic Subjects," I examined the positioned practices through which locality and its entangled complexities are referenced and remade. The chapters in part 3, "Locality Remembered and Dismembered," explored the implications of shifting sociopolitical contexts and experiences for various imaginings of locality and the differently situated practices that sustain it.

Two brief stories guide this book to its conclusion without implying anything of the sort for its subject.

Victor and Luis

When Luis completed high school, he left his rural ayllu to live in El Alto. He was following a path taken by older brothers and sisters, some of whom could provide him with a place to live and contacts for jobs. Indeed, he had arranged to take employment in a store owned by relatives of the family for whom one of his sisters worked as a maid. Before he left for El Alto, he told me, his mother, Modesta, took him to the city of Viacha, where she contracted with a yatiri to prepare an offering (misa) to ensure that all would go well with her son in the El Alto: that he would be healthy, safe, and prosperous.

Modesta's concerns to make the offering were understandable. The offering asserts the translatability of the practices of urban spaces and the cash economy within a ritual idiom familiar from rural life: as misas and other offerings to place deities serve to ensure agricultural abundance and accumulations from wage earning, protection from falls on steep mountain paths and from bus accidents on the streets of El Alto. But Modesta's concern for her son was more poignant. His elder brother by two years, Victor, had embarked upon a similar route to El Alto, where he was murdered the previous year. Victor's murder was not a random act of urban violence, not the dissolution of sociality often ascribed to urban and neoliberal settings. It was rather a chilling transposition to the urban context of tensions in the countryside, tensions exacerbated by the setting of El Alto.

Victor was killed by a group of young men from a neighboring ayllu, classmates of his in a rural school that served a number of communities. The murder occurred a few weeks after his graduation. The immediate context was a wedding between a man from the neighboring ayllu and a woman from Victor's. In the wake of a party in El Alto to celebrate this interayllu union, Victor along with other men from the party stumbled through the streets looking to continue their drinking. The men from the neighboring ayllu turned on Victor, beating him and leaving him to die.

Hernando

When I last saw Hernando, he was preparing to leave his parish for a sabbatical: a time to rest, visit with his family, and perhaps visit missionaries working in other parts of the world. Rumor in Machaqa had it that he might not return to Bolivia or that he might be reassigned to another parish with amenities (including a lower altitude) that placed less stress on his health. After a brief visit with Hernando, I was traveling with two catechists (ministers); sharing the benefits of my rented jeep, I offered to drop them off on my way back to Qhunqhu, where I was staying (in the house I had helped Alejandro build). En route we came across another man who flagged us down for a ride; it turned out that he knew one of the catechists slightly. As we got underway, he turned to me and said, "Excuse me, brother, what is your institution?" Before I could reply, the catechists jumped in explaining my research as an institutional affiliation with the parish. They went on to explain that Hernando was "tired" and would soon "rest" (i.e., as if completing his thaki) and that he would turn the operation of the parish over to the ministers. (I heard similar comments in other contexts from other catechists).

This, of course, clearly captures the catechist's construction of their own thakis as continuous with those of priests; like the machaq mallkus, eligible and poised to advance in their cargo careers, the ministers considered themselves "machaq" priests. For his part, Hernando suggested that his fate was up to his religious order. Moreover, he told me that a new priest had already been assigned to the parish, either to replace him or to work alongside him upon his return. (The Aymara seminarian he was grooming as his replacement had married and left the seminary a few years earlier.) What is more, Hernando said, among the plans for the parish for the coming year (perhaps as a function of having two priests in residence) was a project to open up a satellite pastoral office in El Alto, serving Machaqueños in residence there.

† † †

These vignettes point in a number of directions, not all of them contained by this book. I intend them here as they condense the shifting conditions of locality in Bolivia today.

Victor's murder suggests the complex projection of local ayllu disputes into the Alteño context, and the ways such tensions may be sharpened by other forms of rivalry and measures of self-worth among young migrants. Victor's family suggested that envy was a motive: a number of his attackers had not finished school, nor, it was implied, did they have the employment opportunities that seemed to be opening up for Victor.

In ways I have already examined (for instance the incorporation of urban residents in rural fiesta practices), urban and rural ayllu settings are deeply articulated. Victor and Luis, like many migrants, drew upon a social network that spanned country and city and moved back and forth between them. Family members who have lived for years in El Alto or La Paz continue to claim animals among their family's herds and some return periodically to help with planting and harvesting chores. In 2000, which was a bumper year in Machaqa (following seven or eight years of meager harvests), I had occasion to hear a Machaqueño who had moved to the city and found employment complaining about the abundance of the harvest, which required repeated (and thus costly) weekend bus trips back to his fields to complete the work. It is not uncommon for ayllu authorities to serve in these positions while based in the city, essentially commuting to the countryside when their presence is required. Indeed, a city-based (and savvy) mallku is increasingly an asset. I have heard accounts of entire cabildos from other ayllus housed in El Alto.

To the extent that the murder of an eighteen year old can, the violence of Victor's death makes some structural sense. Ayllu boundaries are conceptual and practical sites of tense but necessary juxtaposition and interaction. Marriages that traverse them are particularly fraught with conflictive potential. Rural schools similarly traverse ayllu boundaries, joining students from a number of locales. This is starkly evident in the massive schools located on the Titiri-Milluni border. The suspicions of fat stealing teachers, children entombed alive in the foundations, and other abominations attributed to such sites surely take some of their force from the risks of permanently mediating such local boundaries. Contexts such as El Alto compel similar forms of mediation. Alongside the kin-based network assisting Victor and Luis is a more generalized Machaqueño presence in the city as migrants with houses take on boarders from other ayllus, while soccer clubs and social centers efface microlocal borders joining together a range of Machaqueños. It is this homogenized Machaqueño community and its complex connections with the variously differentiated spaces of rural Machaqa that Hernando hopes to serve with his satellite parish office. Making sense of these connections is an ongoing challenge. At the celebration of Rosario, the year after Victor's death, as ayllus danced in their separate sayañas on the plaza of the town, enacting the contentious integrity of the region, Modesta ran from the dancers of her ayllu to confront the fathers of her son's murderers. "Where is my son?! Where is my son?!" she screamed. The men, I was told, ran away.

But Rosario offers only one space for making sense of these challenges, for demanding answers to the puzzles of producing locality in difficult and sometimes tragic circumstances. Modesta also went to Viacha. Why go to Viacha when there were perfectly reputable yatiris available in her ayllu and elsewhere in Machaqa? "Secrecy" was the reason given when I asked; Modesta brought Luis to Viacha to find a yatiri so that her neighbors would not gossip about her actions. Secrecy and the sense of public scrutiny is an always presented concern, a mixed blessing of ayllu sociality. (Compare the comments of Alejandro's wife, Rufina, who once complained to me of the sterile (and, perhaps, ominous) anonymity of El Alto and La Paz: "once you leave your house," she said, "you can turn around and not know which door you've just come out of"). Perhaps I should leave it at that.

Yet it seems worth noting both that Viacha stands as something of a gateway to El Alto and that this rather decrepit town has taken on increasing structural importance in the wake of the Law of Popular Participation. For Viacha is the seat of the municipality of which Machaqa is a subalcaldia. Now more than a dusty stop on the way to the city, Viacha is increasingly a focal site of administrative pilgrimages made by mallkus and others from Machaqa seeking access to governmental resources. More than that: the sociopolitical production of Machaqa now involves the placement of machaqueño representatives in Viacha. The regional cabildo appoints a delegation from Machaqa to serve in various functionary positions—guards, doormen—at the mayoral offices. These neomayordomos participate in a social and political landscape transformed by the neoliberal reforms of the 1990s. It was within this transformed landscape that Modesta sought explicitly to position her offerings for her surviving son's safety and prosperity.

It also bears mentioning that these are not one-way pilgrimage routes. The rider in my rented jeep was not the only one in recent years to ask me what my "institution" was—a question I had not encountered during earlier periods of fieldwork. One function of the recent reform laws –which both peeled away various state services to local populations and prescribed paths of access for local populations (codified as territorial base organizations, subalcaldias, and so forth) to limited state resources—has been a proliferation of NGOs under whose auspices a considerable percentage of decentralized nation-state resources are distributed (see Gill 2000). I was being asked to declare my NGO affiliation: an identifier of some import as it is now emerging as a criterion of successful mallku service that an ayllu authority develop a proposal to one of the NGOs serving the region for a community development project during his tenure.

Against these ever emerging entanglements of locality within shifting national and transnational contexts (and of national and transnational developments within local contexts), the catechists' beliefs that they might take over the operation of the parish seem jarringly naive. Their dream of an autonomous locality (a catechist-run parish) is not likely to be in the cards; the destiny of Jesús de Machaqa parish like that of Hernando's career is largely in the hands of the Church hierarchy. And, of course, while pastoral workers lament the dying Andean locality of the elderly, which seems to portend the disappearance of the locality championed by inculturation, Hernando's vision of a satellite parish office in El Alto reflects astutely not the erasure of locality but its shifting constitution in a complexly entangled world. For the production of such localities always involves referencing and asserting their translocal viability in ways resonant in microlocal terms but also deeply compromised and conditioned by additional imaginings and interventions in the production of locality.

‡ ‡ ‡

In the course of their consistently suggestive work, Arnold, Jiménez, and Yapita (1992) and Yapita (1992) following Huanca (1989), have explored an Aymara discursive style they describe as "braiding" or "plaiting." This verbal art is characterized by the "crossing" of multiple narrative themes, which are foreshadowed and then brought into relief by a speaker over the course of a narrative. The resulting tangle of subthemes, elided words, and apparent non sequiturs, while chaotic and scattered on the surface of an abstracted moment of interaction, resolves into a textured relationship of multiple narrative threads for the participants over the longer duration of the interaction. Arnold and Yapita compare the style to textile production. We have seen similar metaphors for the organization of the complex rotation of life trajectories (thakis), the braiding of which, over time, traces the situated and ongoing production of locality.

I have neither the facility in Aymara to adequately appreciate this discursive art nor the literary subtlety to approximate it in my native language. Yet I have found the metaphor a productive one both for thinking about the open-ended project of locality and for pursuing and plaiting the various strands of this ethnographic project. In braiding together an ethnography of missionization, a revisiting of Andean locality, and an examination of Aymara conceptions of embodied subjectivity and personhood, in bringing in and out of focus, and twining into different juxtapositions, foreign missionaries, catechists, and a host of other Aymara, I have sought to simulate a textured reality that I have only partially glimpsed and no doubt imperfectly understood. As a fabrication of coherence, a braid reveals itself most clearly at its end. These last vignettes, drawn from recent field experience and tentatively analyzed here may serve to condense and summarize many of the issues at hand. But they point as well to a future not yet in focus nor fully in hand. For Aymara as for missionaries, for me as for you, grasping these unending and entangled strands is our ceaseless project and singular achievement.

Introduction: Converting Difference

1. Reporting events that took place at about the same time Father Monast's observations were published, Platt describes an "eccentric ex-priest" who related to him with a "wild look in his eye": "These Indians don't believe in God at all. They're not *really* Christians. It's the Sun they worship—the Sun! the Sun!" (140).

2. For theological statements of inculturation, see Damen 1989; Irarrazaval 1988; and Suess 1991. Jordá 1981 remains the seminal work for discussions on the southern altiplano of a *teología andina*; see also Quispe et al. 1987. Birgit Meyer 1994 discusses inculturation in the African context.

3. For these developments in Bolivia, see Albó 1994; van Cott 2000; Paulson 2000. See Hale 1997; Nelson 1999; Warren 1998 for discussions from elsewhere in Latin America. Wilmsen and McAllister 1996 present case studies from other world areas.

4. As a recent reviewer (Pels 1997) suggests, "The study of Christian missionaries has been a major area of innovation in the anthropology of colonialism." See, for instance, the works of Beidelman 1982;Comaroff and Comaroff 1991; Huber 1988; Lattas 1998; Rafael 1988;White 1991.

5. See Adelman 1999 for a set of recent reflections on the colonial legacy in Latin America. For examples of earlier and thoughtful discussions on the same, see Stein and Stein 1970 and Morse 1964.

6. I take as a benchmark the *Handbook of South American Indians* edited by Julian Steward and published in seven volumes between 1946 and 1959 by the Smithsonian Institution Bureau of American Ethnography.

7. See Ortiz 1995 [1947]; Coronil 1995, 1996; Mignolo 2000 for discussions of this counterpoint between colonial centers and local peripheries.

8. See, for example, the work of Appadurai 1996; Gupta and Ferguson 1997; Ong 1999; Miller 1995 for different discussions within anthropology on this topic.

9. See the reflections of Briggs 1996 and Warren 1998, as well as the controversy surrounding the work of Stoll 1999.

10. Some touchstones and examples of this rapidly expanding literature include Appadurai 1996; Axel 2001; Mallki 1995, Ong 1999.

11. These concerns have been voiced most influentially by Orin Starn; see Piot 1999 for a thread of a comparable discussion in the Africanist literature. In coordination with the important questions he has asked of Andeanists, some of the most notable publications in the field in recent years reflect a trend away from community-based studies, focusing rather on regional and national social movements (Starn 1999), the transformations of ethnic identities in urban spaces (de la Cadena 2001), rural schooling (Luykx 1999), as well as transnational commercial networks for indigenous handicrafts (Colloredo-Mansfeld 1999).

12. Miller's insightful discussion of consumption hinges precisely on the constrained position of the consumer taking on things produced *elsewhere,* with limited creative choice.

13. For a sampling of these discussions, concerned with the indeterminacy of abstract (semantic) meaning apart from situated and interactively produced communicative contexts, see Duranti and Goodwin 1992; Hanks 1990; Silverstein 1976; Goffman 1974.

14. In counterpoint to this inherited framing of the problem, recent discussions in the Americanist literature have focused on later moments of colonial administration in the Mesoamerican and Andean heartlands (e.g., Taylor 1996; Mills 1997) as well as situations of later, sporadic, and less or never decisive mission contact at the more long-standing frontiers of Spanish colonialism (e.g., Langer and Jackson 1995).

15. I address this in connection with the Andeanist literature in more detail in chapter 1. For an exemplary effort to grapple with the constitutive force of the primordial colonial moment, see Abercrombie's (1998) discussion of interacting modes of historical knowledge and social memory among the Aymara-speaking ayllu K'ulta.

16. As Freccero (1986) notes, "Conversion can be adequately represented as definitive only by extending what may be simply a moment of self-consciousness into a temporal sequence, which is to say, into narrative form, in which the observing self is separated from the observed."

17. In the same vein, Talal Asad (1996:265) reframes the question of conversion as one of shifting possibilities and constraints for experiencing authentic selfhood, writing

> The *politics* of consciousness, like the politics of personal identity of which it is part, is an entirely modern Western possibility. The *self-conscious* selection and integration of new elements into that identity (which many anthropologists refer to as syncretism or hybridity) is central to that possibility. That is to say, the centrality of self-constructive *action* is due to a specific epistemic structure.

He thus ties the very question of conversion to an ontology of self grounded in Western modernity.

1. ANDEAN LOCALITY REVISITED

1. We should be equally attentive to the complex positions of missionaries who are often subject to control as foreign aliens in Bolivia and subordinates within various hierarchies of the Catholic Church. I examine this in more detail in chapters 2 and 3.

Here let me recall my next jeep trip with Jan, a month later, when we journeyed to an interparish event in Copacabana. The bishop—Jan's boss—would be in attendance and Jan was quite nervous. While Ingrid and I and two of the nuns waited for him in the Landrover, he completed a last-minute shower (a display, to my eyes at the time, of missionary affluence) so as to arrive fresh and clean for his encounter with the bishop. The nuns, clearly amused by this anxious and recently arrived priest, teasingly called him "Don Tranquilo" (roughly, "Mister Mellow").

2. The key historical moments, of course, are the rise of the Incan empire and its eclipse by Spanish colonialism. The legacy of Hispanic colonialism and what was seen as the enduring backwardness of Andean societies with respect to twentieth-century modernity drove many of the founding questions of Andean area studies. For some contemporary statements as well as useful reflections on these early disciplinary moments, see Adelman 1999; Morse 1964; Stein and Stein 1970; as well as the essays in Steward 1946; and Cline 1967.

3. See Manheim 1991 for an extensive examination of history of Quechua since the European invasion.

4. These include forms of forced relocation as well as labor drafts for more temporary periods of service in other parts of the empire.

5. See Grieshaber 1980; Klein 1993; Platt 1986; and Rivera 1986 for a sense of this differential impact and the variation of sociocultural forms—i.e., communities in the historical wake of hacienda expansions versus large intercommunal ayllu structures—between the lake region and the area of Northern Potosí.

6. This theme of "verticality," first stressed by John Murra (1968, 1972), has been an especially fertile one for Andeanists; see Murra, Wachtel, and Revel 1986; Larson, Harris, Tandeter 1995. I find it useful to think with, as the pattern of noncontiguous "archipelagos" of social groups maintaining access to valued distant products is resonant with my interests in the translocal dimensions of local practices. While the theme has likely been misused as a putatively pan-Andean pattern (see Murra's caution [1985]), it is certainly relevant for the altiplano regions at issue here (Choque 1979, 1991).

7. For examples of the larger end of the ayllu continuum, see the work of Albó and equipo CIPCA 1972; Arnold, Jiménez, and Yapita 1992; Platt 1986; Harris 1982b, 1985; Rasnake 1988; and Abercrombie 1986, 1998. For a discussion of ayllu as community, see Allen 1988.

8. At the other extreme, where ayllu tends to denote a limited kin group, below the level of Platt's "minimal ayllu," Isbell (1985:105) reports an informant commenting, "An ayllu can be a barrio [neighborhood], the entire village, one's family, or even the district, the department, or the nation." Ayllu, explained the informant in an oft-cited gloss, "refers to 'any group with a head.'"

9. For contemporary discussions of the MNR reforms and their impact, see Heath, Erasmus, and Buechler 1969; Preston 1978; Marschall 1970; Albó and equipo CIPCA 1972; Bonilla, Fonseca, Bustillos 1967; and Carter and Mamani 1982. Since the mid-1990s a new set of reforms, linked to a global neoliberal trend, have been underway in Bolivia. I treat these developments in most detail in chapter 7 and in the conclusion.

10. See Preston 1978. Rasnake (1988:272) reports the emergence of peasant sindicatos in the Department of Potosí only since 1983, attributing, incidentally, the diffusion of these modernizing reforms to rural capacitation courses offered by Catholic pastoral workers.

11. In this sense now common criticisms of community-based studies as historically naive or insular in their views of Andean locality are insufficient. For examples of community-centered research see Buechler and Buechler 1971; Carter and Mamani 1982; Preston 1978; and Crandon-Malamud 1991. Well-known work outside Bolivia includes Allen 1988 and Isbell 1985. Roseberry's (1995) reply to Starn's (1992, 1994) criticisms of insularity in community-based Andeanist ethnography suggests additional avenues for a more nuanced assessment of mid-century ethnography in the Andes and Latin America more generally.

12. Isbell (1985) adopts this language most explicitly.

13. For examples of ayllu-centered research, see Rasnake 1988; Abercrombie 1998; Platt 1982; Harris 1982b, 1985; and Arnold, Jiménez, and Yapita 1992.

14. See especially in this regard the essays in Murra, Wachtel, and Revel 1986.

15. This risk is not without its rewards. Platt (1987b), for instance, has fruitfully located the colonial moment as not the beginning of Aymara history but rather a watershed event within a longer Aymara history and has thus drawn attention to indigenous cultural resources shaping the Amayra responses to colonial challenges.

16. It was in Peñas that Tupaj Katari—the leader of the southern wave of rebellions that convulsed the colonial Andes in 1781—was executed by the weakened Spanish administration.

17. During research in 1997 and 1999 I learned that the altiplano sur had been reorganized so that it was now under the control of the bishop responsible for El Alto, a rapidly growing city of indigenous migrants located at the very rim of the altiplano above the city of La Paz. This reorganization of pastoral administration—effectively doing away with the fictive distinction between rural and urban parishes—reflects the increasingly intense links between rural Aymara communities and El Alto. I return to this explicitly in the conclusion.

18. See, for instance, the work of Vellard 1963; Bonilla, Fonseca, and Bustillos 1967; Albó and equipo CIPCA 1972; Ticona and Albó 1997; Wachtel 1990; and Astvaldsson 1997.

19. The Urus are a highlands group historically subjugated by the Aymara, inhabiting marginal lands in and around Lake Titicaca and the Desaguadero River. See Wachtel 1990.

20. See Choque 1979, 1986, 1991, 1993; Choque and Ticona 1996; and Wachtel 1990 for the most accomplished early colonial histories of the region.

21. The literature on the Toledan reforms is vast. For historical discussions of the reducciones and their impact on indigenous ayllus, see Spalding 1984 and Stern 1982. For a briefer, more presentist assessment of the role of the reducciones in shaping contemporary Andean communities, see Molinié-Fioravante 1986. The transformative impact of the reforms is crucial to what I identified above as Andeanist attention to the constitutive moment of colonial encounter. Abercrombie (1986, 1998) provides some

of the most informative discussions. Fraser (1990) addresses the reproduction in the Andean landscape of Iberian ideals through the architecture of the towns.

22. To put this sum in perspective, the total capital of the church that year was 7,738 pesos, 6½ reales, including liquid assets of 1,901pesos, 4 reales.

23. AALP JDM/lf.

24. While the strict continuity of pre-Hispanic land holdings and vertical ecological access of the parcialidad Machaqa la Chica is difficult to trace, Choque points out that the valley farms of Acaluco and Timusí that "belonged to the community of Jesús de Machaqa" were declared by Gabriel Fernandez Guarachi in his testament of 1673 to be his property (1979). By the nineteenth century Timusí along with other lands held by the Guarachis were recognized as property of the "indígenas de Jesús de Machaqa."

25. For discussions of La Paz's emerging prominence in the colonial period, see Klein 1993. For general discussions of the status of caciques, see Rivera 1978.

26. Choque and Ticona (1996) report these three dates. Bonilla, Fonseca, and Bustillos (1967) and archival documents I have seen from the nineteenth century invoke the 1645 transactions. These purchases (certainly the seventeenth-century activities) were compelled by the Spanish revenue–generating strategy known as *composición de tierras,* which made lands not immediately in use or held by clear (Iberian) title property of the Crown and subject to sale to the highest bidder.

27. For discussions of these liberal reforms and their impact on free-holding ayllus and communities, see Albó and Bernadas 1990; Platt 1986; and Rivera 1986.

28. Details about the beaterio are sketchy in accounts to date (cf. Burns 1999). For passing mention of the convent, see Gisbert 1980; Bonilla, Fonseca, and Bustillos 1967; and Paredes 1955.

29. ACLP, tomo 259 ff., 185–208v.

30. Klein (1993:120) points out that this investment in local communities occurred at a time of economic "depression" in urban areas linked to the "century-long crisis in silver mining from 1650–1750."

31. This reflects a certain status inflation in recent decades. When the MNR reforms were first implemented, each ayllu was codified as a syndicate, with groups of neighboring ayllus bundled into subcentrals. As we shall see, this bundling grates against other patterns of intraregional social structure. For a variety of reasons, from this structural dissonance to competition among ayllus, by the time of my research no self-respecting ayllu would consider itself anything but a subcentral—though not every one of these communities had the paperwork and administrative infrastructure (technically, three constituent syndicates are necessary) to sustain the claim (cf. Albó and equipo CIPCA 1972).

32. Prior to the emergence of the contemporary zone system, I was told, leaders of the four katus made offerings to four principal place deities (wak'as) of the ayllu.

33. The colonial administration distinguished originario families from forasteros or agregados, assessing higher tribute payments from the former. (Thus some originarios renounced their status to avoid the greater tribute burden.) Forasteros often settled on marginal land or came to have use rights to smaller tracts. In some cases forasteros may have been tenants on excess lands held by originario families.

34. I am also aware of cases in which a man inherited the personhood of his wife's father, effectively switching allegiance between zones. A number of informants stressed this apparently ad hoc nature of the zones—i.e., affiliation is voluntary and flexible— though I suspect this flexibility serves largely to accommodate interpersonal frictions and tensions deriving from inheritance of personhood by a number of sons.

35. That said, it requires some willful effort to confirm an original structure of twelve in the colonial documents. This becomes clear only in the mid-eighteenth century. Even then, it seems the gloss of the region as twelve ayllus ordered a more complex on-the-ground reality. Across this time one also wrestles with the shifting status of regional haciendas such as Chijcha or Qurpa and the shifting status of Jesús de Machaqa pueblo.

36. I observed little formal activity indicating a special contemporary relationship between the two Qhunqhus, though in 1999 I witnessed a delegation of ayllu authorities from Liqiliqi joining the people of Milluni in celebrating the anniversary of the founding of a large primary school located on the border of Qhunqhu Milluni and Sullkatiti Titiri.

37. As I elicited this ranking from an informant in Milluni, Sullkatiti was listed as the "foot." This is likely an intentionally insulting mistake; other accounts place Sullkatiti nearer the top of the intra-ayllu ranking.

38. On this see the work of Kubler 1946; as well as Platt 1987a; and Abercrombie 1986, 1998.

39. The contemporary system I describe here contracted considerably during the 1970s; before this other fiestas were celebrated. A somewhat more detailed review of this history can be found in Orta 1996.

40. It may also be the case that a couple who have completed more senior obligations and are eligible but not ready to "rest" will continue to serve their turns as p'iqi until they retire.

41. The ideal now is that a couple should serve three times as p'iqi before advancing along their cargo path, but this impractical ideal is not strictly enforced.

42. In some ayllus the secretary general is now referred to as *jilaqata*—in Milluni the terms were used interchangeably, with some preference for *mallku*.

43. See Bonilla, Fonseca, and Bustillos 1967; Albó and equipo CIPCA 1972.

44. The production of aynoqa fields is communally coordinated through a three-year cycle of potatoes, quinoa, and barley followed by a fallow period of five to ten years. Alongside the fields used for agricultural production (*pampa aynoqa*) there are in some communities communally regulated highlands grazing areas (*qullu aynoqa*).

45. The size of these qallpas is perhaps the most salient remaining indication of the differences between originarios and agregados—the latter have plots half the size of originario families; see also Bonilla, Fonseca, and Bustillos 1967.

46. In recent years this act of interayllu cohesion has been undercut by some catechists and ministers who perform comparable services in their communities.

47. A series of political reforms implemented in the mid 1990s have set in motion the conversion of rural political and territorial units into municipalities conceived as decentralized administrative hubs through which the disbursal of governmental and

NGO resources would be coordinated. The result has been a shifting tangle of rural municipalities and component municipal districts. The cabildo as I have described it continues to represent Jesús de Machaqa, though now as a municipal district within the municipality headed by Viacha. See Ticona and Albó (1997) for an early assessment of this situation. I return to these developments in chapter 7 and the conclusion.

48. Mayordomo service was a form of forced personal labor. Ethnographies of the 1960s—steeped in the reformist, modernizing ethos of the moment—characterize it as a *pongueaje disfrazado* (disguised *ponqo* service), e.g., Bonilla, Fonseca, and Bustillos 1967. The reference is to forms of personal service once required by hacienda owners of their serfs (ponqos) and outlawed by the MNR reforms. The term comes from the Aymara *punqo* (door)—and evokes a servant waiting in the doorway for his master's orders. Contemporary catechists old enough to remember explicitly contrast their current relations with parish priests with the more strict hierarchy of the past, evoking their present "equality" in terms that directly reference the liberating reforms of the MNR.

49. Bonilla, Fonseca, and Bustillos (1967) describe only mayordomos from one parcialidad participating each year and claim that at one time both did. The most detailed account I collected suggests that six of the "active" mayordomos came from the upper parcialidad and six from the lower one.

50. Echoing toponymic designations of other wak'as, I have heard it referred to as *escaleras negras* (black stairs) as well as *San Salvador* or simply *Niño*.

51. For T'alla, see Bertonio 1984 [1612]; and Abercrombie 1986:171.

52. He later described the wak'a as a stone with writing on it, and I believe he was referring to a cornerstone or plaque that may once have marked the site.

53. Informants listed two other fiestas—Candelaria and Corpus Christi—that were performed until the mid-seventies. A related liturgical event—the festival of the Niño Jesús, the patron saint of the town, in August—also involves the participation of the ayllus in a town-centered celebration and is still observed. However this festival is widely regarded as a mestizo celebration.

54. Rosario is among the last ritual opportunities for men to play qena qena flutes, which are restricted to the dry season. The qenas are put away with the commencement of the rains around All Souls' Day (November 1) in favor of *pinkillus,* which are played through Carnival.

55. These adornments—called *ch'uxña* (green) or *llaqa* (green/leaf)—were available for rent from vendors in the plaza.

56. For more on the current Machaqa case, see Ticona and Albó (1997). See Abercrombie 1998 for a similar process elsewhere in Bolivia.

2. MISSIONARY MODERNITY IN THE POSTWAR ANDES

1. As coined by Fernando Ortiz (1995 [1947]), *transculturation* evokes the reciprocally transforming connection between colonial centers and colonized peripheries. Ortiz is attentive to the localization of global colonial processes as well as to the shifting meaning of the local as fashioned in encompassing translocal contexts. Ortiz's case is Cuba, and he traces the stories of tobacco and sugar as products whose shifting fortunes outline the

global assimilation of colonial products and the local transformations of these social things in emergent global circumstances.

2. McDonough (1992:265 ff.) notes a similarly gendered assessment of Latin American Catholicism on the part of North American Jesuits in the 1940s.

3. See, for instance, Ramos Gavilán 1988 [1621]; Borges 1960:chapter 9; MacCormack 1991:107 ff., 111, 157 ff.

4. For some discussions in this vein, see Escobar 1995; Joseph, Legrand, and Salvatore 1998; and Stein 2000.

5. Barnadas (1976:99) presents a more complete list of the religious orders returning to Bolivia at this time (see also Albó and Barnadas 1990). For this moment of reengagement in wider perspective, see Latorre 1978:14; McBrien 1981:643–48; McDonough 1992:51, 123.

6. See Barnadas 1976:chapter 8; Demelas 1981; and Salmón 1997 for discussions of this period.

7. European pastoral developments such as the theology of hope as well as worker priest movements suggest that important intellectual roots of liberation theology may be found in postwar Europe. Similar correlations with the civil rights movement in the United States might also be productively explored. Not only did much of the theology of liberation emerge in the context of a wave of European and North American missionary activity in Latin America, but many of the Latin American theologians at the forefront of regional pastoral innovation over the 1960s, 1970s, and 1980s received training in Europe (Hugo Assman, Leonardo Boff, Gustavo Gutierrez, Otto Maduro). I offer this not as an effort to reverse the arrrows in a facile monological model of change but rather to underscore the entangled translocal moment out of which these apparently local pastoral transformations arose.

8. See, for instance, Schillebeeckx 1979; Ogden 1982; and Hellwig 1983.

9. In a case I have documented elsewhere (Orta 1990), members of radical Catholic parishes in Nicaragua in 1977 performed liturgical celebrations analogically linking biblical depictions of centurions serving Pontius Pilate with their own experiences of the dreaded National Guard of Anastasio Somoza.

10. The term *conscientization* is taken from the work of the Brazilian popular educator Paolo Freire (e.g., 1974). For anthropological discussions detailing these aspects of liberation theology, see Shapiro 1981; Nelson 1986; Burdick 1993; Orta 1990.

11. The ambiguity and tension of these "two populars" in Latin America has received extensive comment, e.g., García-Canclini 1995; Kselman 1986; Levine 1990; Rowe and Schelling 1991.

12. AALP/CEB, Christmas letter from Bernard Chierhoff, auxiliary bishop, La Paz, 1969.

13. This image of empty evangelical space, like the trope of "abandoned" places, further enables a pastoral construction of a discrete enduring Andean Other.

14. ABEC, "Pastoral de conjunto: altiplano zona sur," September 1973. Translated portions of this document appear in Esquivel 1975.

15. AALP/CEB, "Para la formación de los futuros diaconos."

16. ABEC, "Pastoral de conjunto."

17. As we shall see in future chapters, for contemporary Aymara the memorization and repetition of ritual knowledge is anything but superficial or "mere."

18. AALP/CEB, "Carta de un grupo de sacerdotes de Bolivia a los Señores Obispos reunidos en Tarija: puntos de reflexión sobre el sacerdocía ministerial en Bolivia," April 4, 1970.

19. AALP/CEB "Sobre la restauración del diaconado permanente en Bolivia," 1969.

20. ABEC, "Pastoral de conjunto."

21. AALP/CEB, "Sobre la restauración."

22. Ibid.

23. Ibid.

24. ABEC, "Pastoral de conjunto."

25. For accounts of this period see Aguiló et al. 1991; LADOC 1975; Lerneaux 1980; Berryman 1987:101; Dunkerley 1984:215 ff.

26. AALP/CEB "Carta de un grupo de sacerdotes."

27. The schism among Bolivian pastoral workers was compounded by a period of "crisis" suffered in 1974 by one of the strongest mission teams in the pastoral zone, as a series of developments—from mountain climbing accidents to marriage—reduced a team of Jesuits based in Tiwanaku from eight members to two; see Jordá 1981:39.

28. See, for instance, Annis 1987; Stoll 1990.

3. LOCAL MISSIONS, GLOBAL ALTERS

1. Charles Taylor (1985; cf. Hallowell 1955), for instance, stresses self-interpreting self-awareness as a condition of personhood. I also have in mind work on indexicality and related features of language that function in part to establish a more or less shared "here and now" context as a presupposable point of reference for situated interactants, e.g., Duranti and Goodwin 1992; Percy 1958.

2. Suess 1991 and Damen 1989 present theological overview of inculturations and its emergence; see also Irrarrazaval 1989. Jordá 1981 remains the seminal work for discussions of "Andean theology" on the southern altiplano; see also Llanque 1990; Quispe et al. 1987.

3. See Burdick 1993; Levine 1986; Mainwaring and Wilde 1989.

4. Suess 1991, for instance, cites Hellenic culture as at once the template and limiting condition of evangelization. "This Hellenic culture, as it was the first matrix for the expression of the Faith, limited and determined many times the reexpression of the Faith in other cultures" (185).

5. His recollection of deepening ties to the Aymara was underscored in his narrative when he told me that while in La Paz, he consulted a yatiri—a native of his parish (indeed, the father of one of the catechists) who had a house on the outskirts of La Paz—to divine when he would be able to return to his parish.

6. Courses, particularly those taking place in interparish pastoral centers are heavily structured events. Catechists are often interned for a number of days and immersed in a highly codified routine. An agenda explicitly detailing the times and events that segment the day into periods of working, sleeping, eating, resting, and worship (with

an occasional soccer match thrown in) is prominently posted and copied down by cat-echists in their notebooks. As is the case in other institutional contexts—professional meetings of anthropologists, for instance—these schedules do more that just organize the flow of activity. They assert a uniformity or a sharedness of experience among the participants. Moreover, they also serve as icons of the experience, artifacts (such as a conference catalog) circulated to show others who were not in attendance what the meeting was like. I have heard catechists read portions of these agendas aloud as part of their reports to faith groups.

7. This observation was recorded in 1991. As part of sweeping political reforms im-plemented since 1995, the status of "traditional" or "customary law" and efforts to re-spect community autonomy to a greater degree have become the focus of national de-bate and policy.

8. I observed a small number of women attending these courses in Laja and Toledo; catechists are overwhelmingly male. More balanced gender participation can be found in pastoral efforts focused on the capacitation of Aymara teenagers and young adults (as health promoters or instructors of religion in rural schools). In a few cases women at-tending catechist courses were primarily involved through these other activities with the Church, in others women served as the leaders of the community faith group.

9. Mayordomos were responsible for fulfilling ayllu obligations to the parish, main-taining the matrix church during periodic labor turns. Lutriniros (from the Spanish *doc-trinero,* "parish priest") were old men with knowledge of Christian doctrine who pub-licly catechized young children on certain feast days. A risiri (one who prays; from the Spanish *rezar*) was a community member with memorized knowledge of Christian prayers, called upon to pray during certain ritual occasions, especially those related to the dead. Risiris could also use prayer to attract rain or repel hail and frost, much as yatiris do through other offerings (waxt'as).

10. I am drawing here on Goffman's (1974, 1981) uses of footing and frame to dis-cuss the possible positions an actor in a given context can take, as well as Fillmore's (1985) use of frame to discuss the schematizations of experience that inform a posi-tioned actor's actions and understandings; see also Hanks 1990:79; Duranti and Good-win 1992.

11. For insightful discussions of such mythic narratives, see Dillon and Abercrom-bie 1988; Rasnake 1988; and Abercrombie 1998.

12. The altar held a number of icons, identified to me either as Tata San Antonio or Mama Nieves (the "Virgin of the Snows").

13. I have seen reciprocal visits of Milluni to Titiri, as well as similar practices be-tween other pairs of neighboring ayllus.

14. My closest friends in the community observed my participation with real con-cern. By the time of the 1991 festival, Ingrid and I had formalized our relationship to Alejandro and Rufina by becoming godparents to one of their sons, Ernesto. As I learned later, nine-year-old Ernesto had been charged by his mother with the unenvi-able task of taking care of me. This involved following me around the plaza, assessing when a confrontation was looming (say, when I was talking to someone known as a

particularly belligerent drunk) or when my many cups of alcoholic hospitality seemed to be running over, and devising a pretext ("Godfather, godfather, my godmother needs to talk to you!") to extricate me from the situation.

4. SYNCRETIC SUBJECTS: THE POLITICS OF PERSONHOOD

1. Catechists are classic examples of such brokers. See also Gluckman 1949; Wolf 1965.

2. See Lattas 1992 for an insightful discussion of doubleness in another setting; see also Gilroy 1993.

3. I have in mind discussions in sociolinguistics and cognitive anthropology dealing with the intersection of practice and context, such as those appearing in Duranti and Goodwin 1992; Goffman 1981; Fillmore 1985; Lave and Wenger 1991:32 ff.; Hanks 1990:77 ff.

4. Some recent commentators on Christian evangelization have borrowed from Foucault to characterize Christian conversion as a "technology of self." See Klor de Alva 1999; van der Veer 1996, cf. Asad 1993a; Dumont 1985; Taylor 1989. See my introduction, this volume.

5. See Carrithers, Collins, and Lukes 1985; Giddens 1991; Taylor 1989; cf. Mauss 1973 [1936], 1985 [1938].

6. Some of the parishes I worked in were engaged in various liturgical "experiments" to support this end. The introduction of the ministers in Jesús de Machaqa can be seen as part of this effort to "re-ritualize" at the level of these faith group celebrations. Other priests described efforts to incorporate Aymara symbols in baptisms, or to better correlate Catholic liturgical practices with the agricultural calendar or life cycle. Father Miguel, for instance, told me he was working on a ritual conflation of marriage and confirmation, appreciating the strong links between marriage and public adulthood in Aymara conceptions of the life course.

7. See Huanca 1989 for a discussion of the chuyma in connection with the knowledge of yatiris.

8. Indeed, "soul" is a deeply syncretic concept, a complex of loan words and manifold beliefs stemming (at least) from colonial missionary preoccupations with Andean cults of the dead and the translation traditions of the earliest catechisms; see, for instance, Bertonio 1984 [1612]. For some contemporary discussions of soul in the Andes see Allen 1982; Bastien 1985; Gose 1994a; Harris 1982a.

9. I did not ask him about the "little bird" at the time because I did not glean the details of Oscar's instructions to him until some time later when I transcribed, with the assistance of Demetrio Marca, my tape recording of the event.

10. For marriage also see the account in Albó and Mamani 1980:310. The newlyweds are not named but addressed as "child" and further infantilized by their godparents, who, considering them "tender" and helpless, dress and undress them, feed them, and accompany them when they must go off to urinate. Carter (1977:88) writes of betrothed Aymara couples being "treated as children." Entering mallkus also have guides

or godparents assisting them. They are considered immature during the first months of their tenure and prohibited from speaking forcefully.

11. While a thaki is an individual process, this is not to say that a cargo career is limited to an individual life. As a public manifestation of social and ritual personhood—a performance of chuyma—a thaki may be inherited or otherwise taken on, in essence transferring personhood and, in some cases, conflating two lives within a single performance of personhood. Thus, a woman may continue a thaki in the name of her husband (deceased or migrated); a son may inherit and complete the thaki of his father or, conversely, a father may undertake a second thaki on behalf of his son, who has migrated to the city but wishes to maintain his social legitimacy (and access to land) in the ayllu (see Vellard 1963, plate 21).

12. The herd includes animals belonging to each member of the family, including married adults living in La Paz or other cities. Each ownership is marked by a distinctive pattern cut into the sheep's ear and is extended matrilineally among sheep. The herd thus embodies a family that is extended across space; this event provided an opportunity to remember children, brothers, and sisters who were, in some cases, seen infrequently.

13. Perhaps the most common Aymara sacrifice, a ch'alla consists of spilling a few drops of (typically) alcohol on the ground or flicking them in the air while naming or thinking of a particular place or place deity.

14. The issue of deception came up most often in the context of the regular verbal reports catechists make to the priest and reflects pressures upon catechists to increase attendance at faith group meetings as well as to introduce the theological innovations of inculturation.

15. In addition to the literature cited earlier in this chapter, see Taylor 1985 and Hallowell 1955:80.

16. Early efforts to establish the position of catechists on the altiplano often resulted in communities assimilating the position within their set of yearly cargo responsibilities, to the dismay of priests, who envisioned the catechists as specialists to be formed through an extensive process of courses and pastoral experience (see Orta 1995, n. 15, cf. Marschall 1970).

17. The hierarchy is said to reflect differences in age or seniority, which is held to be a function of participation in mission courses. As one catechist expressed it, "With that knowledge we will advance, to mature a bit from being a catechist." The—typically married—catechists are sometimes abused in their communities for having remained catechists for so many years without a promotion to priest. The sense is that the catechists are wasting their time since they do not accrue any officially recognized prestige over the course of their careers. This is a source of much disaffection among catechists and frustration among pastoral workers.

18. When, in one community, it was necessary to remove an ornate Latin missal from the local chapel—where it was being damaged by mice and leaks—community authorities decided that the local catechist should care for the book in his house. They felt the book was dangerous to other members of the community, but not the catechist, because he was "almost a priest."

19. The yatiri's practice of divination through "looking" (*uñjaña*) at coca leaves is also cast as "reading" (*liyiña,* sp. "leer").

5. ALEJANDRO'S HOUSE: THE POROUS PRODUCTION OF LOCALITY

1. Sayañas are also reconfigured by intrapatriline disputes, as, for instance, the one I have described involving Alejandro. Such cases are sometimes resolved by the creative transformation of technically nonsayaña land into a neosayaña. In two cases I am aware of this involved mobilizing rights to land held by women.

2. Newlywed couples typically receive gifts from well-wishers. The gifts are called ayni and are thus equated with a range of more day-to-day forms of ayni exchange. In this sense the ayni gifts given to the couple at marriage are something of a starter kit of social relations through connections of debt: the gift that keeps on giving. This has moral as well as practical ramifications.

3. More generally, affines stand as unsocialized raw material; brothers-in-law, for instance, are commonly classed as wild antisocial trickster animals (e.g., the fox); Abercrombie 1986; Gose 1994a.

4. Plan International also pairs indigenous families with "sponsors" in Europe and North America, who, in addition to donations that fund the sort of projects I am describing, occasionally send cards to their Bolivian foster child and his/her family.

5. Of course, these connections are reckoned cognatically (and sometimes quite creatively) for the purposes of allowing or disallowing marriage. Still, there does seem to be a certain truncating of matrilineal memory in this patrilocal setting. As for the sort of parallel descent remembered in Arnold's paths of blood and semen, the most comparable data from Jesús de Machaqa concern an event once practiced during Holy Week, in which women would serve food to fellow ayllu members in exchange for prayers for their ancestors, and an extant practice during Carnival, when women and their families of procreation return to visit their natal sayaña.

6. Some catechists report having dozens of *aijados* (godchildren). During a ritual of confirmation I observed, some catechists served as godfather to every confirmant from their faith group. Comparably asymmetric relations of compadrazgo have classically been reported for "mestizos" and "vecinos."

7. Though it should also be noted that this participation was encapsulated by a commentary/homily offered by Bonifacio or Alejandro at each station as well as a hymn performed by the faith group.

8. In Qhunqhu Milluni the capilla is oriented roughly north-south, located at the base of a hill on which the ruins of a calvario are found. The community cemetery is located at the rear of the chapel. To the front is an enclosed space, called a *sacristuyu* (sacristy corral), walled in by high adobe walls, broken up by arched entryways to the east, west, and south as well as a series of windowlike openings. In the southeast corner of the sacristuyu is a *misaqala* with adobe benches along each wall. The southern entryway opens onto another enclosed space, larger than the sacristuyu: the "plaza." It is here that dance troupes perform during fiestas. The low adobe wall bounding the plaza opens to the west and to the south. To the east an

adobe hut (the *tata uta:* lit. "sir/priest house") interrupts the wall. This is a place where visitors may lodge (e.g., visiting musicians during fiestas); I believe this was where visiting priests were fed.

9. In a mass performed by a priest or a deacon, a catechist is usually responsible for selecting the songs; when two catechist preside over a faith group, the junior catechist is given the task.

10. This water is prayed over by the catechist and aspersed in a clear imitation of a Catholic priest—one that like Bonifacio's transubstantiation of the bread at the ayuno exceeds catechists' authority as conceived by the Church. I have elsewhere observed catechists repeat many of the gestures of a priest when distributing communion wafers, as if performing the transubstantiation themselves (lifting the wafers in the air, making the sign of the cross over them). When I asked them to list the parts of the mass they performed, they were careful to exclude this part of the liturgy.

11. In one case a man requesting a liturgy to commemorate his dead wife provided bottles of soft drink for the faith group meal. The generosity parallels the offerings of food made during All Souls Day and may be seen as "payment" to the group, who, after all, had done the work of remembering his wife.

12. Music may also be played during some household-level rites—marriage celebrations, for example. In each case these are highly public occasions performing and affirming relations above the level of the household. Similarly, with the exceptions of lone herders playing flutes or drums while they wander the hills (which I observed rarely and often in the context of practicing for an upcoming event) or household-level groups playing as they climb from their principal residence to one of their herding houses to mark their sheep during Carnival, instrumental music is always performed by groups of men from a number of patrilines.

13. Male and female faith group members sing in a high nasal tremelo characteristic of other Aymara musical practices (cf. Turino 1993:48 ff).

14. The one factor that is not compensated for in faith group practice is dancing, which has classically been associated by the Church with "idolatrous" practice and is strongly linked by faith group members to the consumption of alcohol.

15. The generation of such lists codifying religious knowledge is a classic technique of catechizing, reminiscent in many ways of the strategies of the earliest generations of priests and the *lutriniros* who mimic them (cf. Barnes 1992). Although I did not observe this pedagogical style in the missionary-sponsored courses I attended, it was a technique commonly deployed by catechists in interactions with their faith group. The rote memorization involved also suggests influences from rural schools; cf. Luykx 1999.

16. In a separate context Alejandro described the faith groups to me as in a process of catching up with the *tatar abuelos* (ancestors), "following their footsteps." Here it seems the faith group must achieve through study, by means of the techniques of literacy, what the ancestors already knew.

17. The comment was made during a discussion of Pentecost. The point of departure is the descent of the Spirit upon the apostles who begin speaking in tongues.

6. SEDUCTIVE STRANGERS AND SATURATED SYMBOLS

1. See, for instance, Turner 1957; Gluckman 1960; Geschiere 1997.

2. Rivière 1991 and Wachtel 1994 also discuss some of these events involving catechists.

3. See, for instance, Molinié Fioravante 1991; Salazar-Soler 1991; Wachtel 1994; Weismantel 2001.

4. Aymara I knew were often out and about after dark for a range of benign reasons: checking on their cattle or taking them to water one last time, returning from meetings, or, in the case of a p'iqi, making the rounds of his zone to alert people to an upcoming work obligation, teenagers returning from a rendezvous with girlfriend or boyfriend. A number of people—particular teenagers—reported surprising and frightening apparitions encountered at or near wak'a sirinas, though often with little long-term harm.

5. Discussing similar data from Peru, Gose (1994a) links this sense of productive labor to a form of auto-sacrifice.

6. Although fat as a ritual component is typically offered to wak'as, it also figures as an offering to Catholic saints (and to the dead) in the form of candles. Recall that candles are among the products made from the fat extracted by kharikharis. Consultants consistently described candles as made of "fat" (lik'i). On at least one occasion I saw a homemade candle—a clay dish filled with fat with a wick—being placed before a saint's image. I also observed more conventional candles being offered in this way; the typical offering is for an increase in livestock, though luck and wealth are also objectives.

7. Historically, the term wiraqucha is more ambivalent, serving as a respectful term of address used by abject Aymara encountering hacendados and other worthies. As I encountered the term, it often had a wry undertone, referencing an asymmetry now "officially" nonexistent.

8. The classic example would be a man who doesn't wear a poncho or a hat. It is not clear to me if the term is used with respect to women.

9. Among the activities on this final night of Rosario is a ch'alla recognizing the machaq mallkus (new mallkus), the men who, by virtue of having completed all other cargo obligations, are eligible to serve as mallku for the coming year. The man who demanded the stranger's identity card had just been recognized as a machaq mallku and, in fact, went on to serve as mallku the following year. This public assertiveness was uncharacteristic and likely linked to his changing status (compare Bonifacio's public assertiveness in the ayuno performance in chapter 5).

10. Warisata was an experimental school founded in the 1930s by pioneering pro-Indian educator Elizardo Perez. The massive school building located on the border of Qhunqhu Milluni and Sullkatiti Titiri dates from this time and was build as part of the same educational effort. See Perez 1962; Luykx 1999.

11. At the time (late 1990) this was an especially contentious topic because of the impending arrival in Bolivia of teams of U.S. Marines to train Bolivian troops for the work of eradicating the coca crop and apprehending drug traffickers.

12. This part of my argument emerged in conversations with Stuart Rockefeller.

13. My understanding of cargo cults derives principally from the work of Burridge 1960; Clark 1988; Errington and Gewertz 1994; Lattas 1998; Lawrence 1964; and Strathern 1979–1980.

14. Canessa (2000) makes a similar case for the particularity of kharisiri suspicions.

15. See, for instance, Canessa 2000; Comaroff and Comaroff 1999; Geschiere 1997; Nelson 1999; Weiss 1996.

16. See, for instance, the work of Scheper-Hughes 2000. Compare Nelson's (1999) concerns about anthropological discussions of baby-stealing rumors in Guatemala.

7. Burying the Past

1. While the term *vecino* might be glossed, as I have suggested above, as an ethnically non-Indian or mestizo resident of the town, the emergence of this "rural elite" in the nineteenth and twentieth centuries reflects the merging of early modern Spanish conceptions of social privilege as these informed colonial social hierarchies in the Andes with new forms of socioeconomic power and hierarchy generated by postindependence Bolivian liberalism (Abercrombie 1998; see also Gose 1994a).

2. Choque 1986 and Choque and Ticona 1996 provide the most detailed accounts of the uprising and its aftermath and include illuminating archival and oral historical data. Choque and Ticona (1996:292 ff.) report an oral history recorded in 1990 in which the consultant recounts his father's interrogation by police after the uprising: "This is the way they questioned me," he told me: "'Speak! How did you do it? You ate *ch'uñu* [desiccated potato] stewed in the brains of the vecinos?'" In an account I recorded in 1992, a man who witnessed the event as a young child describe the "roasting" (*kankatpxi*) of the corregidor and other vecinos.

3. See Choque and Ticona 1996:175–186.

4. Most were released over the course of the next decade. As far as I know the Llanquis died free men, although their deaths and the gravesite of the elder Faustino were focal points for the commemorative ritual discussed below.

5. Technically, the 1991 ritual was the third public commemoration of the massacre; Ticona and Albó (1997) note an initial commemorative event in 1989, although this was limited and sparsely attended. At the time of the 1991 celebration, participants described it to me as the second annual performance of the commemorative rite.

6. Roberto Choque Canqui and Esteban Ticona Alejo, respectively.

7. The station has recently (ca. 2000) relocated to El Alto.

8. Like inculturationists, more secular cultural activists draw heavily on the past, valued as a locus of authenticity and cultural integrity, often thought to be repressed by colonial and republican regimes (Harris 1995). The past is also mobilized as an instructive record of the mistreatment of indigenous groups by the state. And in ways that are comparable to the "practical nostalgia" of faith groups discussed in chapter 5, secular indigenous scholars often assert authoritative knowledge of the past as a component of effective traditional sociopolitical authority in Aymara and Quechua communities (Choque and Mamani 2000; Orta 2000).

While some among the secular movement stridently reject the Catholic Church (and one noted indigenous scholar expressed to me his resentment over the participation of foreign pastoral agents in the events commemorating the massacre), there are important convergences as well. A movement of Aymara "cultural promoters," which emerged in the 1970s, has been a source of a range of indigenist scholarship and cultural activism. The history of this movement reflects the institutional collaboration of a number of rural parishes and suggests links between some indigenous scholarship and other forms of popular educations that have been prominent in rural Catholic pastoral work (Calderón, Q'ispe and Reyes 1995; cf. Hurtado 1986; Pacheco 1992). Church-related institutions ranging from the research and development organization CIPCA to the radio station San Gabriel have served as outlets through publication and broadcast for indigenous scholarship, historical radio dramas, and so forth. Such connections continue to be a factor in the currently changing climate of educational reform in Bolivia and the increasing role of NGOs in the country that have resulted in an increasing number of private educational and research organizations training and employing a new generation of indigenous-identified scholars.

For discussions of activist indigenous scholarship elsewhere in Latin America, see Rappaport 1994; Warren 1998; Nelson 1999; and Burdick 1998.

9. Others have examined this tension in states marked by "extreme cultural pluralism" (Errington and Gewertz 1994; see also Keane 1997), where supralocal solidarity entails a specific alignment (sometimes subordination) of local identity with respect to the nation.

10. For the moment, "other" refers generically to non-Machaqueños. As we shall see below, the enactment of memory forms derived from mortuary practices establishes a very powerful deictic center to the commemoration, authorizing the remembrances of a particular Machaqueño community above those of other Machaqueños and, ultimately, limiting the ability of the ritual to be hosted by other Machaqueño communities in subsequent years as intended by the organizers.

11. Recall that marriage is often initiated by an elopement, figured as the loss of the woman to the groom's patriline. In some accounts the bride is led away from her parents' house like a captured herd animal (Carter and Mamani 1982). Community endogamy is preferred; as the cases of Roberto and Hugo recounted in chapter 6 show, marriages across community or provincial boundaries can produce acute tensions and suspicions.

12. Indeed, the attendance list of cabildo authorities read as part of the event itself recites and constitutes a "Machaqa" quite different from that existing at the time of the uprising. Moreover, in recent decades many ayllus from the upper moiety have formally separated from Jesús de Machaqa constituting a distinct administrative unit within the peasant syndicate structure established after the MNR revolution of 1952. As we shall see, this has intensified, under national administrative reforms implemented since 1996, in ways that impacted later commemorations of the uprising. But for now, lest we overestimate the primordial coherence of the Machaqa of the uprising, it should also be remembered that not all of the ayllus participated in the rebellion, resulting in a fair amount of intra-Machaqueño, interayllu feuding in the years after the event. All this

underscores the self-consciously unstable and contentious nature of the Machaqaness mobilized by the commemoration and envisioned by some of the organizers as a model of sui generis regional ethnic solidarity of wider application.

13. See Allen 1988; Berg 1989; Buechler and Buechler 1971; Carter 1968; Carter and Mamani 1982; Gose 1994a; and Harris 1982a for discussions of Andean mortuary practices and beliefs about the dead.

14. Along with the three-year observance of All Souls' Day, the family of the deceased is expected to contract a Catholic Mass for the dead for three years around the time of the anniversary of the death. Thus the mass on the morning of the twelfth complements the vigil and further fulfills the obligations of Machaqueños to their dead.

15. Halbwachs (1980:63, 68) writes: "The child is provided access to an even more distant past by his grandparents. . . . To a much greater extent than is commonly believed, therefore, the life of the child is immersed in social milieus through which he comes in touch with a past stretching back some distance. The latter acts like a framework into which are woven his most personal remembrances. . . . Later on, his memory will ground itself in this lived past, much more than on any past learned from written history."

16. Gose (1986:302, 1994a) refers to this five-generational unit to suggest the ways local mountain spirits (apus, "the term . . . can mean FFFF in Quechua"), are drawn into human kin relations. He similarly links contemporary mountain deities to precolonial ancestor cults.

17. The Law of Popular Participation is often used metonymically to gloss a set of reforms implemented during Sanchez de Lozada's presidency, formalized in a new constitution (1994) and continuing processes of "neoliberal" restructuring set in motion in the mid-1980s. The details of the Bolivian constitutional reforms and their impact in places such as Jesús de Machaqa merit close and separate treatment. For an overview of the reforms, see van Cott 2000 and Healy and Paulson 2000. For assessments of their impact in the region, see Ticona and Albó 1997; Calla 1999. Gill (2000) presents a glimpse of the impact of the reforms in the city of El Alto.

18. "Presidente enfrentó trato descortés en Jesús de Machaqa," La Presencia, March 13, 1994. The confrontation is also described in Ticona and Albó 1997. The latter includes the text of Saturnino Tóla's speech.

19. Tóla's comments are certainly ambiguous. Yet, the rhetorical parallel between the president's staff of office (itself a metaphor of disciplinary power) and the chicote, along with the appeal to Vice President Cardenas's cultural knowledge, further suggests an effort to assert a form of translatability and alignment between Machaqa and the state.

20. In this regard it is worth updating the political vita of Gonzalo Sanchez de Lozada, who, as this book was going to press, found himself confronted by a largely Aymara political mobilization that ousted him from office. After serving out his first term as president (1993–1997), he was returned to office in 2002 in a closely contested election in which his nearest rival was Evo Morales, an Aymara activist who has emerged as a powerful representative of coca growers in the Chapare region. Sanchez de Lozada's first (and only!) year of this second term was marked by intensifying

protests and violent government responses surrounding a range of policies. In October 2003, announcement of a government plan to allow foreign companies to develop and export natural gas through a proposed pipeline to a port in Chile provoked an escalating series of protests. A range of opposition interests from coca growers led by Morales to an organization of altiplano ayllus led by Felipe Quispe, also known as "the mallku," to urban-based Aymara in El Alto staged demonstrations and marches and blockaded key roads into La Paz. Neighborhood organizations in El Alto, some of them forged and strengthened by the decentralizing logic of neoliberal reforms, seem to have played an important organizational role in this mobilization. Deadly repressive measures by the army and other so-called security forces were met by growing public protest leading to Sanchez de Lozada's resignation and flight to the United States. Of course, the local dynamics of this ethnic mobilization remain to be examined. As the complex position of the El Alto neighborhood groups signals, it is likely to be a product of the very neoliberal moment against which it apparently protests. The only thing certain about the future of this coalition of indigenous political interests is that it will be made and remade in the complex contexts of the future.

achachila (Ay.): grandfather; ancestor; mountain place deity.

ajayu (Ay.): soul; life force (compare *alwa/alma*).

alchin alchipax (Ay.): "The grandchild of the grandchild;" describes five generations of patrilineal descent.

alwa (Ay. from Sp. *alma*): soul; used to refer to enduring social identity of the deceased (compare *ajayu*).

amt'asiña (Ay.): to remember.

animu (Ay. from Sp. *ánimo*): spirit, courage; a quality of the soul.

ayllu (Ay., Q.): indigenous Andean social group typically composed of complementary halves and produced and perpetuated through a shared set of ritual and political responsibilities as well as an ethos of exchange obligations connecting people to one another and to shared place deities.

ayni (Ay., Q.): exchange practice characterized by balanced reciprocity; an exchange partner.

aynoqa (Ay.): Agricultural or grazing lands the production of which is coordinated and controlled by ayllu authorities.

ayuno (Sp.): Fast.

cabildo (Sp., Aymaracized as *kawiltu*): Governing council; a body composed of the community authorities (*mallkus* or *jilaqatas*) from the ayllus of a region.

cacique (Sp): from Caribbean term for "chief," extended by Spaniards to refer to recognized indigenous leaders across their colonial holding.

chuyma (Ay.): "lungs," used like *heart* in English to refer to the interior physical seat of the soul and source of will.

compadres, compadrazgo (Sp.): fictive kin ties based originally in Catholic ritual sponsorship and extended to include a range of Andean social practices.

ch'alla (Ay.): libation; a common Aymara ritual gesture of sacrifice.

ch'ama (Ay.): strength.

grupos de fe (Sp.): weekly worship groups organized and overseen by a catechist.

hacienda (Sp.): privately owned estate or plantation

jilaqata (Sp.): Ayllu authority; in some areas interchangeable with mallku.

kawiltu (Ay.): see cabildo.

kuraji (Ay. from the Sp. *coraje*): courage; passion; a quality of the soul.

lik'i (Ay.): fat.

mallku (Ay.): ayllu authority; hereditary position in pre-Columbian Andes; mountain place deity.

marka (Ay.): town; often the centralized reference point for a larger social, political, or ritual totality.

mink'a (Ay., Q.): exchange practice typically involving a group of people laboring for someone else; a work party.

misaqala (Ay.): "table stone"; a flat stone table at the social center of a house compound; guests are served here; used with a curved stone mortar for grinding and preparing some food.

p'iqi (Ay.): "head"; title of lower-level ayllus authorities representing the component "zones" of an ayllu.

reducción (Sp.): Spanish colonial strategy of concentrating indigenous populations in towns modeled on idealized Spanish polities; such a town.

sayaña (Ay.): the land upon which a family lives; to stand.

sindicato (Sp.): a local peasant union; a model of community political organization extended across rural Bolivia as part of the reforms implemented after the 1952 revolution of the Movimiento Nacional Revolucionario.

tayka (Ay.): "mother"; also used to address a female ayllu authority, *mallku tayka* ("mother mallku").

thaki (Ay.): "path"; a metaphor for a number of life processes.

t'alla (Ay.): female ayllu authority, *mallku t'alla* (used interchangeable with *mallku tayka*).

taypi (Ay.): Center or intermediate space; often connotes a microcosmic abundance or completion attained by the mediation of separate elements or qualities.

uta (Ay.): House.

vecinos (Sp.): ethnically non-Indian rural elite; from the Spanish for "neighbor."

wak'a (Ay.): Place deity; condition of power, beneficence or danger.

waxt'a (Ay.): Ritual offering to a place deity

yatiri (Ay.): "one who knows"; ritual specialist often with abilities to diagnose and treat illnesses and mediate offerings to place deities.

ARCHIVAL SOURCES

When relevant the precise location of documents has been indicated by volume (*tomo*) number (t.) and pagination or foliation (f.), specifying recto (r.) or verso (v.).

AALP   Archives of the Archbishopric of La Paz
    AALP/CEB   Documents from the series: Conferencia Episcopal Boliviana
    AALP JDM/lf   Documents from the Libro de Fábrica for the parish of Jesús de Machaqa
ABEC   Archives of the Bolivian Episcopal Conference, La Paz
ACLP   Archives of the Cathedral of La Paz
    ACLP/CC   Documents from the series: Cabildo Catedral

Abercrombie, Thomas A. 1986. "The Politics of Sacrifice: An Aymara Cosmology in Action." Ph.D. dissertation, University of Chicago.

———— 1991. "To Be Indian, to Be Bolivian: 'Ethnic' and 'National' Discourses of Identity." In Greg Urban and Joel Sherzer, eds., *Nation-States and Indians in Latin America,* pp. 95–130. Austin: University of Texas Press.

———— 1998. *Pathways of Memory and Power: Ethnography and History Among an Andean People.* Madison: University of Wisconsin Press.

Adelman, Jeremy, ed. 1999. *Colonial Legacies: The Problem of Persistence in Latin American Histories.* London: Routledge.

Aguilar, Enrique. 1992. "Radio San Gabriel: The Voice of the Aymara People." In Hamid Mowlana and Margaret Hardt Frondorf, eds., *The Media as a Forum for Community Building,* pp. 21–26. Baltimore: Paul H. Nitze School of Advanced International Studies, Johns Hopkins University.

Albó, Xavier. 1966. "Jesuitas y culturas indígenas: Perú 1568–1606. Su actitud, métodos y criterios de aculturación." *América Indígena* 26(3): 249–308 and 26(4): 395–445.

———— 1979. "Khitipxtansa? Quienes somos? Identidad localista, étnica y clasista en los Aymara de hoy." *América Indígena* 39(3): 477–527.

———— 1984. "Dominar o servir? Hitos de una larga búsqueda eclesiástica en el mundo quechua y andino." *Allpanchis* 24:97–130.

———— 1987 "From MNRista to Katarista to Katari." In Steve J. Stern, ed., *Resistance, Rebellion, and Consciousness in the Andean Peasant World, Eighteenth to Twentieth Centuries,* pp. 379–419. Madison: University of Wisconsin Press.

———— 1991a. "La experiencia religiosa aymara." In Manuel Marzal, Ricardo Robles, Eugenio Maurer, Xavier Albó, Bartolomé Meliá, eds., *Rostros indios de Dios,* pp. 201–265. Quito: Abya-Yala.

———— 1991b. "El thaki o 'camino' en Jesús de Machaqa." In Raquel Thiercelin, ed., *Cultures et sociétés andes et méso-amérique: Mélanges en hommage à Pierre Duviols,* pp. 51–65. Provence: Université de Provence.

———— 1994. "And from Kataristas to MNRista? The Surprising and Bold Alliance Between Aymaras and Neoliberals in Bolivia." In Donna Lee Van Cott, ed., *Indigenous Peoples and Democracy in Latin America,* pp. 55–81. New York: St. Martin's.

Albó, Xavier and equipo CIPCA. 1972. "Dinámica en la estructura inter-comunitaria de Jesús de Machaca." *América Indígena* 32(3): 773–816.

Albó, Xavier and Josep M. Barnadas. 1990. *La cara india y campesina de nuestra historia.* 3d ed. La Paz: UNITAS/CIPCA.

Albó, Xavier and Mauricio Mamani. 1980. "Esposos, suegros y padrinos entre los aymara." In Enrique Mayer and Ralph Bolton, eds., *Parentesco y matrimonio en los Andes,* pp.283–326. Lima: Pontificia Universidad Católica del Perú.

Albó, Xavier, Tomás Greaves, and Godofrede Sandoval. 1983. *Chukiyawu: La cara aymara de La Paz.* La Paz: CIPCA.

Albro, Robert. 1998. "Introduction: A New Time and Place for Bolivian Popular Politics." *Ethnology* 37(2): 99–115.

Allen, Catherine J. 1982. "Body and Soul in Quechua Thought." *Journal of Latin American Lore* 8(2): 179–196.

———— 1988. *The Hold Life Has: Coca and Cultural Identity in an Andean Community.* Washington: Smithsonian Institution Press.

Anderson, Benedict. 1983. *Imagined Communities: Reflections on the Origin and Spread of Nationalism.* London: Verso.

Annis, Sheldon. 1987. *God and Production in a Guatemalan Town.* Austin: University of Texas Press.

Anonymous [Un incógnito]. 1926. *La cruzada nacional pro-Indio.* La Paz: Escuela Tipografica Salesiana.

Appadurai, Arjun. 1996. *Modernity at Large: Cultural Dimensions of Globalization.* Minneapolis: University of Minnesota Press.

Arnold, Denise. 1992. "La casa de adobes y piedras del Inka: Género, memoria y cosmos en Qaqachaka." In Denise Y. Arnold, Domingo Jiménez Aruquipa and Juan de Dios Yapita, *Hacia un orden andino de la cosas,* pp. 31–108. La Paz: Hisbol/ILCA.

———— 1997. "Making Men in Her Own Image: Gender, Text, and Textile in Qaqachaka." In Rosaleen Howard-Malverde, ed., *Creating Context in Andean Cultures,* pp. 99–133. New York: Oxford University Press.

Arnold, Denise, Domingo Jiménez Aruquipa, and Juan de Dios Yapita. 1992. *Hacia un Orden Andino de la cosas.* La Paz: Hisbol/ILCA.

Arnold, Denise, and Juan de Dios Yapita. 1998. *Río de vellón, río de canto: Cantar a los animales, una poética andina de la creación.* La Paz: Hisbol/ILCA.

Arnold, Denise, with Juan de Dios Yapita, Luisa Alvarado C., U. Ricardo López G., and Helson D. Pimentel H. 2000. *El rincón de las cabezas: Luchas textuales, educación y tierra en los Andes.* La Paz: Facultad de Humanidades e Ciencias de la Educación, UMSA/ILCA.

Asad, Talal. 1993. *Genealogies of Religion: Discipline and Reasons of Power in Christianity and Islam.* Baltimore: Johns Hopkins University Press.

———— 1996. "Comments on Conversion." In Peter van der Veer, ed., *Conversion to Modernities,* pp. 263–74. New York: Routledge.

Astvaldsson, Astvaldur. 1997. *Las voces de los wak'a: Fuentes principales del poder politico aymara.* Cuaderno de investigación 54. La Paz: CIPCA.

Axel, Brian Keith. 2001. *The Nation's Tortured Body: Violence, Representation, and the Formation of a Sikh "Diaspora."* Durham: Duke University Press.

Barnadas, Josep M. 1976. *La iglesia católica en Bolivia.* La Paz: Juventud.

Barnes, Monica. 1992. "Catechisms and Confessionarios: Distorting Mirrors of Andean Societies." In Robert V. H. Dover, Katherine E. Seibold, and John H. McDowell, eds., *Andean Cosmologies Through Time: Persistence and Emergence,* pp. 67–94. Bloomington: Indiana University Press.

Basso, Keith. 1988. "'Speaking with Names': Language and Landscape Among the Western Apache." *Cultural Anthropology* 3(2): 99–130.

———— 1996. *Wisdom Sits in Places: Landscape and Language Among the Western Apache.* Albuquerque: University of New Mexico Press.

Bastien, Joseph W. 1985. "Qollahuaya-Andean Body Concepts: A Topographical-Hydraulic Model of Physiology." *American Anthropologist* 87(3): 595–611.

Battaglia, Deborah. 1995. "On Practical Nostalgia: Self-prospecting Among Urban Trobriand." In Deborah Battaglia, ed., *Rhetorics of Self-making,* pp. 77–96. Berkeley: University of California Press.

Beidelman, Thomas O. 1982. *Colonial Evangelisim: A Socio-historical Study of an East African Mission at the Grassroots.* Bloomington: Indiana University Press.

Berg, Hans van den. 1985. *Diccionario religioso aymara.* Iquitos: CETA-IDEA.

———— 1989. *La tierra no da así no más: Los ritos agrícolas en la religión de los aymara-cristianos.* Amsterdam: CEDLA.

Berryman, Phillip. 1984. *The Religious Roots of Rebellion.* Maryknoll: Orbis.

———— 1987. *Liberation Theology: The Essential Facts About the Revolutionary Movement in Latin America and Beyond.* New York: Pantheon.

Bertonio, Ludovico. 1984 [1612]. *Vocabulario de la lengua aymara.* Cochabamba: CERES/IFEA/MUSEF.

Bonilla Mayta, Heraclio, Cesar Fonseca Martel, and Oscar Bustillos Hernandez. 1967. *Tradición y conservadorismo en el área cultural del Lago Titicaca: Jesús de Machaca, una comunidad aymara del altiplano andino.* Lima: Instituto del Estudio Peruanos.

Borges, Pedro O.F.M. 1960. *Métodos misionales en la cristianización de America: Siglo XVI.* Madrid: Raycar.

Bouysse Cassagne, Thérèse. 1987. *La identidad aymara: aproximación histórica (siglo xv, siglo xvi)*. La Paz: HISBOL.

Bouysse Cassagne, Thérèse and Olivia Harris. 1987. "Pacha: En torno al pensamiento aymara." In Thérèse Bouysse Cassagne, Olivia Harris, Tristan Platt, and Veronica Cereceda, *Tres reflexiones sobre el pensamiento andino*, pp.11–59. La Paz: Hisbol.

Briggs, Charles L. 1996. "The Politics of Discursive Authority in Research on the "Invention of Tradition." *Cultural Anthropology* 11(4): 435–469.

Buechler, Hans C. 1980. *The Masked Media: Aymara Fiestas and Social Interaction in the Bolivian Highlands*. The Hague: Mouton.

Buechler, Hans C. and Judith Maria Buechler. 1971. *The Bolivian Aymara*. New York: Holt, Rinehart and Winston.

——— 1978. "Combatting Feathered Serpents: The Rise of Protestantism and Reformed Catholicism in a Bolivian Highland Community." In Roswith Hartmann and Udo Oberem, eds., *Amerikanistische Studien,* pp.92–97. St. Augustin: Haus Volker und Kulturen, Anthropos-Institut.

Bühlmann, Walbert. 1978. *The Coming of the Third Church*. Maryknoll: Orbis.

Burdick, John. 1993. *Looking for God in Brazil: The Progressive Catholic Church in Urban Brazil's Religious Arena*. Berkeley: University of California Press.

——— 1998. *Blessed Anastacia*. London: Routledge.

Burns, Kathryn. 1999. *Colonial Habits: Convents and the Spiritual Economy of Cuzco, Peru*. Durham: Duke University Press.

Burridge, Kenelm O. L. 1960. *Mambu: A Melanesian Millennium*. London: Methuen.

Calderón Jemio, Raúl Javier, Justino Q'ispe B., and Javier Reyes A. 1995. "Una nueva investigación sobre la historia de los promotores culturaled aymara (1970–1992)." *Estudios bolivianos* 1:215–223

Calla Ortega, Ricardo. 1999. Educación intercultural y bilingue y flexibilización magisterial: Temas de las reformas educativas en Bolivia." *Bulletin de l'Institute Frances d'Etudes Andines* 28(3): 561–570.

Canessa, Andrew. 2000. "Fear and Loathing on the *Kharisiri* Trail: Alterity and Identity in the Andes. *Journal of the Royal Anthropological Institute* 6(4): 705–720.

Carrithers, Michael, Steven Collins, and Steven Lukes, eds. 1985. *The Category of the Person*. Cambridge: Cambridge University Press.

Carter, William E. 1968. "Secular Reinforcement in Aymara Death Ritual." *American Anthropologist* 70(2): 238–263.

——— 1977. "Trial Marriage in the Andes?" In Ralph Bolton and Enrique Mayer, eds., *Andean Kinship and Marriage,* pp. 177–216. Washington: American Anthropological Association.

Carter, William E. and Mauricio Mamani. 1982. *Irpa Chico: Individuo y comunidad en la cultura aymara*. La Paz: Juventud.

Chamberlain, Robert S. 1930. "The Concept of 'Señor Natural' as Revealed by Castilian Law." *Hispanic American Historical Review* 19(2): 130–137.

Chatterjee, Partha. 1993. *The Nation and Its Fragments: Colonial and Postcolonial Histories*. Princeton: Princeton University Press.

Choque Canqui, Roberto. 1979. "Las haciendas de los caciques Guarachi en el Alto Perú (1673–1734)." *América Indígena* 39(4): 733–748.

——— 1986. *La masacre de Jesús de Machaca.* La Paz: Chitakolla.

——— 1991. "Una marka Aymara: Jesús de Machaqa." *Historia* 21:103–117.

——— 1993. *Sociedad y economía colonial.* La Paz: Hisbol.

Choque Canqui, Roberto and Esteban Ticona Alejo. 1996. *Jesús de Machaqa: La marka rebelde.* Vol. 2: Sublevación y masacre de 1921. La Paz: CIPCA/CEDOIN.

Choque Canqui, Roberto, Vitaliamo Soria Choque, Humberto Mamani, Esteban Ticona Alejo, and Ramón Conde. 1992. *Educación indígena: ¿Ciudadanía o colonización?* La Paz: Aruwiyiri.

Choque, María Eugenia and Carlos Mamani. 2000. "Reconstitución del ayllu y derechos de los pueblos indígenas: El movimiento indio en los Andes de Bolivia." *Journal of Latin American Anthropology.* 6(1): 202–224.

Christian, William A. 1981. *Local Religion in Sixteenth-Century Spain.* Princeton: Princeton University Press.

Clark, Jeffrey. 1988. "Kaun and Kogono: Cargo Cults and Development in Karavar and Pagia." *Oceania* 59:40–57.

Cleary, Edward. 1992. "Evangelicals and Competition in Guatemala." In Edward Cleary and Hannah Stewart-Gambino, eds., *Conflict and Competition: The Latin American Church in a Changing Environment.* Boulder: Rienner.

Clenndinnen, Inga. 1987. *Ambivalent Conquests: Maya and Spaniard in Yucatan, 1517–1570.* Cambridge: Cambridge University Press.

——— 1990. "Ways to the Sacred: Reconstructing "Religion" in Sixteenth-Century Mexico." *History and Anthropology,* no. 5, pp. 105–141.

Cline, Howard F. 1967. *Latin American History: Essays on Its Study and Teaching, 1898–1965.* 2 vols. Austin: University of Texas Press.

Codina, Victor. 1987. Evangelizar 500 años después. *Cuarto Intermedio* 5(November): 34–51.

Colloredo-Mansfeld, Rudi. 1999. *The Native Leisure Class: Consumption and Cultural Creativity in the Andes.* Chicago: University of Chicago Press.

Comaroff, Jean and John L. Comaroff. 1991. *Of Revelation and Revolution: Christianity, Colonialism, and Consciousness in South Africa.* Chicago: University of Chicago Press.

——— 1999. Occult Economies and the Violence of Abstraction: Notes from the South African Postcolony. *American Ethnologist* 26(2): 279–303.

Comaroff, John L. 1987. "Of Totemism and Ethnicity: Consciousness, Practices, and the Signs of Inequality." *Ethnos* 52(2–4): 301–323.

Condori Chura, Leandro and Esteban Ticona Alejo. 1992. *El escribano de los caciques apoderados/kasikanakan purirarunakan qillqiripa.* La Paz: Hisbol/THOA.

Connerton, Paul. 1989. *How Societies Remember.* Cambridge: Cambridge University Press.

Coronil, Fernando. 1995. "Transculturation and the Politics of Theory: Countering the Center: Cuban Counterpoint." In Fernando Ortiz, *Cuban Counterpoint: Tobacco and Sugar.* Durham: Duke University Press.

——— 1996. *The Magical State.* Chicago: University of Chicago Press.

Cox, Harvey. 1984. *Religion in the Secular City: Toward a Postmodern Theology.* New York: Simon and Schuster.

Crandon-Malamud, Libbet. 1986. "Medical Dialogue and the Political Economy of Medical Pluralism: A Case for Rural Highland Bolivia." *American Ethnologist* 13(0): 463–488.

———— 1991. *From the Fat of Our Souls: Social Change, Political Process, and Medical Pluralism in Bolivia.* Berkeley: University of California Press.

Csordas, Thomas J. 1990. "Embodiment as a Paradigm for Anthropology." *Ethos* 18(1): 5–47.

———— 1994. "Introduction: The Body as Representation and Being-in-the-World." In Thomas J. Csordas, ed., *Embodiment and experience: the existential ground of culture and self,* pp.1–24. Cambridge: Cambridge University Press.

Damen, Franz. 1989. *Hacia una teología de la inculturación.* La Paz: CLAR.

Davis, Natalie Zemon and Randolph Starn. 1989. "Introduction" *Representations* 26:1–6.

De la Cadena, Marisol. 2001. *Indigenous Mestizos: The Politics of Race and Culture in Cuzco, Peru, 1919–1991.* Durham: Duke University Press.

Demelas, Daniele. 1981. "Darwinismo a la criolla: El darwinismo social en Bolivia (1880–1910)." *Historia Boliviana,* nos. 1–2, pp. 55–82.

Dillon, Mary, and Thomas Abercrombie. 1988. "The Destroying Christ: An Aymara Myth of Conquest." In Jonathan D. Hill, ed., *Rethinking History and Myth,* pp. 50–77. Urbana: University of Illinois Press.

Dumont, Louis. 1985. "A Modified View of Our Origins: The Christian Beginnings of Modern Individualism." In Michael Carrithers, Steven Collins, and Steven Lukes, eds., *The Category of the Person: Anthropology, Philosophy, History,* pp. 93–122. Cambridge: Cambridge University Press.

Duranti, Alessandro and Charles Goodwin, eds. 1992. *Rethinking Context: Language as an Interactive Phenomenon.* Cambridge: Cambridge University Press.

Ekholm-Friedman, Kajsa and Jonathan Friedman. 1995. "Global Complexity and the Simplicity of Everyday Life." In Daniel Miller, ed., *Worlds Apart: Modernity Through the Prism of the Local,* pp. 134–168. London: Routledge

Elias, Norbert. 1978 [1939]. *The Civilizing Process.* New York: Urizen.

Errington, Frederick and Deborah Gewertz. 1994. "From Darkness to Light in the George Brown Jubilee: The Invention of Non-tradition and the Inscription of National History in East New Britain." *American Ethnologist* 21(1): 104–122.

———— 1995. *Articulating Change in the "Last Unknown."* Boulder: Westview.

Escobar, Arturo. 1995. *Encountering Development.* Princeton: Princeton University Press.

Esquivel, Adhemar K. 1975. "Progress Toward Having an Aymara Church. *LADOC* 61(November-December): 37–43.

Evans-Pritchard, E. E. 1940. *The Nuer: A Description of the Modes of Livelihood and Political Institutions of a Nilotic People.* New York: Oxford University Press.

Farnell, Brenda. 1994. "Ethno-graphics and the Moving Body." *Man* 29(4): 929–974.

Farriss, Nancy. 1984. *Maya Society Under Colonial Rule: The Collective Enterprise of Survival.* Princeton: Princeton University Press.

Fedders, Edward. 1974. "How the Aymara See Our Priesthood." *LADOC* 53(December): 30–35.

Fillmore, Charles. 1985. "Frames and the Semantics of Understanding." *Quaderni di semantica* 6(2): 222–254.

Fraser, Valerie. 1990. *The Architecture of Conquest: Building the Viceroyalty of Peru, 1535–1635.* Cambridge: Cambridge University Press.

Freccero, John. 1986. "Autobiography and Narrative." In Thomas Heller, Morton Sosna, and David E. Wellbery, eds., *Reconstructing Individualism: Autonomy, Individuality, and the Self in Western Thought,* pp. 16–29. Stanford: Stanford University Press.

Freire, Paulo. 1974. *Pedagogy of the Oppressed.* Trans. Myra Bergman Ramos. New York: Seabury.

Froehle, Brian. 1992. "The Catholic Church and Politics in Venezuela: Resource Limitations, Religious Competition, and Democracy." In Edward L. Cleary and Hannah Stewart-Gambino, eds., *Conflict and Competition: The Latin American Church in a Changing Environment.* Boulder: Rienner.

Gade, Daniel W. 1999. *Nature and Culture in the Andes.* Madison: University of Wisconsin Press.

García-Canclini, Néstor. 1995. *Hybrid Cultures: Strategies for Entering and Leaving Modernity.* Minneapolis: University of Minnesota Press.

Gareis, Iris. 1999. "Repression and Cultural Change: The 'Extirpation of Idolatry' in Colonial Peru." In Nicholas Griffiths and Fernando Cervantes, eds., *Spiritual Encounters: Interactions Between Christianity and Native Religions in Colonial America,* pp. 230–254. Birmingham: University of Birmingham Press.

Geschiere, Peter. 1997. *The Modernity of Witchcraft: Politics and the Occult in Postcolonial Africa.* Charlottesville: University of Virginia Press.

Giddens, Anthony. 1991. *Modernity and Self-identity: Self and Society in the Late Modern Age.* Stanford: Stanford Univerity Press.

Gill, Lesley. 1993. "'Proper Women' and City Pleasures: Gender, Class, and Contested Meanings in La Paz." *American Ethnologist* 20(1): 72–88.

——— 2000. *Teetering on the Rim: Global Restructuring, Daily Life, and the Armed Retreat of the Bolivian State.* New York: Columbia University Press.

——— 1994. *Precarious Dependencies: Gender, Class, and Domestic Service in Bolivia.* New York: Columbia University Press.

Gillis, John R., ed. 1994. *Commemorations: The Politics of National Identity* . Princeton: Princeton University Press.

Gisbert, Teresa. 1980. *Iconografía y mitos indígenas en el arte.* La Paz: Gisbert and Cia.

Gluckman, Max. 1949. "The Village Headman in British Central Africa." *Africa* 19(2): 89–106.

——— 1960. *Custom and Conflict in Africa.* Oxford: Oxford University Press.

Goffman, Erving. 1974. *Frame Analysis: An Essay on the Organization of Experience.* Boston: Northeastern University Press.

——— 1981. *Forms of Talk.* Philadelphia: University of Pennsylvania Press.

Gose, Peter. 1986. "Sacrifice and the Commodity Form in the Andes." Man 21(2): 296–310.

—————— 1994a. *Deathly Waters and Hungry Mountains: Agrarian Ritual and Class Formation in an Andean Town.* Toronto: University of Toronto Press.

—————— 1994b. "Embodied Violence: Racial Identity and the Semiotics of Property in Huaquirca, Antabamba (Apurímac)." In Deborah Poole, ed., *Unruly Order: Violence, Power, and Cultural Identity in the High Provinces of Southern Peru,* pp. 165–198. Boulder: Westview.

Gottlieb, Alma. 1998. "Do Infants Have Religion? The Spiritual Lives of Beng Babies." *American Anthropologist* 100(1): 122–135.

Grieshaber, Erwin. "Survival of Indian Communities in Nineteenth-Century Bolivia." *Journal of Latin American Studies* 12(2): 223–69.

Griffiths, Nicholas. 1999. "Introduction." In Nicholas Griffiths and F. Cervantes, eds., *Spiritual Encounters: Interactions Between Christianity and Native Religions in Colonial America,* pp. 1–42. Birmingham: University of Birmingham Press.

Guaman Poma de Ayala, Felipe. 1980 [1615]. *El primer nueva corónica y buen gobierno.* Ed. John V. Murra and Rolena Adorno. Trans. Jorge L. Urioste. 3 vols. Mexico City: Siglo Veintinuno.

Gupta, Akhil and James Ferguson. 1997. *Culture, Power, Place: Explorations in Critical Anthropology.* Durham: Duke University Press.

Gutierrez, Gustavo. 1973. *A Theology of Liberation: History, Politics, and Salvation.* New York: Orbis.

Halbwachs, Maurice. 1980. *The Collective Memory.* New York: Harper and Row.

Hale, Charles R. 1997. "Cultural Politics of Identity in Latin America." *Annual Review of Anthropology* 26:567–590.

Hallowell, A. Irving. 1955. *Culture and Experience.* New York: Schocken.

Handler, Richard. 1988. *Nationalism and the Politics of Culture in Quebec.* Madison: University of Wisconsin Press.

Hanks, William F. 1990. *Referential Practice: Language and Lived Space Among the Maya.* Chicago: University of Chicago Press.

Hannerz, Ulf. 1992. *Cultural Complexity: Studies in the Social Organization of Meaning.* New York: Columbia University Press.

Harris, Olivia. 1982a. "The Dead and the Devils Among the Bolivian Laymi." In Maurice Bloch and Jonathan Parry, eds., *Death and the Regeneration of Life,* pp. 45–73. Cambridge: Cambridge University Press.

—————— 1982b. "Labour and Produce in an Ethnic Economy, Northern Potosí, Bolivia." In David Lehmann, ed., *Ecology and Exchange in the Andes.* Cambridge: Cambridge University Press.

—————— 1985. "Ecological Duality and the Role of the Center: Northern Potosí." In Shozo Msudo, Izumi Shimada, and Craig Morris, eds., *Andean Ecology and Civilization.* Tokyo: University of Tokyo Press.

 —————— 1995. "Knowing the Past: Plural Identities and the Antinomies of Loss in Highland Bolivia" In Richard Fardon, ed., *Counterworks: Managing the Diversity of Knowledge,* pp. 105–123. London: Routledge.

Healy, Kevin and Susan Paulson. 2000. "Political Economies of Identity in Bolivia, 1952–1998." *Journal of Latin American Anthropology* 5(2): 2–29.

Heath, Dwight B., Charles J. Erasmus, and Hans C. Buechler. 1969. *Land Reform and Social Revolution in Bolivia.* New York: Praeger.

Hellwig, Monica. 1983. *Jesus: The Compassion of God.* Wilmington: Glazier.

Helms, Mary W. 1988. "Ulysses' Sail: An Ethnographic Odyssey of Power, Knowledge, and Geographical Distance." Princeton: Princeton University Press.

Herzfeld, Michael. 1997. *Cultural Intimacy: Social Poetics in the Nation-State.* New York: Routledge.

Hickman, John M. and William T. Stuart. 1977. "Descent, Alliance, and Moiety in Chucuito, Peru: An Explanatory Sketch of Aymara Social Organization." In Ralph Bolton and Enrique Mayer, eds., *Andean Kinship and Marriage,* pp. 43–59. Washington, D.C.: American Anthropological Association.

Hobsbawm, Eric and Terence Ranger. 1983. *The Invention of Tradition.* Cambridge: Cambridge University Press.

Huanca L., Tomás. 1989. *El yatiri en la comunidad aymara.* La Paz: CADA.

Huber, Mary T. 1988. *The Bishop's Progress: A Historical Ethnography of Catholic Missionary Experience on the Sepik Frontier.* Washington, D.C.: Smithsonian Institution Press.

Hurtado, Javier. 1986. *El Katarismo.* La Paz: HISBOL.

Irarrazaval, Diego. 1988. "Nueva evangelización andina." *Iglesias, Pueblos y Culturas* 3(11): 71–96.

Isbell, Billie Jean. 1985. "To Defend Ourselves: Ecology and Ritual in an Andean Village." Prospect Heights, Ill.: Waveland.

Jordá A., Enrique. 1981. "La cosmovisión Aymara en el diálogo de la fe: Teología desde el Titicaca." 3 vols. Lima: Facultad de Teología Pontificia y Civil de Lima.

Joseph, Gilbert M., Catherine C. Legrand, and Ricardo Salvatore, eds. 1998. *Close Encounters of Empire: Writing the Cultural History of U.S.–Latin American Relations.* Durham: Duke University Press.

Kagan, Richard L. 1996. "Prescott's Paradigm: American Historical Scholarship and the Decline of Spain." *American Historical Review.* 101(2): 423–446.

Kapsoli, Wilfredo. 1991. "Los pishtacos: Degolladores degollados." *Bulletin de l'Institut Français d'Etudes Andines* 20(1): 61–77.

Keane, Webb. 1996. "Materialism, Missionaries, and Modern Subjects in Colonial Indonesia." In Peter van der Veer, ed., *Conversion to Modernities,* pp. 137–170. London: Routledge.

——— 1997. "Knowing One's Place: National Language and the Idea of the Local in Eastern Indonesia." *Cultural Anthropology* 12(1): 37–63.

Kearney, Michael. 1995. "The Local and the Global: The Anthropology of Globalization and Transnationalism." *Annual Review of Anthropology* 24:547–565.

Klaiber, Jeffrey. 1992. "The Church in Peru: Between Terrorism and Conservative Restraints." In Edward Cleary and Hannah Stewart-Gambino, eds., *Conflict and Competition: The Latin American Church in a Changing Environment.* Boulder: Rienner.

Klein, Herbert S. 1969. *Parties and Political Change in Bolivia.* Cambridge: Cambridge University Press.

——— 1982. *Bolivia: The Evolution of a Multi-ethnic Society.* New York: Oxford University Press.

———— 1993. *Haciendas and Ayllus: Rural Society in the Bolivian Andes in the Eighteenth and Nineteenth Centuries.* Stanford: Stanford University Press.

Klor de Alva, J. Jorge. 1999. "'Telling Lives': Confessional Autobiography and the Reconstruction of the Nahua Self." In Nicholas Griffiths and F. Cervantes, eds., *Spiritual Encounters: Interactions Between Christianity and Native Religions in Colonial America,* pp. 136–162. Birmingham: University of Birmingham Press.

Ksleman, Thomas A. 1986. "Ambivalence and Assumption in the Concept of Popular Religion." In D. Levine, ed., *Religion and Political Conflict in Latin America,* pp. 24–41. Chapel Hill: University of North Carolina Press.

Kubler, George. 1946. "The Quechua in the Colonial World." In Julian H. Steward, ed., *Handbook of South American Indians.* Vol. 2: *The Andean Civilizations,* pp. 331–410. Washington, D.C.: Bureau of American Ethnology.

Langer, Erick and Robert H. Jackson, eds. 1995. *The New Latin American Mission History.* Lincoln: University of Nebraska Press.

Larson, Brooke, Olivia Harris, and Enrique Tandeter, eds. 1995. *Ethnicity, Markets, and Migration in the Andes: At the Crossroads of History and Anthropology.* Durham: Duke University Press.

Latorre Cabal, Hugo. 1978. *The Revolution of the Latin American Church.* Trans. Frances K. Hendricks and Beatrice Berler. Norman: University of Oklahoma.

Lattas, Andrew. 1992. "Skin, Personhood, and Redemption: The Double Self in West New Britain Cargo Cults." *Oceania* no. 63, pp. 27–54.

———— 1998. *Cultures of Secrecy.* Madison: University of Wisconsin Press.

Lave, Jean and Etienne Wenger. 1991. *Situated Learning: Legitimate Peripheral Participation.* Cambridge: Cambridge University Press.

Levine, Daniel, H. 1981. *Religion and Politics in Latin America: The Catholic Church in Venezuela and Colombia.* Princeton: Princeton University Press.

———— 1990. "Popular Groups, Popular Culture, and Popular Religion." *Comparative Studies of Society and History.* 32(4): 718–764.

Levine, Daniel H., ed. 1986. *Religion and Political Conflict in Latin America.* Chapel Hill: University of North Carolina Press.

LiPuma, Edward. 1995. "The Formation of Nation-States and National Cultures in Oceania." In Robert Foster, ed., *Nation Making: Emergent Identities in Postcolonial Melanesia,* pp. 33–68. Ann Arbor: University of Michigan Press.

Llanque Chana, Domingo. 1990. La cultura aymara: desestructuración o afirmación de identidad? Lima: Idea/Tarea.

Lock, Margaret. 1993. "Cultivating the Body: Anthropology and Epistemologies of Bodily Practice and Knowledge." *Annual Review of Anthropology* 22:133–155.

Lofstrom, William Lee. 1987. *La presidencia de Sucre en Bolivia.* Caracas: Biblioteca de la Academia Nacional de la Historia.

Luykx, Aurolyn. 1999. *The Citizen Factory: Schooling and Cultural Production in Bolivia.* Albany: State University of New York.

Lyon, M. L. and J. M. Barbaret. 1994. "Society's Body: Emotion and the 'Somatization' of Social Theory." In Thomas J. Csordas, ed., *Embodiment and Experience: The*

Existential Ground of Culture and Self, pp.48–66. Cambridge: Cambridge University Press.

McBrien, Richard P. 1981. *Catholicism.* Minneapolis: Winston.

MacCormack, Sabine. 1984. "From the Sun of the Incas to the Virgin of Copacabana." *Representations* 8:30–60.

———— 1985. "'The Heart Has Its Reasons': Predicaments of Missionary Christianity in Early Colonial Peru." *Hispanic American Historical Review* 65(3): 443–466.

———— 1991. *Religion in the Andes: Vision and Imagination in Early Colonial Peru.* Princeton: Princeton University Press.

McDonough, Peter. 1992. *Men Astutely Trained: A History of the Jesuits in the American Century.* New York: Free.

Mainwaring, Scott. 1989. "Grass-roots Catholic Groups and Politics in Brazil." In Scott Mainwaring and Alexander Wilde, eds., *The Progressive Church in Latin America.* Notre Dame: University of Notre Dame Press.

Mainwaring, Scott and Alexander Wilde, eds. 1989. *The Progressive Church in Latin America.* Notre Dame: University of Notre Dame Press.

Mallki, Liisa H. 1995. *Purity and Exile: Violence, Memory, and National Cosmology Among Hutu Refugees in Tanzania.* Chicago: University of Chicago Press.

Mamani Capchiri, Humberto. 1992. "La educación india en la visión de la sociedad criolla." In Roberto Choque Canqui, Vitaliano Soria Choque, Humberto Mamani, Esteban Ticona Alejo, and Ramón Conde, eds., *Educación indígena: ¿Ciudadanía o colonización?* La Paz: Aruwiyiri.

Mannheim, Bruce. 1991. *The Language of the Inka Since the European Invasion.* Austin: University of Texas Press.

Maravall, José Antonio. 1986. *Culture of the Baroque: Analysis of a Historical Structure.* Trans. Terry Cochran. Minneapolis: University of Minnesota Press.

Marschall, Katherine Barnes. 1970. "Cabildos, corregimiento y sindicatos en Bolivia después de 1952." *Estudios Andinos* 1(2): 61–78.

Martínez, Gabriel. 1983. "Topónimos de Chuani: organización y significación del territorio." *Anthropologica* 1:51–84.

———— 1989. *Espacio y pensamiento: Andes meridionales.* La Paz: HISBOL.

Massey, Doreen. 1999. "Philosophy and Politics of Spatiality: Some Considerations." *Geographische Zeitschrift* 87(1): 1–12.

Mauss, Marcel. 1973 [1936]. "The Techniques of the Body." Trans. Ben Brewster. *Economic Sociology* 2:70–88.

———— 1985 [1938]. "A Category of the Human Mind: The Notion of Person; the Notion of Self." Trans. W. D. Halls. In Michael Carrithers, Steven Collins, and Steven Lukes, eds., *The Category of the Person,* pp. 1–25. Cambridge: Cambridge University Press.

Mendoza, Zoila S. 2000. *Shaping Society Through Dance: Mestizo Ritual Performance in the Peruvian Andes.* Chicago: University of Chicago Press.

Meyer, Birgit. 1994. "Beyond Syncretism: Translation and Diabolization in the Appropriation of Protestantism in Africa." In Charles Stewart and Rosalind Shaw, eds., *Syncretism/Anti-Syncretism: The Politics of Religious Synthesis*, pp. 45–68. London: Routledge.

Mignolo, Walter. 2000. *Local Histories/Global Designs*. Princeton: Princeton University Press.

Miguez Bonino, Jose, ed. 1984. *The Faces of Jesus: Latin American Christologies*. Maryknoll: Orbis.

Miller, Daniel. 1995. "Introduction: Anthropology, Modernity, and Consumption." In D. Miller, ed., *Modernity Through the Prism of the Local*, pp. 1–22. London: Routledge.

Mills, Kenneth. 1997. *Idolatry and Its Enemies*. Princeton. Princeton University Press.

Molinié Fioravante, Antoinette. 1986. "The Andean Community Today." In John Murra, Nathan Wachtel, and Jacques Revel, eds., *Anthropological Histories of Andean Polities*, pp. 342–356. Cambridge: Cambridge University Press.

———— 1991. "Sebo bueno, indio muerto: La estructura de una creencia andina." *Bulletin de l'Institut Français d'Etudes Andines* 20(1): 79–92.

Monast, Jacques. 1972. *Los indios aimaraes: ¿Evangelizados o solamente bautizados?* Buenos Aires: Carlos Lehle.

Morse, Richard M. 1964. "The Heritage of Latin America." In Louis Hartz, ed., *The Founding of New Societies: Studies in the History of the United States, Latin America, South Africa, Canada, and Australia*, pp. 123–177. New York: Harcourt, Brace and World.

Munn, Nancy. 1990. "Constructing Regional Worlds in Experience: Kula Exchange, Witchcraft, and Gawan Local Events." *Man* (n.s.) 25(1): 1–17.

Murra, John V. 1968. "An Aymara Kingdom in 1567." *Ethnohistory* 15:115–51.

———— 1972. "El control vertical de un máximo de pisos ecológicos en la economia de las sociedades andinas." In John V. Murra, ed., Iñigo Ortiz de Zyñiga, inspector, *Visita de la provincia de León de Huánuco en 1562*, 2:429–476. Huanuco: Universidad Nacional Hermilio Valdizán, Facultad de Letras y Educación.

———— 1975. *Formaciones económicas y politicas del mundo andino*. Lima: Instituto de Estudios Peruanos.

———— 1985. "'El archipiélago vertical' Revisited." In Shozo Masudo, Izumi Shimada, and Craig Morris, eds., *Andean Ecology and Civilization*, pp. 3–13. Tokyo: University of Tokyo Press.

Murra, John V., Nathan Wachtel, and Jaques Revel, eds. 1986 [1978]. *Anthropological History of Andean Polities*. Cambridge: Cambridge University Press.

Nash, June. 1979. *We Eat the Mines and the Mines Eat Us: Dependency and Exploitation in Bolivian Tin Mines*. New York: Columbia University Press.

Nelson, Diane. 1999. *A Finger in the Wound*. Berkeley: University of California Press.

Nelson, Susan R. 1984. "The Kingdom at Hand: Religion and Politics in Highlands Bolivia." Ph.D. dissertation, University of Michigan.

———— 1986. "Bolivia: Continuity and Conflict in Religious Discourse." In Daniel Levine, ed., *Religion and Political Conflict in Latin America*, pp. 218–235. Chapel Hill: University of North Carolina Press.

Ogden, Schubert M. 1982. *The Point of Christology*. San Francisco: Harper and Row.

Ong, Aihwa. 1999. *Flexible Citizenship.* Durham: Duke University Press.

Orta, Andrew. 1990. "Iconoclasm and History: Remembering the *Via Crucis* in a Nicaraguan *Comunidad Eclesial de Base.*" *Nexus: The Canadian Student Journal of Anthropology*, no. 7 (supplement), pp. 79–139.

———— 1993. "Language, Conversion, and Idolatry: Franciscan Missionary Pedagogy in Sixteenth-Century Yucatán." Paper presented at the annual meeting of the American Society for Ethnohistory, November 4–7, Bloomington, Indiana.

———— 1995. "From Theologies of Liberation to Theologies of Inculturation: Aymara Catechists and Contemporary Catholic Evangelization in Highlands Bolivia." In Satya R. Pattnayak, ed., *Organized Religion in the Political Transformation of Latin America,* pp. 97–124. Lanham, Md.: University Press of America.

———— 1996. "Ambivalent Converts: Aymara Catechists and Contemporary Catholic Missionization on the Bolivian Altiplano." Ph.D. dissertation, University of Chicago.

———— 1998. "Converting Difference: Metaculture, Missionaries, and the Politics of Locality." *Ethnology* 37(2):165–185.

———— 1999. "The Promises of Particularism and the Theology of Culture." Paper presented at the ninety-eighth annual meeting of the American Anthropological Association, November 18, Chicago, Illinois.

———— 2000. "Syncretic Subjects and Body Politics: Doubleness, Personhood, and Aymara Catechists." *American Ethnologist* 26(4): 864–889.

Ortiz, Fernando. 1995 [1947]. *Cuban Counterpoint: Tobacco and Sugar.* Durham: Duke University Press.

Ossio, Juan M. 1973. "Ideología Mesiánica del Mundo Andino." Lima: Ignacio Prado Pastor.

Pacheco, Diego. 1992. *El indianismo y los indios contemporaneos en Bolivia.* La Paz: HISBOL/MUSEF.

Paredes, Manuel Rigoberto. 1955. *Tiahuanacu y la provincia de Ingavi.* La Paz: Antonio Paredes Candia.

Pascual, Thomas and Frederico Aguilo. 1968. *Sociografía eclesiástica de Bolivia.* La Paz: Universidad Católica.

Paulson, Susan, ed. 2000. "Identity Politics in Bolivia Nueva of the 1990s." *Journal of Latin American Anthropology* 5 (2; special issue).

Pels, Peter. 1997. "The Anthropology of Colonialism: Culture, History, and the Emergence of Western Governmentality." *Annual Review of Anthropology* 26:163–183.

Peña, Milagros. 1995. *Theologies and Liberation in Peru.* Philadelphia: Temple University Press.

Percy, Walker. 1958. "Symbol, Consciousness, and Intersubjectivity." *Journal of Philosophy* 55:631–641.

Perez, Elizardo. 1962. *Warisata: La escuella-ayllu.* La Paz: Burillo.

Piot, Charles. 1999. *Remotely Global: Village Modernity in West Africa.* Chicago: University of Chicago Press.

Platt, Tristan. 1982. *Estado boliviano y ayllu andino.* Lima: Instituto de Estudios Peruanos.

———— 1986. "Mirrors and Maize: The Concept of Yanantin Among the Macha of Bolivia." In John V. Murra, Nathan Wachtel, and Jaques Revel, eds., *Anthropological History of Andean Polities*, pp. 228–259. Cambridge: Cambridge University Press.

———— 1987a. "The Andean Soldiers of Christ: Confraternity Organization, the Mass of the Sun, and Regenerative Warfare in Rural Potosí (Eighteenth-Twentieth Centuries)." *Journal des Société des Américanistes* 73:139–192.

———— 1987b. "Entre ch'axwa y muxsa: Para una historia del pensamiento politico aymara." In Thérèse Bouysse Cassagne, Olivia Harris, Tristan Platt, and Veronica Cereceda, *Tres reflexiones sobre el pensamiento andino*, pp. 61–132. La Paz: Hisbol.

———— 1997. "The Sound of Light: Emergent Communication Through Quechua Shamanic Dialogue." In Rosaleen Howard-Malverde, ed., *Creating Context in Andean Cultures*, pp.196–226. New York: Oxford University Press.

Poggi, Luigi. 1974. "Letter from the Nuncio to the Bishop of Juli-Puno." *LADOC* 5:26–27.

Pratt, Mary Louise. 1992. *Imperial Eyes: Travel Writing and Transculturation*. London: Routledge.

Preston, David A. 1978. *Farmers and Towns: Rural-Urban Relations in Highlands Bolivia*. Norwich: University of East Anglia.

Quispe, Calixto, Xavier Albó, Diego Irarrazaval, Franz Damen, and Fanny Geyamont. 1987. "Religion Aymara liberadora." *Fe y Pueblo,* 4(18): 1–52.

Rafael, Vincente L. 1988. *Contracting Colonialism: Translation and Christian Conversion in Tagalog Society Under Early Spanish Rule*. Ithaca: Cornell University Press.

Ramos Gavilán, Alonso. 1988 [1621]. *Historia del Celebre Santuario de Nuestra Señora de Copacabana . . .* Ed. Ignacio Prado Pastor. Lima: Ignacio Prado Pastor.

Rappaport, Joanne. 1994. *Cumbe Reborn: An Andean Ethnography of History*. Chicago: University of Chicago Press.

Rasnake, Roger. 1988. *Domination and Cultural Resistance: Authority and Power Among an Andean People*. Durham: Duke University Press.

Rivera Cusicanqui, Sylvia. 1978. "El mallku y la sociedad colonial en el siglo XVII: El caso de Jesús de Machaqa." *Avances*, no. 1.

———— 1986. *Oprimidos pero no vencidos: Luchas del campesinado aymara y qhichwa, 1900–1980*. La Paz.

———— 1990. "Liberal Democracy and Ayllu Democracy in Bolivia." In Jonathan Fox, ed., *The Challenge of Rural Democratization: Perspectives from Latin America and the Philippines*, pp. 97–121. London: Frank Cass.

Rivière, Gilles. 1991. "Lik'ichiri y kharisiri . . . a propósito de las representaciones del "otro" en la sociedad aymara." *Bulletin de l'Institut Français d'Etudes Andines* 20(1): 23–40.

Robbins, Joel. 2001. "Introduction: Global Religions, Pacific Island Transformations." *Journal of Ritual Studies* 15(2): 7–12.

Roseberry, William. 1995. "Latin American Peasant Studies in a 'Postcolonial' Era." *Journal of Latin American Anthropology* 1(1): 150–177.

Rowe, William and Vivian Schelling. 1991. *Memory and Modernity: Popular Culture in Latin America*. London: Verso.

Sahlins, Marshall. 1985. *Islands of History.* Chicago: University of Chicago Press.

Salazar-Soler, Carmen. 1991. "El pishtaku entre los campesinos y los mineros de Huancavelica." *Bulletin de l'Institut Français d'Etudes Andines* 20(1): 8–22.

Sallnow, Michael J. 1987. *Pilgrims of the Andes: Regional Cults in Cusco.* Washington, D.C.: Smithsonian Institution Press.

——— 1991. "Pilgrimage and Cultural Fracture in the Andes." In John Eade and Michael J. Sallnow, eds., *Contesting the Sacred: The Anthropology of Christian Pilgrimage,* pp. 137–153. London: Routledge.

Salmón, Josefa. 1997. *El espejo indígena: El discurso indigenista en Bolivia, 1900–1956.* La Paz: Plural.

Salomon, Frank. 1981. "Killing the Yumbo: A Ritual Drama of Northern Quito." In Norman E. Whitten, ed., *Cultural Transformations and Ethnicity in Modern Ecuador,* pp. 162–208. Urbana: University of Illinois Press.

——— 1991. Introductory Essay." In Frank Salomon, ed., *The Huarochirí Manuscript: A Testament of Ancient and Colonial Andean Religion,* pp. 1-38. Austin: University of Texas Press.

Sapir, Edward. 1924. "Culture: Genuine and Spurious." *American Journal of Sociology,* no. 29, 401–429.

Scheper- Hughes, Nancy. 2000. "The Global Traffic in Human Organs." *Current Anthropology* 41(2): 191–224.

Schillebeeckx, Edward. 1979. *Jesus: An Experiment in Christology.* Trans. Hubert Hoskins. New York: Crossroad.

Schrödinger, Erwin. 1956. *What Is Life? And Other Scientific Essays.* Garden City: Doubleday.

Scott, James. 1985. *Weapons of the Weak: Everyday Forms of Peasant Resistance.* New Haven: Yale University Press.

Seligmann, Linda. 1989. "To Be in Between: The Cholas as Market Women." *Comparative Studies of Society and History* 31(4): 694–721.

Shapiro, Judith. 1981. "Ideologies of Catholic Missionary Practice in a Post-Colonial Era." *Comparative Studies in Society and History* 23(?): 130–149.

Shaw, Rosalind and Charles Stewart. 1994. "Introduction: Problematizing Syncretism." In Charles Stewart and Rosalind Shaw, eds., *Syncretism/Anti-Syncretism: The Politics of Religious Synthesis,* pp. 1–26. London: Routledge.

Silverstein, Michael. 1976. "Shifters, Linguistic Categories, and Cultural Description." In K. Basso and H. Selby, eds., *Meaning in Anthropology,* pp. 11–57. Albuquerque: University of New Mexico Press.

——— 1988. "The Indeterminacy of Contextualization: When Is Enough Enough?" Unpublished MS.

Solomon, Thomas. 2000. "Dueling Landscapes: Singing Places and Identities in Highland Bolivia." *Ethnomusicology* 44(2): 257–280.

Soria Choque, Vitaliano. 1992. "Los caciques-apoderados y la lucha por la escuela (1900–1952)." In Roberto Choque Canqui, Vitaliano Soria Choque, Humberto Mamani, Esteban Ticona Alejo, and Ramón Conde, eds., *Educación indígena: ¿Ciudadanía o colonización?* La Paz: Aruwiyiri.

Spalding, Karen. 1984. *Huarochiri: An Andean Society Under Inca and Spanish Rule.* Stanford: Stanford University Press.

Starn, Orin. 1991. "Missing the Revolution: Anthropologists and the War in Peru." *Cultural Anthropology* 6:63–91.

———— 1992. "Antropología andina, 'Andinísmo,' y Sendero Luminoso." *Allpanchis* 39:15–71.

———— 1994. "Rethinking the Politics of Anthropology: The Case of the Andes." *Current Anthropology* 35:13–38.

———— 1999. *Nightwatch: The Politics of Protest in the Andes.* Durham: Duke University Press.

Stein, Stanley J. and Barbara Stein. 1970. *The Colonial Heritage of Latin America.* New York: Oxford University Press.

Stein, William. 2000. *Vicisitudes del discurso del desarrollo en el Perú: Una etnografía sobre la modernidad del Projecto Vicos.* Lima: SUR.

Stern, Steve J. *Peru's Indian Peoples and the Challenge of Spanish Conquest.* Madison: University of Wisconsin Press, 1982.

Steward, Julian H., ed. 1946. *Handbook of South American Indians.* Vol. 2: *The Andean Civilizations.* Washington, DC: U.S. Government Printing Office.

Stewart, Charles and Rosalind Shaw, eds. 1994. *Syncretism/Anti-syncretism: The Politics of Religious Synthesis.* London: Routledge.

Stoler, Ann Laura. 1989. "Rethinking Colonial Categories: European Communities and the Boundaries of Rule." *Comparative Studies of Society and History* 31(1): 134–161.

Stoll, David. 1990. *Is Latin America Turning Protestant? The Politics of Evangelical Growth.* Berkeley: University of California Press.

———— 1999. *Rigoberto Menchu and the Story of All Poor Guatemalans.* Boulder: Westview.

Strathern, Andrew J. 1979–1980. "The Red-Box Money Cult in Mount Hagen, 1968–71." *Oceania* 50(2): 88–102, 50(3): 161–175.

———— 1996. *Body Thoughts.* Ann Arbor: University of Michigan Press.

Suess, Paulo. 1991. *La nueva evangelización: Desafíos históricos y pautas culturales.* Quito: ABYA-YALA.

Taussig, Michael. 1987. *Shamanism, Colonialism, and the Wild Man: A Study in Terror and Healing.* Chicago: University of Chicago Press.

Taylor, Charles. 1985. "The Person." In Michael Carrithers, Steven Collins and Steven Lukes, eds., *The Category of the Person,* pp. 257–281. Cambridge: Cambridge University Press.

———— 1989. *Sources of the Self: The Making of the Modern Identity.* Cambridge: Harvard University Press.

Taylor, William. 1996. *Magistrates of the Sacred: Priests and Parishioners in Eighteenth-Century Mexico.* Stanford: Stanford University Press.

Thomas, Nicholas. 1991. *Entangled Objects: Exchange, Material Culture, and Colonialism in the Pacific.* Cambridge: Harvard University Press.

———— 1994. *Colonialism's Culture: Anthropology, Travel, and Government.* Princeton: Princeton University Press.

Ticona Alejo, Esteban and Xavier Albó. 1997. *Jesús de Machaqa: La marka rebelde.* Vol. 3: *La lucha por el poder comunal.* La Paz: CIPCA/CEDOIN.

Trexler, Richard C. 1984. We Think, They Act: Clerical Readings of Missionary Theatre in Sixteenth-Century New Spain. In Steven L. Kaplan, ed., *Understanding Popular Culture,* pp. 189–227. Berlin: Mouton.

———— 1987. *Church and Community: Studies in the History of Florence and New Spain.* Roma: Storia e Letteratura.

Turino, Thomas. 1993. *Moving Away from Silence: Music of the Peruvian Altiplano and the Experience of Urban Migration.* Chicago: University of Chicago Press.

Turner, Terence. 1988. Ethno-ethnohistory: Myth and History in Native South American Representations of Contact with Western Society." In Jonathan D. Hill, ed., *Rethinking History and Myth: Indigenous South American Perspectives on the Past,* pp. 235–281. Urbana: University of Illinois.

———— 1994. "Bodies and Anti-bodies: Flesh and Fetish in Contemporary Social Theory. In Thomas J. Csordas, ed., *Embodiment and experience: The Existential Ground of Culture and Self.* pp. 27–47. Cambridge: Cambridge University Press.

Turner, Victor W. 1957. *Schism and Continuity in an African Society: A Study of Ndembu Village Life.* Manchester: Manchester University Press.

Urban, Greg. 1991. *A Discourse-Centered Approach to Culture: Native South American Myths and Rituals.* Austin: University of Texas Press.

Urioste de Aguirre, Marta. 1978. "Los caciques Guarache." In *Estudios bolivianos en homenaje a Gunnar Mendoza L.* pp. 131–138 La Paz.

Urton, Gary. 1997. *The Social Life of Numbers.* Austin: University of Texas Press.

Van Cott, Donna Lee. 2000. *The Friendly Liquidation of the Past.* Pittsburgh: University of Pittsburgh Press.

Van der Veer, Peter. 1994. "Syncretism, Multiculturalism, and the Discourse of Tolerance." In Charles Stewart and Rosalind Shaw, eds., *Syncretism/Anti-syncretism: The Politics of Religious Synthesis,* pp. 196–211. London: Routledge.

Van der Veer, Peter, ed. 1996. *Conversion to Modernities.* London: Routledge.

Vellard, J. 1963. *Civilizations des Andes: Evolutions des populations du haut-plateau Bolivien.* Paris: Gallimard.

Wachtel, Nathan. 1977. *The Vision of the Vanquished.* New York: Barnes and Noble.

———— 1986. "Introduction: Between Memory and History." *History and Anthropology* 2(2): 201–244.

———— 1990. *Le retour des ancêtres: Les indiens Urus de Bolivie, XXᵉ–XVIᵉ siècle. Essai d'histoire regressive.* Paris: Gallimard.

———— 1992. Chipaya: La guerra de los dioses. *Cuarto Intermedio* 27 (May): 41–73.

———— 1994. *Gods and Vampires: Return to Chipaya.* Chicago: University of Chicago Press.

Warren, Kay. 1989. *The Symbolism of Subordination.* Austin: University of Texas Press.

———— 1998. *Indigenous Movements and Their Critics: Pan-Maya Activism in Guatemala.* Princeton: Princeton University Press.

Weismantel, Mary. 1988. *Food, Gender, and Poverty in the Ecuadorian Andes.* Philadelphia: University of Pennsylvania Press.

———— 2001. *Cholas and Pishtacos: Stories of Race and Sex in the Andes.* Chicago: University of Chicago Press.

Weiss, Brad. 1996. *The Making and Unmaking of Haya Lived Worlds.* Durham: Duke University Press.

White, Geoffrey M. 1991. *Identity Through History: Living Stories in a Solomon Islands Society.* Cambridge: Cambridge University Press.

White, Louise. 1997. "Cars Out of Place: Vampires, Technology, and Labor in East and Central Africa." In Frederick Cooper and Ann Laura Stoller, eds., *Tensions of Empire,* pp. 436–460. California: University of Californial Press.

Wilk, Richard. 1995. "Learning to Be Local in Belize: Global Systems of Common Difference." In D. Miller, ed., *Modernity Through the Prism of the Local,* pp. 110–133. London: Routledge.

Williams, Brackette. 1989. "A Class Act: Anthropology and the Race to Nation Across Ethnic Terrain." *Annual Review of Anthropology* 18:401–444.

Wilmsen, Edwin N. and Patrick McAllister, eds. 1996. *The Politics of Difference: Ethnic Premises in a World of Power.* Chicago: University of Chicago Press.

Wolf, Eric. 1955. "Types of Latin American Peasantry: A Preliminary Discussion." *American Anthropologist* 57(3): 452–471.

———— 1965. "Aspect of Group Relations in a Complex Society." In Dwight B. Heath and Richard N. Adams, eds., *Contemporary Cultures and Societies of Latin America,* pp. 85–101. New York: Random House.

Yapita M., Juan de Dios. 1992. "Kunturinti liq'uchinti: Análisis lingüístico de una sallqa de Oruro." *Latin American Indian Literatures Journal* 8(1): 38–68.

Zajonc, Arthur. 1993. *Catching the Light: The Entwined History of Light and Mind.* New York: Bantam.